ECOLOGY IN THE 20TH CENTURY

ECOLOGY IN THE 20TH CENTURY A HISTORY

ANNA BRAMWELL

Yale University Press
New Haven
and
London
1989

Set in Linotron Palatino by Best-set Typesetter Limited, Hong Kong and printed and bound in Great Britain at the University Printing House, Oxford By David Stanford, Printer to the University.

Library of Congress Cataloging-in-Publication Data

Bramwell, Anna.
Ecology in the twentieth century: a history
p. cm.
Bibliography: p.
Includes index.
ISBN 0-300-04343-0 (cloth)
0-300-04521-2 (paper)
1. Ecology—History. I. Title.
OH541.B7 1989
574.5'09'04—dc19

Contents

Acknowledgments

Much of the research for this book was carried out while I was a Research Fellow at Trinity College, Oxford. I am grateful to the fellows of Trinity College for their hospitality, and for their interest in my work. In particular, Lord Quinton, then President of Trinity, made many useful suggestions about the manuscript and recommended books. John Wright introduced me to the other green world of the word processor, and was very helpful in making facilities available at a time of domestic crisis, while Michael Inwood kindly answered my questions concerning German philosophy. I am grateful too, to Jan Martin, librarian of Trinity College, for her help.

Of the scholars who discussed modern green thinking with me, I am particularly obliged to Geoffrey Ahern, Mark Almond, Andrew Dobson, John Durant, Rodney Needham, Hagen Schulze, Sir Keith Thomas and Paul Weindling. Stephen Cullen, of Nuffield College, kindly made his unpublished thesis on the ideology of the BUF available to me. For discussions many years ago with the then energy advisor to the Friends of the Earth, John Price and his wife Jani, I am grateful. I benefited inestimably from conversations with Professor Juan Martinez-Alier and Klaus Schlüppman at an early stage of my research. They most generously made drafts of their book, published later as *Ecological Economics. Energy, Environment and Society* (Oxford, 1987), available to me. Neither is in any way responsible for my interpretation of ecologism.

Some of the ideas in this book were presented at seminars at the University of Oxford. I would like to take this opportunity to thank John Gray and Charles Webster, at Balliol and the Wellcome Unit for the History of Medicine respectively for their hospitality and stimulating comments and also the late Edwin Ardener, through whom I was able to present some of my material to Oxford anthropologists at St John's College, Oxford.

Lord Beloff and John Farquharson kindly spared time to read the manuscript, and made many welcome suggestions and corrections. I am grateful to Alan Crawford for a meticulous criticism of the manuscript. Robert Baldock, my editor at Yale, encouraged the project from its inception.

Some of the ideas in this book appeared in articles in the *Times Higher Education Supplement*, and in the *Journal of the Anthropological Society of Oxford*. I would like to thank the editors of these journals for permission to reprint some of the material.

Preface

This is an examination of the origins of and ideas behind the growth of the ecological movement, from 1880 to the present day. I argue that today's Greens, in Britain, Europe and North America, have emerged from a politically radicalised ecologism, based on the shift from mechanistic to vitalist thought in the late nineteenth century. It was the fusion of resource-scarcity economics with holistic biology that gave force and coherence to ecological ideas. Thus, they depended for their success on the wide dissemination of scientific ideas, as well as on the more obvious aesthetic and moral values. Political ecology therefore implied the existence of an articulate and scientifically aware group of activists.

The following chapters will examine the thinkers who represent most significantly the roots of ecological ideas. They are located in the biological and physical sciences, in geography and land planning, and in some works of literature.

Perhaps unusually for an academic book, I have tried, deliberately, to include my own views in the analysis. It seems to me that it would be unfair to the reader simply to present a selection of writers, without trying to relate them to our present-day condition. However inadequate, the mirror of one mind does at least avoid the pitfalls of generalised or sociological explanation sometimes offered for alternative, naturist, rural and Back-to-the-Land movements. The ecological critique and its resultant policies are too important to be thus explained away. Works on political ecology have been written either by sympathisers or by sociologists, and a study which is analytical but which also takes the subject seriously is needed. Although this book examines ecologists with a critical eye, and categorises people, an act which is of itself both distancing and critical, I have avoided sociological modes of explanation. This is an act of exploration, of seeing, more than anything else, and it is a voyage I hope will be of interest and use to the reader as it has been to me.

One final word. I refer in passing in this work to the harmony and beauty of nature. I have taken this as given. No-one brought up in a town, as most are today, will deny the attraction of the countryside, whether or not various policies to protect, preserve or destroy elements in it are found acceptable. I have not formally addressed or endorsed the reality of the claim that rural life is in some way morally superior. I have, however, felt it throughout as an underlying argument, hard to prove, not academically acceptable, yet residing within the assumptions of our culture. I felt it with a particular poignancy, because in the early 1970s I moved into a working, yeoman Herefordshire smallholding, and got to know the former occupants before their death. The experience did not entirely confirm urban romanticism about country life. I learned from them something about the hardships, the bitterness and the loneliness of making a living in this way. But I also learned of the unquantifiable pleasures, and, through knowing the ex-farmers, something of the unique quality of faces untouched by television expressions, or modesty, unselfconsciousness and worth, – *virtu*. Had I not known these – possibly last – representatives of a dying race, I would not have recognised what it was that so many ecologists were trying to preserve. Paeans of praise for the yeoman spirit fall easily into cliché, and while such people were in evidence, it was hardly necessary to delineate their virtues in detail; it was a common presumption of the culture of the time, and like all such presumptions, it was not – it did not have to be – articulated convincingly. Now that they are largely gone, it is easy to dismiss their image as a fiction. I am fortunate to know that it was not, and although my knowledge is not of a kind that can be conveyed in an academic text, it has been a constant memory and inspiration to me in its creation.

PART ONE

A POLITICAL THEORY OF ECOLOGY

CHAPTER ONE

Introduction

This work does not examine real pollution problems, nor does it suggest answers to them. It looks for the roots of political ecology, and traces a school of thought up to the present day.

My theory about ecological ideas falls into three parts. Firstly, their strength is not directly linked with actual problems. The issue I examine here is not the cause of soil infertility or pollution, or suggestions for preserving forests, but why it was only from the mid-nineteenth century on that the European 'thinking classes' worried about such matters. The ecology movement represents a new political consciousness and direction. It has been struggling to see the light of day since the third quarter of the nineteenth century. Like all half-smothered things, it wailed sometimes for mother, sometimes for food, sometimes for companionship. Or, to put it less picturesquely, ecological ideas borrowed different political labels from time to time. Secondly, propounders of ecological ideas came from the educated Western classes; thinkers, intelligentsia, what you will. To make full political ecology possible, many conditions had to be fulfilled, and combined at the right time. That is why I locate the origins of normative ecology in the latter half of the last century. In doing so I must, since people so wilfully refuse to fit into a clear chronological framework, omit interesting individuals; Cobbett and Thoreau come to mind. Thirdly, two key shifts in mentality were needed, in the biological and in the physical sciences. Because these are the crucial roots of ecologism, other subsidiary but important elements of the ecological ethic, such as the animal rights movement and vegetarianism, are omitted from my discussion.

As I concentrate on those phenomena which are involved in my theory, I occasionally include material which may offend purists. Fears about finite resources have spilled over into utopian novels, science fiction and popular fiction. I have drawn on works of this kind where they were relevant to my theme. I have not attempted to quote every reference to the beauties of nature, or to the pleasantness or bestiality of peasants. In order to qualify for inclusion, such works have to be 'ecological' in nature. Even given this limitation there are too many recent science fiction novels to be included.[1] These show how, like a brush fire, the ecological world-view has spread and taken hold.

This book is a political and spiritual history of the tributary streams that now flow together in the ecological movement. The final river is already polluted. It is remote from the purity of its origins. Nonetheless, the creation of a large-scale ecological political movement represents a significant break from the past. The egg is hatched.

DEFINITION OF ECOLOGY

The distinctive qualities of ecologism arose in the late nineteenth century, and consisted of two distinct strands. One was an anti-mechanistic, holistic approach to biology, deriving from the German zoologist, Ernst Haeckel. The second strand was a new approach to economics called energy economics. This focused on the problem of scarce and non-renewable resources. These two strands fused together in the 1970s. The scientific element in energy economics gave impetus to the biologically based ecological movement, which had lost credibility because of its links with Germany. The two categories, biological and economic, had a certain degree of cross-membership. There was contact between individuals, and forefathers are still cited. It is the combination of the intensely conservative moral and cultural ecological critique with the full apparatus of quantitative argument that has rendered ecologism the powerful force it is today.

The word ecology is widely used today in the normative sense, not in the biological sense. The science of ecology is one that considers energy flows within a closed system. The normative sense of the word has come to mean the belief that severe or drastic change within that system, or indeed any change which can damage any specie within it, or that disturbs the system, is seen as wrong. Thus, ecological ideas have come to be associated with the conservation of specific patterns of energy flows. These patterns can be relatively small in scale, such as a one-acre wetland site; or it can be the weather pattern resulting from the Amazon rain forests, or larger patterns that affect the continuity of human existence.

The place of man within this hierarchy of patterns is no longer seen by ecologists as predominant. A recent theory is that the earth is not just a dead planet which contains a valuable closed system, but is itself alive. According to this belief, 'Gaia', the earth, has its own serene ecological balance, its own will to live. It is capable of preserving its own existence. It can shrug off disturbing intrusions, whether from comets or from man. Like any other species, Gaia has its own natural term. It lives and it will die.[2]

The countries where ecological theories have been most prominent are Britain, Germany and North America. Although the intellectual community responsible for disseminating and provoking these theories included French and Russian scientists and political activists, England and Germany today present the most striking picture of mobilised environmental groups. North America has both inspired radical, alternative ideas and received them again, in somewhat altered form, from Europe.

The persistence of this 'ethnic map' of ecologists, which has been noted by several observers, deserves comment.[3] Britain, Germany and North America all had different rates of industrialisation. In their demography and patterns of land settlement, too, they have little in common. North America in 1890 was a small town continent, as rural as Russia. Germany had many provincial capitals, the largest being Berlin. England alone was heavily urbanised overall. However, all three had a large, educated middle class, possessed of a strong liberal and Protestant culture. These cultural roots will emerge as a constant theme in my exposition.

The historical manifestations are, of course, profoundly different in the different countries under review. In Germany, there existed a dissatisfaction with and uncertainty about German identity. The shifting political and territorial boundaries of the nation led to a search for a more 'authentic', earth-bound identity. The hunt for anti-mechanistic values meant opposition to big institutions and size as an end in itself. German ecologism well predated National Socialism. It formed part of a generic cultural phenomenon that was in part diverted into the Third Reich as an underlying theme. It re-emerged, well after the Second World War, in more obviously left-oriented groups. The insecurity of German national identity had no exact parallel in Britain, but the British political ecologists also demonstrate a sense of a lost folk heritage, as well as a cultural criticism. The North American radical tradition, of which its ecologism is a native development, differs in its optimism. Theories of post-scarcity abundance, and a libertarian anarchic trend, characterise the American commune movement. In all three countries there was a sense of loss of the past, associated with, but not confined to, the passing of the old, rural world. This fused with critiques of orthodox, liberal economics and mechanistic biology to produce the ecologists, and their later flowering, the Greens.

THE ECOLOGICAL CRITIQUE

Many aspects of ecological ideas have now impregnated our collective unconscious. Claims which, a few decades ago, would have demanded an analytical response now quickly become clichés, part of our mental furniture. Clearly ecologism met a need.

> Ecology was the science which could interpret the fragments of evidence that told us something was wrong with the world – dead birds, oil in the sea, poisoned crops, the population explosion...What it meant was – everything links up...Here was a new morality, and a strategy for human survival rolled into one.[4]

This was written in 1972. On the other hand, ecologists claim that the sense of something wrong has resonated over the centuries. How recent is cultural criticism? We find the same kind of criticism in the early nineteenth century. Did it refer to the same kind of wrongness? Or has there been, as I will argue, a change in the way in which we look critically at the world? A sense that something is wrong is not a reliable guide for constructing specific and revolutionary policies. On the other hand, it is an intuition which needs investigation. No matter how many explanations there may be for the location and growth of ecologism, they would in the last resort be irrelevant to the value of their claims.

What are these claims? Man's vision of his place in the world, the question of the objective existence of that world and his relation to it, is fundamental to Western intellectual life, with its awareness of transience, the tension between past and future, being and becoming, ego and other. It affects the largest questions: the source of historical change, the nature of man, the why and how of man's history. It is intimately bound up with the problem of causality, affecting especially the question of the source of innovation and creativity. The validity of objective science, and the possibility of a social science, these all hinge on the stance taken towards man's place in nature.

Further, there are political implications. Over the centuries,

Nature has oscillated between being hero and villain. A study of the changing attitudes to nature and environment, and the vision of balance between them known as ecology, shows that the axis man-nature provides a set of political categorizations which are fruitful, useful and relevant to today's political scene. But the picture is not a simple one.

Put baldly, nature-based ideas are seen as legitimising social Darwinist, red-in-tooth-and-claw beliefs. The role of nature in German vitalist philosophy and philosophical anthropology between 1890 and 1933 has been associated with the growth of National Socialism, while irrationalist and 'cranky' movements have claimed a special relationship with Nature and Mother Earth. Conservative and reactionary movements have often looked back to the peasant-landowner relationship as a source of national strength. However, the essential characteristic of ecology, while it does not fit happily into any one ideological category, is that it draws many of its conclusions from scientific ways of thinking, and is not conservative.

Political ecology, which began towards the late nineteenth century, started as a progressive, science-based, anti-democratic movement. Kropotkinite anarchists as well as Spencerian individualists, all based their politics on recent theories about biology and physics. Between the wars, a number of positions were associated with ecological ideas, dominated this time by a fear of erosion and famine, and including, in England, the High Tory movement of Hugh Massingham and Lord Lymington. Technophiles and technophobes have always warred within ecologism. Technological optimism was more common in North America, where the late 1960s saw an anarcho-communard green movement. The most successful green movements today, though, are of the radical Left, and there are Greens today who feel unease at some of their ideological forebears.

The complexity is this; it is possible to assert that if man is part of the natural world, subject to the same laws as the animals, then he is, like them, entitled to compete to survive. Because he cannot hope to escape from his animal nature, he is justified in aggression. This is the social Darwinist argument associated by many with a politics based on nature. It assumes that man's survival cannot be taken for granted; he is never secure. The counter-image is that man is so special, so malleable and adaptable in his nature that the laws of the natural world no longer apply to him. Man's intellect and self-awareness, in this mode, meant a qualitative change in his status, and removed him from the biological law of selection and evolution. If his behaviour is not controlled by instinct, then man is adaptable enough to be made over in any image. The model of improvement through social and environmental change is generally a progressive and left-wing model.

However, one can also argue that it is precisely because man partakes of the earthly burden that he should help nurture the earth, rather than despoil it. His 'natural' role is that of a shepherd. Nature embodies stasis and harmony. Man should therefore accept, runs this argument, his limitations, and fit into the given pattern of energy flows. This is, on the whole, the ecological viewpoint, that man is the shepherd of the earth. And an ecological conclusion has been drawn from the premise that man does not have inbuilt limitations. This conservative variant points out that it is precisely man's lack of a fixed genetic inheritance that makes stable institutions essential as a substitute. Because man's culture has to be learnt afresh with each generation, those traditions, such as the family, which embody memory and habit, must be preserved. The belief that man is born without a genetic template for, say, the Church of England, makes continuity in social institutions more important and not less; makes progressive aims more dangerous, precisely because man can be stripped of his non-genetic endowment, his cultural heritage, by well-meaning destruction of existing structures. So man's capacities for improvement and change are finite, and he should beware of attempts to strain the boundaries of what is natural to him.

Thus, it is an over-simplification of ecological politics to think that nature-based thinkers have to be social Darwinist, while believers in man's malleability must reject nature from their analysis. The political stance of ecologists has been more complex, just as other political categories shift and change over time.

ECOLOGISTS AND GREENS

The cultural and political criticism known as political ecology involves substantial ethical and moral claims, and proposes drastic and apocalyptic remedies. Today's green parties have carved out a political niche which receives between seven and eleven per cent of national party votes. The European Parliament has a Green section which has more members than has the Communist Party. Green parties have flourished in Northern and Central Europe, in a wedge stretching from Finland to Austria, to Belgium. Britain, too, has a Green Party (formerly the Ecology Party, and the first to be so named, founded in 1973), and there has been growing 'entryism', especially within the Liberal Party and middle-class Labour constituencies. The Conservative Party is under considerable pressure to protect rural values, and the National Front went Green in 1984.[5] Greens have to be moles in Britain, because of the two-and-a-half party system; but even so, in Britain alone some three million people are alleged to be members of environmental and other ecological groups.[6]

The green tendency has aroused unease in some political quarters, dismissal in others. The Right today tends to be pro-American, pro-nuclear power and conservative. It suspects enthusiasm. The hard Left, despite recent efforts to capture green ground for Marxism, has tended to write off ecologists as trivial, irrelevant, or doomed to failure. One social historian describes Richard Jefferies, the nineteenth-century self-educated farmer's son and naturalist, as 'the Tory transcendentalist writer', and sees his ideas as 'a refuge from unpleasant realities'.[7] In one typical structuralist criticism, ruralist ideas are seen as having 'a fatal flaw . . . like ecological ideas, they were not made to mobilise the masses'.[8] A fatal flaw indeed, but the evidence seems to be that the masses are being mobilized none the less. When cultural criticisms are combined with political action, it is time to examine the phenomenon seriously. The best way to start is to create a history of ecologism. Surprisingly, this has not yet been done.

For many young, uncommitted observers, the idea that ecologists pre-date the 1970s would come as a surprise. Others, working for environmental causes for decades, see the recent growth of media interest in the Greens with some cynicism, or even irritation. Ecologists themselves locate their roots variously. Some believe there has been an alternative, holistic tradition running through Western culture since the Middle Ages. There is already a substantial literature, dominated by American feminists, which propounds the virtues of an alleged pre-patriarchal, pre-exploitative Golden Age, run by female market gardeners and moon worshippers.

Academic studies usually confine their studies to one country. Armin Mohler, historian of recent German conservatism, thinks the ecological 'package-deal' (*Gedankengut*) derives from the conservative romantic reaction of the 1920s. He cites Friedrich Georg Jünger, brother of the better-known Ernst, as a key figure.[9] The historian of geography, David Pepper, finds two main roots of environmentalism in Britain, a scientific root derived from Malthus and Darwin, and an unscientific romantic concept stemming from Matthew Arnold.[10] The American Donald Worster, in the most comprehensive work of its type to date, concentrates on America, and the influences of Thoreau and Emerson. He also finds two strands of ecologism: an Arcadian theme and a more classificatory, dominating attitude.[11] Juan Martinez-Alier's history of energy economics deliberately confines itself to authors who offer specific calculations of calorific values and resources. This naturally excludes biological ecologism, as well as philosophical or mystical ruralism.[12] A standard work on modern British environmentalists, by Jane Lowe and Philip Goyder, notes the parallel developments in North America, Europe, Britain and the White Dominions, but they confine their study to British politics.[13] There is no work which ties together the geographers, land planners and biologists in all three countries, and relates them to the present. Although the present study, too, cannot expect to be comprehensive, it will, I hope, provide a broad framework in which to consider our heritage of ecological ideas.

Almost a third of this book concerns the German connection. In one way this is not surprising. Ecology was formulated in Germany, and many 'alternative' ideas, in the field of medicine, sun-worship, vitamins and homeopathy come from German-speaking countries. During the Third Reich, refugees brought to Britain that tradition of holistic medicine, often bound up with an anti-liberal criticism surprisingly similar to that enunciated by those who remained and were thus associated with the Third Reich. But it is not this connection which will be found in the literature to date. When ecologists sit down and muse about their origins, the scope can be breathtaking but inaccurate. The place of Germany within their framework typifies this, but points to an intriguing problem.[14] Nietzsche, for example, is frequently described as an important figure. Why should this be? In reality, he does not conform at all to the model ecologist, nor is he a German Romantic, – he espoused anti-nationalist and rationalist causes for most of his life. But misinterpretations of Nietzsche are an important force. The symbolic misuse of Nietzsche means: – values, extreme individualism, nationalism, the blood, anti-modernism, Dionysian irrationalism and the superman. It is illiberalism based on existentialism. For many ecologists, these ideas are alien. Yet still Nietzsche hovers, worrying but relevant. For he puts man in God's place, with the responsibility as well as the fun that implies. He is a forerunner of vitalism, and these ideas, attacked by the intellectual establishment, do have a perpetual appeal. They fill a lack. Goethe, Nietzsche, Bergson, Driesch and Heidegger together form an anti-analytical, holistic canon, and escapees from the arid desert of linguistic philosophy often find themselves wandering in their epistemological ether.

Although he spoke against science, especially dismal science,

Nietzsche picked up a scientific image of his time when he described man as a flame-like being.

> Yes! I know from whence I spring,
> Never sated, like a fire,
> Glowing, I myself consume.
> All I seize and touch makes light,
> All I leave behind me ashes,
> Surely, flame is what I am.[15]

Man the creator, man the destroyer; man whose touch produced light and death – what clearer image could there be of the exploitative, dominating Promethean? It was a later German philosopher, Martin Heidegger, described by George Steiner as the 'metaphysician of ecologism' who wrote a surprisingly modern-sounding critique of consumerism in 1944; he called on man to be the shepherd of the earth, to accept his humble role as part of the world, to avoid technology, domination and the role of exploiter.[16] Clearly, a philosophical tradition which produces such opposed interpretations of man as the Promethean and the Shepherd is a complex one. It seems worthwhile, therefore, to examine the recent German nature tradition and its various strands, and its experience in tragic practice.

The question of National Socialist absorption of ecological ideas arises here. I touched on it in a previous book, where I pointed to the existence of ecological arguments so similar to today's in the Third Reich and asked whether it was significant or just an embarrassing accident.[17] Although I examined the issue seriously, and offered supporting evidence, still I did not do more there than outline the problem, and urge that it be taken seriously. This is a suitable work in which to re-examine the problem, with all its implications for our view of Nazi ideology, and for the future of support for the Greens. As this is not a specialised book on Nazi history, I will concentrate on two questions; why, as one historian has already asked, the Nazis were the first 'radical environmentalists in charge of a state':[18] and secondly whether the Nazis succeeded in their attempt to keep the small farmer on the land. This is an ambition of today's Greens, especially those concerned with the Third World. So is autarky, another concern of the German agrarian radicals. It is important to separate the effects of non-specific historical phenomena from the effects of the peasant experiment. I therefore compare various European fascist doctrines, including those of Mosley's fascists in Britain, to see whether the ecological component in Germany can be seen as ethnically specific rather than politically contingent.

Recent years have seen an increasing trend towards the historicisation of National Socialism. Comparative studies have been carried out in fields such as welfare policy, crime, policing and architecture.[19] Various observers, including Thomas Mann, have already pointed to the rural values lying, as a style or rhetorical tendency, behind much of Nazi ideology.[20] There is now concrete evidence to support this intuition. However, there were distinct strands of agrarian ruralism, ecologism and agrarian modernism which need to be differentiated clearly, while it is also important to distinguish between essential and accidental similarities.

Because of the alternative nature of the ecological criticism it has already been subject to a certain degree of polemical criticism which the evidence here may help to fuel. The pacifism and hostility to nuclear power inherent in the Greens renders them the automatic enemy of today's Right. Further, today's Right fears what it perceives as an element of anti-rationalism, together with the inherently destabilising and oppositional nature of ecologists, with their conservative moral values and non-conservative means. The frequent attacks on alternative science, medicine and evolutionary theories launched by luminaries from the scientific establishment clearly display this fear; together with its corollary, that the oppositional, anti-establishment and radical nature of the Greens could lead to revolutionary phenomena.[21] Of its essence, the fear of anti-rational revolution is the fear of a Pol Pot as opposed to a Lenin. A Lenin is seen as working, however destructively, within a recognised and familiar Western framework. The revolt of the peasant, however, is boundless, formless and terrible. Yet ecologism is based on a belief in objective truth and values. Ecologists reject the humanist act of faith for the best of reasons – because their humanism is grounded in what they perceive as immutable natural law. For this reason alone it has been attacked under its guise of social Darwinism as sinisterly anti-progressive.[22] An argument which is used by both establishment-oriented conservatives, together with members of the socialist academic establishment, is that ecologists are a danger because they reject reason and a danger because they believe in reason. This is either deeply wrong or profoundly right. To attack a philosophy because it claims to overthrow progressive aims through its objectivity and closer grasp of reality, and to attack it because it appears to do away with rationality, does seem to mean that there is a confusion somewhere. It may be a valuable pre-paradigm-breaking confusion, or perhaps a sign that existing institutions are under attack, – but certainly it is something that warrants investigation.

My own hypothesis is that the apparent contradictions of the ecological movement can be resolved by seeing it as forming a new political category in its own right, with a history, right wings and left wings, with leaders, followers and a special epistemological niche all to itself. In this book I seek to provide the evidence to prove this theory.

THE ECOLOGICAL BOX

To explain what I mean by a political theory of ecology I must define an ecologist, and explain his beliefs. Then I must show how he occupies a special political niche, and what are the epistemological consequences of that occupation. One way to do this would be to assume that we are all agreed on who and what were ecologists. No such agreement exists. The history of ecologism is not only in its infancy, but what exists has largely been written by believers. Its historiography is divided into uninvolved histories and very much involved histories. This is not to criticise involvement in itself. A philosophy should affect the life of its time, while a subject is only of interest if it relates to our sense of values, whether aesthetic or political or moral, or all three. However, engagement produces problems for the historian of ideas. It means that some works are considered as subjects for academic dissection, while others are written by co-dissectors. This distinction between comrades and victims does not reflect any difference in quality, but in objective and in self-definition. In defining what an ecologist is, what he thinks is his own history is obviously relevant. Here, then, a specific historiography becomes part of the syndrome it defines.

Ecologism is a political box. It is a new box, into which many distinguished and important thinkers fit who fit only partially into other, better-known boxes. 'Thinkers' they must be, since an acquaintance with scientific ideas, available to specialists in other disciplines but not widely disseminated, is an essential part of ecologism. The box began to attain its current shape and size around 1880 in Europe and North America. Self-definition about belonging in this box arose later, in the 1920s. It was not until the early 1970s that the box acquired a proper name, and earlier ecologists saw what they had thought their very own box expropriated. Over the last hundred years the clarity of the box's outlines was obscured by the presence of other, bigger, better-known boxes, some of whose corners were tucked into our ecological box – that is, they shared policies and aims, but temporarily, and variably, since non-ecological boxes fluctuate in their degree of concern for ecologism.

How is one to define a man-made category, and how far back is one to trace its ancestry? At what stage does it cease being pre- or proto-, and become, as it were, *sapiens*? Conservatism, Socialism and Communism too go back only so far. How far is a matter of dispute, and depends on whether one accepts self-definition by members of these categories. Such self-definition is itself a constantly changing, live political issue. The argument for continuity of ecological opposition is held by many ecologists. They believe that an alternative ecological idea dates back millenia. How is one to judge the validity of such a claim? One may feel that some violence is done to a historically specific concept by linking together disparate cultures and eras, by spotting collectivism among Pythagoreans and laissez-faire ideology among the victims of Diocletian. We realise that each historical epoch is unique, and we do not, therefore, expect to find duplicates of historical phenomena in each period. At the same time, we know that there are human constants and similarities. Much of ecologism lies in looking for these. We know that continuities exist. The historian walks a tight-rope between these two conflicting realities, both of which are true. We step and step not into the same river.

However, change and development there must be. Therefore, new fusions can be created from ancient human instincts and habits. In normal terminology, the political categories mentioned earlier are confined to the recent past. We trace Conservatism and Socialism back certainly to before the exact definitions and party systems as we know them today arose. Not too far back; probably to a few decades at most, a short time before people recognised themselves as being 'it', and we allow for the fact that full-blown 'its' can still change substantially within the usable time-span, as Tories changed to Conservatives, and Marxist Social Democrats changed to liberal Socialists. By analogy, therefore, one would expect the ecologist to emerge shortly before the word became used normatively. As the first normative use of the word that I have found dates to 1915, it seems reasonable to place the creation of the ecological box in about 1880, some thirteen years after the scientific term was first coined.[23]

Conservatism and Socialism have, in general usage, an association with the words which form their root: conserving and *sozial*. Similarly, ecologism arises from the concept of *Oekologie*. Ecologism does not involve the web of life alone; it was used originally as co-terminous with ethology, the study of animal behaviour in its environment, and with *oekonomie*, the concept of 'economical' household management. This implies that the use and conservation of resources is a moral activity as well as an economic one; and a morality closely bound up with the survival of the group.

But, although the terms rest on Greek roots – some ecologists find this link with early classical Greece itself significant – the words refer to a set of biological, physical science and geographical ideas that arose separately around the mid-nineteenth-century. Biological holism showed that man and animals were interdependent in and on a balanced environment. It implied that there was a scientific truth that lay outside man's perceptions, but on which man depended. The physical sciences learned that the dissipation of energy might endanger man's existence, or even that of the planet itself. Geographers examined land settlement and use from the aspect of resources. Land itself became perceived as endangered, and its finiteness, always known as a truism, began to matter.

How and when did ecologism manifest itself? A theory about this is not provable in the scientific sense. The method I propose to follow is to describe, explain and analyse together. I start from the position that we are aware that something exists which is to be examined, using observation, common sense and empathy. The form of the examination will help to define the phenomenon. At this stage I want to sketch out the qualities of an ecologist, and show what the potential political consequences were.

The First World War brought apocalypse to a generation already intellectually alienated. It showed that real disaster, real loss, was possible. In the 1920s ecologists began to define themselves as such. It had taken about that long for the scientific roots of ecologism to merge into a political discipline, to become an ideology.

The existence of this ideology has been obscured because it took on varied political forms. Most controversially, in the 1920s and 1930s, an alternative, anti-capitalist stance meant that the apparently alternative, anti-capitalist 'Third Way' National Socialist and Fascist parties attracted ecologists. After the Second World War the ideal lay dormant for a period. It then revived, still in an alternative anti-capitalist form, with similar ideas, programmes and beliefs, but with a self-defined leftwards tinge. The political shift was partly because the 'soft centre' moved from right to left during this time. It was also because American anarchists and Marxists in the late 1960s took up ecological ideas as part of 'alienation'.

Ecologists themselves are divided between those who believe that ecologism sprung up fully formed in the late 1960s, and those who see an underground, green tradition that always existed in Western history. Some place its origins in early Greek times; some in the Bronze Age. Heidegger believed that society went wrong in the transition from Greek to Latin, so that Greek concepts were translated into Latin but misunderstood. To give an account of beliefs that rationality has always battled with intuition as a source of our civilization would take too long at this stage; I will only say that it is *ecologists* themselves who argue this. The belief itself is a symptom of being an ecologist, and will be treated here on that level. Similarly, the hunt for a scapegoat who *made* society go wrong is a symptom of ecologism. Much of the literature consists of accusation and counter-accusation hurled to and from the scapegoats of other ecologists' Manichaean analyses. It is unusual for the historiography to be part of the subject itself.

Ecologists believe in the essential harmony of nature. But it is a harmony to which man may have to be sacrificed. Ecologists are not man-centred or anthropocentric in their loyalties. Therefore, they do not have to see nature's harmony as especially protective towards or favouring mankind. Ecologists believe in an absolute responsibility for one's actions, and for the world in general. There is no God the Shepherd; so man becomes the shepherd. There is a conflict between the desire to accept nature's harmonious order, and a need to avert catastrophe because ecologists are apocalyptical, but know that man has caused the impending apocalypse by his actions. Ecologists are the saved.

As part of their sense of responsibility, ecologists know that there is no free lunch. Everything has a cost; everything a place. The saved are better able to plan man, space and the environment than existing institutions. Bureaucracies are wasteful and slothful, as Kropotkin pointed out; but man's unplanned actions are destructive and can be aesthetically unappealing.

For, although non-anthropocentric, ecologists are not passive in their stance towards the world. They care intensely about how things look, feel and are, and feel a responsibility to indicate the way to the truth. Aesthetic values, then, are vital to ecologism. But not only the sensuous pleasures of nature, the importance of which to ecologists varies from decade to decade and from to country to country. There is hostility to the elaborate, the formal, despite the belief in benevolent planning. The civilization of the latifundia is resented as much as the civilization of megalopolis. The aesthetic values of the ecologists include the spiritual value of the one-to-one contact between man and object; between the history and meaning of a thing and the thing's maker, and the user or purchaser or owner of the thing. Ecologists prefer a direct link between man and object; both the object and the contact with it are then seen as more real. This opposition to 'reification', as the Marxists call it, involves in Marxist terminology the alienation between man and what he makes, and is an attack on the factory system, as well as alienability of land and property. Here, Marx was tapping a pre-capitalist vein of social criticism. But the criticism is deeper and a more spiritual one than Marx makes, and is not confined to the factory system or to capitalist society. The poet Rilke in one of his letters refers to his belief that the thingness of things was dying away, through mass consumerism. If there is to be no interposing mechanism between man and man, man and thing and man and nature, neither must there be any wasteful, artificial state mechanisms, no bureaucracy, no unproductive 'Thing', in Cobbett's words.

Since the ideal moral and aesthetic relationship between man and the world is what is local and intimate, trade is the part of the market economy, or indeed, any economy, that is most alien. Production can be in the form of small-scale craftsmanship, but trade cannot be anything other than a distancing between man and product. Most ecologists are opposed to trade *as such*, for moral reasons. Given that belief, programmes are erected to show that trade damages buyer and/or seller. But the belief is not dependent upon the rationale.

Some of the apparent contradictions of ecologism can be reconciled by perceiving its underlying moral stance. Ecologists are optimistic, in the sense that there is no original sin and nature is harmonious. However, they are also pessimistic, fearing waste, irreversible decline and the ruin of the environment, because nature is harsh, not man-centred and is unforgiving, as reality is unforgiving. And there is no God of the kind needed to step in and put things right.

Most ecologists are not formally religious. Ecologists who began in irreligious rebellion are sometimes converted to a 'strong' religion, but a pantheistic religious feeling is the norm. Mediaeval Christian mystics are cited; such as Joachim di Fiore and Francis of Assisi. Ecologists often tend towards the Asiatic religions, Buddhism and the Way of Lao-Tzu. Confucius is too worldly. In a post-religious culture, some ecologists who have religious yearnings choose Catholicism, be it Roman or Anglo-. The leftwards politicization of ecologism, together with its alternativeness, has brought in the Quakers. Regeneration of the countryside and Back-to-the-Land were Liberal Quaker causes in late nineteenth-century Britain.

The ecologist believes that nature embodies eternal reality, and also that the scientific method provides a means of uncovering the truth. There is a scepticism about 'traditional' science, but no rejection of objectivity. There are philosophical problems concerned with the fact that man's standpoint does not comprise that of the universe. But even if truth can only be attained incrementally, it is still possible eventually to get there. Any holy lies or golden myths that lurk in the way to the truth are seen as merely lumber.

This rejection of the existing, traditional system, whatever it might be, together with its upholders, does not seem conservative, despite the similarity in some values between the conservative and ecologist. What political beliefs reject the interposing mechanism, of owner or of state? Anarchism, of course, and individualism; a dislike of involvement in party systems, and a rejection of any existing mechanism for mediating and legitimising the claims of interest groups on the production of others. It is an alternative, apolitical stance, but placed here at the service of a larger unit than man, namely the world.

Politics can be defined in many ways. It is the legitimation of structured force, or of a monopoly of force located in one area. It is the description of the processes by which men conduct their affairs. It is the way in which men rule themselves or each other. It is the ordering of disorderly impulses. It is war by any other means. It is a way to distributive justice, the maintenance of the polity. It is the shadow on the cave. Whichever definition you may choose, ecologists go outside the political process. But, like Marxists, whose revolutionary dialectic is equally unpolitical, their non-political nature becomes itself a new political category. Ecologists strain at the bounds of ordinary political discourse, and in doing so extend it.

The categories 'Right' and 'Left', or 'Conservative' and Socialist', have constantly shifted in their attitude to nature, and its acceptance or transcendance, what one might call the naturist axis. In Table 1 I give an example of how the axis Nature/Transcending Nature shifted political contexts at the end of the last century. Similarly, Table 2 shows how apparently straightforward political issues, like equality, have represented different things to ecologists.

The need for an unequal, though not necessarily hierarchical society, was earlier derived from nature. Equality as a priority for human survival in a world of finite and shrinking resources is a more recent derivation. Equality used to be the progressive technocratic ideal; but a creative inequality emerges from Jacques Monod and Noam Chomsky's work as 'natural'. I am not arguing not valid in all spheres but important here.) These radicals managed to drop out even from their own radical allegiances. So putting one's individual judgment ahead of party allegiance, even of the most fanatical kind, is another hallmark of the ecologist. As well as being saved, he is a Protestant. As marginalised escapees from Lutheranism, that is not surprising.

CHAPTER TWO

The Manichaean Ecologist

The true ecologist could not have arisen until the middle of the last century. There are two stages to this argument; the first is to demonstrate the essential qualities and ideology of the ecologist, and show that there has been a continuity of form and content of this ideology since then. The second step is to look at earlier variants of naturistic thought, and see what connections and similarities there are to my model.

There are two axes to the historiography. The first is chronological; when did ecologism (and variants, such as environmentalism) start, and how is the image of the ecologist structured? Effectively, the ecologist is defined by many writers in terms of his opposite, the enemy of nature. When the enemy is clearly portrayed, then the naturist emerges as his victim.

In his study of man's picture of his place in nature, the historian of geography, Clarence Glacken, decided to end his study at 1800, because after that date a qualitative change began in man's view of his place in the world. He saw George Perkins Marsh's synthesis, *Man and Nature* (1864) as expressing the 'new perspective', followed by late nineteenth-century human geographers. 'With the 18th century there ends in Western civilization an epoch in the history of man's relationship to nature. What follows is of an entirely different order, influenced by the theory of evolution, specialization in the attainment of knowledge, acceleration in the transformation of nature.'[1] Glacken argues that the 'utilitarian interpretation of earth and animals persisted' until the mid-nineteenth century.[2]

The conclusion that emerges from historians of science is that earlier epochs all have something in common; they are able to see the earth as man's unique domain precisely because of God's existence. Before, both religious *and* natural theology were impregnated with the idea of a God-centred world. When science took over the role of religion in the middle of the nineteenth century, the belief that God made the world with a purpose in which man was paramount declined. But if there was no purpose, how was man to live on the earth? The hedonistic answer, to enjoy it as long as possible, was not acceptable. If man had become God, then he had become the shepherd of the earth, the guardian, responsible for the *oekonomie* of the earth.

One historian of science, Donald Worster, places the origins of the ecological spirit in the eighteenth century, with Gilbert White, the naturalist of Selborne, and John Ray, the biologist, as forebears. He argues that their work emerged from a nature-centred, pastoral natural science qualitatively different from what had gone before.[3] White and Ray, though, do not fit the ecologist typology described earlier, and it appears anachronistic to put White into the ecologist category. Indeed, Worster himself hints as much by indicating that 'the Selborne cult' was used in the later nineteenth and twentieth centuries to 'locate a compelling image of an alternative world and an alternative science'.[4]

Lowe and Goyder, in a study oriented towards the structures of political action and mediation, argue convincingly that environmentalism took organised form in the mid-nineteenth century, although they find isolated examples of conservationist sentiment as far back as the Middle Ages, and prophetic pleas for preservation which were far in advance of their time.[5]

They chart three main waves of conservationist sentiment from 1865 onwards. The first was from 1880 to 1900. The second was the inter-war years, and the third period began in the late 1950s. These authors see parallel movements in Canada, the United States (by 1900), Germany, France, Switzerland and Sweden. As they point out, throughout Europe in the late nineteenth century groups and institutions began to safeguard buildings as well as natural areas. They asked why, given that animal protection, nature protection, building preservation and footpath pressure groups were linked, as evidenced by interlocking membership of pressure groups, similar phenomena occurred in different countries? They attribute the environmental protection groups to a new attitude to what was being lost and a new attitude to changes, to a decline in the belief in progress, and a rejection of the ideas of the Enlightenment.[6] But many ecologists themselves believe there has always been a hidden, alternative, green history, that a justified protest against the despoliation of the environment has always existed. They search for the moment when a harmonious, benevolent, nurturing balance vanished, and seek the agent responsible. The rationale behind this search is that man, being one with nature, should sit in his natural niche without ecological destruction. Being, as is tautologically true, one with nature, man yet escapes from nature's laws. Either man, alone among nature's creations, has been created able to escape nature's domination, or some wrong spirit, group or movement has disrupted man's behaviour towards nature. It is not only mutual aggression that concerns the ecologist. It is man's apparently uncontrollable effect on the environment around him, through population growth and consequential growth in resource consumption.

Given the paradox that natural man behaves unnaturally, what went wrong? Various explanations put forward have in common the tendency to point to a guilty party. There are several different guilty parties in common usage. These are Christianity, the Enlightenment (with atheism, scepticism, rationalism and scientism following on), the scientific revolution (incorporating capitalism and utilitarianism), Judaism, (via either the Jewish element in Christianity or via capitalism), Men, the Nazis, the West, and various wrong spirits, such as greed, materialism, acquisitiveness, and not knowing where to stop. The wrong spirit is a twentieth-century explanation, usually confined to the West, and derived from the puritan element in Protestant and dissenting Christianity; therefore it is found mainly in Northern Europe and North America. According to this ethic, 'bad' spirits are located in Western man, who is seen as the unsaved, expansive, nonecological dominator of nature. Only by rejecting the materialist heritage of the West will men be saved.

Like the problem of locating the English Revolution, analysis of the seeds of anti-nature suffers from a bewildering variety of historical locations and cruces. These can only briefly be summarised here.

The belief that Christianity led to an anti-nature position derives from the Old Testament promise that gave man dominion over beasts, sea and land. In an influential article, Lynn White argued that it was anthropocentric Christianity, backed by an apparent mandate from above, that was responsible for man's tendency to exploit nature.[7]

However, it could be argued that the New Testament suggested a humbler acceptance of the world. A self-abnegating humility is implicit in the gospels. For many, man's traditional sense of intuition and balance disappeared with the rationalism and scepticism of the eighteenth-century Enlightenment. Man substituted mental processes for the world of feeling. Man became the centre of the universe, displacing God and his harmonious handiwork. The taboo against exploitation of animals and land was broken. As Enlightenment liberalism is supposed to have paved the way for the untrammelled totalitarian state, so it broke the mould of propriety, of man's proper feeling for nature. Talmon thinks that the eighteenth century idea of the 'natural order' meant an order in which man was sovereign.[8]

The scientific revolution is seen as one result of the decline of mediaeval religious communality, and located in the seventeenth century. According to this viewpoint, the Renaissance destroyed the matriarchal, compassionate, whole harmony of the Middle Ages. The birth of science brought a mechanistic, rapacious, inorganic attitude towards nature. This interpretation links the 'bad' scientific spirit with Men, or the masculine spirit, which this feminist interpretation links, in crude gender orientation, with men. Francis Bacon, especially, is supposed to have lauded the exploitation of the earth, while Isaac Newton, Leonardo da Vinci, John Dee, and the mechanistic, individualistic philosophers of industrial capitalism, Locke and Hobbes, legitimized the new masculine domination of female earth. This scientific revolution is sometimes conflated with patriarchal Christianity. Bacon, for example, is accused of viewing nature in a detached way because of the influence of Christianity.[9] But most writers link atheism or at least scepticism, not Christianity, with the scientific revolution. The shift from the Aristotelian rationalism of the Middle Ages to the mysticism of Dee and Newton is ignored by these writers. The influence of Hellenistic anti-Christianity on Bacon and other prominent early modernists is also ignored, probably because the Greek spirit is generally seen as a 'good' spirit by ecologists. The golden mean, the ideal of balance, is an ecological ideal. Glacken stresses Bacon's demand for humility towards nature, because it is God's creation. One should 'approach with humility and veneration . . . to study it in purity and integrity'.[10]

So atheism as the guilty party is connected with the Enlightenment and scientific revolution categories. There are elements in gospel Christianity (its Greek element, according to Schopenhauer) which support the morality of acceptance. St Francis of Assisi is presented as an antidote to the Pauline tradition. Rudolf Bahro sees the Franciscan ethic as an 'alternative'.[11] The Christian critics of anti-nature place its spirit in an untrammelled, progressivist rejection of God. Eighteenth-century Tories like Bolingbroke saw the Whig spirit as representing this exploitative potential, and twentieth-century writers like Massingham, G.K.

Chesterton and the Oxford Inklings (the group led by Tolkien and C.S. Lewis) linked a dark destructive greed with evil. In C.S. Lewis's attack on the Olaf Stapledon, H.G. Wells figure, in *That Hideous Strength*, he paints a world where rationalism destroys itself, where, by ignoring human (here, God-given) values and instincts, the final product of the atheist scientist is the talking head, the skull in the machine.

The ecologist's emphasis on a sense of balance, of acceptance, is linked with a need to accept nature's apparent cruelty. Some writers argue that the life of animals in nature can never be as horrible as when man intervenes: others that the cruelty of the carniverous life applies only to the sick, the weak, and those ready to die. Horror at the carnivore was attributed by Hugh Massingham and Lord Northbourne to a sickly, progressive, urban creed of science, that shrank from a robust understanding and acceptance of life's burdens. The attempt to escape from nature's necessity was, he argued, part of man's futile attempt to forget his own forthcoming and inescapable death. It was part of an atheistic package-deal that wanted eternal progress and expansion.

The belief that 'good' Christianity was Greek- or Buddhist-inspired sometimes led to an anti-semitic picture of a patriarchal, exploitative, materialistic Jewish Christianity. Feuerbach, Marx and Schopenauer all linked capitalism and utilarianism with the Jewish spirit. The existence of Spinoza, the pantheistic Jewish philosopher who was expelled from his synagogue, and whose holism influenced later German philosophers somewhat marred this picture. T.H. Huxley, who was reluctant to accept the anti-vivisectionist argument, nonetheless preferred him to Descartes; he feared the suffering to animals if Descartes's belief that they did not feel pain turned out to be wrong.[12] Spinoza is virtually omitted from Caroline Merchant's study of early modernist philosophy, perhaps because he opposed the Cartesian dualism she claims typifies the period. Buddhism, as the good spirit in this Manichaean framework, remains an inspiration now, but was interpreted in a more war-like spirit before the Second World War. Francis Yeats-Brown, author of *The Bengal Lancer* and member of Mosley's British Union of Fascists, studied yoga and was a practising Buddhist; however, he opposed pacifism. Buddhism for him offered a noble warrior ethic.

Before organised feminism took up the idea of an underground green matriarchal spirit, the idea that patriarchal societies, (either from the Iron Age or from Roman times onward), had destroyed society's balanced communion with nature (represented either by a Bronze Age Northern Europe or by an idealized Greek city state) was already current. J. Bachofen, a mid-nineteenth-century anthropologist, stated that most pre-historical societies had been matriarchal, and dominated by a mother-goddess figure.[13] The image of the overturned mother goddess joined the image of the dead boy-Christ in the study of comparative religions. Robert Graves' *The White Goddess* was a more recent example of this tendency. He argued that popular European folklore into Shakespeare's time concealed a coded history of the lost goddess and the oppressed European tribes. The Nazis supported Bachofen and his matriarchy theory. Pro-Nazi anthropologists in the Nordic countries in the 1930s supported the culture of the Bronze Age over that of the Iron Age.[14]

For some time this theory encountered patriarchal incredulity. However, with the growth in feminism, a new historiography was rapidly accepted. 'Now', wrote Carolyn Merchant, 'ecology and the women's movement have begun to challenge [their] values.'[15] The challenge moved rapidly from scholarly polemic, as in Carolyn Merchant's book, to rabid polemic like Mary Daly's *Gyn/Ecology*, which argued that American women were all being tortured, and drew comparisons with the extermination of the Jews by the Nazis.[16] (There were bizarre side-effects. The feminist witches of PAN (Pagans Against Nukes) worshipped at the same pagan standing stones as the pagans of the Third Reich. They pointed out that the stones really represented the spirit of women, but that the Nazis had been too partriarchal to understand the truth.[17]) With the publication of Marilyn French's book, *Beyond Power. Men, Women and Morals* (1985), the belief that women had once presided over a world of compassionate, moon-worshipping, nurturing matriarchs was widely accepted. It is a commonplace of popular literature today.

Henry Adams, who was an energy ecologist perturbed about finite resources, also wrote on the mediaeval cult of the Virgin Mary. He helped to created a favourable picture of the Middle Ages through his works on Mont St Michel and Chartres. He argued that American society had rejected the feminine, womanly aspect of life.[18]

Rudolf Bahro is a feminist Green. He links 'the industrial system, the dynamic of capital, the European cosmology, patriarchy, i.e., the whole mental drive of the spiral of death' in his definition of Exterminism 'the tendency towards mass destruction of all life'. This tendency, although contained in 'the genotype' of human beings can be controlled by overturning our patriarchal civilization and following feminine, or feminist values.[19] In *Build-*

ing the Green Movement he defines the 'patriarchal character' as 'expansive, progressive,' etc., moving 'forward' and 'upward', 'away from the Earth', while 'feminine spirituality' is directed downwards, into the earth. Quoting a fellow Green, Luise Rinser, he argues that the 'condition of salvation' is that 'men should submit to the feminine part of their nature'.[20].

For many, Nazism was the essence of exploitative, nihilistic anti-nature. The feminist interpretation of ecology links the patriarchal spirit with Nazism as its essence. Griffin argues that the Nazis equated the Jew with the feminine (partly because – she thinks – Jews in Germany wore the kaftan, and this was seen as a woman's garment).[21] Klaus Thewelweit studied the memoirs of right-wing German generals, and decided that they ignored women throughout, including their own wives, as an attempt to ignore the feminine in themselves.[22] However psychologically persuasive, the interpretation is not historically convincing. In their propaganda, ironically, the Nazis presented themselves as the victimized, oppressed, ravaged woman figure, one with the forests and with nature, exploited by the demonic, capitalistic spirit.[23]

SPIRIT OF PLACE, SPIRIT OF RACE

Geographic determinism has vied for centuries with cultural, religious and racial determinism as an explanatory force. Interpretations of conflicting racial spirits continue today as an explanation of what went wrong. For a long time they replaced the 'geographic march of history', whereby the fresh spring of man was in the East, and the decline of man in the West.[24] Jean Bodin, Hegel, Spengler and even Giraldus Cambrensis believed that civilization moved inexorably from one part of the globe to another, changing as it went. Today's North and South dichotomy expresses the same perversion of early enviromentalist theories. Where the 'West' is concerned as villain, this geographical expression usually covers a racial analysis. This is clearly seen when the 'West' or the 'North' is used to cover Australia and New Zealand.

Johan Galtung, a Norwegian economist, is one of many today who sees capitalism as the expression of a specifically 'European cosmology' which derives from the 'Indo-European prehistory of Western culture'.[25] Through the Germanic conquest of most of Europe, this patriarchal, expansionist ideology 'made North-Western Europe especially effective for capitalism'. [26] Here, both monks and scientists shared the unfettered freedom of the rich conqueror, the entrepreneurial spirit which led to exploitation and despoliation. This is the death drive, says Bahro, unique until recently to the 'Northern White Empire', but now affecting the Japanese and 'even the Russians'.[27]

When Indo-European history became interpreted as the fight between two forces, patriarchal, Iron Age, anti-nature, versus Bronze Age, matriarchal nature, it was a short step to recreating a racial dichotomy to express the conflict. For Robert Graves and D.H. Lawrence, the Etruscans and other pre-Roman Mediterranean peoples were earth-bound, blood-oriented, small, russet-coloured matriarchal tribes. The Dorians, Achaeans and other Northern tribes who swept down and wiped out the matriarchal tribes were the tall, blonde Aryans. [28] The argument that the blonde Aryan represented culture and civilization through the Greco-Roman world, propagated by Gobineau and Houston Stewart Chamberlain, is generally rejected today. However, it is not seen as racialist to argue that they represented a negative, destructive patriarchy; which substituted the rule of the sword for that of the corn spirit. The anti-Aryan creed, which was taken up by Celtophiles in the nineteenth and twentieth century, has today mutated into a generalised anti-Western belief. The craving for the Other identity of the Protestant North middleclass (Germany, the Nordic nations, to a lesser extent Switzerland, Austria), which led in the 1920s to a yearning for the non-national pan-Aryan, leads today with equal ease to a longing to merge with the masses of the Far East.

In any case, although the precise location may change, the essence of mechanistic, exploitative anti-nature is usually located by ecologists in the Other. From the time of the rediscovery of the Druids, first the Romans, and then the non-Celtic Europeans began to be seen as guilty. Celts and Celtic propagandists appropriated the natural for themselves, and claimed a special relationship with pre-Christian supernatural forces.[29]

OUTSIDE THE EGG

Capitalism, the utilitarian spirit, the teleological spirit (interpreted as the belief that nature was governed by purpose), Christianity, the masculine desire to ravage nature, the scientific attempt to get outside the egg; despite the different agents ascribed to these explanatory theories, they appear to have something in common, for at different times all have been ascribed to connected groups. For example, capitalism has been ascribed to Christianity, but also to atheistic, expansionist scientism.

Even an interest in the natural world, the desire objectively to observe and categorise the world around us, has been attributed to a fundamentally hostile anti-naturism. Some argue that the growth of the natural sciences helped to break an earlier sense of correspondence between man and nature. No matter how affectionately scientists and naturalists regarded nature, the process of catching, killing and labelling was an aggressive and dominating one, based on a feeling of apartness and superiority. Keith Thomas argues that the growth of the natural sciences in the seventeenth and eighteenth centuries produced a separation between ourselves and the world, as observers defined themselves as being apart from the objects they observed.

> In place of a natural world redolent with human analogy and symbolic meaning, and sensitive to man's behaviour, they constructed a detached natural scene to be viewed and studied by the observer from the outside, as if peering through a window, in the secure knowledge that the objects of contemplation inhabited a separate realm.[30]

This may seem paradoxical. Why would an *interest* in nature mean detachment from it? Because the act of objective observation assumes that it is possible to stand away from nature, and study it objectively. The very awareness of nature as an Other signifies man's loss of an organic connection with it.

The assumption that the world can be seen objectively is challenged by Hayek.[31] He claims that scientific and technological education produced the scientistic heresy.[32] According to this, trained scientists believe that the organic and spontaneously creative world of man can be controlled, planned and organised much as man treats the inanimate and animal world. Like Glacken, Hayek places this shift to the belief that man can and should control the earth in the early to mid-nineteenth century, but attributes it to the influence of Comte and Jeremy Bentham. Hayek does not express an opinion about the way in which man treats the natural world. He only argues that the claim to be 'outside the egg', to understand processes and ends better than those living them, is unjustifiable.

However, there was an 'outside the egg' anti-naturism that flourished into the nineteenth century (it continues, of course, to this day, through the new libertarian philosophers and physicists). The onus was on the scientist to prove that biological analogies were relevant to man, and eventually a dissatisfaction with mechanical models produced organic biological thinking, and helped to legitimise true ecologism. Hayek argued that it was methodologically impossible for man, part of the world he studied, to make accurate judgments and predictions about the carrying capacity of the earth. He specifically attacked what he called the 'social energetics' of Wilhelm Ostwald and Lancelot Hogben.

It is certainly an important paradox that some ecologists, despite their concern for what is whole, balanced and sufficient, display the characteristics of the scientific, global planner. This applies especially to economic ecologists, and the contradiction between their 'small is beautiful' values and their belief in global planning is their most striking feature. Despite their awareness of their alienation from nature, their method of returning to the natural world involves mass planning and coercion. One root of this tendency to look for global coercion as a solution lies in the influence of Marx.

The most influential 'outside' philosophy of the mid-nineteenth century was that of Karl Marx. The apparently contradictory claim that Marx was the first ecologist has also been made. By the 1970s not only had Marxists evolved a variant of ecologism but Marx was hailed as the first ecologist.

MARX AS AN ECOLOGIST

The main exponents of this view are H.L. Parsons and Marcel Prenant.[33] A comparison of their arguments shows that the basic analysis of Marx's views has not changed much over fifty years. Parsons claims that the relativism of Engels, the dynamic, 'historically specific' development theory of Marx, is a forebear of ecologism; indeed, he calls Marx, not Haeckel, the first ecologist.[34]

He presents Marx as a kind of early Monist, confirming the unity of man and nature through materialistic doctrine. Parsons rests his case on an identification of man's 'dialectical relations with nature' and the man-nature relationship of the ecologist.[35] This does not sound like true ecologism, because in this analysis man's role is too active, but there is a sense in which the dynamic concept of the dialectic can be equated with ecological processes.

What does 'balance' in nature mean? Balance implies symmetry. It implies two or more symmetrical parts, in equilibrium. It also implies stasis; some element of to and fro movement to keep the system balanced, but not more. The wonderful polarity of nature displays symmetry; there is Left, and there is Right. Magnetic fields face North, then they face South. However, there is change in nature, sometimes exogenous, sometimes endogenous. In one model nature moves from one state of equilibrium to another via a state of change or excitation. In the eighteenth century, the problem of change in nature was met by a model that incorporated symmetrical change; nature was a sphere, and the sphere turned. There was a hierarchy within nature, but the hierarchy could be upturned. Natural scientists made this picture more sophisticated by picturing the natural world as a fixed sphere; within its transparent walls lived our known universe, and matter was moved and transmuted from top to bottom, and back to the top again. For example, rain moved down from the skies to land, rising up again as mist. But the overall balance remained.

Although this may at first seem similar to today's picture of a balanced ecology, for example the cycle of energy consumption, the eighteenth-century picture was not a dynamic one. Dynamic nature emerged in the nineteenth century. What Parsons is implying is that the process of clash, change, and new equilibrium that Hegel described in his dialectic parallels the new vision of unidirectional, asymmetrical, stadial change that the physical and human sciences perceived at this time. Progress, surely, implies that you never arrive at a state of equilibrium. The concept is open-ended. The ever-shifting pattern of natural life moves through dissonance to temporary equilibrium back to change (or 'contradiction').

Parsons argues that when Marx describes dialectics, from which I extrapolate here my account of the dialectic resolution of asymmetric phenomena, he is describing nature; more, he *means* nature whenever he says 'dialectic process'.[36]

Certainly Engels, especially, was interested in the problem of man's relationship with nature. In his *Dialectics of Nature* he argues that it is man's nature to be able to dominate. But the domination is only apparent. His mastery over nature is accompanied by increasing immiserisation. The unforeseen effects of his actions overwhelm his intentions. Engel's critique is not directed to the tendency to dominate, but to the flaws in the system he produces. These flaws, according to Engels, derive from man's animal nature, which must be overcome. Engels goes on to claim that

> Only the conscious organisation of social activity with planned production and distribution can give man his social freedom

> and *liberate him from the remnants of his animality*, just as production itself gave him his *biological freedom*.... From the achievement of this organisation will date a new era of history, when man, and with him all branches of his activity (natural science in particular) will take on such a brilliance that all that has gone before will be thrown into deep shadow.[37]

Prenant, who is concerned here to establish the scientific nature of biological theory, and its importance as a foundation of society, quotes Marx in *The German Ideology*: 'As long as men exist the history of Nature and the history of men mutually determine each other.'[38] Prenant advances the economically ecological argument that the 'social application' (of biology) 'has... lagged sadly behind scientific knowledge', and cites deforestation, alcoholism and hunger as evils caused by capitalism, which do not exist in the USSR (this was written in 1938). The sentence from *The German Ideology* is taken somewhat out of context, since there Marx stresses the non-existence of a pure nature, and the irrelevance of the concept to society. However, by stating that 'Marxism dares and knows how to dominate all known physical and biological laws' Prenant expresses the man-over-nature philosophy behind Marxism.[39] Both mechanists and vitalists are criticized by Engels, for the same reason; they do not appreciate the 'richness and regularity' of the laws which underlie 'Nature, where chance seems to reign'.[40] By looking at Prenant's interpretation of Marx's attitude to nature, we can see that in the 1930s Marxism was held by its advocates to represent the triumph of human reason and organisation over nature and necessity, while a distributive utopia was believed to exist in the USSR of the time.

But, assuming Parsons' more recent parallel between dialectic and natural law to be valid, is it enough to make Marx an ecologist? Ecologists are not anthropocentric; Marx is.[41] After all, man is a major agent in his theory of historical development; 'man makes his own history', even with the aid and intrusion of other factors. Marx supported a progressive ideal that rested on Lewis Morgan's stadial theory of civilization. Primitive tribes were backward and barbarous, not admirable. Marx specifically attacked the 'primitive and irrational form of exploitation' practised by French peasants in his '18th Brumaire'.[42] Further, despite Parson's evocation of long walks on Hampstead Heath, it is clear that Marx does not *like* nature.[43] He agrees with today's ecologist that the countryside falls victim to the town, that capitalism destroys rural life, that capitalist agriculture destroys the peasant. But there is an undoubted note of pleasure in this prophecy. It is not made in any serious value-free spirit. No-one can read Marx's description of the Indian peasant without realising that he despises and yet fears what he describes.[44] The Communist Manifesto calls for the abolition of the countryside rather in the way that Old Testament biblical prophecy promises that there will be no more sea.[45] Marx ably argues the case that pre-capitalist rural life has its own rules and values, that go under when capitalism triumphs; but his expectations of a socialist victory rest on the necessity of capitalism. He does attack capitalism for its success in creating a productive agriculture. ('The cleanly weeded land and the uncleanly human weeds of Lincolnshire are pole and counterpole of capitalistic production.'[46]) It exploits the peasant, and appropriates the peasant's surplus. The capitalist loots the graveyards of Europe to spread phosphate on English fields. But Marx is not claiming that this amounts to over-use of natural resources, nor is he saying that farming without intensive fertiliser-use is better than farming with it. He attacks capitalist success in farming because his theory must attack capitalism, and predicates the success of capitalism, in any sphere, on exploitation.[47] He did not want the peasant world to survive. However admirable the pre-capitalist world might be, where it could be compared with capitalism to the latter's detriment, it could not, by definition, continue into capitalism and beyond, into socialism.

Marx's argument against nature on the grounds of the necessity of historical development is, indeed, overwhelmingly subsumed in his resentment of unaltered nature. Even his covert anti-semitism is mellowed when he contemplated with pleasure the role of the Jew in forwarding capitalism, and thus helping to destroy nature. Like Schopenhauer, Marx argued that the capitalist, and utilitarian spirit was linked with the Jewish spirit.[48] Like Feuerbach, he argued that the Greeks had been pro-nature (Marx's doctoral thesis was on this subject) the Jewish spirit being of a dominating and utilitarian kind.[49]

So to interpret Marx's vision as 'ecological', Parsons has to reinterpret his words. For when it comes to the question of man's survival on the earth, Marx explains that given a choice between nature and man, of course man would come first. No true ecologist would support this belief. Ecologists are not speciesist.

We return again to the multiplicity of cruces offered for the anti-nature revolution; the Iron Age's victory over the Bronze Age; the shift from Greek to Roman concepts, the end of the Middle Ages, the growth of individualism and capitalism in the seventeenth century, the eighteenth century and the nineteenth century. This difficulty in settling on the exact moment when man went wrong can be interpreted in various ways. It may mean that there was no move away from nature at all, that all these shifts are imaginary. It may mean that there was a series of significant shifts. As with all attempts to use history as polemic, violence is done to the facts, the spirit and the subtleties of past eras by the varied conspiracy theories of the ecologist.

The quest for the origins of what went wrong coincides with the quest for a better way for man to live on the earth. Recently, ecologists have tended to stress an original state of virtue whence these falls took place. Many anthropologists, like earlier pre-historians, have claimed that the non-Westernised tribes who still survive live in a golden age. Agriculture itself is seen as the origin of exploitation. In a recent study of self-sufficiency ideals, Allaby and Bunyard think that agriculture was a luxury not a necessity, arising from well-fed societies. The argument here is that desperately poor societies do not get round to developing agriculture. Lewis Mumford argues that the first ploughing was a religious ceremony, not a practical one, with phallic overtones.[50]

If South American Indian tribes are not only better, but happier, than Western man, with the leisure to sit around gossiping and appreciating life, then this is a strong argument for ecologists against agriculture and in favour of the hunter-gatherer way of life.

However, the hunter-gatherer tribes lacked that crucial component of the ecologist, an articulate intelligenstia. The only lament remaining to us on the transition from one way of life to another is the parable of Cain and Abel. The speech of a nineteenth-century Red Indian chief to an American President on the proposed purchase of Indian land has become a totem for fundamentalist ecologists like Rudolf Bahro (at a recent Schumacher Conference, this speech was cited several times by different speakers). It is indeed a moving speech, that talks of the unquantifiable splendour of nature (it seems to be purely a verbal tradition). Yet the most fundamental change in the earth's environment caused by man took place when small hunter-gatherer tribes began to move over the continents, using slash and burn agriculture as they went. But in any case, when the hunt for the scapegoat lands in the Paleolithic era, it seems fruitless to pursue it further. I will only note that Manichaean world-views tend to produce, eventually, an Inquisitorial reaction from the harassed victim.

It may well be that the source of man's griefs lie in his distant past. Others, apart from ecologists, have argued that some wrong turning, some crime, even, took place millenia ago.[51] Such a search for lost traditions has frequently been intellectually and spiritually fruitful, while radical movements often evoke a lost past to justify revolution. But a specifically ecological lament for a lost past began more recently.

PART TWO

A HISTORY OF ECOLOGY, 1880–1945

CHAPTER THREE

Biology and Holism

> While occupying ourselves with the ideal world in art and poetry... the real world can be truly known only by experience and pure reason. Truth and poetry are then united in the perfect harmony of monism.
>
> (Haeckel, *The Wonders of Life*, p.157)

Ecology is now a political category, like socialism or conservatism. Political categories always have a dual meaning. They can be used to describe parties, policies or governments as they are, or they can describe an ideal type, an ideology. Here, ecology displays an important difference from conventional political categories. The empirical sense of the term ecology derives from the natural sciences. It has not developed from observation or prediction about human societies, but required an ethic which saw man and animal as comparable before ecologists could extend their observations to human society. This is crucial to the political implications of ecologism.[1]

In this chapter I will look at the origin of the word and the political developments associated with its founder. I will also examine the attitudes of the natural sciences before 'ecology' appeared, why it was that holistic biology developed in Germany and not elsewhere, and whether it was true that a Goethean holism was responsible.

ECOLOGY; THE ORIGINS OF THE WORD

In evolving a theory of ecology, the origin of the word is as good a place to start as any. It was used by Ernst Haeckel (1834–1919) in his *Generelle Morphologie* in 1866.[2] Haeckel's role in the history of ecology is both important and ambiguous. He coined the word, and in the context of nineteenth-century science it expresses the shift to a contextual and holistic biology. He was also a political figure, whose reforms sprang directly from his scientific belief. In this, he was the precursor of a wave of such scientists, fired with the belief that their expertise in their own discipline would enable them to re-order political life.

When Haeckel coined *Oekologie* he was referring to the web that linked organisms and their surrounding environment. His own definition of the term was was 'the science of relations beteen organisms and their environment'.[3] Ecology looked at organisms in their context; their life-cycle, their environment and their place in the cycle of energy use. Haeckel's use of the term was as a descriptive tool. It is still so used today, for example, in studies of the ecology of plants and streams, or the ecology of plants in a field.[4] Ironically, Haeckel himself did not fully develop his own invention for his own discipline. One author argues that 'he does not display any notable insight into the dynamic principles of ecology'.[5] The full development of plant ecology owed more to plant geographers such as Eugenius Warming, who published on plant communities in 1895.

The scientific mentality of the period was ready for the concept. The idea of geographically as well as biologically inter-related organisms had appeared in different countries and different disciplines at almost the same time. Biologists contemporary with Haeckel whose political and reformist interests resembled his included Isidore Geoffroy Saint-Hilaire. His 'fundamental biological notions' (1854) included 'General facts, relationships and organic laws concerning organised beings seen either as a whole or via their organs.'[6] An important inclusion in his biological relationships was 'ethological laws relating to instinct, *moeurs*'.[7] The general facts included the 'successive and current distribution of organised life on the earth's surface'.[8] Nikolai Danilevsky, the famous pan-Slavist, was a geographer and botanist, who, inspired by Saint-Hilaire, made nine major ichthyological expeditions between 1853 and 1885.[9] His political and ecological essays were published in 1890.[10] Anton de Bary's symbiosis concept was also fruitful for ecological science.

Haeckel has been compared to Amerigo Vespucci – he discovered the name of the 'continent' not the thing itself.[11] He was a zoologist who specialised in microscopic and amoebic forms, where the intricate connections of parasite and food were less apparent. But his love of nature and his propagation of the creed of pantheism left a mark on his era. His works were translated into English and had a mass distribution. Their influence on English-speaking countries was enormous. For self-educated working men, his two-shilling works with titles such as *The Riddles of the Universe*, or *The Wonders of Life*, published by the Rationalist Press Association, were a life-line to political awareness through scientific knowledge. In this he was on a par with Darwin and Karl Marx.

The resonances of the new term went beyond biology. It carried overtones of the Greek word *Oekonomie*. As used by Aristotle, this originally meant the proper functioning of a household unit, the *oekos*. A soundly organised working household was the basis of a viable state. It was as self-sufficient as possible. It husbanded its resources, and avoided waste and disorder – as we still say that something is done with economy. It was not a methodologically individualist concept, but implied a self-contained group; the nation, the tribe, the organism. This connection between the meaning of ecology and of economy was made in 1928 by Walter Johnson, biographer of the great eighteenth-century naturalist Gilbert White of Selborne.[12]

Further, ecology was at first used co-terminously with ethology, the science of animal behaviour. North American scientists like Charles Whitman in the late nineteenth century, followed by Julian Huxley, revolutionised zoology by meticulous observation of birds in their natural habitat. The idea that animal behaviour could be understood by close observation in the wild found opposition. It was difficult to carry out controlled experiments in these conditions. An imaginative and empathic attitude was needed. When the idea of inbuilt or instinctive behavioural drives emerged, a theory was needed to explain its source. By the First World War, the field was split between vitalists and behaviourists. The split between theories of mechanical causation and vitalists, who postulated a life-force, stimulated Konrad Lorenz (1903–   ), originally a behaviourist in sympathy, to study animal psychology in depth. Vitalists believed that the life-force was responsible for inexplicable behavioural factors, such as route-finding in pigeons, care for the young, mating, nest-building and so on. Ethologists searched for precise mechanisms, either in-built or partly learned, that would explain the advanced and complex 'culture' displayed by animals.

'Biological' ethology was the science of character based on the study of animals. It overlapped in meaning and area of study with Haeckel's ecology.[13] It extended the web of relationships from the physical sphere, energy and resources cycled between sun, water, plants and animals. It showed that habitat and animals, group and individual, instinctive drives and learned adaptations, had to be seen together and in context, if animals, and by implication man, were to be understood.

HAECKEL THE ECOLOGIST

If Haeckel failed fully to develop this key concept, then it is obviously necessary to justify his inclusion as a founding father; the invention of the word itself could be a trivial connection. Indeed, in creating a new box in which to fit apparently disparate thinkers, the methodology presents a problem. Why should one particular man matter?

Intellectual history always runs the risk of degenerating into a mere list of quotations or an exploration of bizarre side-alleys. But Haeckel, though, little known as he is to-day, matters in several ways beyond the invention of ecology, which by itself would not necessarily be crucial. His political influence was considerable, through the Monist League, which he founded late in life, and through his pupils, who included prominent reformers and political agitators, as well as scientists. His political legacy will be discussed later, but Haeckel, in his republican atheism and his nature-worship directly influenced D.H. Lawrence. Through Lawrence, Haeckel's ideas influenced several early founders of the Soil Association as well as vitalist nature-lovers in Britain. His theory of recapitulation provided further direct inspiration for the 1920s Back-to-the-Land movements inspired by neo-Lamarckian environmental ideas. Many who were interested in biology found in him scientific backing for the prevailing sense in turn-of-the-century Europe of dissatisfaction and alienation. He offered an alternative which was programme, hard evidence and religious wisdom rolled into one creed. He created the biological root of today's ecologism, which was to stimulate philosophical anthropology as well as ethologists. Finally, he was a North German nationalist, of Protestant origin, thus fitting the ethnic and religious characteristics which I outlined in the last chapter. Let me at this point recapitulate the main points of my earlier definition of ecologism.

The specific characteristics of political ecology are that it is a normative philosophy, that it is a total world-view which does not allow for piece-meal reform, that it believes truth to be attainable, and its attainability to be desirable; it fears the dissipation of energy and resources, and is not anthropocentric.

Man's existence should not be considered primary for a moral stance towards nature. As second-order characteristics, ecologists want to reform man, society and their relation to the world. The reform is motivated by their scientific knowledge (or theories) about man and the world and their fundamental reverence before the beauty and order of nature. They fear the loss of soil fertility, due to erosion or pollution.

Although Haeckel did not express fears about pollution and soil erosion, and was not an energy ecologist (although one of his chief followers, Wilhelm Ostwald, was an important one) none the less he was an ecologist in three important ways. Firstly, he saw the universe as a unified and balanced organism. Space and organic beings were made of the same atoms. Hence his Monism, whether defined as all-matter or all-spirit. He also believed that man and animals had the same moral and natural status, so was not man-centred. Thirdly, he preached the doctrine that nature was the source of truth and wise guidance about man's life. Human society should be re-organized along the lines suggested by scientific observation of the natural world. Through his influence, he enabled ecologism to become a viable political creed.

HAECKEL; HIS BACKGROUND AND IDEAS

As a student, Haeckel was devoutly religious. His social attitudes were progressive; he disliked strong class barriers, and till his death he remained a believer in progress, thinking that science and truth would always prevail. He criticised university learning for what he saw as its hidebound nature, and opposed the practice of duelling, still fashionable among German students. He was a meritocrat. Like many upwardly-mobile middle-class German intellectuals, he was involved in the expansionist, nationalist Pan-German League. Later, however, he joined the German Peace Movement. He failed to join fellow-academics and intellectuals in the near-universal celebration of the outbreak of the First World War.[14] Nobel Prize winning chemist, Wilhelm Ostwald, Haeckel's most important successor as Monist, was also a pacifist. Unlike Haeckel, he continued to be one even during the First World War. Haeckel lost his religious faith in his early twenties. It was replaced by what he was to call Monism, the belief that 'the real world, the object of science, can be truly known only by experience and pure reason'.[15] Haeckel believed in a holistic world-view, that is, he rejected the concept of a mind-body split. He contrasted Goethe and his (alleged) pantheism with Kant, but hoped that the traditions deriving from their two views might eventually live in harmony. This unlikely event was to come about through the unifying quality of Monist doctrine. Monism's opposition to dualism was that mind and matter were one, because the universe existed on only one level. No non-physical spirit or force could exist. Towards the end of his life, Haeckel decided that while all was one, the one could just as well be spirit as matter. This did not prevent him being attacked in English religious and spiritualist journals as the most dangerous atheist of all time. The tendency to an all-spirit view was there as early as 1884, when he defined Monism as 'one spirit in all things...one common fundamental law', and argued that one could not 'draw a sharp distinction between the two great divisions of nature'. He rejected creeds that distinguished between the natural and the spiritual sphere. All were one, whether 'mechanical or pantheistic'. He claimed various heretics and atheists as scientific forebears. As well as Goethe, there were Lucretius, Bruno and Spinoza. He argued that they had all shown 'the oneness of the cosmos, the indissoluble connection between energy and matter...mind and embodiment...God and the world'. In 1905 he quoted Goethe on 'God-Nature'. Thus, the spiritual element in Monism was always potentially there.[16]

Even in his *Confession of Faith of a Man of Science* he was thinking as an ecologist. He pointed out that the energy level in the universe was constant. According to the first law of the conservation of matter this implied that matter and energy were both constant, and were the same thing. There was no such thing as empty space; it was filled by the ether and by atoms. This constant level of matter was the fabric of the universe, and had to be the stuff of the mind as well. There was no room for an extraneous element. Nothing came out of the universe: nothing came in.

Haeckel also thought that animals should be seen as equal to man: at least, to some men. The 'first beginnings of reason' could be discerned in 'the most highly developed vertebrates', together with 'the first traces of religious and ethical conduct... the social virtues...consciousness, sense of duty and conscience'.[17] He saw the higher vertebrates as equal to 'primitive man', and like him they had no 'higher degree of consciousness and reason'.[18]

Haeckel argued that although matter itself was immortal, because of the law of conservation of energy, there was no after-life and no soul. He paid lip service in his middle years to what he described as a 'younger Christianity', that is, less custom-bound and petrified; he was also interested in Buddhism.[19] In this, he expressed what was to be a continual theme among ecologists and those interested in animal rights. The appeal to ecologists of a religion that gave equal status to all species is obvious.

Later in life, he attacked Christianity for putting man above animals and nature. 'It has contributed not only to an extremely injurious isolation from our glorious mother 'nature', but also to a regrettable contempt of all other organisms.'[20] If there was no mind, where did values and emotions come from? Haeckel argued that it was rational to worship Nature and live by Nature's laws. Man was isolated from the world. This was wrong, and, more especially, it was unscientific. Man had forgotten his social rules; egoism to preserve the self; altruism to preserve the family and society. Monistic sexual ethics were more natural than Christian puritanism, which was anti-family and anti-sex – though Haeckel was careful to distance himself from dangerous Socialist ideas about free love. He believed that it was reason that led to an appreciation of the beautiful, the true and the good. Emotions he thought irrelevant to his analysis.[21] This was odd in view of his emotional nature-worship.

THE RELIGION OF NATURE

The extraordinary influence of Haeckel and his successors can be attributed, in part, to the quasi-religious appeal, the incipient pantheism of his picture. But there is a deeper appeal; the return to a god-impregnated nature, which had been banished from the North by Christianity. This void, apparently not felt by other Europeans, could now be filled, and filled by a convincing science-oriented ethic, that did not depend on received myths.

Christianity is considered by historians of science to have been traditionally anti-nature. Since it is split into sects, arguments have arisen as to whether Catholicism or Protestantism is the most hostile.[22] I referred in the last chapter to the examination of alleged Greek, Buddhist or Jewish strands in Christianity as explanations. Worster describes Christianity as a pro-scientific creed, that places the earth in a profane domain, where it can be utilised for man's ends.[23] Glacken interprets Christianity as the shepherding creed; nurturing the earth as a reflection of God's being.[24] Now that ecology has become more widely discussed, a number of Christian ecological apologists have emerged, who offer re-interpretations of the Genesis story, and the Franciscan tradition as evidence.[25]

Over Christianity's two thousand years, it has undergone

many metamorphoses, and has varied in different countries and cultures. Its monastic heritage has stimulated and preserved as well as hampered free enquiry. The Protestant ethic also contains opposing strands. The scientists concerned with ecology, whether biological or economic, came mostly from Britain, Germany and North America, areas with a Protestant tradition. This suggests that there was some lack felt in the religion of Protestant countries that was not felt elsewhere. It might be a reappearance of ancient resentment at the cutting down of the sacred groves 'or it might be the loss of the mother spirit' that led to the search for the life-force that infused nature.

This rebellion was not new. The eighteenth century had begun with a belief in an 'integrated order', which functioned like a harmonious, orderly machine, and was designed by God.[26] There was a vitalist reaction. The concept of a 'Soul of the World' and 'the Spirit of Nature' was used by Henry More and John Ray. In 1749, Linnaeus (1707–78), the great Swedish naturalist, described the 'Economy of Nature', using 'economy', in the way described earlier.

Linnaeus's nature presided over a fixed cycle of water moving through the system; water rose up from the earth, and returned as rain and snow. While nature was benevolent, her regime was fixed. Hierarchy and rules were inevitable. Within the cycle of the natural economy, each species had its place.[27] So naturalists in the eighteenth century were vitalists. They had a vision of a stable, circular-flow world. It was fixed and hierarchical, but elements within it were cyclically mobile. By the early nineteenth century, unilinear progress had burst the bubble.

The vision of the suspended, self-contained sphere, working with dazzling efficiency but unchanged over time, was destroyed by the atheism, the evolutionary and geological science of the early nineteenth century. But the ethics of natural theology were replaced by the ethics of natural law. The expansion and confidence of the great era of Victorian science destroyed the idea that all was fixed. But progress was a new law. Order, Right, Duty, – these were still the desirable ends, and without a fixed natural order and an omnipresent Creator, scientific principles could be used to create a utopia. This shift of vision was not yet ecological. The natural scientists T.H. Huxley, Francis Galton, Charles Darwin, Herbert Spencer and the early Geddes, put man first. Huxley, Spencer and Galton all saw the dynamics of natural development as potentially valuable to man's well-being; while Galton wanted to establish a scientific priesthood. Darwin showed 'how plants and animals, most remote in the scale of nature, are bound together by a web of complex relations', but did not draw man-oriented conclusions from his work; indeed, he avoided including man in his scheme for as long as he could.[28]

However, Huxley did draw such conclusions. He interpreted the *Origin of Species* as

> Harmonious order governing eternally continuous progress, the web and woof of matter and force interweaving by slow degrees, without a broken thread, that veil which lies between us and the infinite – that Universe which alone we know or can know; such is the picture which science draws of the world.[29]

The metaphor of the veil returns constantly during this century. In Schiller's series of 'veil' poems, the image was of a veiled nature. When rash man tried to life the veil, he died. The interpretation which emerges from this marvellous series (which, it should be stressed, can only be a coarse rendering of a subtle work of art) is that the lone voyage of self-discovery by the free spirit leads to suffering and death. But by Huxley's day, the veil was our ignorance of nature, which could and should be pierced. The naturalist Hutton talked of the 'veil of Nature'.[30] Natural law had replaced God, so nature's laws must become known so that man could follow them. The new pantheism had a somewhat dominating Nature as its centre, a Nature expected to educate and guide humanity.

This optimism became harder to maintain as people realised the implications of the second law of thermo-dynamics, that energy was always dissipating. Clearly, a world where waste and decay and irreversible decline were the law could not be a world of progress. It was a world centred on death.

The religion of nature was salvaged by the new vitalism. Will, spirit, the life-force, all were renewed by neo-Lamarckian concepts. Haeckel himself was a neo-Lamarckian. Several scientists believed that there was an immortal germ-plasm. Dr Alexis Carrel, a tissue-transplant specialist, believed he had kept non-cancerous cells alive for several decades. His book *Man the Unknown* expressed a religious faith in the unity of man and nature. Like Haeckel, he was an inspiration to the inter-war ecologists in Britain. In fact, he was a personal friend and acquaintance of many. Dr Paul Carus was polymathic editor of the Chicago *Monist*, an influential journal of general science unconnected with Haeckel. Carus argued for a consistent 'unitary world conception' and an unflinching search for nature's rules for man. The objectivity of morals and ethics was a common belief for Monists. Carus argued that the criterion of a valid ethical system was its objective reality, – truth was the criterion of ethics.[31]

The clear distinction between the ecological scientists and the man-oriented ones is shown by comparing Haeckel with T.H. Huxley. Huxley, like Haeckel, was a republican and an atheist, who studied natural law for human guidance. But, far from believing that man should live more closely to natural laws, he believed that man's civilization could only be maintained by artificial and deliberate means. He used the analogy of the gardener, who weeds and tends to preserve the garden. He concluded that civilization *should* be maintained, despite its 'artificiality'. It was the good way for man to live. He was anthropocentric, and adopted a mechanical model of nature. Haeckel, though, deduced from cell-theory that 'all matter was sensate'.[32]

It would be over-simplifying matters to place Huxley at one end of a pole, and Haeckel at the other. Both had faith in the wisdom and benevolence of nature's laws. Huxley's vision of Darwinian evolution is a moving evocation of natural order. It is a vision, however, that assumes that man is the centre and aim of this beneficence. Huxley's attitude to animals is another divide. Haeckel, as mentioned earlier, gave animals the same status as man. Huxley saw Descartes's picture of unfeeling, non-volitional animals as strengthened by the results of modern work on reflexes, brain and spine, although he did not advocate full-scale vivisection because of the terrible pain that would be caused to animals if Descartes was wrong.[33] Lacking proof that some vital life-force existed, and rejecting the notion that the universe was all spirit, he decided for an advanced version of the mechanical model.

HAECKEL, NATURE AND SOCIAL DARWINISM

Haeckel is sometimes seen as a conservative figure, and Bölsche was described as a reactionary by Martinez-Alier.[34] It is part of my argument that those who want to reform society according to nature are neither left nor right but ecologically-minded.

Nineteenth-century ecologists believed in progress (a belief that began to decline during the twentieth century), and in the power of man's will to change himself, so long as his will was used as a 'good' will, that is, in accordance with nature's laws. The American *Monist* argued for man's power to reshape himself.

> The new factor introduced with man is a voluntary co-operation in the process of evolution, a conscious upward striving towards a higher condition, a pressing forward toward an ideal. Man, contrary to all else in nature is transformed, not in *shape* by external environment, but in character by *his own ideals*.[35]

This capacity, unique to man, came from man's awareness of his relation to the infinite, and the attempt to realise the divine ideal in human character. Man was part of nature, and nature was beauty and order. For Haeckel, nature meant the spirit of freedom. He saw the natural order as progressive and optimistic. He was probably the first naturalist to derive human morality from animal instincts. 'Do unto others as you would have them do unto you' and 'love thy neighbour as thyself' he described as 'ethical instinct...derived from our animal ancestors'.[36] Human societies had to survive, that was their function, as with animal societies. The instinctive rules and codes evolved by both, Haeckel argued, were the same. This led him to a belief in co-operation and altruism. He criticized Nietzsche and the individualistic anarchist Max Stirner for substituting a religion of strength for universal charity; for, added Haeckel significantly, this was a 'biological error'.[37] The same belief in biological fitness led him to argue for eugenics ('racial hygiene' is the literal translation from the German) and for euthanasia. Yet, like Prince Kropotkin in *Mutual Aid*, he derived 'sympathy and altruism' from 'natural principles'.[38]

Our general impression of social Darwinism does not include the belief expressed by Haeckel that 'Love is the supreme moral law of rational religion.'[39] But Haeckel's nature was benevolent. And if it was benevolent, then contradictions and divisions had to be 'unnatural'. Haeckel went out of his way to oppose the Christian belief in inevitable sorrow and grief.

> Monism teaches us that we are...children of the earth who, for one or two or three generations, have the good fortune to enjoy [its] treasures...to drink to the inexhaustible fountain of its beauty, and to trace out the marvellous play of its forces.[40]

He put his faith in education, which would reveal the wonder and beauty of life, and Monism, which emphasised its poetry. Social Darwinism is sometimes seen as a mechanism to legitimise the power-holding classes, and certainly social Darwinists opposed class warfare. However, Darwinian and neo-Lamarckian reforms were demanded by natural scientists and social reformers who did not perceive themselves as part of the ruling élite. They saw the rulers of society as irrational, reactionary, hide-bound and war-mongering. Their own loyalties were to their beliefs and consciences, not to institutions.

Despite its apparently innocuous emphasis on the beauties and wonders of Nature and Truth, Monism was potentially a subversive creed; not only because of its rejection of organised religion, but because of its rejection of social traditions. This point is sometimes submerged by the apparently rigid and conservative image of the organic, cell-state. Haeckel, like Herbert Spencer and biologist Virchow, of the Progressive Party, deduced the ideal state from an organic analogy. Like the brain and nervous system, the ideal state would be centralised. This was not because, as conservatives would argue, hierarchy had virtues in itself, but because nature's work showed it to be the most harmonious and efficient means of ensuring survival. Haeckel's ideal state was not coercive, but he combined his belief in co-operation with a belief in duty. He was the first biologist to argue that duty was a biological impulse.[41] All living organisms, amoeba, apes, primitive and cultivated man, were bound by a law of care for the family and collective and the desire to survive.

Existing human society should be rejected because it lagged behind scientific advances. If the laws of biology were followed, the result would be a humane, efficient, peaceful state. As we saw earlier, that radical social change should be implemented according to nature's laws is a typical ecologists' view.

As I shall argue later that German National Socialism had a strong ecological element, it might be a good moment here to discuss the charge, levied in 1971 in an influential book by Daniel Gasman, that Haeckel inspired Hitler and Nazi ideology. The charge is based on the assumption that Haeckel was a Darwinian, and ignores the fact that he was a neo-Lamarckian. Haeckel is supposed to be a *völkisch* thinker, although this is quite untrue, and the work, which has combed the most obscure and little-read books by Haeckel, is forced to rely on an unsubstantiated journalist's report in 1918 as evidence. Haeckel is supposed to share an anti-Enlightenment bias with Hitler. Yet the Enlightenment in no way rejected a politics based on nature and biology; on the contrary, Kant himself accepted Linnaeus's classification of animals and applied it to man, recognising distinct races of man, whereas the *völkisch* Herder rejected it, and argued that man was one race, separated for a few hundred years. Then the chain of evidence is weak. Hitler may have read Haeckel, but there is no evidence that he did, although we have abundant evidence about his reading in general, including lists of books borrowed from libraries. There is no direct contact traceable in the way there is for D.H. Lawrence. Hitler was not sympathetic to the 'green' wing of his party. Haeckel's creed was pacifist by inclination, while Hitler's was not. Haeckel was a nationalist for progressive reasons; the centralized state would, he thought, sweep away the conservative, particularist, Catholic and reactionary remnants of militarist states. The Third Reich did not support Darwinian evolutionary theories, and Hitler is supposed, by Rauschning, to have referred to Bölsche as an urban absurdity.[42]

THE POLITICS OF MONISTIC ECOLOGY

We have now examined Haeckel's biology, his Monism and his belief in a positive progressive nature. This section will examine his politics and his political heritage, and argue that it is in accord with the typology of political ecology discussed earlier.

It was not until 1905 that Haeckel became chairman of the Monist League, but it had always been inspired by his ideas. Monism and Haeckel's writings were from their inception attacked by Christian and conservative groups in Germany and England. They were widely disseminated through almost universal literacy and cheap printing. One popular magazine, *Gartenlaube*, with some five million readers, carried chatty notes on natural science. The liberal impulses stifled in the German empire found expression through natural science, and its tone was anti-establishment. Several of its best-known exponents were forty-eighters, that is, banned after the revolutions of 1848. Although Monists have been described as right-wing because most were eugenically-minded, their political affiliation was for the most part firmly on the left. Karl Vogt, who taught biology to Houston Stewart Chamberlain, among others, was a left-wing socialist materialist, and with Moleschott was forced to lecture in Switzerland. Indeed, one of Dostoievsky's most horrible terrorists read the works of Karl Vogt. The editor of a popular science journal was another old forty-eighter, and his magazine was banned in Prussia for years. The works of Darwin himself had been banned by one conservative journal in Germany, and were welcomed by liberals.[43]

But the easiest way to discover the League's political slant is to examine its membership. Many belonged to the German Social Democratic Party. They included ex-Marxist and eugenicist

Ludwig Woltmann, who became a popularizer of Gobineau, and the Swiss August Forel, who taught Ploetz and other eugenic communards, and who was drowned with Ludwig of Bavaria. One of Wilhelm Bölsche's early novels describes a young man, a left-wing activist, tempted by a utopian and spiritual paradise, but who rejects it in favour of a working-class fiancèe and the class struggle. Haeckel and Darwin were on August Bebel's reading list in prison, as with most enlightened and progressive souls. Darwinian biologists were often internationalist and pacifist, whereas *völkisch* German nationalists were anti-Darwinian. Chamberlain himself was on the point of completing his Vogt-inspired doctorate in biology when he was converted to neo-vitalism. Forel during the First World War protested to Haeckel about pro-war poems in the Monists' journal. But he also wanted modern science to list races in order of their potential service to mankind.[44] There was a move by Monists to merge with the Social Democratic Party. Carl von Ossietsky and Magnus Hirschfeld, both prominent left-wingers, were Monists.[45] Wilhelm Ostwald thought that all Monists must be oriented against conservatism, orthodoxy and ultramontanism. Few Monists became Marxists, because class conflict was seen by them as wasteful and pointless. Ostwald's *Natural Philosophy* ended with a call to class co-operation based on the gradual disappearance of all groups but the skilled worker. One day all would be technocrats.[46] Haeckel's followers in the Monist League belonged to the optimistic, progressive, scientific Left. The university-educated eco-socialists active in today's German Green Party derive from this tradition.

Haeckel's enormous popularity was partly due to his biographer, the man who played Boswell to his Johnson, Wilhelm Bölsche. They both appealed to a generation of republican, socialist atheists, who were anxious to believe what was in effect a new religion. Haeckel's emphasis on what was both wondrous and rational was persuasive. This humanism seems a world away from the other, better-known German tradition of idealism and relativism, of Engels and Dilthey. But in its belief in the human will, together with the vision of society as an organic whole, it lent scientific validity to relativism. The political relevance for Germany was to be far in the future, decades after the collapse of the Third Reich, when the educated middle-classes began to support the Greens.

Haeckel and the Monists did not support democracy, partly because they did not trust untrained scientists to understand man and society. In this they resembled the Fabians, the scientific social reformers of the same period. The nuclear physicist Frederick Soddy, Bertrand Russell and H.G. Wells all wrote with scorn of the pettiness of politics, the superior capacities of the scientific mind. They rejected the notion of political science and philosophy, because society was too important to be left to the compromise, bargaining and jockeying for power that characterised the political process. Comte had influenced many. He thought that committees of trained experts were more competent to govern than elected representatives (not to think of pre-democratic modes of government). Experts were apolitical and meritocratic. The art of politics would be replaced by a knowledge of man. Anthropology would render the pettiness and self-seeking of politicians unnecessary. This rejection of traditional politics is typical of the world-view of today's ecologists.

Thus, Haeckel's link with ecology is not confined to the verbal accident of inventing the term. Ecology, as a conceptual tool, was a term that contained the kernel of its normative usage from the beginning. Its founder became heavily involved in politics. Both his politics and his scientific work touched on concerns fundamental to today's ecologists. They did not touch on *all*; on the other hand, his immediate followers extended Haeckel's interests to cover soil erosion and resource conservation. Haeckel's most important legacy was his worship of Nature, the belief that man and nature were one, and that to damage one was to damage the other. He offered scientific 'proof' that harmony and benevolence were intrinsic to the world, and that man must fit into its framework, while cherishing and caring for nature's wonders.

In many ways, he was more entitled to be regarded as the direct founder of the movement than the holistic biologists who form the subject of the next section. Their scientific contribution is, however, more relevant to man's behaviour and social organisation.

MATERIALISM AND VITALISM

One of the missing links of nineteenth-century biology was the gap where the soul or spirit had previously lived. Scientific materialism was the first answer. The world was all one; man was part of the world. There was no tangible soul, therefore all was matter. Monism, the unitary man-nature philosophy propagated by Haeckel, opposed the dualism between man and soul, body versus spirit, emotion versus reason, that had been so strong a part of Western and Christian philosophy. The revolt against scientific materialism, which appeared earlier in Germany than elsewhere, was, however, characterised by the same rationality and optimism. The vitalists argued that it was the wonders of science themselves which showed that anything was possible. The greatest wonder of all was organised and complex life, which could not be satisfactorily explained by materialism. Vitalists were agnostics; pending scientific proof of a life-force, of, in effect, a God, they predicated its existence. This attitude makes more sense if one remembers that during the nineteenth century a mental posture of considerable credulity was needed to believe the bizarre discoveries of the natural scientists. Schopenhauer thought that different laws governed different 'provinces of nature'. Where gravitation and similar laws had been valid for what he called 'the province of the mechanical', new laws were needed for 'chemistry, electricity, magnetism and crystallisation'.[47] If marvels like invisible bacteria and hypnotism could affect body and psyche, or elements in an immortal germplasm determine one's character, what hidden powers could not be omnipresent? The very fact that science had uncovered such miracles meant that the boundaries between possible and impossible – even or perhaps especially for the trained scientific mind – became fainter.

Here, too, Haeckel's role was crucial. Monism began as a materialistic creed. Before Haeckel's death, it had moved to a vitalist position, where all was one, but all was spirit. Haeckel's last work was *God-Nature,* published in 1914. One of Haeckel's students was Hans Driesch, Professor of Philosophy at Heidelberg. He also lectured at Scottish and English universities up to 1913. In 1907 and 1908 he gave the Gifford Lectures, on natural philosophy and evolution. Driesch was the most important neovitalist of his day, described by his English translator as having many admirers in England and Germany. His pupils included Ernst Jünger and Ortega y Gasset, both radical nationalist conservatives. As late as 1970 he was cited as an inspiration by members and supporters of the Soil Association, along with Bergson.[48] He postulated the existence of what he called a 'dynamic teleology' behind organic life. Inorganic objects were governed by a 'static teleology'. Teleology simply meant inherently purposeful. His distinction between dynamic and static argued that the vital force operated at a more intense level with animals, but that the same principle was at work through everything in the universe. Life was governed by will and purpose; the higher the life-form, the higher the level of purpose within it. Driesch thought that the only way to explain the marvels of human consciousness and animal life was that some thing or being had intended it so to be. This purpose he called the life-force. Driesch distinguished his neo-vitalism from the earlier nineteenth-century vitalism. Darwin's demonstration of evolution had made earlier vitalism untenable, but had not explained the increasing specialisation and complexity of life forms. If amoeba could survive as they were, why shoud they mutate or develop eventually into human beings? He freely admitted that there was still no proof of the existence of a life-force; however, he saw the mechanical, accidental causation of life and evolution as an obviously untenable hypothesis.

Driesch's *The Philosophy of the Organic* was published in 1909. Vitalism retreated into philosophy, and lost its status in mainstream science. It remained as a vigorous sub-culture, finding expression in existentialism, as well as in popular science after the Second World War. What made life distinct, if anything, remained a vexed question, one illustrated by Karl Popper's dispute with Schrödinger, the physicist. Schrödinger argued in *What is Life* (1967) that life was qualitatively different from the non-living. He thought that the difference was shown by life's capacity to contradict the second law of thermo-dynamics; life resisted entropy. He defined living organisms as those that 'feed on negative entropy'.[49] Life could organise its own energy production and consumption. It could 'suck orderliness from its environment'.[50] Popper denied that there was any such difference between life and non-living organisms. To him, 'every oil-fired boiler and every self-winding watch may be said' to do the same thing.[51]

Popper apparently missed Schrödinger's point. Man shovelled coal into the steam engine and it moved. But what moved man? That which lived could feed, convert and use energy sources to create a structured life form without external intervention. It could reproduce itself. Through collecting and using energy, focused and usable energy was created by the organism. A steam engine could not do that. Popper's dismissal of Schrödinger's definition hints at a deep antipathy towards what can be seen as an anti-materialist argument.

The religious and spiritual overtones of the 'life-force' seemed to make it unacceptable generally to the irritable materialism of accepted scientific discourse. In the natural sciences, genetics was to offer a physical explanation of national selection, while behaviourism promised an explanation of animal behaviour that ignored self-generating activity.

ETHOLOGY; LORENZ AND HIS HEIRS

Scientific holism was not dead, however. In 1909 a German physiologist, Jacob von Uekhüll, first used the term *Umwelt*. By this word, used today as 'environment' in German, he meant 'the subjective or phenomenal world of the individual'.[52] The concept of interaction between observer and observed continued into the 1920s, when the success of *Gestalt* philosophy added to the force of non-behaviourist types of explanation. It was an attempt to merge different ways of studying perception. It showed that animal and human visual perception fastened on specific elements in a picture or scene, and completed the picture from non-observed assumptions. The gap beween man and animal was further weakened by the development of ethology. Köhler's chimpanzee studies suggested that animals thought. They even had the equivalent of the Eureka exclamation, which Köhler charmingly calls the 'Aha' expression. This appeared when a problem was solved.[53]

The split between mechanical causation and vitalism had stimulated attempts by ethologists at experimental validation of both hypotheses. Ethologists searched for precise mechanisms, both in-built and learned, to explain instinct. Without the concept of ecology, the relation between organisms and environment, ethologists would not have been inspired to see the animal in its natural habitat, and, true to our ethnic map, ethology flourished in England, America, France, Holland and Austria. One gifted Afrikaner, Eugene Marais, studied in such hostile isolation, far from the mainstream of academic life, that he finally committed suicide.

The idea that animal behaviour can best be understood by examining it in its 'natural' surroundings seems obvious today, but its exponents were fighting the laboratory paradigm, which denied feeling, spirit and individualism to the animal kingdom. Such ideas were dismissed as anthropomorphism. The zoo was the source of many animal studies. It was paradoxical that environmentalists failed to ask themselves whether an animal stripped of its intended environmental stimuli would be typical, whether a beast in prison was the proper subject for analysis. Although ethologists were to be criticized for extrapolating from animal to human, behavioural psychologists did so too. Again, was the laboratory experiment the correct way to understand the complex and subtle interactions of animals and men?

For obvious reasons, it was hard to study birds in imprisonment or in laboratories. Perhaps for this reason, it was birds who were first studied in the wild. The most famous ethologist in this tradition was to be the Austrian naturalist Konrad Lorenz. Brought up by the Danube, he observed birds in their habitat from childhood. He first became famous outside Germany with his book *King Solomon's Ring*. This anecdotal account of animal behaviour conveyed the endearing picture of a Dr Dolittle, and the German title of the book, 'He talked to the Animals.' emphasised this. But Lorenz also offered convincing explanations of its causes. The theory of instinctive drives might be complex. But anyone who had ever observed their own cat could understand the concept of displacement activity. In place of the behaviourists' passive animal, born with a blank mind, to be affected by electric shocks, bright lights, bells and food withdrawal Lorenz suggested a set of inborn templates, designed to guide behaviour along a certain line. The development could be thwarted or altered, but the pressure on the animal to perform certain actions would produce observable phenomena as a result. However, animals could learn from and respond to changes in their environment.

Lorenz had begun as a behaviourist, who followed the mechanical explanation, namely that animal behaviour had reducible physical causes. He was also inspired by the excitement and romance of biology, as interpreted by Wilhelm Bölsche's books, such as *Love-Life in Nature*.[54] Because Bölsche was a devout Haeckelian, it was Haeckelian neo-Lamarckian evolution that appeared in his picture of nature, not Darwin's more mechanical process. Although Sir Charles Elton's famous text *Animal Ecology* was first published in 1927, Lorenz appears not to have come across it. Elton was always aware of the parallels between man and animals in their interaction with their environment, and for this reason was active in establishing the Nature Conservancy Council.[55]

Lorenz's ethology contained normative elements from the start. Animal and environment were seen as a unit. The feedback between specie and habitat was part of the study. On the other hand, it was not determinist. Each animal was an individual. Animals learned, changed and loved, like humans. Some paired for life; some flirted and got divorced. They felt surprise, jealousy and pain.

The idea of explaining human behaviour by comparisons with animals had not been taken seriously before. Such comparisons had been largely polemical or ironical. Now the comparison could be made on the basis of the new science, and it appeared to prove that the gap between species was not as great as had been thought. The door was open for scientific anti-anthropomorphism, leading to 'anti-speciesism', the belief that it was wrong to distinguish between the moral or even legal standing of different species.

Lorenz first entered political controversy with his book *On Aggression*. This argued that all animals displayed signs of something like aggression, but which had a purpose for their survival. The most striking was that animals would defend their territory and their kin-group. Animals defending someone else's territory tended to lose the fight; one could almost say that they knew they were in the wrong. Lorenz accounted for the untrammelled nature of human aggression by arguing that it was precisely because man was a fundamentally peaceful being, who had not developed innate mechanisms for controlling aggressive behaviour. He instanced wolves, who would stop attacking as soon as the victim made a surrender gesture. Man, like the turtle-dove, had no inbuilt stopping instinct. The exploratory, inquisitive drive was another 'animal' trait in man, responsible for much of his cultural achievements.

Lorenz believed, like T.H. Huxley, that if man's animal nature were recognised, it would be easier to solve his political and social problems. His book was an impassioned call to avoid war. It was, however, taken as a justification of violence. The argument that man had innate tendencies was seen as determinism. He was interpreted as arguing that man was innately violent.[56]

The debate between nature and nurture concerned genes and the possibility of genetic transmission of behaviour patterns. Many historians of science saw an implicit racialism in the sociobiological position. However, it is clear that genetic programming would presuppose a universal, species-oriented approach to human behaviour. If humanity had genes for any specific quality, all humans would have them. But resistance to the idea that the human species, like animals, owe their mind and emotions to physical factors, was powerful. When one of Lorenz's students, Irenäus Eibl-Eibesfeldt, claimed to have found a universal body-language of expression and gesture, it was countered by the behaviourist psychologists' claim that frowns, smiles, etc., were firstly non-universal expressions, and secondly if they were 'universal' it was because such expressions came most easily to the human musculature. A baby learned to express surprise by raising its eyebrows because a baby surprised by something would naturally look up at it. Eibl-Eibesfeldt countered that this hardly accounted for the universal baby habit of pouting, stamping its feet and banging its firsts when angry. He produced photos of

Amazon Indian girl children pouting and turning away when their shells were taken by little boys. Not only sex, motherhood and violence, but the very nuances of social behaviour were, argued human ethologists, genetically programmed for mankind.[57]

Many conservatives found these conclusions disturbing. What use were traditions and institutions, those guardians of the collective memory, if human qualities were programmed? Because ethology seemed to work with the lowest common denominator of behaviour it was seen as anti-culture, claiming that man was only his propensity to mate, nest and hunt. Lorenz saw the wonders of human culture as a direct result of his animal qualities. In his 1973 work on the theory of knowledge, developed from his years of meditating on Kant while a prisoner-of-war, he cited Toynbee's theory of history as the first example of history which examined cultures as organisms.[58] Lorenz described culture as a historically unique process; like a species, it developed independently. Its evolution was not controlled by man's will, or by his power of abstract thought. Lorenz concluded that 'the cognitive function of culture, the acquisition and accumulation of knowledge, emerges through processes that are parallel to those which occur in phylogenetic development'.[59] Lorenz now seemed to be accepting man's uniqueness. At some time in his development, man had experienced a 'creative flash' that had produced self-aware intelligence and consciousness.[60] But man's capacity to create a culture was still natural, built in by nature. And if man could understand his own nature, then, for the first time, the forces that 'have destroyed all earlier civilizations' could be warded off.[61] 'A reflecting *self-investigation* of a culture has never yet come into being on this planet, just as objectivating science did not exist before the time of Galileo.'[62] Without specifically articulating his debt, Lorenz, like the holistic and vitalist philosophers before him, referred to Goethe's inspiration, – combined with error, through not understanding that 'the creative force is life itself', not 'the reflection of some pre-established harmony'. Lorenz claimed that Chomsky, who had shown that the grammar of language and thought was innate, and found in identical form in all humanity, owed a debt to Wilhelm von Humboldt, who had expounded this in 1827. As Lorenz admired Chomsky and his work, this was not intended as an attack. It was a reference to the German tradition, so alien to Lockean liberalism, of holistic universality.[63]

The development of human ethology has proceeded since the Second World War. The belief that man's thoughts, beliefs and ideas are unconnected with his physical animality will possibly seem one day as bizarre as biblical anti-Darwinian arguments seem to biologists today. But critics are right to stress the connection with older strands of German philosophy. For though with pouting children and monogamous geese we may seem to have travelled some way from the roots of ecology, important links emerge.

The first is the anti-anthropomorphic stance. The ecological vision of man as an animal no longer depended on a moral position. Ecological values were backed up by a new science.

Ethology did not deny man's special nature, his capacity to be self-aware and change his environment. Neither did it abandon man as the evil spirit. It offered solutions to the eternal problem of how man should live in the world. One might adduce as evidence connecting Lorenz with ecology his statement that he supported Rachel Carson's work, and considered himself, in the political sense, an ecologist.[64] But that by itself would underrate his importance.

It is in his solutions to man's separate and unique position on earth that Lorenz approaches most closely to our quest. The same philosophical questions that preoccupy ecologists appear in Lorenz's work. Even the problem of entropy, of the dissipation of energy versus the increasing complexity of life, appears in his meditations.

> The most amazing function of the life process . . . is that it seems to develop from the simplest to the highest . . . However, none of the laws of physics, even the second law of thermodynamics, is broken by this. All life processes are sustained by the flow of energy being dissipated . . . in the universe . . . Life feeds on negative entropy.[65]

Lorenz gave as examples of positive feedback, the snowball and the flame, which by devouring, increased. But was man doomed to behave like a flame, magnificent, but leaving only ashes behind him, as in Nietzsche's ironical poem? Lorenz thought not. Man, unlike flame, could avoid such uncontrolled growth, because nature herself in effect separated man from animals in kind as well as in degree through his cultural traditions. His explanatory, open nature, which was itself his genetic heritage, meant that he could understand and control himself. At this higher level of integration, man would co-operate with and understand natural processes. His very alienation from the earth fitted him, it seemed, to become the shepherd of the earth that Heidegger had demanded he become.

BIOLOGICAL ECOLOGY

This chapter has traced elements in German biology that bear on the development of ecological ideas. The explicit anti-anthropomorphism of Haeckel and his vision of energy flows were developed and expanded by ethologists, including Lorenz. Although the vitalism of Driesch was left behind by mainstream science, some of its questions stimulated holistic thinking in later decades.

Vitalism between the wars also affected the scientific picture of the earth itself, as well as man's life upon it. As a historian of geography has noted, the biological vitalism of Bergson and Driesch, as well as holistic philosophy, produced not merely an organic analogy, but a system in which 'the earth was a functionally related, mutually interdependent complex which... remained in an equilibrium condition'.[67]

Theories of the earth as organism had a long history. The mid-eighteenth century as well as the landscape Romantics of the nineteenth century offered a rhetoric of the living earth. The geographers Alexander von Humboldt and Carl Ritter described the earth as a functioning organism. The biological analogy fitted Friedrich Rätzel's belief that man and land had an indissoluble, mystic bond. The geopolitics of Halford Mackinder, enthusiastically adopted in Germany, argued that geographical factors inexorably affected man's social, political and economic conditions. In 1905, A.J. Herbertson described the earth as a 'macro-organism...the soil itself the flesh, the vegetation, its epidermal covering...and the water its circulating life-blood'.[68] Herbertson, however, presented this picture as 'comparison' only. What gave the metaphor a scientific basis was the argument against entropy and the development of systems theory. If the earth was sustaining an equilibrium of energy, then it was interacting with its source of energy, and responding to its energy loss. Kenneth Boulding, originator in the 1960s of the famous 'Spaceship Earth' phrase, saw systems theory as the dynamic behind ecological ideas, because it offered a theory as to how complex biological organisms worked. Boulding by 1941 had evolved an ecological-economic theory which used his earlier work on population dynamics. He was a founder member of the Behavioural Sciences Centre, Stanford, together with biologists and physicists. Paul Ehrlich wrote of the self-organising earth, and used systems theory to explain it.[69]

In the 1920s, British geographers explained the geological pattern of a region as being equivalent to man's 'germ-plasm', while 'the cultural landscape reflects the activities of a living, throbbing individual'.[70] In 1920s Germany similar arguments were heard.

Eduard Suess's (1831–1914) nineteenth-century coinage, the 'biosphere', was revived in the 1920s by a Russian biologist, who was also active as a geochemist, mineralogist and natural philosopher. Vladimir I. Vernadsky published *La Biosphère* in 1926, introducing the new theories of energy and chemistry. P. Theilhard de Chardin coined the term 'noosphere' after meeting Vernadsky in Paris.[71]

The force behind vitalist theories had been the perception that energy did not only dissipate, but could, under certain circumstances, appear to synthesise. There was a stubborn belief that, in biological terms man could be considered as displaying 'life against entropy'. The geographer Bernard Brunhes thought that while the physical sciences showed a world wearing out, the life sciences showed a world steadily improving, growing perfect.[72] Cultural conservatives like Henry Adams had a more pessimistic approach. While believing that man's history consisted of the search to use and control energy, and that knowledge was increasing exponentially, Adams saw man as subject to entropy. For an organism, entropy resulted in death.[73]

The fusion of biological vitalism and organic geology seems to have been a prerequisite for the global vision of ecologists today. Optimists and humanists supported the idea that the life-force opposed entropy. The apparently paradoxical presence of optimism and humanism among today's ecologists can be traced to this intuition.

The question of man-animal equivalence had a dynamic whose consequences were neither predicted nor accepted by most ethologists. Equivalent rights and status, it was argued recently, belong to the animal world, the plant world, and even, recently, the inanimate world.[74] The last of these claims is the most startling, but it conveys one of the most important parts of the ecological vision. It is clear that rights in this context is a misuse of the idea, which strictly speaking relates to a judicial-political status, not a moral claim to consideration.

And it is possible to argue that distress over man's dominant-manipulative relationships with animals and inanimate objects simply sidesteps the responsibility of worrying about real and difficult political issues. However, this is to miss the point of the non-political nature of the claim that we should treat all objects in the world with a reserved and discreet love. The call to deny all dominant or potentially dominant relationships – including affection – is as dramatic and novel a moral ideal as earlier was chastity. While the ideal of chastity has never been obeyed in its entirety, it has over the past two thousand years inescapably affected our morals, social ideals and culture.

The belief that any alteration of another's being is wrong, even if inspired by care and affection, may or may not be *true*; but an awareness of the potentially sadistic aspect of being object to subject, once stated, lingers. The tension between status and friendship, paternalism and power, the mutation of cruelty we call affectionate teasing, is in our biological fabric, is involved in our attitudes to children, siblings, equals, sexual partners and the old. To cease from dominant-inspired relationships would be as violent a social and familial change as the attempt to refrain from sexual congress was at the turn of the first century A.D.; yet once a moral ideal has been proposed – and believed – it creates its own reality, its own validity. That is the hallmark of a religious revival, and it is an element in ecological thinking that became first possible then acceptable through the new discipline of ethology.

CHAPTER FOUR
Energy Economics

> Nature possesses properties and forces whose discovery and right use appear to be among man's highest tasks, because they have the power to make his labour more fruitful.
>
> (Von Thünen, *The Isolated State*, pp.245–7)

SCARCE RESOURCES AND SOLAR POWER

Ecological economists are claimed by some writers to be the first *real* ecologists. Certainly the call to conserve scarce resources is today perhaps the strongest green argument. Economists have begun to look at the problem not only of allocation of resources but also of inter-generational allocation of resources. The existence of fixed, non-renewable resources was first seen as a problem when the implications of the theory of dissipation of energy (the second law of thermo-dynamics) were understood.[1] The universe was now seen as a closed system: nothing came in, nothing came out. Therefore, the energy that was dissipated, changing its form from usable to unusable energy, could never be replaced. If finite energy resources were not conserved, the result would be waste and loss; eventually, famine and disaster. Wilhelm Ostwald expressed this view when he wrote in 1911 that 'the free energy accessible can only decrease, but not increase'.[2] Today, this mental picture is everyone's common sense view. However, it depended on a complex scientific argument, and it was not until the theory was grasped by natural scientists working outside physics that it was seen as presenting a danger to human society. This shift of vision paralleled the disappearance of Say's Law as a serious economic concept.[3] In physics as in economics, the self-contained, closed system was no longer viable without a stringent programme to prevent a leakage of energy.

The intellectuals who wrote about this problem were usually trained natural scientists. They tended to switch disciplines and pursue reform in areas remote from their original field, but which seemed to present the same kind of problems. Some were also interested in biological ecology, and were mentioned in the last chapter: others were human geographers, architects, economists or chemists. This disparate group included left-anarchists and Marxists, but tended not to be 'party men' of any orientation. What they had in common was their independence of establishment thinking, and a somewhat bloody-minded persistence in alternative ideas. They were not so much motivated by the emotional identification of nature and beauty found in the biologists discussed earlier, nor by the Romantic or sensuous response to landscape found in the United States and England; rather it was a vision of future collapse of human societies, and a sense of injustice over what they saw as inequitable distribution of energy resources. They drew from nature recommendations for egalitarian co-operation. Kropotkin 'urged people to uncover the laws of the environment and to act in accordance with them'; he argued that intervention should be based on a 'respect for and understanding of the natural world'.[4]

Although for the most part they held socialist and egalitarian principles, the disciples of energy economics never quite made the socialist text-books, perhaps because their works did not express the humanitarian impulse that characterized nineteenth-century bourgeois socialism, but a science-based fear for the future of human survival. Like those of all movements fed by fears of apocalypse, their solutions were draconian. They included restructuring society into a system which controlled resource allocation and resource use, in order that the burden of shortage be equally shared. As the one major source of renewable, 'free' energy is human labour, suggestions for reform usually included the compulsory direction of human labour, which would be managed by a committee of wise scientists. Where Back-to-the-Land settlement plans or plans to establish communes were the hall-mark of the small-scale, anarchist dream, of Right or Left: the scientific plan was global. Both involved a eugenic ideal. Selective breeding was the key to future progress for the Platonic socialism of J.D. Bernal and Hermann Muller.[5]

LAND , PRODUCTIVITY AND THE PLANNERS

Some energy ecologists had a positive attitude to the possibilities of technology, but as the nineteenth century used coal, clearly a non-renewable resource, the technology suitable for a planned energy intensive eco-system would have to be of a kind as yet unknown. Existing ways of producing energy from water and windmills were seldom seen as serious alternatives to coal-produced steam. Several early science fiction or fantasy novels were written by this group, suggesting new ways of managing society, with a view to conserving finite resources. The content of some of these works reveal the ways in which scientists were thinking. One science fiction novel by a professor of chemistry, A.J. Stewart, described a world in which a man-made bacteria escapes and kills all grass. A millionaire with vision establishes a secure bacteria-free zone based around Glasgow – at that time teeming with resources, skilled manpower, coal and successful industry, – in which he stockpiles food. He recruits up to a million healthy, hard-working, socially responsible inhabitants, and organizes their labour 'properly' and productively, to find food and energy substitutes. When the loading capacity of the area is reached, no one is allowed in from outside. Internal strikes are crushed ruthlessly. Eventually the world outside collapses, and the perfect social system created by the benevolent but social Darwinist visionary inside the Glasgow commune can expand into the outside world.[6] This was an early example of survivalist futurism: a variant of the pull-up-the-drawbridge mentality which is more common in today's ecological commune movement than in the early twentieth century.

The fear of land shortage, of a failure to produce enough food to feed the population, haunted energy ecologists. An entire discipline grew up based on the problem of intensive food production. Studies in the mid-nineteenth century showed that in terms of energy units used, peasant productivity was greater than that of large, capitalist farms. Belgian and Dutch writers studied Flemish peasants to learn from their frugality, endless hard work and patriarchal morality. Productivity per hectare became the standard, as opposed to productivity of labour, capital or technology: – land was visibly a fixed resource, whereas population sizes were not. Not only was maximising production from land the logical response to a fear of food and fertility shortage, but independence from trade and capitalistic market relations would free what socialist economists regarded as wasted resources for more useful tasks. The deep distrust of the speculator, the middleman, or the trader, made autarky desirable. Peasants were seen as the source not only of social cohesion and conservative values but of ecologically sound agricultural improvement. They were seen as less likely to exploit the soil than capitalist or mercantilist farmers, more likely to conserve soil fertility for future generations.

The belief that small farms could be more efficient than large contradicted liberal economic beliefs in the economies of scale and the virtues of capital investment. It also contradicted Marxist and Social Democratic prophecies that small-scale farming was doomed to give way to large farms because economies of scale made the latter more efficient. Effective pressure, indeed, was put on British governments throughout the twentieth century by Fabian planners and Quaker economists, such as Astor, Rowntree and Lamartine Yates, to support large farms on the grounds of superior efficiency and social tidiness. The collectivist *Zeitgeist* of the 1930s and 1940s found these arguments appealing. But market-oriented peasant farming on the continent proved surprisingly adaptable and efficient in its own terms.[7] German peasant advocates argued that if all inputs were correctly costed, and energy costs, import costs for machinery (or the raw materials needed to make it), fertiliser and fodder added to the net costs of agricultural production, then the virtually self-sufficient peasant was more productive in terms of the social and economic costs of the resources involved than was the large landowner, who could afford to buy in artificial fertiliser and machinery and hire labour. Autarky was impossible without self-sufficiency in food production, and autarky was in some cases part of the opposition to trade and mercantilism held by socialist and anarchist reformers.

While agrarian economists differed as to the value of machinery on small-holdings (of course, nineteenth-century steam tractors were unsuitable for small farms, and disproportionately damaged the soil), it was agreed that land under peasant cultivation benefited from the intimate care and knowledge of the peasant. Peasants were prepared to work for a real return on their labour so low that no capitalist farmer would accept it. 'It is the small cultivator only who, spade in hand, can fertilise the waste and perform prodigies. . . His day's work he counts for nothing', was the hard-headed sentiment of the time, an argument encountered today.[8] Apart from Kropotkin's arguments, kept alive by the anarchist movement, this awareness of the economic argument for self-sufficiency seems to have been lost, subsumed in a belief in a late nineteenth-century 'drive back to nature', caused simply by a 'reaction to the growing industrialization of the age'.[9]

PATRIOTS AND PEASANTS

The urge for a more equitable distribution of production appealed to early variants of Distributism. One writer argued that in capitalist agriculture, a produce of one thousand units would be distributed thus;

One landlord 200 parts
One tenant 100 parts
14 labourers 700 parts (50 each)

Whereas if the same area of land was worked by sixteen small owners, each receiving 60 parts of the total produce, the extremes of poverty and opulence, 'the parents of vice in private and revolution in public life' would be avoided.[10] The Flemish peasant let nothing go to waste: human sewage, animal manures, river mud and bones for phosphate.[11]

This analysis was more serious and more economically radical than the glorification of the simple peasant practised by Rousseau (who apparently based his assessment of the economic superiority of the independent Swiss peasant on erroneous observation).[12] The gut reaction to praising peasants was that it was a crack-pot notion, practised by cranks and sentimentalists. But when economists and social scientists produced acceptable models of improved welfare via peasant productivity, the debate was lifted onto a more convincing level. And in this instance peasant societies were proving surprisingly durable. In the flat alluvial plains of Northern Europe, the late nineteenth century saw a real growth of peasant productivity in Flanders, Denmark and North and North-East Germany. In Denmark, small farm agriculture was capital intensive. In Germany it was labour intensive, and in Flanders both. But in all three countries, innovation and response to market conditions was needed as well as the bitter stubbornness needed to work heavy soil with hand tools most months of the year. This theme of the forward-looking peasant, as opposed to the reactionary landowner, was to be prominent in Northen European peasant ideology. Knut Hamsun's picture of Isak, the Norwegian frontiersman, shows him as 'A ghost risen out of the past to point the future, a man from the earliest days of cultivation. . .and withal a man of the day.'[13] De la Vigne Eckmannsdorf, a Silesian landowner and supporter of Walther Darré, the radical Nazi Minister of Agriculture, saw the role of the peasant as the core of a new culture, a new world, untainted with the vices and errors of the old, but retaining the folk wisdom of the past.[14] The peasant's role was to reclaim new ground and to make poor and difficult land fertile. To some agrarian ideologues, peasant production meant more self-sufficiency and less reliance on paper money and trade, but to others, it meant a greater reliance on market mechanisms and more flexibility of land use and crop rotation.

The first writer to argue the relative merits of small farms and latifundia from the production point of view seems to have been a German diplomat based in St Petersburg, Count Bernhardi, who published a study of their comparative advantages in 1849. This work was re-published in 1925 in Germany, during a revival of this debate. Possibly this isolated and early example of such a study was stimulated by Russian populism. Indeed, the Russian *mir*, and its perpetuation in the Russian agricultural reforms of the 1860s, with its collectivist morality, was praised by Prussian landowners. Several doctoral theses on the subject of comparative productivity of small and large farms appeared in Germany between 1890 and 1900, and most of the them opted for peasant production as economically superior.[15]

In England, experience with the intractable peasant problems of Ireland and India had helped to dilute *laissez-faire* with a hapless imperial paternalism. All the political parties toyed with smallholding programmes.[16] Nor was it only the Tory tradition that wanted to protect the yeoman against the Whig landowner. Despite the continental belief, prevalent to this day, that free trade meant an anti-peasant policy, and that the repeal of the Corn Laws introduced an era of utter desolation to English farming, many staunch free trade liberals also supported the vision of a smallholder economy. Richard Cobden, free-trader and Manchester economist, argued for the forty-shilling freeholder. Liberal thought supported the responsible individual, and claimed that food production overall would rise, not decrease, through encouraging yeoman farmers. Not only visionary politicians but practical liberal theoreticians supported the yeoman. Herbert Spencer thought that land reform was a necessary reform on which to base a free and efficient society. John Stuart Mill 'devoted five chapters of his *Principles* (1848) to peasant tenures, and sang a paean to small ownership' whilst he also supported an emigration scheme to settle Britons in the colonies, with the proviso that it be eventually self-financing.[17] Despite the popular support for such a movement, Lloyd George, once in power, failed to implement it, except for the Small Holdings and Allotments Act of 1907, which he believed could have little effect. Lloyd George's own programme was allegedly liberal, but incorporated many of the étatist features, such as state-aided afforestation, state development funds, and a government-backed 'central, rational and concerted effort', of the later British Union of Fascists programme.[18]

The anti-state, anti-organization nature of the peasant-yeoman life and spirit made it attractive to anarchists as well as to *laissez-faire* liberals and liberal nationalists. Prince Peter Kropotkin, the Russian anarchist, had written a master plan for the economic development of Siberia while on military service as a youth. It disappeared permanently into his General's filing cabinet, but the practice was useful for his later anarchist programme. He was offered the secretaryship of the Russian Geographical Society in 1871, but turned it down to pursue his political aims.[19] His practical training and experience produced plans for reform that were less utopian and messianic than earlier anarchists', such as Fourier, and for this reason more influential. In *Mutual Aid as a Law of Nature and a Factor of Evolution* (London, 1902) he drew attention to examples of co-operation and altruism among animal societies, suggesting that a law of mutual aid was as important as the law of competition. Nature proved that human altruism was 'natural'.[20] One author comments that 'Kropotkin laid the conceptual foundation for a radical theory of human ecology. He viewed nature and people in nature as organic, interrelated wholes.'[21] He wrote in *Fields, Factories, and Workshops Tomorrow* (London, 1899), that per hectare productivity was the crucial factor, and that improved technology combined with peasant ownership of land would bring about increased food production. Kropotkin placed his land reform and productivity proposals in the context of the small, independent artisan and worker, and supported the small business if it could be decentralised. He argued that small industrial production had continued under capitalism, in Britain as well as in France and Germany, where guild and corporate protection for the artisan was greater, and claimed, correctly, that the German SPD expectation that small businesses would be unable to compete with large conglomerates had been disproved. Each new techological advance, each large firm, spawned thousands of small firms who supplied often hand-made parts and spares. 'Small Industries and Industrial Villages', as one of his chapter titles ran, were the productive areas of the future. Man would return to the land in fruitful and co-operative harmony, not as primitive ruralist, but as educated artisans. Not only would yeomen understand technology but, as Kropotkin rightly pointed out, engineers, inventors and entrepreneurs themselves initiated technology which, in a healthy society, came 'from below'. This was a further argument in favour of small, decentralised, independent schooling, an anarchist demand then long before the days of Ivan Illich, and part of the Schumacher Society programme today.[22]

This book, with its wealth of up-to-date statistics and its sober argument, influenced Tolstoy, Gandhi and Mao Tse-Tung. At a lower level, it inspired the wartime Penguin guide, *Your Smallholding*. Lewis Mumford praised Kropotkin's grasp of the implications for decentralisation of the (then) modern technology. Ebenezer Howard's *Garden Cities of Tomorrow* (London, 1902) used Kropotkin's figures. The socialist Robert Blatchford's *Britain for the British* (London, 1920) suggested that if Kropotkin's statistics were correct Britain could feed herself. If the soil was cultivated as intensively as in Belgium, there would be enough food for thirty-seven million inhabitants.[23]

THE FRONTIER ECONOMY

Continental liberalism tended to become polarised between Left and Right as soon as it appeared. However, during the nineteenth century, the expanding settlement of North America helped to perpetuate the liberal-oriented yeoman cult, with its implications of independent freedom. Thomas Jefferson had written that the most stable and prosperous republic was that formed by prosperous farmers. Jefferson was elected honorary President of the Bavarian Peasant's League in 1810. Inspiration between the USA and Europe flowed the other way, too. John Quincy Adams (later President of the United States), despite his sarcasm about bug-ridden, smelly peasants in Bohemia, was impressed by Silesia's experimental farming methods and pedigree cattle when he journeyed to North-East Germany to learn from its farming and manufacturing techniques.[24] The frontier economy became a potent symbol of freedom and independence for an increasingly radical European farming population. As expansion to the American West began, the vision of free land for the pioneer created a new school of political economists. Its first major exponent combined liberal economics, including a belief in free trade, with the aim of supporting an agricultural economy based on the free, non-rent-paying farmer.

Johann von Thünen (1785–1850) was an economist and geographer who owned an estate near Rostock. He wrote *The Isolated State* in 1820, and revised it several times up to 1840. This book, still well-known to geographers and those interested in geo-politics, presents a theoretical model of ideally efficient land use, based on the picture of an 'isolated state', set in a flat plain. Von Thünen was also the founder of neo-marginalist economics, but was overshadowed by the better-known Carl Menger and W. Stanley Jevons. But in his economic modelling, von Thünen took pains to differentiate clearly between factual and counter-factual postulates, and stress the need for a relativist approach: all theories should comprehend and assimilate truths which contradicted one's own cherished ideals. 'Without abstracting from reality, we can attain no scientific knowledge', he explained. None the less, 'in the real world, the steady state cannot exist'.[25] Von Thünen was concerned at the poverty and landlessness among the over-taxed agricultural labourer. He worked on a theory that would maximise human freedom of action, whilst maximising well-being among this most crucial of classes, the farmer. Although reviled by some Marxist economists as the founder of what they saw as ahistorical, inhumane marginalist economics, von Thünen cared enough about his labourers to leave his estate to them. He was claimed by both the National Socialists and the post-Second World War East German communist intellectuals as the 'first German socialist'.[26]

Von Thünen foreshadowed later, fully-fledged ecologists in three ways: first, he extrapolated from his picture of the natural laws of the scientific world a political prescription which had to be followed to prevent disaster; second, he saw the rural sector as the key determinant of moral, economic and social life; and third, he pursued a (somewhat incremental) search for truth through deductive reasoning.[27]

Von Thünen set out to discover what, given the model state, the pattern of agricultural cultivation would be, and also which part of the farm's return determines cultivation. He concluded that the unique quality possessed by the agricultural sector was that capital formation was determined by agricultural settlement on the margin. His model was based on the family farm, run by an individual who, during one lifetime, should produce sufficient capital to provide for his old age. Typically for a classical economist, he envisaged capital in a literal form, as corn, walls and roads, to be converted by the prosperous farmer into interest-bearing funds.

Thus he combined a picture of a non-feudal and non-capitalist smallholder economy with a world of capitalistically fluid relationships. Mobility of labour and fluidity of capital were essential for the improvement of the labourer's standard of living, and the increase of the national wealth. How to ensure that the labourer could be mobile, without losing the link between man and soil?

Von Thünen argued that the expansion of cultivated land was a sign of national wealth, and free trade was needed to ensure the most efficient (and hence most profitable) use of land resources. The economic use of land was a long-term aim, because of the gradual and conservative development of farming patterns.[28] However, over time, demographic movements would respond to rates of wages and interest, and affect farming patterns. On the frontiers of the State, transport costs would increase and rent fall. The frontier wage for the labourer *and* capitalist was the 'natural wage' earned on non-rent-paying land, that level of renumeration below which he could not provide for his old age. The special role played by the frontier wage was that it was a wage where none of the surplus went on rent, but was kept by the worker: and lent out to others, who in turn would clear fresh ground, living off this capital, until the ground was productive. Von Thünen formulated the proportion of wages to be paid to a new group of frontiersmen as 'the geometrical mean of the essential subsistence needs of the worker, measured in grain or money, and his product. This wage will maximise everybody's income.' The resultant formula was inscribed on his tombstone.[29]

However, this benevolent condition did not currently exist in Europe, where according to Von Thünen the broad pattern of landholding was to hold from a landlord, whether the state, the church or the private landlord, and labourers could not reject low wages in favour of new, uncultivated land. He contrasted the situation in Mecklenburg with that in North America, with unlimited fertile land. He advocated mass emigration of agricultural labourers to the USA, but pending that time, thought that a similar 'frontier' could be created in European conditions by adopting free trade. What was needed for the frontier wage was not so much unlimited land, as a sufficient diversity of conditions of cultivation. Then changing conditions would produce a 'frontier' somewhere or other at any one time. The existence of the non-rent-bearing wage would help to keep up wages in the non-frontier sector, and, by analogy, this process would apply worldwide, while the artistic and intellectual attractions of the city would exert a counter-pull to the high-wage margin, and prevent overcrowding at the frontier.

This astonishing call for a fluid, dynamic state of human development predated libertarian ecologism by over a century, but uses a symbiotic argument. Free trade and free thought need not be the enemies of rural values, but enable them to be brought to their fullest use. The division between capitalist and landowner disappears – every farmer becomes his own capitalist – and no barrier is placed before the inevitable change of technology and society. Man could not prevent such change, which was part of his adaptation to nature, but could avoid stasis. 'Nature reveals her secrets only slowly; and since every great discovery brings changes, perhaps even total changes, to the life of society, it follows that in the process of reaching the goal, industrial activity is itself subject to change.'[30] The implications of this liberal economic philosophy for agrarian reform were temporarily submerged by the state socialism of later agrarian philosophers, such as Karl Johann von Rodbertus-Jagetzow, who inspired protectionists Adolf Wagner and Gustav Ruhland. Rodbertus, a Liberal in the Frankfurt Parliament of 1848, and first exponent of the theory of surplus value, thought the desire for private property in land would disappear given proper ethical education. Both the anti-capitalist paternalist Rodbertus and the freedom-loving von Thünen were attacking the landowning basis of the Prussian state, though from analytically opposite angles. Both had followers in the twentieth century who read into them the belief that agriculture was the primary economic sector for moral as well as for structural reasons, and used their arguments for a more 'economic' use of resources. The German economic historian Richard Ehrenberg helped launch the *Thünen-Archiv* in 1906 with a call for the state to control the use of natural resources.[31]

RESETTLING THE PLANET

That apparently most positivistic of sciences, geography, produced numerous social reformers apart from Kropotkin. It was a short step from describing land use and structure to recommending specific reforms. Geo-politics, the deterministic discipline invented by Halford Mackinder and taken up by Karl Haushofer, kept to defining the source of imperial power. Another geographer and anthropologist was Friedrich Ratzel, who, in 1880 invented the term human geography, considered by one historian of geography to have been inspired by the historical relativism of Dilthey.[32]

The fear of soil erosion and loss of mineral resources led to the concept of *Raubwirtschaft*, which translates as something like 'exploitative economy'. Scientists in the nineteenth century, including Liebig the chemist, Surell the forestry expert and George Perkins Marsh, whose *Man and Nature* (New York, 1864) examined man's impact on the natural environment, had already pointed to deforestation and other destructive results of human action.[33] Élisée Reclus (1830–1905), the French anarchist and geographer, wrote a nineteen-volume work on world geography in between plotting terrorism at the First and Second International. He was described as 'wonderfully tolerant' to 'nearly everyone on the far left of the political spectrum'.[34] He argued in 1877 that man's effect on his environment had been almost exclusively destructive. Reclus, son of a French Protestant pastor and educated partly in Germany, was influenced by Fourier, Ruskin and Comte, as well as inspired by Carl Ritter's geography lectures, and the utopian and millenarian background of his theological training. He wrote an early work on 'nature sentiment', and had a small farm in Colombia, an experiment which failed.[35]

For a scientist to examine the changing structure and face of a landscape with regret for man's involvement was a new phenomenon. One French naturalist, de Triboulet, listed the number of species which had disappeared under man's rule. Sometimes such environmental destruction was attributed to primitive tribal behaviour: for Ratzel, it was nomadism, an implicit criticism of non-Western lifestyles, and especially what was seen as the Arab destruction of the once flourishing Roman Mediterranean. The decline of Rome was attributed to the disappearance of the peasantry and a loss of soil fertility. It was used to point out the dangers of a loss of peasantry and fertility for the uncaring contemporary European empires. Others thought that Western culture was implicitly exploitative. A Franco-Russian scholar, Eduard Petrie, wrote in 1883 that the Western-style colonization planned by Russia in Siberia would destroy not only the physical environment but the culture and spirit – ethnocide – of the primitive tribes there. The belief in stadial development and inevitable progress which had propped up so much scientific endeavour since Lewis Morgan was rejected by these ecological geographers. Another Russian geographer, Alexander Voeikof, wrote critically of the impact of man's activities on his environment (1901) while Eduard Hahn thought that the self-sufficient agriculture of the Incas was superior to the Western, captialist agriculture of his day. The expansion of the global trade economy meant not only the loss of non-renewable resources but the destruction of the pastoral peoples.[36]

Raubwirtschaft found little echo in England or America. But the dust-bowl experience meant that the specific fear of erosion was exported back to Europe. One German explorer, with the unGerman name of Colin Ross, a poet and soldier of the First World

War, described the exploration and conquest of the United States and its abandoned mid-West farms in the early 1930s. William Morris Davis attacked the destruction of nature in 1899, while the dangers of deforestation were emphasised by Nathaniel Southgate Shaler in his 1896 article, 'The Economic Aspects of Soil Erosion'.[37]

One of the first writers to connect the destructive effects of human action with the possibility of unbalancing a biological equilibrium was the German geologist Ernst Fischer, killed in the First World War. He tried to quantify existing mineral and animal resources, and concluded that economic growth must outgrow natural resources and produce pollution. Even small alterations to the ecological balance would have an enormous effect. He traced the growth of organic life from the rocks to the water to the biosphere and thence to the zooshpere; the most complex level of interaction, where equilibrium was most fragile. The theory of thermo-dynamics inspired an American bio-chemist, Lawrence Henderson (1913), to look at the long-term inevitability of loss of energy resources.[38]

The household model of the economy had given way to the dynamics of neo-classical economics and marginal theory. Only in the biological sciences, or in the ideas of those trained as biologists, did the term 'economy of nature' seem to retain the old implications. This led to trained biologists taking their global vision of balanced interaction into other fields. One man earlier influenced by Comte and Fourier was Nikolai Danilevsky (1822–1885), the nineteenth-century inspirer of pan-Slavism. A believer in organic cycles of history, Danilevsky conforms to the picture of a political ecologist. Like the later Ostwald, he categorised societies according to their level of scientific knowledge, and claimed that human society had always been inherently scientific rather than barbarous or superstitious. Man had always looked for the true laws of nature, and once empirical science had emerged, in about 1800, according to Danilevsky, the potential for technological and social change was unlimited. He foresaw the use of electricity for communications and flying vehicles, while at the same time he defined history as a quest for human communion with nature. He was a scientific optimist, who rejected the idea of a struggle with nature.

> In nature itself, the struggle of elemental forces is only apparent, and every set of contradictions is resolved into a harmony of a higher sort. . . The result of the contradictions found in nature is their unification into a harmonious third pheno-

> menon...called cooperation or love...Man does not struggle with nature, but adjusts himself to her; he does not free himself from her power but, learning her laws more and more deeply, finds them identical with the laws of his own nature... In submitting himself to the laws of nature, he acts only in accordance with his own aspirations.[39]

He was associated with statistics as well as biology and wanted to reform Russia according to modern scientific principles, the principles of a purposeful nature. However, to him these principles were already embodied in Russian rural life, needing only to be encouraged and trained by educated and scientific helpers. He supported Fourier's phalange, the association of communal villages, especially Fourier's belief that man was intended for variety in his work patterns. Danilevsky's interest in both statistics and geography led him to study the patterns of inherited diseases in man as well as the distribution of plant and fish life. He wrote a two-volume criticism of Darwin and the theory of gradual evolution. He preferred a theory of evolution by 'jumps'.

Like the Monists and most of the energy ecologists discussed here he was a socialist, but, influenced by Slav cultural-racialism, not a reforming one. He predicted a revolution in Russia that would presage an efficient, modern, authoritarian state. Danilevsky was variously described by different authors as liberal, totalitarian, messianic and racialist. Socialists who are anarchically oriented, authoritarian and supporters of Russian (or other) peasant life do not fit in with orthodox political classifications. The prevalence of such thinkers among those trained as biologists is further evidence that here we are dealing with a special category, one found in societies and states as different as Russia and Scotland, but based on an international European scientific community.[40]

Another member of this community was Patrick Geddes (1854–1932), town planner and supporter of Back-to-the-Land decentralization. He was also a member of the Kibbo Kift Kin. A biologist who studied under T.H. Huxley, he became interested in the statistical classification of human and animal populations. He saw society as living within fixed physical limits. Energy came in and was modified by the organism and its activities, both physiological and economic. Energy then escaped from the system. He hoped to produce a grand chart of matter-energy conversion among human and animal societies, and evolved a classification of societies based on their type of energy use. But unlike Wilhelm Ostwald, who thought that efficiency in energy use was an index of the status and progress of a civilization, Geddes hoped that society would switch to a 'biological' use of energy. He saw village societies as the natural human social unit.[41]

Geddes' forebears included Reclus, (to whom he became close in Reclus' last years), Kropotkin and George Perkins Marsh. He ardently believed in Marsh's theory of deforestation as a contributory factor to the decline of past civilization. Geddes read Comte, Ruskin and Spencer. From Ruskin he took his criticism of capitalist values and neo-classical economics: from Comte, his belief in the benevolent powers of the apolitical, disinterested planner. Spencer's essentially libertarian approach led him to support the decentralized village. He moved to Montpellier after the First World War, and tried to make it the centre of a new village revival. He wanted to start a rural university. Marxism and Fabian socialism he described as too urban, 'mechanistic and pecuniary by turns'.[42] After a visit to India in 1914, Geddes supported the British presence in India on the grounds that the British were best suited to managing the forests and reclaiming the land. He felt the same way about the French presence in Algeria. He argued that their sensible and productive land use justified their colonial policy. He foresaw, indeed, the anti-peasant policies of post-colonialist governments. Geddes supported the garden city movement, and influenced the town planning movement through his lectures and books.[43]

Geddes expressed his Back-to-the-Land belief most clearly in two articles written in 1927 and 1929 respectively. In 'The Village World; Actual and Possible', he praised the efforts of Rabindranath Tagore in Bengal and 'Æ' (George Russell) in Ireland to revive rural comunities. He thought that material and cultural renewal of villages was needed, calling it 'Village Eutopia'. The drift to the land could only be halted by re-afforestation and the cultural and intellectual programmes he supported at Montpellier. In 'Rural and Urban Thought; a Contribution to the Theory of Progress and Decay', he complained that the 'biological and evolutionary' sciences had not been given a chance to improve the world. His own invention, the Regional Survey, had not been applied seriously.[44] Geddes did not say exactly how it had failed, or how it should be put into effect. This vagueness about details seems typical of the ecological reformer.

To be a town planner was not, of course, necessarily to be an ecologist. Geddes, though, was seen as evolving a science of human ecology.[45] He believed that a viable sociology could only be created on the basis of biological knowledge. He divided civilizations into phases of technology, of which what he called the 'biotechnic' was the most advanced. Mumford interpreted him to mean that in a biotechnic civilization, 'The biological sciences will be freely applied to technology, and...technology itself will be oriented toward the culture of life.'[46] One historian of Geddes' ideas puzzled over why his dynamic, holistic, vitalist and unitary town planning had not triumphed. He concluded that it was because Geddes failed to explain his ideas in a sufficiently coherent way.[47] The fact was, however, that dynamic, holistic, vitalist and unitary ideas could not easily be implemented by committees of town planners, however benevolent. Planning itself meant either a coercive approach to human activities, in that the plan involved people doing what they would otherwise not have done, or a miraculous piece of positivistic prophecy, in which case it was entirely redundant. To admire the mediaeval town did not mean that its virtues could easily be reproduced. 'Dynamic planning', indeed, was a contradiction in terms. That Geddes' pre-First World War belief in town planning, based on an admiration for the city fathers of Renaissance Florence and for the vitalism of Bergson, should have been perverted into the rigidities and corruptions of the later town and country planning acts, was unsurprising. This contradiction is present in all libertarian socialism, but becomes more noticeable in the work of those who had made specific recommendations for changing the physical and social infrastructure. The more specific the proposal, the more evidently it demanded 'from above' action of a kind which could only be taken by the state. Geddes' support for the small scale community, for the burgher 'folk' was echoed by many twentieth-century ecologists, but the inherent problem of reform from below by action from above was ignored by reformers whose politics ranged from far left to far right.

Geddes' stand at the Town Planning Exhibition of 1910, crammed with a 'hotch-potch' of postcards, 'crude old woodcuts', newspaper cuttings and diagrams, was rendered 'wonderful' by his personality and powers of exposition.[48] There is something touching about the Scottish individualist, who thought that the green leaf was the foundation of all life, and which compares with the German green anarchist Gräser, whose visiting card was a blade of grass, and who lived in a cave, to save energy.[49] His flailing attacks on 'war-lords, greedy politicians and slothful bureaucrats', and his claim that they resulted from the loss of rural ideals and work-ways, convey an intemperate vagueness, rather than the kindred spirit of Goethe, to whom he was compared at the time. He complained that in Western culture, 'agriculture and engineering' were cut off from 'religion and culture'.[50]

Geddes was interested in man, his biological nature and his use of energy. In this he combined two separate inspirations for the ecological world-view. Biological ecologists had not previously criticised human over-use of finite resources. If ecological equilibrium was part of nature, so was man. Biological ecologists tended to respond to the problem of man's destructive or negative influence on other species and on nature with appeals to man to evolve a sensitive and appreciative response to the natural world. Economic ecologists responded differently. They too, like Haeckel, Spencer and Virchow, used organic analogies. However, the answer of the finite resource economists was the purposive organism. Human capacity for chaos and destruction needed tighter, though more subtle, social control. The World State would be like a hive community, run by boards of experts. The geographical element in ecologism led to an emphasis on land use and regional structures. The idea of a large-scale organised planning of human homes and industries took root in the early twentieth century. It expressed a cultural criticism of what was seen as existing waste and untidiness. But it also implied an optimistic belief in the power of human planning to create a society where human values and capacities would be enriched and liberated.

These human values were seen as essentially rural ones. In Germany the belief in modern, rural simplicity became entwined with an aesthetic criticism of wasteful, reactionary, illogical architecture. It combined with a reaction against the grand – the urban – the powerful. The truthful, honest approach to society and its artefacts was by its nature oriented away from the past. The past was seen as a series of myths. Civilization as it was known expressed a malevolent obfuscation of real values. Modernists could talk of

> A century cold as steel and glass. . . the great creative brain. . . the new style of the twentieth century which, because it is a genuine style as opposed to a passing fashion, is totalitarian. . . the glass walls. . . the steel frame is hard. . . a world of science and technique, of speed and danger, of hard struggles.[51]

This Ernst Junger-like paean of praise to what David Watkin aptly calls 'the collectivist outlook and its affinities with Bolshevism and National Socialism' attracted support from those who revolted from Megalopolis.[52] German Modernists supported decentralization; some a Back-to-the-Land movement. Nikolaus Pevsner approved of the Boy Scouts.[53] English Modernists had stronger anti-urban elements. The architectural historian, William Lethaby was a romantic populist, and exponent of the Arts and Crafts Movement. He praised the (alleged) collectivist harmony of the Middle Ages. He announced that 'the best forms of civilization' were 'simple housekeeping in the country, with tea in the garden; boy-scouting and tennis in flannels': along with the 'beauty of efficiency' possessed by a naval squadron.[54] Modernism followed Ruskin and Morris in believing that the physical artefacts of man's domestic life, the style of the houses he inhabited, helped mould his spiritual and social life.

From planning houses and villages to planning regions was a reasonable step: to the planning of a nation's space another. Lewis Mumford was a disciple of Geddes. He was a regional planner under Roosevelt, and supporter of a Ruskinite communistic planners' paradise, inspired by mediaeval communalism. He was cosponsor and author with Herbert Agar of a call for a world government in 1940.[55] Mumford's aim was no less than to reorder the earth's population, in a more resource-efficient and also more beautiful way.

> One of the major tasks of the twentieth century is the resettlement of the planet. The past three centuries have been centuries of random exploration...spontaneous and guided by insufficient knowledge; and much of the work of settlement remains to be done over again...Population that spread with no more *social direction* than the surface tension which gives definition to an ink blot, must be re-grouped and nucleated in a fashion that will make possible a co-operative, civilized life. Industries...must now flow out into new centres...*conscious scientific intelligence must determine the new loci of industrial advantage*.[56] [My italics]

There is no evidence from Mumford's illustrated books that the architecture and planning he approved of had anything to do with the mediaeval world, as they consist of Le Corbusier-like terraces, of the kind being pulled down all over the Western world today as unbearable for human beings to live in.

He defined Geddes' 'bio-technic' stage as one where the key inventions, aeroplanes, contraceptives, the cinema, were derived from 'a study of living organisms', and in which knowledge of the biological sciences would enable full – and, of course, benevolent – control to be exercised over man's life and artefacts.[57]

The positivist rebuttal of this programme, that man cannot be improved by an improved environment, is unconvincing. Naturally, people *are* affected by their surroundings. However, their surroundings are the creation of their own time and culture; the problem is, rather, who is better able to create the environment than those living within it? Has the attempt to alter natural patterns of land use by planning helped or hindered? Was it inevitable that twentieth-century architecture and town planning should have taken its disastrous course, or was this due to the malevolent cultural spirit of so-called Modernism? One historian of art, Giles Auty, sees 'Modernism' as 'the unofficial art' of the post-Second World War Western world, an excuse for 'cultural meddling'.[58] The fact that Le Corbusier's architectural utopias were disastrous does not mean that the Ruskinian and Morris-influenced garden cities would be disastrous too. What does seem to have failed is the artificial transplantation of urban dwellers to rural areas, but even this failure was a slow one. The ecological rural dwellers of today are less arrogant than those of the past, who thought that the objective social science was a reality. They ask only the freedom to be unaffected by bizarre and failed experimentation. The paradox is that political ecology has maintained the belief that man is capable of benevolent interference in man.

'ALL IS ENERGY'

Another British economic ecologist who was inspired by calculations about the carrying capacity of the earth was Frederick Soddy (1877–1956), who worked on radioactive disintegration with Rutherford, and won a Nobel Prize in 1921. Among other achievements, Soddy predicted the discovery of the isotope. He was made a Fellow of the Royal Society in 1910, and a Professor at Oxford in 1919.[59]

Soddy was another disciple of Ruskin. He believed that positive science was a myth, and wanted scientists to be 'responsible'. At first he hoped that atomic physics would prove an economic blessing through its energy-producing potential. Later he foresaw the atom bomb, and was attacked by colleagues as a crank for this reason.

Ruskin's influence turned Soddy to considering orthodox economics, by which he seems to have meant classical and neo-classical liberalism, a category in which he included Marx. Soddy was right to see Marx as a classical economist, as Marx's economic model as laid out in *Capital* assumes the perfect market and perfect information characteristics of the classical school – although it is not for this aspect of his model that he is remembered. He quoted approvingly Marx's appropriation of William Petty's

Physiocratic description of material wealth, that 'labour is its father and the earth its mother'. But it was the 'determinist or ..."the ultra-materialistic"', aspect of Marx that he opposed.[60]

Soddy argued that the economist should be trying to answer the question, 'How do men live?' The answer to this question was that energy was the fundamental 'means of production'. The language of the economist, with its terms like capital, rent and interest, obscured this basic truth, with disastrous results. Capital did not 'grow': rather, as stored wealth, it was subject to the laws of entropy, and withered away. Still less did it produce interest or rent. A sack of corn was capital: but its store of energy gained from the sun diminished unless used.[61] He roundly declared that it was the power source, not the capitalist, engineer, mechanic or manager, who made things work. And all energy came from the sun. Coal, wood, food and human energy depended on sunlight.

This idea had of course been expressed by other scientists, including Ostwald, whose comments about the sun as the source of energy have been taken out of context and presented as evidence that he was a sun-worshipping, occultist crank. Soddy was familiar with Ostwald's work but seems to have come to the same conclusions about energy use independently.[62] Furthermore, he was not content with creating a theory of the growth of civilization based on energy use, or of imperial decline based on deforestation. He wanted to tackle what he saw as a simple error in human thought and organization that had led to waste and poverty. He spent the last forty years of his life in trying to reform this error. The great discoveries of the first and second laws of thermo-dynamics had passed by the closed minds of economists. It was necessary for the trained scientific mind to step in and correct them. By an intellectual confidence trick, economists had persuaded governments and people that there were laws of debt, interest and capital. But assets were 'real' only if they helped to tap energy sources. Soddy thought that the fallacy of orthodox economics led to wars as well as to poverty.

He demanded a reform of the banking system. Debt, for him, and the way in which it was created, was the main enemy. The belief in the 'spontaneous increment of debt' was 'an absurd human convention', whereas the 'spontaneous decrement of wealth' was a real natural law.[63] Compound interest, especially, was madness, leading to ruin and usury. In *Wealth, Virtual Wealth and Debt* he repeated his argument that economics should be founded in thermo-dynamics, and that energy, based on the sun, was the paramount factor. The private banking system created money, which it lent out at interest. There was no requirement that banks should keep reserves equal to the credit they created. Credit creation was done by fiat, and meant a free benefit for bankers at the cost of the community as a whole. Soddy demanded that banks should switch to 100 per cent reserve requirements, and that the State should issue all money. (Presumably Soddy meant *credit*, as the issue of notes and coins was already a quango monopoly.) Credit would be issued according to a national price index, kept by a National Statistics Council. During a boom, taxes would be raised or gilts sold, and during a depression, taxes would be lowered, according to the level of the index over time. Finally, there should be no gold standard, and all exchange rates between nations should float freely.[64] The inflationary implications of the Social Credit national dividend were carefully avoided, in theory at least, by this plan for a fine-tuned credit creation run by a council of wise men.

The demand for a state-controlled creation of credit was similar to the demand by other monetary reformers in the 1920s, including Silvio Gesell and Gottfried Feder. Soddy's rationale differed in its techicalities and emphasis on energy from that of Major Douglas, founder of Social Credit. Douglas believed in the creative power of credit, as long as it was issued by non-malevolent agencies. The picture of a flawed circular flow, with purchasing power (Douglas) or energy (Soddy) 'leaking out', was very similar, and some of the reforms suggested were the same. Loss of faith in Say's Law, the classical economic model in which factors of production must always equal factors of consumption, paralleled the loss of faith in the cycle of constant energy. Just as usable energy levels were constantly being depleted, so usable credit was constantly being devalued by interest and usury. Soddy, though, opposed Douglas and Orage's proposal to widen share ownership and a stake in the economy by creating a kind of national 'company'. They believed that the wealth and prosperity now enjoyed by a handful of people could be widened to the community at large, in the form of a national dividend. But Soddy saw wealth as strictly finite, limited, essentially, by the amount of available, and in the last analysis, in however long a term, solar energy.[65] So dividends, however distributed, were a confidence trick.

Soddy can be defined as an ecologist in the way he perceived agriculture as the 'key industry', and the cycle sun-soil-food as 'the internal energy of life'. Soddy did not influence the land use economists and reformers referred to above, nor did the anarchists adopt his ideas. Because Soddy's anti-banking feelings led him into attacks on Jewish bankers, he may have become an embarrassment to other monetary reformers, as the 1930s saw the rise of Nazism. He also wrote about the dangers to the white race from a future shortage of energy. In this he reproduced the 'endemic Euro-centrism and anti-semitism' of his time and place, and it would probably be wrong to attribute too great a share to them in his thinking.[66] In the early 1920s his ideas did interest a surprising group of people, Montagu Fordham, the Guild Socialists and Social Creditors, John Hargrave, Rolf Gardiner and later Hugh Massingham. This diverse group was to support Nordicism, Tory anti-semitism and eugenics. But although quoted by these ecologists as a source of ideas, Soddy never seems to have acquired a school or a party. He remained a difficult, 'alternative' figure, who praised Marx, but opposed Soviet Communism and Soviet possession of the atom bomb.

Soddy's energy vision may at first seem a surprisingly materialistic one. What could be more physical than energy and matter? Indeed, Soddy called his own economic theory 'Cartesian Economics'. The title implied a mechanistic, anti-vitalist view of life untypical of the scientists considered so far. But Soddy refused to join in the materialist versus spiritualist controversy. He described scientific discoveries and philosophical speculation as stretching out to infinity along two special axes: in the middle ground lay the 'problems of life', among them economics. The laws of human nature were not the laws of nature. In this assertion too Soddy differed from ecologists. 'Life,or animate mechanism' was 'a dualism', both halves of which were equally essential to man's life.[67] The special aspect of human nature was that man possessed a powerful aesthetic drive. Orthodox economics failed to allow for it in suitably Ruskin-like terms.[68] Soddy's adoption of Ruskin's aesthetics was accompanied by a faith in scientists amounting almost to arrogance.

> The laws of energy. . . might furnish a common scientific starting point from which all men concerned with the public rather than with their own private interests might start to rebuild the world more in conformity with the great intellectual achievements which have distinguished the present age. The first step towards such a scientific Utopia would be the due delimitation of the rights of the community's creditors – the curbing of the demon of debt which masquerades among the ignorant as wealth.[69]

ENERGY AND UTOPIAN SOCIALISM.

In the late nineteenth century reformers emerged who wanted to reorganize economic theory to take account of energy values. In

1880, a Ukrainian socialist and landowner, Serge Podolinsky, wrote to Marx and Engels. He earnestly requested them to study the theory of value in terms of its energy, rather than its labour content. Engels told Marx that Podolinsky seemed to be merely regurgitating Ricardo's ideas, and the point of the suggestion was missed. This is surprising, as Marx was usually in the forefront of the scientific thinking of his time. He was inspired by stadial and progressive theories of civilization, Darwin and natural selection and scientific racialism. He also sympathised with the pre-capitalist criticism of money: that unlike land as a source of wealth, the mobility of financial wealth made it inherently irresponsible.

However, he seemed to lack the tinkering, technological, experimental mentality of the engineer, and substituted a purely heuristic approach. He was aware of the existence of the problem – how should man live on the earth? – but preferred a millenarian approach to the answer, placing an undefined utopia in an undefined future of plenty.[70] Several of his sympathisers and followers, though, continued to direct their focus to the energy problem.

Josef Popper-Lynkeus (1838–1921) came from the same small Bohemian town as Karl Popper's family, and was possibly a distant relation. His works were found in any educated middle class Viennese socialist home, along with those of Marx, Kautsky, Darwin and Weininger. Indeed, when Karl Popper was asked to give the William James lectures at Harvard in 1949, he thought he had been taken for Popper-Lynkeus and invited by mistake.[71] Josef Popper was an inventor, a pacifist, an atheist and a philosopher, and addressed an unconvincing Rawlsian critique to hierarchical and Darwinian theories: that the theorists would not have adopted their ideas if they had believed that they might themselves end up in a weak position, or be eliminated by natural selection. In 1912 he published *Die allgemeine Nährpflicht*, which suggested a form of civilian conscription. Men would labour for twelve years, women for seven, to provide the basic subsistence minimum to be distributed to all. 'Extra' resources and labour would be directed to a second economic sector, the market economy, although each businessman would be able to hire only a limited number of employees. The conscription period was calculated according to Popper-Lynkeus's idea of the productive capacity of Germany's economy and agriculture. Karl Popper categorised this suggestion for slave labour merely as 'piece-meal social engineering', which suggests the fundamentally socialist slant of his views, formed as they were in pre-First World War Vienna. Popper-Lynkeus wanted to diminish the use of exhaustible resources, and substitute wind and water power, as well as human energy, as far as possible, to achieve a 'viable' or static economy, which would not have growth as an aim. He was more pessimistic than Kropotkin about the possibility of increasing food and renewable energy products (Kropotkin had suggested intensive greenhouse potato production) and criticised Kropotkin's technophile proposals on the grounds that more energy units would be required to increase production than would be produced for use. The Friends of the Earth opposed capital intensive dairy farming for the same reason in 1974: they argued that the amount of finite energy units required to build a milking parlour would not 'pay' for itself in increased finite energy units. In his egalitarianism, and desire to spread the burden of the (alleged) scarcity of resources, Popper-Lynkeus anticipated the red-green 'entryism' of the late 1970s, rather than the optimistic post-scarcity anarchism of Bookchin.[72] When the Green Party recently suggested a 'Social Wage', Popper-Lynkeus was given as a progenitor of this idea.[73]

For his figures on energy use, Popper-Lynkeus used work by Karl Ballod-Atlanticus, (1864–1933) a more technophile writer of science-fiction. His *Der Zukunftstaat (The Future State)* appeared in 1898, inspired by Francis Bacon's *New Atlantis* and Plato's *Republic*. It was revised and re-published in 1927. Ballod, another 'scientific utopian', admired both Henry Ford and Marx, and wanted to show how a technocratic socialist state could function. Ballod, who was German, shared the German preoccupation with food production per hectare. He suggested that land be divided into farms averaging 500 hectares, each worked by several families. Each farm would support a local community as well as its farmers. One may ask how this pattern would differ from normal market agriculture: the novelty seems to be that Ballod wanted land distribution and farming to be based on a computation of soil fertility and fertiliser requirements, and aimed to retain, if not increase, current levels of soil fertility. Cities would be no larger than 100,000. Their sewage would be returned to the farms to be used as fertiliser. In his revised version he argued that all firms should be publicly owned and run, on a state, province and communal level, by a highly paid technocratic élite. Ballod was Eurocentric, as is shown by his suggestion that Europe's energy balance should be made good by importing vegetable oil from outside Europe. This would be used to power tractors, which in turn would enable land to grow food for humans, not horses.[74]

Ballod's novel heavily influenced Bogdanov, and through him Lenin. Possibly, Lenin's collectivisation schemes were partly inspired by Ballod's anodyne-sounding calculations. Ballod, like most urban utopians, saw the farmer as merely the passive vessel for reform. Early anarchists had planned their anarchist communism around the belief that peasants would bring free food to the wayside and leave it there.[75] Chayanov, the Russian agronomist who became Minister of Agriculture under Lenin, also wrote a science-fiction novel in which self-sufficient peasants would fly into cities to attend concerts, and then return home to milk the cows. Against what must have been the evidence of his own eyes, Chayanov pictured the Russian peasant as uninterested in money and unmotivated by market forces.[76] While peasants and farmers are generally dissatisfied with the profit on their crops, whatever, it is, this does not signify a distaste for vulgar cash, so much as a sense that a money return for their produce is not an equivalent exchange of value for value.

Despite his interest in technology, Ballod opposed the private car, which he believed would use up available oil within a few decades. The complete rejection of market forces as a motivation for human conduct went along with a blank rejection of individualism. However, it did not entail a lack of aesthetics. Ballod set aside one hundred thousand workers in his ideal state to make pianos! Ballod died before Hitler's motorways and before his ideal *Erbhof*, the peasant farm of 7.5 to 125 hectares, was implemented. He would have disliked both, yet the presumption of land scarcity and need for peasant technology had stimulated Nazi thinking on agrarian problems. There was a department for wind energy production in the Third Reich which was studying windmill technology till the end of the war, while methane gas plants were seen as an energy source of the future.[77] Ballod's belief in a technocratic élite was also weirdly fulfilled under Hitler. In agriculture, farm advisors were used at local and provincial level. In other sectors, the engineering and scientific developments were taken over by a cadre of inspired, often SS-run middle management. Ballod's interest in synthetic rubber and synthetic fabric also foreshadowed the characteristic *ersatz* production of the Third Reich.

THE BENEVOLENT PLANNERS

By the Second World War, ideals of planning were widely accepted in government circles in Britain as well as in North America. The urban messiahs of the day were to triumph in both countries, but the aim of land-based ecological planning was promulgated in research institutes. One curious by-product of war-time planning and controls was a sense of omnipotence, the spirit that inspired the United Nations and other supra-national bodies.

Sir George Stapledon (1882–1960), whose achievements as a plant biologist revolutionised farming practices all over the world, and who left an unpublished book on human ecology behind him, was among those who meditated on the future of man and the earth during the war. His conclusions were remarkably similar to those of today's ecologists. Like them, he was anxious 'to husband the bounty of nature' and care for posterity.[78] He used the findings of biological ecology to argue that man must be in balance with his environment. A world dominated by machines and a polluted environment damaged man.[79] His 1935 book, *The Land, Today and Tomorrow*, had argued for state intervention in agricultural production and marketing, for intensive farming based on rotation of arable and grass crops, for prevention of erosion and healthy soil from fertile land. In 1943 he called for a 'British land improvement commission' to centralise the 'splendid' work of the War Agricultural Committees. One body would oversee forestry, national parks, reclamation of hill land, and have powers of compulsory land requisition.[80]

Stapledon, himself a scientist, combined his love for the land and admiration for robust English yeoman with a large faith in scientific knowledge. Of course, given an educated population motivated by good-will, ability and honesty, his scheme for an enlightened state planning authority might have worked. Like other 'High Tories', though, he failed to understand the urban bias of the 'New Jerusalemers'. He worked towards a global planning authority which he thought could be run by the same type of man who had run the Indian Civil Service; incorruptible, paternalistic, wise. To his question,

> What do we desire to do with ourselves on this planet, and how do we wish to develop ourselves and the resources of our planet? These are the great questions. How best to distribute ourselves over the vast surfaces of the globe and how to utilize the bounty of nature to the best advantage of every man...[81]

he gave the answer that bio-regions must be created.[82] Monoculture in agriculture and industry should be avoided. Decentralisation, 'planned and regulated', he stressed, would

> bring together in close harmony people who are employed in widely-different pursuits and...permit of the maximum possible of interchange between the employment of individuals and particularly of different individuals in one and the same

> family (all living in the same home) in rural and in industrial enterprises.[83]

Stapledon's programme must have seemed over-ambitious to many readers at the time.

> We must first look to the possibilities and potentialities of every country of the world with a view, as far as may be possible, to the arrangement within each of a just balance between agriculture and industry and between different industries. . . The various limiting factors to achieving balance in every case demand an immense amount of unbiased research conducted from an entirely new point of view.[84]

This belief was, in theory at least, to find its instrument in the human ecology and land planning section of the United Nations. However, its work was overwhelmed by the devotion to third world developments, big projects, and modernisation, financed by grants and loans from the World Bank. The governments of newly independent countries wanted large dams not small windmills; they wanted to develop wild areas, not preserve them. None the less, Stapledon's ideals remained a factor both in supranational planning bodies, and in land planning faculties in many universities today.

Stapledon shared his belief in global re-development with Patrick Geddes and Lewis Mumford. Although Stapledon was a biologist, he was not inspired by the cell-state organic analogy used by Mumford, who praised what he saw as the organic, collective harmony of the Middle Ages, and believed that a new world order would reproduce the efficient and harmonious working of the human body. The world planning authority envisaged by Stapledon would not interfere with local customs and styles of government. Stapledon was specific about the value of the British Empire in this task, and Britain's experience in settling the colonies and the White Dominions. The Nation was a fine thing; but 'to achieve world harmony and world efficiency is a still greater work of art and a work of time – a work of art in time painted against the background of space.'[85] The divisions between Mumford and Stapledon, – one, after all, a Communist sympathiser, the other a patriotic British imperialist – are here less noticeable than the similarities. Both assumed that a complete re-organisation of the planet's resources, human and non-human, was possible and desirable. Both assumed the expertise and goodwill and honesty of the educated classes. Both were optimistic about popular response to this programme of relocation and change.

Both saw the use of physical resources, the avoidance of erosion, as crucial.

This faith in planning and the planners existed across the political spectrum, and, although inspired by the propagators of the white empires (especially in Britain and the United States) was also fuelled by Communist utopianism. The hostility to individualism and especially what was seen as the exploitative and greedy individual businessman, was almost ubiquitous.[86]

The energy ecologists provided bases for calculating the future of human societies. They have often been overtaken by events, of course, but were founded on convincing-sounding computations of the carrying capacity of the earth, and the need to retain the fertility of the soil. Most were Euro-centric, but some were as globally aware and anti-West as ecologists today. They varied in their specific values. Some were libertarian socialists inspired by Morris or Ruskin, who liked villages and peasants, while others were egalitarian socialists inspired by Marx, who wanted to exploit them. The American geographers described earlier were often Thoreauvian woodsmen. However, they shared a faith in reform based on scientific calculations and in their own visions of loss and disaster. Nearly all had read Comte, and rejected existing political institutions and traditions for Comtean reasons, that is, that the government of men by men should be replaced by the government of men by rational, apolitical institutions. Some wanted to remodel human society according to biological laws, but most did not, opposing social Darwinism through egalitarian and internationalist dogma rather than reason. When the oil crisis threatened the West in the early '70s, the same arguments about finite resources reappeared, and the same plans to re-structure society so that the most economical use could be made of land and energy.

CHAPTER FIVE

Communes and Communards

Utopian plans for communes are as old as utopias, and owe much to the same sense that society could be made to work more efficiently and delightfully.[1] Of course, not all communes are just ecologically oriented. Religious, anarchist, communard, socialist and racialist motives all exist, and sometimes fuse. The self-sufficiency element has obvious links with ecological autarky though, as has the desire to work the soil without artificial pesticides and fertilisers. While there is a substantial literature on communes in the nineteenth and twentieth century, they are seldom differentiated, the subject lying still in a magical twilight between history, polemic and journalism. It is one of the most important aspects of ecologism, though, because it touches most of us. It is an area where almost everyone at one time or another has longed to live a purer, more real and freer life, to go back to the land.

Colonies in the New World were the chiliastic answer to moral and economic problems. The line between the planned experiment, which we mean by 'commune', and the process of demographic expansion is not always easy to draw. Coleridge and Southey dreamed of servantless freedom by the banks of the Susquehannah. Their wives mused on the fact that they would have to do the housework.

The cultural criticism that marks ecologists, together with the belief in self-sufficiency and improved land use, leads to communes as a practical method of improvement. A commune implies a rural setting. The Quakers and other dissenters maintained their faith in an urban setting, and a parallel hierarchy of education and business activity emerged. During the nineteenth century, religious communities were established in the North American countryside which tried to minimise links with the outside world. However, the Oneida commune and other religious experiments survived by becoming profitable trading groups and losing their controversial experimental elements. Other religious minority groups, such as the Amish and the Doukhoubours, survived because they were transplanted as homogeneous groups from their country of origin, and owed their survival potential to tribal as well as religious bonds, rather than novel experiments.[2]

The twentieth century saw a growth in the commune movement, inspired by anarchist, radical, religious, revolutionary and ecological ideals. However, in England there were estimated to be some one hundred working communes only in 1970; in the United States and Mexico, however, the figure for rural communes alone was two thousand.[3]

The failure rate this century in non-religious communes has been high. This can be attributed to enhanced demands for technology from the communard, with less prospect of self-sufficiency; to some basic flaw in the concept of free association, or to financial strain induced by high rates and property costs. The urge to communicate one's belief, to affect society, does not always co-exist with self-sufficiency in a remote Welsh smallholding, without typewriter or electricity. The Mexican commune that combined dance theatre with summer farming seems a form of transhumance, a reversion to pastoral life, rather than real self-sufficiency.The evangelical nature of the ecologist makes complete withdrawal difficult.

The need for cheap land means that North America has always been the obvious place for starting a commune. Also the United States had a tradition of *practical* closeness to the land, even before the opening of the West in the mid-nineteenth century. Thoreau described in *Walden* not only the beneficent effects of woodland life, but how to live well off society's leavings and discards.[4] Bricks, doors, windows, glass, all could be 're-cycled'. The idyll of the Red Indian and his ability to live off and with the land was another constant theme. When the 'deep ecologists' recently praised the speech of a Red Indian chief this was the latest example in a long line of romanticising the pastoral North American tribesman.[5] Britain's Boy Scout movement developed from Ernest Thompson Seton and his Woodcraft Indians, a movement intended, *inter alia,* to train city youth in Red Indian techniques. This was partly survivalist; and the summer camps to which American children are still sent owe much to the ideal of independence and self-help of the last century. However, what gives Seton's activities its characteristically ecological scientific rationale was the belief that boys went through the stages of civilization as they grew up, and that the 'cave-man', primitive hunter-gatherer stage had to be developed, not repressed.

American libertarian traditions combined sun-worship, nudism, health-and-nature cures, with self-sufficiency. Benjamin Tucker, editor of *Liberty* from 1885, supported rural decentralization and settlement. There is a strangely modern air about two Seton-inspired science fiction novels written in 1902 and 1904 by the anarchist J. William Lloyd. Above his desk hung pictures of Darwin, Thoreau, Morris and Whitman. The author of a study on him comments that this was a strange combination, but the reader of this book will by now immediately recognise its proto-ecological nature.[6] The hero of Lloyd's novel *The Natural Man. A Romance of the Golden Age* lives off the land. His group call themselves the 'Simplicists', or the 'Tribe'. They wear Red Indian clothes, and one member, – a German immigrant, significantly enough – goes naked in the woods and talks to animals. He is a spiritualist. They swing from tree branches but read Greek and Latin. They are healthy, happy, intimate with nature and free. Animals are killed only when hunger makes it necessary. In a key passage, the hero argues that 'the entire population of the planet could support itself in this pastoral way from poor soil', and that land belongs to 'those who used it and while using it'.[7] He quotes Whitman, Thoreau and Emerson, and expresses a Monist view of the world; 'the whole universe was One great Life' in constant evolution. The Tribe recycles its sewage, and takes care not to pollute streams. They avoid waste. In the second novel, man the tool-making animal triumphs over man the naturist, – the development and conflict of personality is very well done – and the hero excuses the shift to a planned, collectivist, technocracy by arguing that the brain is natural too. What is natural is to express; the repressed is what is unnatural.

America provides other threads of continuity which lead to today's ecologists. While the 'counter-culture' of the 1960s claimed to be unique, observers saw threatening historical precedents in the 'frighteningly alien' eruption of Nazi youth.[8] A more accurate precedent would have been the pre-Nazi German youth communes and Messianic and artistic communes of the 1920s. But in any case a 'distinctive tradition of cultural radicalism' had existed for a hundred and fifty years; not only had Utopian communities been founded by native Americans and recent European immigrants, but a strain of Asiatic mysticism and occultism among communards had an equally long history.[9] The nineteenth-century Indian Sri Ramakrishna was just one of a line of Eastern gurus: in his case Whitman and even Emma Goldman, Russian-born anarchist leader, were admirers, while Thoreau was affected by 'mystical literature from India'.[10]

Another reason for the symbolic as well as the practical significance of North America for experimental groups was that radical beliefs seemed inherent in her culture. Early radicals supported the liberal Anglo-Saxon rights of Tom Paine. Social theories were founded on a belief in a conflict-free harmony of real interests. Inward, other-worldly, pacifist movements, stimulated by idealised versions of Asiatic religions, found fertile soil here. The existence of this tradition was obscured by those German and Russian anarchist and communist immigrants who were urban and union-based after 1880. It mutated into the drug culture of the 1960s. Perhaps not many readers of Louisa May Alcott realise that she grew up in a commune, somewhat similar to, but less successful than, that described in the sequel to *Little Women, Little Men*. When George Orwell describes the lyrical innocence of mid-nineteenth-century Eastern America, it is this combination of space, rural freedom but taut social and religious discipline that we remember, exactly the kind of breeding ground for social experiments inspired by a love of nature.[11]

Land reform, the movement led by Henry George, called for the nationalisation of rent, so that land could be distributed equally to the people. George's *Progress and Poverty* was inspired by overcrowding in the immigrant slums of New York, and was not meant especially to apply to rural land, which was still available for American settlers. George prefaced his work with a paean of praise for the successes of progress and capitalism. A stranger on earth would ask himself, he wrote, how it was that such wonders could exist as telegraph and steamship, sewing machine and gas-lights. Given such plenty, what had gone wrong? He concluded that land was misused because of monopoly ownership of a scarce resource.[12] Georgite movements sprang up in Europe, especially Britain and Germany. In both countries they concentrated on urban land, and led to local government reform in Britain and the decentralisaton of industry in both countries after the First World War. Herbert Spencer thought a just society could only begin if land was first re-distributed. Alfred Wallace, the biologist, adopted a socialist Georgism. He was also a follower of Theosophy.[13] The Land Restoration League was Georgite. Single tax colonies inspired by George were founded in Australia and Mexico as well as the United States, where one Georgite was fond of quoting the Bhagavad-Gita.[14] But for many of George's followers, it was by no means self-evident that the country was preferable to the town. Towns were cleaner. They had mudless roads, pavements, sewage, lighting and shops. There were hospitals, doctors and transport, education and harbours. The tension between rural populist Georgites and the local government and urban reformers of the middle classes persisted until the First World War.

The apparent contradiction between ideals of rural life and optimism expresses too the Hayekian paradox of the American commune ideal. On the one hand there is an intentional effort at cultural rebirth, on the other hand a belief in the spontaneity of cultural creation which cannot cry halt to technical progress. Both anarchism and religious mysticism inspired American communes, and after 1880, when anarchist movements became more urbanised and revolutionary, only a few Back-to-the-Land groups survived, until a new ecologically conscious generation began again in the 1960s. Both anarchist and religous groups were based on optimistic assumptions. The mystics saw the Divine in each human being, needing only to be awakened. The anarchists believed that no conflict need exist between rational men.[15]

Rejection of the town and progress was not inherent in the commune ideal. It came, not from studies of lead poisoning or cholera, but largely from the works of Ruskin. I referred earlier to the specifically aesthetic nature of the ecologist. The Art Nouveau movement in Northern Spain was influenced by Ruskin and Morris. Ruskin was too unscientific, too religiously moral in his political prescriptions to qualify as an ecologist, but his influence on the political ideals of British ecologism can scarcely be overestimated. He wanted the public sphere to be beautiful: the private one to be spartan. He appropriated all the values of purity and visual harmony for the cause of social reform. He gloried in the idea of manual labour, and even persuaded Oxford undergraduates to build a road one summer. He started the St George's Guild, which financed small farms and village settlements, as well as rural industries – as long as they did not involve such industrial artefacts as sewing machines.[16]

We saw how Ruskin's rhetoric inspired in Soddy a dislike of and rejection of unrooted money. Ruskin's ideal Platonic society, the rulers guided by the public weal, co-operation and harmony among the ruled, appealed to the Comtean scientific mind. He called for aesthetic integrity, for the artistic morality of truth. Despite Ruskin's praise of Italian cities and Renaissance civilization, it was the pro-rural vision not the city-state one that was absorbed; his attack on the waste and ugliness of industrialization rather than the call to beautify cities.

Unlike the later Henry Williamson, Ruskin was not personally involved in the farm settlements but he gave practical support to them in others, and continually expounded the value of the simple rural life. Ruskin influenced William Morris, a more gifted and competent craftsman, who developed a peculiarly English brand of rural folk socialism. His rhetoric of class hatred went unnoticed by many, because Morris, like Ruskin, was inspired by the ideal of Englishness, the heritage of beauty expressed in well-wrought things; the gardens, embroidery, stone-work, music and art of the long-silenced, oppressed native English. Celts and Saxons had long vied as the under-dogs of European history, both seen as in possession of natural harmony. It was easy to perceive and demonstrate that harmony in the English village and English countryside. Both were living works of art. Ruskin and his followers were too blinded by their vision fully to realise that their survival depended on economically successful agriculture as well as the spirit of place and people.

Morris, though also not an ecologist, (the young Morris was inspired by Richard Jefferies, but became a revolutionary Marxist at the age of fifty) was moved by the longing to use resources properly, economically and beautifully.[17] There was a darkness behind his optimism, what Armytage perceptively described as the fear of the destructive power of time. 'Save the grief that remembers the past,' Morris wrote, 'And the fear that the future sees.'[18] The poem prefigures the darkness, the fear of irrevocable loss that characterises the ecologist.

Morris disliked the notion of the state-commune, developed by Edward Bellamy from Ruskin, and preferred semi-agricultural communes instead. In the 1890s, colonies and private smallholding associations sprang up everywhere. Often located in Southern England and near to towns, they were intensively farmed market gardens. Rider Haggard, the best-selling author and landowner, was also a farmer. He took on several run-down Norfolk farms at a time of falling grain prices and worked them himself. He campaigned for agricultural protection, compulsory life insurance and old age pensions, and better wages for agricultural labourers. When he mentioned that his Norfolk farm was short of labour, hundreds of impractical applications reached him from townsmen. He commented ironically that Carlyle's and Ruskin's works should be banned, because they inspired people to throw up their secure jobs and go farming.[19] Some four hundred smallholding colonies were started during this time. The Ruskin movement produced Guild Socialism which originally had a rural bias, and opposed 'big business'.

Ruskin and Morris had wanted to rescue the submerged ten

per cent, while Huxley represented the scientists who demanded a 'socialist autocracy', the compulsory distribution of food to prevent inequality of suffering. Kropotkin wrote *Mutual Aid* to refute Spencer's competitive evolutionism. He opposed Huxley's 'scarcism' with what the called 'The Coming Reign of Plenty', which would be characterised by optimistic and benevolent bounty.

Distributism, the creed publicised by G.K. Chesterton, was one inter-war rural land planning solution to what were perceived as the evils of urban life and plutocratic capitalism. Chesterton took over his brother's defunct Distributist journal in 1925. Contributors were Catholic or High Anglican; many were socialists who had become admirers ot the Middle Ages, others were Tories opposed to industrialisation. The Distributist League supported small-scale private property and small business, not because it was small, but because such ownership was immediately relevant to and under the control of the individual. One Distributist and friend of Hilaire Belloc was Father Vincent McNabb, who wanted a religious movement 'seeking not wealth but God [to] pioneer the movement from town to land'.[20] Belloc observed that it was the artist, writer or potter, like Eric Gill, who could opt out, while industrial workers could not.[21]

Chesterton wrote an introduction to Cobbett's *Rural Economy* which praised him as an independent yeoman spirit. His yeoman ethic was a thorn in the side of progressive Socialists like Orwell, who repeatedly accused Chesterton and his allies of being on the wrong side of history, against the inevitable march of progress.[22] Chesterton's idea of Back-to-the-Land was rather different from Ruskin's. There was no co-operative sandal-making, no free education and primitive crafts. Chesterton described his idea of decentralization as a 'sortie from a besieged city, sword in hand'.[23] His unhappy prediction of the inexorable victory of mediocre urbanism in *The Napoleon of Notting Hill*, was accompanied by claims that the towns would collapse of their own accord as the financial and political plutocracy collapsed.

Tolstoyan pacifism and naturism also stimulated the commune ideal. There were 60,000 British pacifists in the Second World War. A number were brought up in Christian pacifist communes. The pacifist religious ideal inspired writer John Middleton Murry as well as Eric Gill. John Brewer Paton, a Congregationalist, founded the English Land Colonization Society in 1892. Tolstoy inspired Hugh Massingham, while D.H. Lawrence planned communes through most of his life. (Some years after his death a site in North America was found for a Lawrencian commune, but the war intervened.)[24] Artists who tried to make a living from chicken farms in Cornwall became a cliche in popular British literature between the wars – one of their number was usually murdered. The character-improving effects of the farm colony were shown by the Salvation Army, who established groups for down-and-outs, recidivist convicts and trainee emigrants before the First World War.[25]

In Germany land was scarce, and in East Prussia entailed estates, re-established after 1851, made land purchase difficult. The emigration of agricultural labourers since 1820 had worried *völkisch* nationalists and tax commissioners alike. To reverse this process was the aim of the Prussian Settlement Commission in 1880. At first, German idealists inspired by Georgite ideals went abroad; their communes were in North and South America. Alfred Ploetz, who supported eugenics and temperance, and was a doctor of medicine, part of the circle of socialist reformers forced out of Germany by Bismarck's anti-socialist laws, emigrated to Minnesota with his wife to start a eugenic and vegetarian commune. The native Minnesotans, of German stock, spoke an earlier German dialect, and resented the Ploetzes as urban newcomers, with 'foreign' accents and bizarre ideas. Eventually they returned to Switzerland.[26]

The kibbutz ideal in Israel was rooted in the German nature tradition as well as Russian populism, although the left-wing Ruthenian and Ukrainian nationalists exiled in Vienna who praised the old Cossack tribal unit, possibly also helped to inspire it. Theodore Hertzka, a follower of Henry George, started a commune called *Freiland*, – and many Georgite communes had the same symbolic name. Michael Flursheim and Adolf Damaschke were ardent exponents of decanting town dwellers back on the land. The commune movement at this time attracted those interested in the 'social problem'; that is, urban unemployment and poverty, slums, the declining birth rate and so on. Bernhard Förster, Nietzsche's brother-in-law, and later an ardent Nazi, started a commune in Paraguay, where there was already a large German population. Africa was the favoured home for many commune plans.[27] But besides eugenics and temperance ideals, religious mysticism played a large part in the German commune movement. One such group, the Bruderhof, started by the secretary of the Student Christian Movement, derived its ideals from Fichte, Goethe, Boehme (the Bohemian mystic) and Tolstoy. After the Nazi takeover in 1933 they gradually trickled out to England, and by 1937 the Cotswold Bruderhof had been established. It was so successful that another was built in 1938. Under threat of internment, its members left for Paraguay during the war, and by 1960 'Bruderhof' groups were flourishing in Connecticut, Germany, Paraguay and England.[28]

Within Germany, the aesthetic movement was submerged by 'Life Reform' groups which practised organic farming, vegetarianism and nudism. As with the Youth Movement, the communards represented every extreme of the political spectrum. One writer divided them into eight kinds; communistic, feminist, *völkisch*, anarcho-religious, evangelical, Quaker, Anthroposophical (followers of Rudolf Steiner) and Jewish. Colonies of agricultural labourers were also a specific answer to the problem of landless refugees from ethnic German settlements. The anti-Polish, *völkisch* Artamanen (Guardians of the Soil) dreamed of re-settling 'the German East'. Constantly harassed by police, with no status as German nationals after the Aliens Act of 1921, they existed on hand-outs of clothes and food, and worked on farms in eastern Germany without payment. They encapsulate the mixed political parentage of nationalist youth communes in the 1920s. They combined quotes from Tolstoy and Gandhi with the swastika banner inscribed 'To the Eastland will We Go', and a rejection of the West and its civilization. However, they formed barely a tenth of the total membership of the youth movement. These existentialist and revolutionary groups were also licensed and limited companies, – as it were the Direct Action Terrorist Squad Public Company Limited by Guarantee- and had to keep accounts. Their activities and numbers can therefore be checked. The small size of the groups is a good corrective to their all-embracing rhetoric: they were not typical.[29]

Gandhi inspired less exotic groups, such as Willy Ackermann's bio-dynamic commune near Hamburg in 1930. Here the land was farmed without machinery, and they built their own huts. This small commune deserves some attention, since it survived the Nazi period and is still going strong. The most long-lasting communes appear to be the religious communities in North America, and the organic farming, Anthroposophist groups in Germany. Both worked in a disciplined fashion, with strong leadership and strict financial accounting.

One commune which fuses religion and ecology was the Findhorn community in Scotland. Like the mystic communities of North America, it was established to nurture 'the Divine within men', but also to wait for the 'New Age', the new culture that would be born when men realised their place in nature. Members of Findhorn had to work in harmony with the elemental world, that is nature spirits, and also guardian angel-type figures. There was an angel for each physical phenomenon, including winds. The belief that a hidden spirit world shadowed each physical entity, that angels were not confined to man but were common to all living things, is similar to the popular 'morpho-genesis' of Rupert Sheldrake. Sheldrake took up the problem of the apparent transmission of cultural knowledge, and argued that once something existed on the earth, whether a pattern of behaviour or a new form of crystal, a spirit existed that held the ideal form of that object or pattern. Thus, techniques like bicycle riding became easier over generations, because an ideal pattern of bicycle riding existed, and was accessible to the collective unconscious.[30] The Findhorn commune claimed that pollution would destroy that other, spirit world, and that the world we know would become a desert, an ecological disaster, for if man 'violates God's law, man may be seen by nature spirits as a parasite,' and withdraw the life force from the planet.[31] The Findhorn experiment has lasted some eighteen years, and impresses visitors with the fertile growth on a windy Scottish island.

The strain of technical optimism that characterised the anarchist communes of the late nineteenth century returned in American ecological communes after 1960. Independent libertarianism, survivalism and anarchic radicalism: *laissez-faire* and LSD: all merged with an ardent idealism about the land.[32] 'It may take a thousand years before we know the spirit of place which animates this continent', commented one ecologist communard in 1968.[33]

Given the tradition in the United States of interest in agrarian communes, it would have been unsurprising if Roosevelt's New Deal had followed Germany in trying to resettle the unemployed on the land. But despite the bias towards land planning among his staff, and the existence of *Lebensraum* in plenty, only some four thousand settlements were created in his time. However, the British experience with state-funded smallholdings was eyed with interest.[34] As unemployment became more and more a problem of the ethnic minorities, Back-to-the-Land was quietly shelved as even a theoretical solution. Black communes followed the same pattern of radical mysticism as white, but were urban. One of the oddest existed in Chicago during the Second World War, publishing a journal called *World Philosophy*. It featured a swastika on the front cover, whether in tribute to the Buddhist inspiration, or a reference to their occult interests is not known.[35] But such groups were rare, and the ethnic pattern of the communes remained largely of European origin. In photo features of hippy communes in the 1970s, the camera portrayed row after row of blonde, thin, hairy heads; small, tow-headed children were rocked by their mothers. It was for all the world like the opening up of the West. According to studies made of communes, the ethnic homogeneity of the long-lasting commune is partly because members are volunteers, self-selected, and partly because of the middle-class, educated nature of most communards. Not only do they have to have a family background comfortable enough to be worth escaping, but it has to have an element of *old* affluence in it to turn the children to the spartan aesthetics of ecological communes.

The commune movement linked with the ecological movement in more ways than the obvious ones of caring about pollution and self-sufficiency. They shared an anarchist heritage, a belief in individual values, and a tendency to spiritualism. It at first seems strange that the rationalist urge which led American youth to construct solar power pumps and equal-temparature domes might be directly linked with a belief in occult or mystical phenomena. Yet the evidence seems there. One New Mexico commune established in the early 1970s, of the authoritarian ecological type, followed bio-dynamic organic gardening techniques: the works of Ehrenfried Pfeiffer were on the shelves. Other books included Stanislavsky, Buckmaster Fuller, Robert Ardrey, Lewis Mumford, and works on Gurdjieff and Ouspensky. Even more significantly, the group went out of its way not to acquire knowledge or techniques from orthodox sources, such as libraries, universities or newspapers. They preferred to experiment for themselves, to hypothesise, to follow rumour. A general incredulity and scepticism about the 'normal' world was combined with an eager credulity about their own.[36]

This conforms to the theory of one sociologist that an interest in occultism, popular science and 'Danikenism' results from the failure of either religion or received science to offer a coherent fact-and-ethic mythos. Religion lost its faith, and science doubted its facts. Ethno-centric religion had been lost to the European peoples since Christianity, it was part of the stolen folk heritage.[37] The result was that a generation brought up in the optimistic liberal heritage of the United States, together with the faith in reason of the educated middle class, found that no coherent, credible world-view was available. In the words quoted in the introduction, something felt wrong with the world, and ecology explained everything. It brought everything together; the dishonesty and irresponsibility of government; the corruption and short-sightedness of business and industry. The post-war faith in the American mission to help the Third World progress mutated easily enough into the mission to protect its forests and soil. The same proseletysing force lay behind both. However, this could only be morally acceptable if ecologists in the United States could live in a less resource-heavy way. As Webber points out, the growth of more egalitarian class structures under American capitalism removed much of the critical bite from socialism, while at the same time socialism went mainstream. This left anarchic do-gooders in a quandary; they had to do good by example, to find the divine within themselves before emerging for their mission.[38]

Empirical studies show that this has not happened yet. Communes are generally not independent. Self-sufficiency even in vegetable growing is rare. Parental contributions and welfare payments are the norm: sometimes a generous patron or idealistic reformer underwrites the project. Increasingly, the mission of the commune provides not only the impetus but the salaries. Part-time lecturing, journalism and other propaganda helps to pay for the videos and clothes dryers. It would be unfair to claim that as the ferocity of ecological propaganda increases so does the irresponsibility of its exponents. And it would be a pity if the golden dream of the free man on his own soil were to wither into a mere intellectual fashion. The American continent has the land available for voluntary social experiments, and it might yet be that some leap emerges, or that real developments in economic resource use are discovered. The fact that the longest-lived communes are religious ones (including Anthroposophy here as a religion) suggests that the development will be in this direction.

CHAPTER SIX

Back To The Northland

> Economists, philanthropists, humanitarians, improvers of the condition of the working class, organisers of charity, members of societies for the prevention of cruelty to animals, temperance fanatics, hole-in-corner reformers of every imaginable kind...
>
> (Marx and Engels, *Communist Manifesto,* p.113)

In the late nineteenth century rural life became linked with physical and moral welfare in the minds of many. With the First World War the belief in the regenerative power of contact with the land took on even greater force.[1] It seemed that a new era had arrived in which the whey-faced poor in their rotting slums could be re-settled in suburban villages and garden cities. All over Europe, soldiers about to be demobilized were promised smallholdings. If the evils of urban living were avoided, physical and mental health would be improved. This belief focused on the fate of urban children, the seed-bed of the new world. What had been tentative and utopian pre-1914 ideas about reform through country life now seemed a practical possibility.

The 1930s saw the full development of the group of ideas we call ecologism today. It was characterized by that global perspective which is an integral part of ecological, as opposed to environmental thought. Calls for ecological awareness, the need to live according to ecological ideas and maintain ecological balances; these became widespread among a small, inter-knit group described here as High Tory.

Environmentalism and ecologism took different paths. Ecologists called for complete social and economic change worldwide. They prophesied erosion and total soil pollution if all countries did not follow their recommendations. And like all ideologues, they claimed that unless everyone played by their rules, the game was up.

On the other hand, organised environmental protection groups in Britain went in for specific problem-solving. The Council for the Protection of Rural England was established in 1928, with an active local branch structure. The first Town and Country Planning Act was passed in 1932, largely as a result of lobbying by the Council. (The first town planning act had been in 1909, but it did not include rural planning controls.[2]) The Ramblers Association was formed in 1935, and again had a strong local structure.[3] These manifestations of environmentalism implied the belief that local government, in its Fabian guise of benevolent Platonic Guardian, was the suitable means for reform. This cast of mind was to be labelled that of the 'new Jerusalemers'.[4] But a more total and radical social criticism came from ecologists of the time. They rejected political lobbies as irrelevant to the real problems. These were seen as loss of fertility in the soil, soil erosion, loss of resources, such as the phosphates contained in human sewage, depopulation of the countryside, pollution of water and the spread of urbanism. The solution was to restructure society, especially its trade and economy.

High Tory ecologists were anti-capitalist and opposed to *laissez-faire*. Many were pro-German, and remained so throughout the inter-war period. But if there had ever been a moment when anti-capitalism, eugenics, racialism and rural values could have fused into an English version of National Socialism, deep differences now showed themselves. Ecological ideas in England split into two separate styles. The more radical edge of this cultural criticism was not politicized in the 1920s. D.H. Lawrence did not stand for Parliament. In the 1930s, some of his equivalents did, but the existence of the Third Reich, and its claim to support rural values, acted both as spur and bridle. It polarised the movement into admirers and abhorrers, and, eventually, as with the Chicago school of organic biologists, disheartened and silenced it.[5]

GREEN SHIRTS

One pervasive manifestation of these Back-to-the-Land ideas in the 1920s was the growth of new scout movements, offsprings of Baden Powell's Scouts, which had been designed to teach children about the countryside and form responsible characters and leaders. The Woodcraft Folk was intended to give working-class children experience of the outdoor life. It was inspired by the Woodcraft Indians founded in America by emigré Ernest Thompson Seton (1860–1946) – he later became Chief Scout under Baden Powell. In 1916 a Quaker, Ernest Westlake (1856–1922) started a breakaway scout movement, the Order of Woodcraft Chivalry. It wanted more emphasis on forestry and less on warfare. The Order maintained links after the war with the German Youth Movement, who admired its pro-mediaeval stance. Patrick Geddes was on the committee. It founded a forest school in 1928. The Order remained small and obscure, and by 1945 had faded away.

A breakaway scout group was led by John Hargrave (1894–1982). He too was a Quaker, but one who was profoundly concerned that urban life and the First World War had produced a mentally and physically deficient race, while the élite failed to breed sufficiently. These fears about the degenerative effects of civilization and war were most common among socialist reformers. Hargrave found the Scouts too warlike and too conservative. He developed a collection of ideas which to-day sound oddly matched. He was a pantheist who was also interested in Eastern religions, but yet believed in an Anglo-Saxon nationalism, and wanted to go back to English roots. He was a socialist and a pacifist, and also had strong eugenic beliefs. He spent two years as a stretcher-bearer in the First World War, and was then invalided out, so that unlike the founder of the Woodcraft Folk, he belonged to the lost war generation.

Hargrave's mixture of folk roots and a craving for Oriental religion resembled the alternative, counter-culture developed in Germany between 1890 and 1933, as did his pacifism. Both the post-war German Youth Movement and the Kibbo Kift were inspired partly by a revulsion against war, and a desire to restructure society so that such horror could never happen again. Hargrave's books were translated into German during the 1920s, and extensively read.[6] Like Tolkien and the Scandinavian novelists, such as Selma Lagerlöf, Hargrave wanted to create a national myth, a substitute folk-memory for that destroyed by those false gods *laissez-faire* and industrialisation.

He founded a movement which meant to do more than merely introduce children to open air life: it was to establish a counter-society, and especially a potential counter-government, in the form of the Kibbo Kift Kin. The Kin consisted of a network of leaders, regionally based. Geddes, again, was an advisor to the Kin, and so was H.G. Wells – Hargrave was apparently inspired by his 'New Samurai', and wanted the Kin to be a similar élite.[7] Rabindranath Tagore, the Indian mystic, Theosophist and poet who was received with rapture in Berlin in the 1920s, Julian Huxley, zoologist, Arctic explorer Vilhjalmar Stefansson, Havelock Ellis, and Frederick Soddy were also 'Kin'.[8] Rolf Gardiner, organic farmer and Nordic racialist, was briefly 'gleemaster'. Their annual council was called the Althing, and their uniform was a Saxon cowl and jerkin, and a Prussian army cloak.

The spiritual progenitors of the Kin were D.H. Lawrence and William Morris, but where Morris and other Nordicists were inspired by the ideal of 'Teutonic democracy', Hargrave sought a Teutonic élitism. Lawrence, through his wife, Frieda Weekley, (formerly von Richtofen) had come into contact with the 'counterculture' of the artists' colony of Ascona, where Hesse and other German intellectuals created a world of Eurythmics, pacifist *Wandervögel*, anarchy and green proto-Nazism. Through Lawrence's books, the distinctive German brand of serious nature-worship and sun-worship affected the English nature tradition.[9]

The presence of Tagore as patron demonstrates the 'soft' element in Hargrave's programme, and the confusing synthesis of political attitudes that existed in the 1920s where communard and idealist movements were concerned. Tagore, poet, millionaire, Nobel Prize winner in 1913, and agrarian reformer, developed village communes and agricultural schools in Bengal. He saw India's future as one of agricultural reform and supported the peasants. One of his pupil assistants, Leonard Elmhirst, the son of a Yorkshire missionary, married the radical American heiress, Dorothy Whitney Straight. They started Dartington Hall, a mixture of co-operative rural regeneration and experimental education, later a home for Communist activists, and refugees from all over Europe. It was Tagore who recommended the fertile and beautiful South Devon countryside to Elmhirst (the local Rector decided they had been sent by the Devil).[10] One of the founders of Ascona, Rudolph Laban, fled to Dartington in 1938 after managing theatres and operas under the Nazis. The circle of élite, alternative intellectuals embraced any alternative political creed. The Argentinian poetess, Victoria Ocampo, met Elmhirst and Tagore in Bengal; both become close friends with her and contributed to her journal, along with another close friend, Drieu la Rochelle.[11]

Hargrave's policies at first attracted other Quakers and co-operative socialists. However, his emphasis on Social Credit policies and Anglo-Saxon pageantry began to alienate Labour Party supporters. These dissidents began a Woodcraft Folk movement.[12] Perhaps surprisingly for a movement that is still part of today's Labour Party, the Woodcraft Folk also shared a 'Volk' feeling with the German Youth Movement. The founder, Leslie Allen Paul (1905–) was attracted to Nietzsche, Whitman,

Jefferies and Thoreau. Their constitution was called the Folk Law. Like Hargrave, Paul wanted to improve the race by eugenics as well as by healthy exercise. None of these groups had any discernible anti-semitic element, but they were certainly consciously looking for Anglo-Saxon racial roots and methods of social organisation. Hargrave's ideas were to be imposed by an élite fired by mystic communion as well as by common ideals and comradeship: the Woodcraft Folk pursued policies such as a national health service, employment protection, subsidised child-bearing and better nurseries and playing fields. Both groups adopted the theory of recapitulation, as it was called, derived from Haeckel's theory that 'ontogeny recapitulates phylogeny'. The American psychologist, G. Stanley Hall, argued that the developing adolescent recapitulated the history of man. Between the ages of ten and fourteen, the primitive hunter was dominant.[13] This formative phase should be used to educate and train the adolescent youth, – we encountered this idea as a rationale behind Seton in Chapter Five.

Hargrave absorbed his Social Credit ideas from Rolf Gardiner, who was briefly a member of the Kin and a friend of D.H. Lawrence. Hargrave and Major C.H. Douglas, (1879–1952) founder of Social Credit, both wrote for Gardiner's paper, *Youth*. Social Credit policies were similar to G.K. Chesterton's Distributism. They opposed the payment of interest, and wanted all credit to be issued by the state. If credit were a state monopoly, like currency, deflationary collapses would be averted, and malevolent financial interests controlled. The economic theory evolved by Douglas was a variant of criticisms of Say's Law. Jean Baptiste Say thought that supply must always equal demand, because the money that went into production remained in circulation to create purchasing power. Marx had implicitly attacked this theory through his model of surplus value. Keynes was to point out that depressions could develop because in times of deflation people preferred saving to expenditure (although he did not explain what happened to money saved that prevented it going into circulation via the banking system). Douglas saw the 'leakage' of purchasing power as caused by finance capitalism. His A+B theorem became famous. This argued that wages, salaries and dividends (A) paid by one firm, would be never enough for purchasing the firm's product (B). The B was money paid elsewhere as, for example, interest charges and bank charges. The state should issue credit to make up the difference, thus providing sufficient purchasing power to keep the economy going, and providing it to the productive worker. Finance capitalism was unproductive, because under it, interest left the productive sector. International finance damaged national economies (the term multinational was not then in use: probably, Douglas would have used it). Like today's green anti-trade, anti-finance-capitalist theories, Social Credit lent itself easily to a blanket condemnation of mercantilism, greed, materialism, and exploitation, although it emphasised the value of the productive craftsman, entrepreneur and farmer. Douglas argued that as long as there was spare capacity, state-issued credit would not be inflationary.[14]

Douglas spent most of his working life as an engineer in India, South America and other non-European areas. During the First World War, he was Assistant Director of the Royal Aircraft Works at Farnborough.[15] He had the simple but unconventional folk wisdom of the outsider. His followers included the Tory, anti-Whig lobby, but also appealed to those with a puritanical dislike for unrooted money, or who had suffered financial or emotional loss from modernization. Douglas, however, was an individualist, and believed in the value of technology. In fact, he saw existing financial institutions and bankers as obstacles to technological progress, as a dead hand. Here, as with Henry Williamsom, and many inter-war fascists, was the Wellsian vision of clean, efficient, unwasteful technology, hampered by traditionalists and vested interests, yearning to be set free by sensible engineers and trained bureaucrats.[16]

Social Creditors opposed usury and the banking system, and believed in the 'just price'. Support for this creed came from farming communities in the Dominions, as well as from fundamentalist Protestant groups and right-wing Catholics. Silvio Gesell, monetary reformist, inspirer of Keynes and member of the Munich Soviet, believed in a form of Social Credit, as did Gottfried Feder, the early Nazi. Social Creditors, once won over to the blinding simplicities of the A+B theorem, perceived themselves as the good, the sane, the normal, in opposition to the destructive and malevolent creators of 'the system'. It was a short step from opposing finance capitalism to opposing what were seen as the destructive effects of exploitative, utilitarian untramelled capitalism on the physical, valued world. Social Creditors cherished conservative values.

The Kin depended on Hargrave's dynamic and inspiring leadership, but he was too much of an individualist to keep such a group together, much less expand it. His increasing belief in occult forces, his slogan that 'All is Energy' came to seem more and more irrelevant after the Depression began. In fact, Hargrave merged the Kibbo Kift with a group of unemployed workers in

Coventry, formed in January 1931 into a 'Legion of Unemployed', with an inner ring known – ominously – as the Iron Guard. Later, the Legion was known as the Green Shirts. The similarity of names between the Legion, the Iron Guard and Green Shirts of Rumania is striking, and can hardly be coincidental, but whether Hargrave knew of or understood the implications is uncertain. The Legion also demanded a just price, a national dividend and national credit. When the groups merged, the Kibbo Kift adopted the green shirts and dropped some of their Anglo-Saxon archaisms, while in January 1933 it changed its name to the Green Shirt Movement for Social Credit. It saw itself as a populist but non-violent movement, which would reform society directly, not through parliamentary democracy.[17]

Hargrave's abilities as a propagandist and creator of pageantry kept the Green Shirts alive for a few more years. In 1935, inspired by the success of the Social Credit Party in Alberta, Canada, the Green Shirts changed their name again to the Social Credit Party of Great Britain. They put up a candidate in South Leeds who polled a respectable 11 per cent. After this Hargrave, thinking himself more powerful than he was, began to attack Sir Montagu Norman, Governor of the Bank of England. Major Douglas withdrew his support from the new party. It then came under the ban of the 1936 Public Order Act, which outlawed uniformed marches. Although the Social Credit Party still exists, the days of the Green Shirts were over. Like other pro-rural groups in Britain, they had suffered the constant jeers of the more fashionable intellectuals. By 1944 they were dismissed by the later notorious Tom Driberg, Socialist MP and representative of the new urban left, as a 'small, fantastic cult of nature-worshippers'.[18]

The Green Shirts saw themselves as a third factor in politics, neither communists nor fascists, neither capitalists nor socialists. Candidates stood against the British Union of Fascists; in Liverpool, Green Shirt candidates were attacked by a fascist activist after beating him in a local election.[19] Rhetoric about a Third Way was common to the radical Right and revolutionary conservatives in Europe at this time. However, the Green Shirts had an element of Quaker niceness, of world unity pacifism, that failed to attract a loyal constituency. Hargrave's book of oracular sayings has a positive and preaching tone and a vacuous and somewhat self-indulgent content. The group has been defined as occultist, or 'illuminated', in the sense of claiming a secret knowledge: although one ex-member of the Kibbo Kift Kin is quoted as fearing that it would eventually have led to a religious fascism, the group seems to have been in essence apolitical.[20] Apart from an urge to return to Saxon roots and revive the countryside, it had no policies. D.H. Lawrence's comment on Hargrave was:

> I agree with him on the whole...but he knows there's no hope...so he's full of hate, underneath. But, for all that, on the whole, he's *right*. If it wasn't for his [Hargrave's] ambition and his lack of warmth, I'd go and Kibbo Kift along with him...But by wanting to rope in *all* mankind it shows he wants to have his cake and eat it.[21]

'Kangaroo', the fascist leader in Lawrence's novel of that name, published in 1923, strangely parallels Hargrave. In the book Somers/Lawrence is drawn to the dictator, but rejects Kangaroo's embracing, comradely love in words similar to those used about Hargrave. Although it was not the inclusiveness but the intensity of Kangaroo's love which alienated the writer, the tone of the objection is very similar, as is the sympathy extended towards an existentialist criticism of hedonism.

> 'You see', he [Kangaroo] said, 'Christianity is a religion which preaches the despising of the material world. And I don't believe in that part of it...I believe that the men with the real passion for life, for truth, for *living* and not for *having*, I feel they now must seize control of the material possessions, just to safeguard the world from all the masses who want to seize material possessions for themselves blindly, and with nothing else. The men with soul and with passionate truth in them must control the world's material riches and supplies; absolutely put possession out of the reach of the mass of mankind, and let life begin to live again, in place of this struggle for existence, or struggle for wealth.'[22]

The Kin's ideology of local cells and leadership excluded serious parliamentary efforts to gain political power, which was surely correct in a two-party system, but hardly left much lee-way for action, given the rejection of terrorism, violence or a coup (assuming for the sake of argument that these would have had any prospects of success). They were neither a special interest group nor a mass movement nor a powerful, behind-the-scenes clique. However, like the Woodcraft Folk, their hiking and camping activities inspired loyalty and comradeship. By providing a platform for 'alternative' financial ideas, and a network of luminaries who could be kept in touch with each other, the Kin possibly helped to keep alive and stimulate a belief in English rural roots. It is an interesting commentary on the differences between England and Germany that whereas in Germany such a movement only began to succeed following the Depression, in England, the

Depression finished it off. Perhaps the British Union of Fascists picked up too much of its support. The Green Shirts are mentioned in police records as taking part in anti-B.U.F. marches and demonstrations, while the Woodcraft Folk occasionally supported Soviet Russia in the 1930s. Perhaps it fell between two stools: the aim of unpolitical propagation of Anglo-Saxon nationalism on the one hand, and the desire to organise a new social force on the other. A Quaker inspired by Indian Scouts, Nietzchean energistics and New Zealand Social Credit, was probably the nearest England had to a Hitler. His poems and slogans like 'All is Life. There is no Life but Life', came close to self-parody. Without an identifiable scapegoat figure, his movement was not likely to or designed to capture serious nationalist-cum-green support. Exclusivist nationalism does not work if you try to include everybody.

THE SAXON KINSHIP

The group we shall look at now consisted of more specific exponents of ecological ideas, who had an understanding of the dangers of soil erosion. They supported whole food and organic farming decades before such matters became common currency. Two of them, Rolf Gardiner and Lord Lymington, were founder members of the Council of the Soil Association in 1945. These two also wanted closer links with Germany. What was the German connection? Among Haeckel's converts was D.H. Lawrence. According to the memoirs of a childhood friend, Lawrence as a boy was influenced by Haeckel's rationalism and nature-worship, which he read in one of Haeckel's popularized scientific works, *Riddle of the Universe*. It may seem strange that a writer associated with an irrational creed of 'blood' should have been so inspired by an evolutionist, but Haeckel believed will and beauty played a role in descent: Lawrence later rejected the idea of determinist evolution, but this was not necessarily a reaction against Haeckel, who supported the theory of mutation through 'cell irritation' (i.e., not slow selection via survival). Certainly, one author attributed to Haeckel a major role in Lawrence's best-known works, and to the development of his cosmology, especially his combination of 'causal evolution with Nature mysticism'.[23] Lawrence was not a programmatic ecologist, as I have defined it, but his intellectual background was saturated with a mixture of nature-worship and anti-anthropomorphism. He later came into contact with the sun-worshipping colony of artists and anarchists at

Ascona, mentioned above. One author goes so far as to say that the Leavises' articles in praise of Lawrence, English village life and Richard Jefferies resemble the articles published in *Die Tat*, Diederichs' *völkisch* journal.[24] (Diederichs was a neo-Conservative, nationalist German who published many young National Socialist intellectuals, such as Ferdinand Fried, Ernst von Salomon and Giselher Wirsing.) Although Lawrence profoundly influenced the pro-Nordic Gardiner, this comparison appears to me problematical. It brings out the problems of the necessarily retrospective historian. It is possible to quarry Lawrence for exciting references to race, eugenics, blood, and so on,[25] while the famous end of *The Rainbow* expresses an anti-urban, and indeed, anti-mankind critique that approaches nihilism.

> She saw...the amorphous, brittle, hard edged new houses advancing from Beldover to meet the corrupt new houses from Lethley...a dry, brittle, terrible corruption spreading over the face of the land, and she was sick with a nausea so deep that she perished as she sat...And the rainbow stood upon the earth. She knew that the sordid people who crept hard-scaled and separate on the face of the earth's corruption were living still.[26]

Birkin's desire to see man destroyed, if only 'this beautiful evening with the luminous land and trees' is preserved, has the same illiberal, anti-human force.[27] Certainly, Lawrence's intuitive but detailed perceptions of landscape, and the people embedded in that landscape, have the *total* nature defined earlier as essential to the ecological package-deal and appear to resemble the language of proto-Nazis. However, the apolitical quality of Lawrence's vision, the puritan individual morality, his refusal to engage in domination or submission, removes his work from the world of political radicals and reformers. Ecologists wish to avert apocalypse. Lawrence did not.

Lawrence, though, was a powerful influence on the ideas and style of Rolf Gardiner (1902–1972). As Gardiner was an early ecologist, this is an example of continuity of ideas, but also of their mutation. Gardiner's active political career began early. He was born in London into a wealthy trading West Country family, which had estates in Malawi, and a family business in London. His father was an Egyptologist. His mother was half Swedish and half Austro-Hungarian Jewish.[28] He became a Guild Socialist while at Cambridge, where in 1923 he began to edit a magazine, *Youth*, to which he brought a strong leaning towards the German Youth Movement and Social Credit, and in which he attacked the philosophy of the Bloomsbury Group and Keynes. He was founder of the Cambridge Social Credit Study Circle. He was a founder member of the Soil Association, and member of its Council. Well after the Second World War, he was still active in promoting organic farming, and was engaged in a vigorous correspondence about Ronald Blythe's *Akenfield* in the *Observer* in 1969.[29] He later criticized his involvement in the Kibbo Kift, which he dismissed as 'mummery', a mixture of 'political idealism' borrowed from H.G. Wells and Major C.H. Douglas.[30]

Like several pro-Germanist ecologists between the wars, Gardiner leads a strange sort of double life in literature about the twentieth century. Readers of Griffith's *Fellow Travellers of the Right* will have come across him as a fervent supporter of Nazi rural policies and paganism, but those interested in ecology will have found warm-hearted support of Gardiner from John Stewart Collis, in *The Worm Forgives the Plough*, a description of his wartime experiences working on the land which includes admiring references to Gardiner as an employer and dedicated ecologist. Embarrassed academics still recall Gardiner – who loved music – singing a song to the corn spirit when his daughter married an Oxford don, but an expert on the nature tradition in English literature found Gardiner's contributions 'impressive'.[31] He was High Sheriff of Dorset between 1967 and 1968, while giving lectures to the Radionic Association. He bought an estate in Dorset in the 1920s and farmed it organically. He planned to start a rural university there. His children did not take up country life. However, the estate, Springhead, at Fontmell Magna, survives as a centre for rural studies and organic farming.

Gardiner's first work was a booklet, privately published in London, and published in Dresden by a German journal, *Die Hellerau Blätter*. It was written while he was still an undergraduate, after he took a folk-dancing troop to Germany in 1922. It described his love of folk-dancing and the spiritual importance it had for him. At a time when Morris dancing is seen as a precious folksy idea, tied up with every kind of absurdity, too stale to be a funny joke even in the days of the Ealing comedies, it is hard to realise the electric excitement that underlay the discovery of English folklore, music and dancing before the First World War. The movement soon split, with the English Folk Dance Society attacked by the more militant, for being fuddy-duddy. 'It has become respectable, and respectability in England is the death warrant of any vital enterprise. . .and individual enterprise is the hall-mark of life, of creativeness.'[32] Gardiner's account restores some of the thrill of discovery and new meaning: it is not concerned so much with anthropology or the Folk as with a philosophy of life. He draws from the living dance lessons on man's attitude to nature, to the soil, to sex and to politics. His emphasis on life and creativity, on harmony and balance, included the suggestion that Folk Dance could bring back to us 'a liberty, a harmony of existence, for lack of which we are now most brutally suffering'.[33] He attacked 'the black soul of a selfish individualism' in favour of the 'naturalness, communality, and freedom' of the folk dance.[34] He yearns for a self-forgetfulness that will take the bearer above himself. 'The sword dance...above all an emotional unity, [it] set in voltaic commotion every electron in the souls and bodies of the dancers, till they are consumed...by one blind, electric, purging flame of ecstacy, an exaltation, a cathartic frenzy,...'[35]

He stressed the joy of fusion again in the Morris dance, the surging, electric fluid...fusing the whole six of you...yet at the same time each individual dancer is himself, distinct, apart'.[36] Dance and song as a purgative, regenerative mixture was, again, an Asconan cult. Rudolph Laban's mistress invented eurythmics at Ascona. The American Martha Graham and the Communist Margaret Barr were to pursue it at Dartington Hall. Gardiner's longing for a patterned communality might have led him to Marxist Socialism or the Christianity of C.S. Lewis, but the pull of the land was to be a stronger influence, towards dreams of a united and pagan England and Germany. In a later article, 'Meditations on the Future of Northern Europe', he wrote of man's need to search for 'the country of his heart, that place or region where he can ultimately take root and bear fruit like a tree, and which for him becomes symbolic of the unseen home whence he is sprung, and whither he will return.'[37] He produced that apparently omnipresent demand among right-wing rejecters of capitalism, a 'third way'.

> The Christianisation of Europe has been the spirit-urge, the Christian urge, which in its later stages becomes the urge of Science...The moot point is, whether human beings are going to reverse direction and switch back to the old, unconscious way of living, the way of peasants, of savages, or evolve a third way of life, a sort of synthesis of consciousness and unconsciousness, a living not from the blood nor from the intellect, but from some principle more central and more eternal than either.[38]

Describing the power of nature's laws, he wrote,

> We live on a plane whose life marches to one dominant rhythm. Setting aside all disparities, we can discern a law

> governing our earth-existence, cyclical recurrence...life... ebbing and flowing in mysterious processes of contraction and expansion; even the human heart has its systole and diastole.[39]

The Lawrencian influence is obvious here, and Lawrencian ideas ran through Gardiner's semi-religious work, *World Without End* (London, 1932), which began, interestingly enough, with an epitaph from *Kangaroo*, and a dedication to Lawrence for freeing Gardiner and his generation from 'dead tradition'. This work attacked party politics, and the attempts to escape existing party structures which Gardiner called 'New Partyism'. He opposed this along with European fascist parties, as 'middle-class attempts at restoring male power, common, vulgar, mean, urban...' the 'pathetic attempt by suburbia to re-establish itself in the soil'.[40] The spirit of the age was so strong that one could escape it only by personal spiritual re-birth, a theme that was taken up recently by Rudolf Bahro, the German 'fundamentalist' Green, who saw any compromise with politics as damaging the ecological cause. Gardiner was to quote Lawrence again in 1943:

> 'We must plant ourselves again in the universe.' This, verily, is the need of a human race impoverished by abstraction, and living more and more like the machines it has invented. Here is our whole programme, the discipline of organic relationships and organic growth. The study of ecology, in this extended sense, now becomes our most imperative science.[41]

Lawrence had written to Gardiner in 1928 praising the more 'physical' German youth, and the creed of 'song, dance and labour'.[42]

Gardiner emphasised the organic metaphor: 'But it [living according to an ecological law] means the subjection of ourselves and our tools to a larger organic authority, the authority of the Natural Order, which is based on rhythmic laws.'[43] In this wartime book, Gardiner produced plans for a Back-to-the-Land programme, and farmers' co-operatives. He quoted from Richard Jefferies and Rudolf Steiner on the need to replenish a debilitated soil with decayed organic matter. 'The life-quality or vital essence of plants and animals are all important for the well-being of men.'[44]

Gardiner's pro-German politics continued alongside his interest in nature and organic farming. In 1928, he was co-editor of a symposium, *Britain and Germany*, published as *Ein Neuer Weg*, (*A New Way Forward*) in Germany by a Youth Movement publisher, the *Bund der Wandervögel und Pfadfinder*. It included a calendar of Youth Movement activities between 1922 and 1928, as well as discussions of Anglo-German relationships. Gardiner claimed a non-political and independent stance for the book, but he called for 'a new union of Celtic-Germanic peoples, from the Adriatic to the Arctic, the Vistula to the Atlantic.'[45] In *World Without End* he talked again of a Baltic union, of an England joined to Prussia, but not, at any cost, to places influenced by Latin culture, like Heidelberg and Munich.[46] Anyone who yearned for past imperial glories or the White Dominions, he continued, should realise that Europe was Britain's destiny.[47] This was an unusual stance, especially among conservatives, in a time when the Empire dominated British politics.

Essays in the 1928 symposium described a visit to Northumberland by German student groups from Hanover and Brandenburg; the programme included sing-songs and talks on 'The Order of Woodcraft Chivalry'.[48] Erich Obst wrote about the British character. He was Professor of geo-politics at Hanover, and Herbert Backe, responsible for German agriculture between 1942 and 1945, studied under him in the 1920s. Kingsley Martin, later the pro-Soviet editor of the *New Statesman*, also contributed an essay. Gardiner rejected 'any nonsensical racial theory, such as a dogmatic belief in the 'Nordic Race'...We restrict things to Northern Europe and a common Germanic sympathy...the practical and spiritual possibilities are here, and not elsewhere.'[49] Despite this disavowal, Gardiner was enthusiastic about the Nazi takeover early in 1933.

A selection of Gardiner's writings published by the Springhead estate lists his tours and visits abroad with folk dancers and choirs, but omits any reference to Gardiner's visits to Walther Darré, or any mention of pro-German sympathies. Yet these were not accidental ornaments to his beliefs, but fundamental to them.

Gardiner became attached to the circle around Lord Lymington, later the Earl of Portsmouth, who, like Gardiner, visited Walther Darré, Nazi Minister for Agriculture, in the 1930s, although it was Gardiner who was Darré's house guest. (In 1943, he broadcast a kind of recantation of his acquaintance with Darré on the BBC, arguing that Darré's ideals had been betrayed by the Nazi Party.) Wyoming-born aristocrat and land-owner, Gerard Lymington was an Anglo-Saxon nationalist, although his inspiration was less recondite than that of Hargrave. In 1930, he became leader of a group formed to revive English customs and provide a network of similar-minded sympathisers, the English Mistery. He went on to form a similar but more activist group called the English Array in 1936 which, while it opposed war with Germany, also opposed disarmament. They held meetings at Gerard

Lymington's country home, and, up to 1938, concentrated on soil fertility, erosion and pollution.[50] The Array was formed mainly from landowners and ex-army officers, – it included Reginald Dorman-Smith, Minister of Agriculture in 1939, and later to be Governor of Burma. Membership was especially strong in East Anglia.

In 1938, Gardiner became a contributor to a new journal called *The New Pioneer*, a magazine edited by Lymington and Beckett, ex-member of the National Socialist League. Members of the League believed that Mosley was in the pay of international financial interests and that the B.U.F. was too soft on the Jews. They wanted to rouse the masses to overthrow democracy. Unlike Mosley, who supported Mussolini, but believed in gaining power through Parliament, Beckett and his ally, William Joyce (later 'Lord Haw-Haw') were radical Nationalists. They had been members of the National Socialist League. Beckett resigned before joining Lymington. They were disillusioned with Mosley, who had expelled them from the British Union of Fascists, and were opposed to the foreign nature of fascism and its foreign funding. Presumably a pro-German sympathy was the link between these men – too extreme for Mosley – and the High Tory nationalists, two groups who were widely separated by education, class and style. Beckett had originally been an Independent Labour Party M.P., and shared a real socialist commitment with William Joyce. He does not seem to have had much influence on the *New Pioneer*. Contributors included A.K. Chesterton, who had recently resigned from the B.U.F., Major-General J.F.C. Fuller, the expert on tanks and other advanced military tactics, and various anti-war and B.U.F. supporters. However, Gardiner dominated the journal, which devoted much of its space to calls for a Back-to-the-Land programme.

In its attitude to Germany the journal took a fairly moderate tone at first and then became more strident.[51] However, its emphasis on healthy soil, healthy food and rural regeneration was constant. Although the existence of Nazi Germany's peasant ideology must have been known to the contributors, no overt link was made in the articles. Lymington himself had written *Famine in England* in 1938. It prophesied a future of soil erosion and degradation in an England unable to feed herself, or to buy in food. It aroused considerable interest, and led to the formation of his group Kinship in Husbandry. The Kinship included many organic farmers, followers of Steiner's bio-dynamic agricultural method, grass experts, seed-breeders and nutritional experts.

Nearly all the issues of *New Pioneer* dealt with these and similar ecological questions. In May 1939, the work of Seebohm Rowntree and Viscount Astor, who had written a typical Fabian tract on agricultural economics which opposed smallholdings as outdated and inefficient, was attacked for not mentioning humus. The edition of June 1939 talked about soil erosion and the need for land reform, which would allow 'responsible initiative in peasant ownership', while 'controlling the land in the interests of the nation'.[52] The issue of July, 1939 drew an analogy between farm and nation: 'like a farm, a country should be one organic whole', and talked about the deleterious environmental effects of imported food.[53] The *New Pioneer* was agriculturally nationalist. It called for more resources for British farmers. It complained that ten million pounds was given to re-settle Czech refugees, but that nothing was given to compensate Hampshire smallholders when their crops were ruined by storms.[58] There was a strong Fosterian note in this:

> The New Pioneer is the man who faces inwards. His is not the new world to conquer, but the old world to redeem...His are not the illimitable lands, forever beckoning, but his to find the pass across the lost horizon of our own purpose. Earth's perimeters will go to other races unless we are reborn at home.[40] Redemption...will come by fanning the spark of flourishing life that survives in ourselves.[55]

England had to

> Restore Health, which means wholeness to our people. Therefore health must be both physical and moral. For health and security we are concerned with the care and development of our soil. Without a healthy and productive soil we cannot have physical health, we cannot have economic security and we cannot have the sense of reality and real values that will give us spiritual health.[56]

Haeckel's teaching affected the English 'Youth Movement' in one specific way that seemed to contradict its strong racial element. His theory that phylogeny recapitulates ontogeny, that the child growing in the womb recapitulated all the stages of evolution, inspired positive, environmental health and education measures. It helped support a strong belief in the value of environmental improvement, especially pre-natal treatment. This interest, which had led to the formation of experimental preventative and total health groups such as the Peckham experimental 'Pioneer Health Centre', was part of the *New Pioneer* ethos; indeed, the founders of the Peckham experiment took part in

Kinship in Husbandry meetings.[57] Recommendations for good pre-natal feeding included food grown in healthy soil, wholemeal bread, eggs and vegetables. Articles contrasted 'The England of to-day as symbolised by the mass-produced tins of the centralised milk factory; and the England we wish to see symbolised by the pigs bred in the cottage garden. . .and the manure from the pigs returning to enrich the soil', while the erosion fears of the period were emphasised.[58] The fundamental history of civilisation was, they argued, the history of the soil. The collapse of civilisations was due to the soil becoming desert when cities 'forget the soil on which they fed'. 'Man, being an animal,' was 'bound to the soil'. The city-dweller, cut off 'from one side of his cosmic nature', lost wisdom. The decline of Rome was a favourite example.[59]

Erosion was a major issue for the ecologists of the 1930s. One of the first uses of the word in its normative sense was in a geographical survey of soil erosion world-wide, with particular reference to North America, *The Rape of the Earth* (1939). This influential work discussed the need for an ecological equilibrium which was further defined as the 'ecological balance of the original flora and fauna'.[60] It was wrong for man to upset the equilibrium of animal ecology, while land reclamation by ecological methods, that is, enclosing and leaving alone, was the cure. Price support and price controls for agriculture, social security, action to prevent rural unemployment, were also part of the programme. But the emphasis remained on a healthy, organically nourished soil. The cycle of nutrients, from soil to vegetables to animal to soil, was seen as a wholeness we had lost, a chain whose most important link had been broken. Books by Dr G.T. Wrench received a sympathetic hearing in the *New Pioneer*, which shows, again, the emphasis on environmental rather than eugenic influences. Wrench argued that 'a mother of C3 class, if undiseased herself, may ensure a A1 baby',while the discovery of untouched Indian tribes in remote valleys had led to investigations to discover the causes of their superior teeth, health and longevity.[61] Indian village compost-making, the re-cycling of rotted animal and human wastes was the cause. Stone ground wheat meant that the whole grain, with all its nutrients, was ingested, and European rats were compared unfavourably by this writer with Indian rats which ate organic breadcrumbs. 'One feels that the [European] rat would sooner sit and work at a bench or at a desk than make his muscles glow with hard work upon the field.'[62]

Lord Lymington, in his autobiography *A Knot of Roots*, claimed that 'by 1928, I was probing into the problems of Rachel Carson's *Silent Spring*, and leaping by instinct rather than knowledge towards some of her 1962 conclusions'.[63] During a visit to Germany in 1931, he visited one of the Kaiser Wilhelm agricultural stations. He was impressed by their phylloxera-free vines, sweet lupin for cattle fodder, and early ripening maize, but found that the only common language for discussion was Latin. Lymington knew Ehrenfried Pfeiffer, one of Rudolf Steiner's early agricultural lieutenants, and possibly acquired some of this ecological awareness from him. Although Pfeiffer's book on biodynamic farming was not translated into English until 1938, he ran two bio-dynamic farms in Walcheren, Holland, and Lymington went there each year from 1935 to 1939, once with Sir Albert Howard.[64]

The interlocking circles around Gardiner and Lymington spanned British National Socialists, men with ugly hair cuts and razor-scarred faces, researchers and experimenters like Sir George Stapledon, the grass breeding specialist at Aberystwyth, who helped form the revolution in farm productivity after the Second World War, and Sir Albert Howard, who ran an agricultural research institute in India. They included the pro-German writers described by Griffiths, such as Edmund Blunden, who typified the intellectual middle-class love affair with Germany, and who, when war broke out, expressed the sneaking desire to one of his pupils at Oxford that Goering might become Protector of England, because he would restore blacksmiths to every village.[65] There were country gentry who wanted peace with Germany, and rowdy baronets. The poet and playwright Ronald Duncan was another close friend of Lymington and Gardiner, as was Arthur Bryant, the historian.

Lymington entertained and corresponded with believers in wholeness, health and preventative medicine such as Ananda Coomaraswamy, author of a history of art and nature in India, China and mediaeval Europe. The Lymington circle included Dr Alexis Carrel, of the Rockefeller Institute. Carrel, of French origin, was a Nobel Prize winner who specialised in tissue transplants. His book, *Man the Unknown*, stressed the need for a holistic medicine, for seeing the human organism as a whole. Lymington believed that Carrel had lost his Rockefeller laboratory through his holistic message, but his Rockefeller file shows, apparently, that he retired to Vichy France and had an institute there. He died in 1944. Lymington was a Conservative M.P. between 1929 and 1934, and was part of a Young Tory group in 1930, based on himself, R.A. Butler, Harold Balfour and Michael Beaumont.[66] He resigned in 1934 over British agricultural policy, and admitted he was lucky not to be interned under Regulation 18B during the war, as happened to various members of the

B.U.F. and the Anglo-German Fellowship. He became head of a local agricultural war board. The post-war welfare state and its grey atmosphere did not suit this extraordinary patriot and adventurer, and in 1950 he emigrated to Kenya.

Lymington also contributed to the *Anglo-German Review*. This was not concerned with rural problems or ecology, although there was one article on the German agricultural settlement programme, 'Escape from the Slums', which praised the cottage and allotment schemes.[67] Lymington supported a benevolent dictatorship and a united Europe; he appreciated the freemasonry of international aristocracy that he found on his visits abroad.

RECONSTRUCTING RURAL ENGLAND

In a recent edition of Kropotkin's call for intensive land settlement, the editor discussed the viability of Kropotkin's arguments, and traced their influence through Sir George Stapledon, Hugh Massingham, and the Rural Reconstruction Association started by Montagu Fordham.[68] The anarchist prince seems an odd source for a group that includes High Tories, but this cross-fertilisation between apparently disparate people is common among ecological thinkers.

The idea that the farmer or labourer should own the land was part of early twentieth-century ecologism. Because land reform meant redistributing the great estates it was seen as a left-oriented movement. Followers of Henry George had begun with the demand to nationalise rents; they proceeded to call for the nationalisation of property. Land reform groups had a professional and upper-middle-class membership; Alfred Wallace was one supporter, as was Cardinal Newman's brother.

But to support the peasant, the yeoman or the agricultural labourer in England was an emotionally conservative position, usually backed by a deep sense of specifically English patriotism. Ecologists tend to be international, because of the global vision of their ideas. However, they also have a local sense of place, a feeling for the village or for a tribal patriotism. In pre-First World War England, to be an English nationalist *was* to opt for a localised patriotism, just as to be a Welsh nationalist would be today. Normal nationalism was located in the Empire, especially the White Dominions.

An example of this English patriotism is to be found in Maurice

Hewlett, lawyer and best-selling novelist of his time. After writing several historical novels, Hewlett wrote two romances in the first of which the hero gave away his money, forsook an ordered, normal life, and wandered the earth collecting plants and living off the land. In the second, published in 1912, he returns to Sussex and lives a self-sufficient and vegetarian life in a goat-herd's hut, eventually establishing a rural school for the local children.[69] So far this seemed merely an uncoventional Edwardian romance that caught the popular fancy, but in 1916 Hewlett emerged as a surprisingly radical, 'blood and soil' nationalist. He published a verse chronicle of the English labourer, a work meditated for ten years. It was a *Puck of Pook's Hill*-like survey of key moments in English history, seen through the eyes of the dispossessed English farm labourer. Hewlett commented that decorum forbade him to call his poem *The Hodgiad*, thus revealing his debt to Richard Jefferies' portrayal of the long-suffering farm worker. The Chronicle was dedicated 'To England'. It attacked the Norman Conquest, the Normans and the landowners, and argued that the sufferings of the English 'Peasantry' during the war entitled them to free land and government support when they returned. The Introduction stated,

> A certain man, being in bondage to a proud Conqueror, maintained his customs, nourisht his virtues, obeyed his tyrants, and at the end of a thousand years found himself worse off than he was at the beginning of his servitude. He then lifted his head, lookt his master in the face, and his chains fell off him.[70]

The poem ended with the declaration, 'Thus Hodge at last shall win his land.'[71]

This post-colonial emphasis sounded odd from a man so much a part of the established order as Hewlett. He was later to be a member of the Kibbo Kift Kin.[72] H.N. Dickinson was another novelist who sought Tory justice for the labourer. In *The Business of a Gentleman* (London, 1914), the sporty, land-owning hero has to take over a factory owned by his wife. He finds it run on Manchester Liberal lines, with strikes formented by socialist do-gooders. Inspired by his experience of running an estate, he turns the factory into something similar. Under paternalist leadership, inspired by loyalty, duty and higher wages, the workforce makes the factory profitable. Dickinson's book attributes every social evil to urbanism.

Montagu Fordham shows how hard it is to classify ecologists.

They sit stubbornly in their pro-nature box while political categories swirl around them. His main interest was the rural reconstruction of England's agriculture. He perceived it as derelict, and thought that the answer was to reconstruct it on a smallholder basis. His writings spanned thirty-eight years, from *Mother Earth* in 1907 to *The Restoration of Agriculture* in 1945. A Quaker, he began with an agrarian programme acceptable to the pre-First World War Liberal Party. His second book was published by the Labour Publishing Company in 1924.[73] He formed the Rural Reconstruction Association, and one of its last works incorporated articles by ex-Mosleyites. One was Jorian Jenks, agricultural adviser to the British Union of Fascists, and editor of the Soil Association's journal after 1944. Fordham scrapes into the ecologist category through his pro-peasant programme. His support of the peasantry had mystical dimensions. He stressed their instinctive knowledge of God's and nature's laws, their direct wisdom and their 'strong and vital faith in spiritual things'.[74] He opposed any trade in food, and believed that nations should be self-sufficient. He spoke of 'the devastation of the fertility of the land in countries that had been concerned in providing us with food', complaining that the international food trade caused unemployment and poverty 'in newly developed countries'.[75]

In the early 1920s Fordham worked on a Society of Friends relief mission to Cossack refugees and peasant villages devastated by the Soviet-Polish war. He was to write surprisingly favourably about Stalin, describing his policy as 'devastating common sense'.[76] He praised Rolf Gardiner and Lord Lymington, as well as the then moderate centrist, Harold Macmillan.[76] He attacked *laissez-faire* economics, and regarded the Guild Socialists, Tawney, Penty, Sidney Webb and especially Frederick Soddy as exponents of the 'new economics and sociology' which should be taught in village schools.[77]

The Rural Reconstuction Association was founded in 1926. It called for 'the restoration of agriculture to its rightful place in our national life.'[78] Despite Fordham's earlier mysticism about Mother Earth, its arguments were kept on a level of practical policy. It called for farm price support, and attributed the Wheat Act of 1932 to its agitation.[79] By 1945 its board included Sir George Stapledon and Lord Lymington, and it was chaired by Michael Beaumont, ex-member of the English Mistery and Conservative M.P. for Aylesbury between 1929 and 1938. Thus, between 1907 and 1955, the Rural Reconstruction Association and its founder had received support from the Liberals, the Labour Party, ex-members of the B.U.F. and High Tories, as well as from apolitical agrarian economists.

DOWNLAND MAN

Hugh J. Massingham (1888–1952) was one of the Kinship in Husbandry circle. His books on the English countryside and rural crafts are still read, and much loved. He saw himself as a Cobbettian democrat. In his autobiography, Massingham discussed the political inspiration that led him to turn to rural values.[80] He had adopted a theory known as Diffusionism from W.J. Perry, an anthropologist who deduced from his studies of primitive man that man was by nature innocent and non-predatory, 'an entirely pacific being'.[81] This view of man's relationship to nature was sketched in the introduction to this book, where I suggested that it was possible to draw many different political conclusions from the idea that man was a natural being. Massingham argued that nature was benevolent, and that man, as part of nature, in his natural state, was unaggressive and co-operative. We had misinterpreted nature by seeing her as red in tooth and claw: there was sudden death in nature, all animals preyed on each other or on plant life, but this was something to be accepted and even appreciated as a moral duty. It was the inherent burden of existence that energy was recycled in this way, that life lived on life, that life must have an end. Death in nature was, indeed, more merciful, quicker and easier, than the conscious cruelty of civilized man[82]. It was the attempt to avoid the natural course of life that led to grief. Darwin's theory of evolution assumed constant progress, which Massingham thought absurd and undesirable. Huxley and others who talked of cruel nature were sentimentalists. H.G. Wells was typical of those who wanted to escape from nature into a hateful Utopia, where man would be so remote from his real nature that he would lose his desire to live. He disagreed with Hobbes' natural state of conflict theory, and believed in 'the psychic unity of mankind', inherent in Diffusionism. This creed attributed all the ills of civilized humanity to man's social background and institutional environment. His nature was sound at the core: 'It was not in our stars but in ourselves that we were underlings, slaves to the machines and the ideas that it generated...but...in the organised institutions of civilized society.'[83] Massingham wanted a Europe based on small regional groupings, and blamed Germany's lack of greatness and aggressiveness on her 'unnatural unification'. In his memoirs, he stressed culture, rather than race, as the determinant factor in human history, and while this may have been in part a reaction to Nazi racial theories, it was also inherent in his Diffusionist beliefs, as well as in his High Anglicanism (he converted to Catholicism in 1940).

Looking back on his childhood, Massingham observed a deep unhappiness that had no obvious cause.

> Was it that, all-unknowing, we were afflicted with the malady of the age that had reached and passed its apogee of material prosperity and had begun to descend, deeper and deeper into unsuspected depths, into the abyss of the 20th century? Or was it that we were uprooted from our homeland, and sickening, withering in our urban pot and de-oxygenated air? We were 'hydroponics'...nothing to offset the deadening effects and mechanical processes of the mental factory.[84]

Massingham shared his dislike of a formal education with Henry Williamson. He complained particularly that the classics taught him 'entirely failed to be ecological'.[85] It was his private reading of literature and history that inspired in him a love of the English countryside which he compared to that taught at the Danish Folk Schools – the rural education centres introduced in the 1920s. He became a self-taught naturalist, and drifted into journalism, writing for the *New Age* and *The Nation*. (From 1938 until his death he was correspondent for *The Field*.) The *New Age*, edited by A.R. Orage, also a patron of Ezra Pound, supported Social Credit policies, the ones advocated by Rolf Gardiner as a young man. It attacked usury, Whig history and heroes – William of Orange, Adam Smith, Malthus, Cobden and Darwin – and supported a society based on crafts and Guilds. Chief villain of the 'money power' was the Bank of England. The fact that both Cobden and Adam Smith supported 'small proprietors' (Smith) and 'forty-shilling freeholders' (Cobden), was ignored in this analysis.

Guild Socialist ideas were Catholic in inspiration, though not always in denomination, and deeply religious. Materialism was a blind alley, and man was not an end in himself.[86] Massingham and his pre-First World War circle of Guild Socialists formed part of a group of writers and artists, many of whom were to be killed in the war, and replaced by the negative, flippant and sterile culture known as Bloomsbury. His friends included T.E. Hulme, the philosopher, Gaudier-Brzeska, the artist, and Epstein. Another nature-lover, the poet Ralph Hodgson, supported

Nordic racialism, according to Massingham, but generally this group was not pro-German. Massingham's opposition to determinist racial theory was typical of his religious, essentially conservative cast of mind. But he could write angrily about 'traders whom for months we had been pillorying for the knaves and Judases of German Jews they undoubtedly were'; he blamed them for opposition to the Plumage Bill, an attempt to protect wild birds along lines started by W.H. Hudson, whom Massingham admired.[87]

Opponents of 'the money power' always had a tendency to drift towards an anti-semitic position because of their association of bankers and finance houses with Jews. Massingham's role in the Plumage Bill campaign hardened his attitudes. He began to distrust special interest groups and parliamentary democracy; more, it gave him an insight into 'the true meaning' of 'the conquest of nature', which he contrasted with the aim of 'wholeness, which is holiness'.[88]

> . . .impossible for so hellish a commerce to have persisted as it did if the human relation to nature were not resting on a false basis. . .It was predatory and acquisitive only. Was it man's customary attitude to nature? Was man the instinctive matricide? Was his only thought of his maternal heritage to rob, exploit and spend to his own vulgar gain the natural riches. . . lavished upon him? Or was this approach to nature the expression of some widespread mental disease, contrary to the nature of things and man's own health of mind, but induced and fostered by an economic system (in this part of) Western civilization? Was it, in other words, a birthright from Nature, herself predacious, or was it the effect of historical causes and sequences? Is Nazi Nihilism its ultimate fruit?[89]

Massingham was to develop the idea that Nazism was the fruit of a scientistic, nihilistic creed, the antithesis of conservationist values and traditions. He was encouraged in his interpretation by the writings of the Conservative German emigré Hermann Rauschning, ex-President of the Danzig Senate, who described the Nazis as nihilistic and destructive. Rauschning felt he, along with other farmers and land-owners, had been hoaxed into supporting the Nazi peasant programme. 'Nazi propaganda articulated a language that touched the most sensitive nerve of the peasant', and exploited their desire to escape from a liberal agrarian policy.[90] Like Massingham, he opposed the 'rationalised farming' of the nineteenth century, which he associated with positivism and Darwinism, and had read of world-wide erosion in *Rape of the Earth*.

He wrote that on his family's East Prussian farm, after a hundred years of chemical farming, without manure, the soil had lost much of its humus, and yields were down some fifty per cent. Massingham described Germany in 1943 as the 'Satanic-Teutonic state', whose father was 'Hobbes not Hitler'.[91]

Despite this difference between him and Rolf Gardiner, the two men agreed on the need to regenerate the countryside, and develop a new class of yeomen peasants. Although Gardiner's efforts to make Springhead 'a nucleus for land settlement based on subsistence-farming by co-operative groups' failed, Massingham was deeply inspired by Gardiner's Springhead estate, and the Springhead Ring, 'a new regional growth arising spontaneously from our native earth' which reminded him of the candle-flame of Iona during the Dark Ages (surely an image that Gardiner, who preferred the pagan Dark Ages to the Christian ones, would have rejected). 'That this blossoming of the ancient thorn of wisdom should have been at Paladore, the last resting-place of the martyred Edward...what did it not mean to me who had had my solitary vision of the Wessex of Aldhelm and Arthur and Alfred?'[92] The rural feasts, songs and celebrations, the songs and masques performed at Springhead were more than a means to help make England self-sufficient in food, they were a 'means (to win) the soul of England back to herself'. Massingham felt that Springhead showed that under a new economic system land could be redistributed to a million new smallholders. 'What nobler opportunity for the landlord to redeem the crime of the Enclosures and for the nation to redeem itself?'[93]

Enough has been quoted to show the strength of Massingham's belief in the values of rural conservation, ecology and settlement. The food shortages of the Second World War seemed to vindicate advocates of land-use maximalization through peasant cultivation. Massingham joined Kinship in Husbandry, and edited a book on the small farmer in 1947 which included studies of co-operative groups, homesteading and ecological problems. His hatred of bureaucracy, the artificial, the mechanical, the non-craftmanslike, was Cobbettian in its fanaticism. A sense of loss and waste permeates all his writings. The best men were being lost to the land: soil fertility was swept out to sea. The campaign to use more artificial fertilisers was backed by armament firms. 'The woodlands pass.'[94] His often moving rhetoric was based on this dark dread of desertification and homelessness. It drove him to an ethic of service, service to nature and to England, and also service in the more hierarchical context of man to man, which was founded in concepts of Christian duty.

But, again, if man and nature were one, whole, pacific and benevolent, what had gone wrong? Man was one with nature, but man had made the chaos. For Massingham the problem remained unresolved, which keeps his assertive rhetoric self-indulgent. 'The law of nature, *be it truly interpreted*, expounds the divine law.'[95] (My italics.) Perhaps Massingham was unhappy with the logical results of his own analysis. His dislike of rigorous analysis is clear from his work, despite his feeling for exact naturalist detail and description of crafts. The National Socialists, consistent at least, were to attribute the spirit of mechanistic, exploitative technology, *bad* technology, to the Jews. Their dichotomy, their causation, was clear. The great error, the wrongness, of the path Western civilization had taken, was caused by the cultural effects of Jewry. Massingham, despite his anti-semitic outbursts, could not have agreed with this analysis. But there had to be a scapegoat, a *reason* for the wrong path the West had taken since the Middle Ages. For Cobbett, the enemy was the mercantile, lobbying, alien, urban Quaker, and the state-pensioned parasite. For Massingham, as for Knut Hamsun, the enemy was the capitalist, Protestant spirit, the Whig liberal, and the free market economic system associated with it. Individualism meant an atomized, exploitable work-force, and an exploitative attitude to all natural resources. By regaining the knowledge of our ordered, craft-oriented country roots, man would rescue himself from the trough of urban despair.

This was an 'enemy' whose elusiveness was equal to its strength. The greater the opponent, the more profound, and even violent, the need for counteraction. But the violent counteraction in this case was back to an allegedly more pacific natural man, away from imposed violent structures. How to combine problem and answer? Massingham's eventual answer, to retreat to the country, and each man to create for himself a core of sanity, was Gramsci-ite. A change of human, spiritual consciousness was needed.

To see the 'enemy' as the Western capitalist, Protestant ethic is today perfectly acceptable, fitting in not only with the need to blame somebody, but providing the perfect scapegoat, the white, Western, Protestant male, who, as Wyndham Lewis says, is too chivalrous to defend himself against being bitten to death. Yet, as Massingham himself knew, the Victorian era saw a degree of care for future generations that has not since been surpassed. It was the century of the long view, when houses were sold on 99-year leases in the sure knowledge that the family would still be there to plan land use when the leases expired, and when the planting of woods and copses was discussed with one's son and grandson to ensure their approval and understanding of the project. It was the death of this long view that Schumpeter mourned along with the death of capitalism. Nonetheless, the enemy as the insensitive Western capitalist is a concept still often expressed today by Third World representatives and more especially by Greens. It is a racialist viewpoint with idealist overtones. Franz Fanon identifies the white man's spirit as the spirit of untrammelled exploitation and destruction.[96] For this reason, Massingham has remained exempt from the kind of attacks launched on his fellow-ecologists who took a pro-German position in the 1930s.

Massingham's conservationism, and its rejection of economics as motive or structure, was tied to a programme of peasant cultivation, guilds, land distribution, Social Credit, wholeness, and mediaeval folk religion. He always felt it was a lost cause, and this may account for the choleric melancholy which suffuses his work, and his constant retreat into wrestling with religious apologias: – his identification of the 'rural Christ' with the peasant destroyed by Rome, his belief that pre-Puritanical Christianity fused nature with doctrine. In a curious way, this pessimistic conservative longed to believe the views of an optimistic naturist, but never achieved it. His positive values are persuasive, but his identification of his enemies, – Hobbes, Satan, the Teutons, is less so.

FELLOWSHIP OF THE NORTH

The last and most influential flower of the seed of Catholic Distributism was Tolkien's *Lord of the Rings*. His manichaean presentation of good and evil has persuaded admirers to try to identify Orcs and Hobbits, the Dark Lord and Gandalf. Many believe that Tolkien was moved to write his powerful parable by the Second World War, and that the spirit of arid, mechanistic darkness, which poisons water and kills trees, expresses his feeling about Nazism and the German treatment of the Jews. However, he is also seen as a Northern European nationalist, and this interpretation is especially strong in Italy, where far-right groups print Hobbit tee-shirts, and have Hobbit summer camps which teach bomb-making and runes. According to Tolkien's biographer, though, the original inspiration for the picture of the Shire despoiled, the poisoned water, the tainted loyalties, the good perverted and bought, lay in his experience of the industrialization of parts of the West Midlands countryside just after the First World War. The Shire was originally Worcestershire, 'Bag End' his aunt's farm, and it was the pollution of parts of this beloved countryside that Tolkien resented. Other familiar rural scenes became Birmingham suburbs. German art played another role. A late nineteenth-century German painting, the *Berggeist*, which showed a white-haired traveller on a rock under a pine-tree, talking to a fawn on a mountainside, gave him the inspiration for Gandalf.[97]

As an undergraduate, Tolkien mourned the loss of an essentially English cultural history, especially a mythical history. William Morris's Norse epics resonated in his mind. Of the Finnish folk epic, the Kalevala, he said, 'Would that we had more of it left, something of the same sort that belonged to the English.' He compared it to a 'primitive undergrowth', slowly cut down by European literature.[96] Like Hargrave, and, indeed, C.S. Lewis, Tolkien saw an England stripped of its myths, and deprived of its folk memory, especially its Northern, Nordic folk roots. Where Hargrave had temporised unsuccessfully with the 'Althing', Tolkien set out, with *Lord of the Rings*, to fill the gap.

> Once upon a time. . . I had a mind to make a body of more or less connected legend, ranging from the large and cosmogonic to the level of romantic fairy-story – the larger founded on the lesser in contact. . . which I could dedicate simply: to England; to my country. It should possess the tone and quality that I desired, somewhat cool and clear, be redolent of our 'air' (the clime and soil of the North West, meaning Britain and the hither parts of Europe; not Italy or the Aegean, stil less the East), and, while possessing. . . the fair, elusive beauty that some call Celtic (though it is rarely found in genuine, ancient Celtic things), it should be 'high', purged of the gross, and fit for the more adult mind of a land long steeped in poetry.[99]

At the time of the Munich agreement, Tolkien was more anxious about Soviet Russia's intentions than those of Germany. He 'had a loathing of being on any side that include[d] Russia. One fancies that Russia is probably ultimately far more responsible for the present crisis and choice of moment than Hitler.'[100]

Of course, Tolkien was in no way sympathetic to Nazism. But he did not express the anti-German feeling that overtook so many civilians during the war. 'People in this land seem not even yet to realise that in the Germans we have enemies whose virtues (and they are virtues) of obedience and patriotism are greater than ours in the mass,' he wrote in 1941. Hitler had perverted, ruined and misapplied 'for ever that noble northern spirit, a supreme contribution to Europe, which I have ever loved, and tried to present in its true light.'[101]

The mysterious delays in finishing off the *Lord of the Rings* were perhaps due to this sense that it had become difficult to create a Nordic myth for England while she was fighting a country whose guiding ideology included that myth. The cleansing of the Shire (carried out, one notes, by the radical working class Sam Gamgee, while the paternalist Tory Frodo waits for death and resurrection) can be interpreted in several ways. The trees that were cut down are replanted again, the dark, smoky mills are demolished. The bearers of exploitative capitalism are chased out by the sword and the fist. The victims turn on their oppressors with the aid of the returning *Auslanders*. The strawberries ripen in the field, elf dust stimulates the crops like bio-dynamic compost. The crop of new babies are stronger, bluer-eyed and blonder-haired than ever before. Was this Blake? Or was this Wagner, one of Tolkien's inspirations? As Martin Green writes, what shows as an acid reaction in one country shows as alkali in another. But, he adds, 'there can surely be no question that the Englishmen are saying exactly the same things as the Germans.'[102] By the time the book was issued, the possible implications of voicing Norse myths so convincingly in a country recently bereft of empire, identity and homogeneity, went unperceived, except by the politically sensitized on the far Left and far Right. Enraged Marxist professors at Sussex University attacked Tolkien's rural fantasy world, for its irrational appeal, for detracting attention from the evils of capitalism. Nice conservatives fell with relief on Tolkien's 'values', while *Lord of the Rings* joined pirated translations of Alfred Rosenberg's *Myth of the Twentieth Century* in right-wing fringe book lists. Its greatest appeal was to the deracinated hippy generation. Gandalf and Middle Earth became code words for drug fantasies, signs that pot was easily available in World's End shops. Tolkien became a California fad. The full implications of the Tolkien cult belong in a later chapter, but enough has been said to show his links with the pro-Nordic spirit of the early twentieth century, the sense that England's cultural roots had been snapped and her countryside polluted.

CHAPTER SEVEN

The Literary Ecologist

INTRODUCTION

Who are the writers of the ecological movement? For me, as for many others relying on a small public library, the outstanding figures to write about the smallholding ideal were two men who apparently had nothing in common in age or nationality; Knut Hamsun and Henry Williamson. Again, like many others, I had no idea when I read *Growth of the Soil* by Hamsun or *The Story of a Norfolk Farm* by Williamson, that either author had been involved in politics, still less what their politics had been. From the point of view of literary criticism or theory, again, they have little in common. Williamson was a prolix writer, who worked and reworked his stories, over decades or, as with *Tarka the Otter*, before publication. He used his own experience for material. The power of his work comes from his total recall, his eye for detail and the unsparing truthfulness of his writing. Hamsun was a genius with prose, whose power emerges even in translation. Unlike Williamson, he cannot be parodied. Both men were seen as 'modern' and revolutionary, in style and content, in their day. Both were self-taught as artists.

It seems a curious and perhaps coincidental expression of the spirit of the age that two literary giants should, quite separately, have writen works on the small farmer. Hamsun published *Growth of the Soil* in 1917, when he was 60. He had returned to his native North Norway for ten years and farmed there. Williamson had tried to restore and reclaim a Norfolk farm through the time of depression and war. The experience was described once in *The Story of a Norfolk Farm* (1941), and, more truthfully and in greater detail, but as fiction, in three volumes of his *Chronicles of Ancient Sunlight*, completed in the 1960s. Despite the gap of some forty-five years, both writers express the ideology of the peasant or small farmer, independent, individualistic and nationalistic. The relevance for ecological ideas, and especially its political economy, is that both trace the most basic possible experience of what they see as the crucial component of a nation, the man on the land.

Both writers were originally left-wing. Both became nationalist and autarkic, but in the special, anti-capitalist, pro-farmer sense common among ecologists. Williamson, immediately after the First World War, was a Leninist Communist. Hamsun began as an anarchist. Both ended by supporting extreme parties, but for different motives and through different experiences. However, as with my typical ecologist, who rejects party politics and orthodox political categories, both men were always anti-political, and saw the movements which they supported as equally anti-political. This may be the explanation why the two great exponents of literary ecologism in this century displayed (though at different times in their lives) similar political tendencies.

The inter-war link between the search for rural values and some nationalist parties has emerged very strongly. It does, I think, demonstrate that the 'alternative' movement tended to take a particular form between 1914 and 1945 which it does not take today. No modern parallel (at the time of writing) seems to exist. It is an argument in favour of continuity that today's vision of ecological smallholder settlement was alive between 1917 and 1945, and was presented with the same arguments as it is today. On the other hand, the change in political categorization is striking.

'THE SUN SEES NO SHADOWS'

Williamson is part of an extant tradition of English nature writing. Nature is embedded in our literature, and it would be hard to find a conventional chronicle written in the last three decades that did not stress something of the beauty of English countryside before the First World War.[1] A study of the moral role played by nature in English literature would certainly include E.M. Forster and D.H. Lawrence. Naturalists who were also writers include Gilbert White, W.H. Hudson, and, outstandingly, Richard Jefferies (1848–1887). Observers of village life include Mary Mitford and Hugh Massingham. Henry Williamson belonged in all three categories. His special interest for the ecologist is that he twice went 'back to the land' himself. As a twenty-three year old he left a frustrating job as a journalist, and lived rough in a cottage in

North Devon, surrounded by wild animals. After success with his nature books, he decided to restore a family farm, and retreat from the worldly world.

In both, he was inspired by Richard Jefferies. We noted earlier that Jefferies had been described both as a 'Tory transcendentalist' and as an inspirer of William Morris's utopian socialism.[2] This apparent contradiction is resolved by seeing him as an early ecologist. Jefferies was a gifted farmer's son, a journalist who remained a country dweller. Author of *Hodge and his Master*, he saw and described the harsh life of the agricultural labourer without losing his pantheistic love of nature. Thus, he offered evidence for those who sought agrarian reform, while inspiring the lover of nature.

Surprisingly for a nature writer living in rural Berkshire, Jefferies was not only aware of scientific developments but welcomed them enthusiastically. He was one of those for whom theories of evolution fuelled a sense of transcendental unity with nature.[3] In *Nature and Eternity* (1895) Jefferies exclaimed,

> It is probable that with the progress of knowledge it will be possible to satisfy the necessary wants of existence much more easily than now, and thus to remove one great cause of discord...All living creatures, from the zoophyte upwards... strive with all their power to obtain as perfect an existence as possible.

Progress meant not only the 'fuller development of the individual' but improvement of the species, and even the development of new, superior races. 'Part and parcel as we are of the great community of living beings, indissolubly connected with them from the lowest to the highest by a thousand ties, it is impossible for us to escape from the operation of this law.' Besides this law of progress, Jefferies welcomes the law of heredity.

> The physical and mental man are...a mass of inherited structures...He is made up of the Past. This is a happy and inspiriting discovery...which calls upon us for new and larger moral and physical exertion...wider and nobler duties, for upon us depends the future.

The discovery of laws governing man's nature brought, as Jefferies saw it, a new potential for perfectibility. Biology and science together meant progress, but a genius was needed to point the way. 'The faith of the future...will spring from the researches of a thousand thousand thinkers, where minds, once brought into a focus, will speedily burn up all that is useless and worn out...

and evoke a new and brilliant light.' Jefferies described this fusion of scientific genius as 'converging thought', which was rendered possible by greater means of communication.[4] So, as one author points out, his worship of nature was not 'an atavistic rejection of progress in favour of primitivism'. Jefferies favoured 'the light of the future' as long as it was derived from nature.[5] Jefferies, therefore, saw nature as powerful, benevolent, and a force with whose laws man must abide. But nature was not interested in man. It was 'a force without a mind'. This lack of 'directing intelligence' meant that 'all things become at once plastic to our will'. So the power of nature at once confined man's potential and set man free from a dominant authority. All political authorities and traditions became unnecessary with nature's guidance. Jefferies had, like Williamson, a concern for truth and accuracy.[6]

D.H. Lawrence read W.H. Hudson as well as the North American transcendentalists, such as Emerson, and earlier we saw that Haeckel influenced him. However, Williamson seems not to have come across Hudson's works at a formative age, and he was not the influence that Jefferies was, in seeing the agricultural worker as central. Stylistically, too, Williamson followed Jefferies, and their habit of using the sun and sunlight as an image mirrored a similar cast of mind and ethic.[7] Jefferies' works are saturated with light.

'THE RHINE AND ITS ANCIENT TRIBUTARY THAMES'[8]

Henry Williamson (1896–1977) is well known as a nature writer. His book *Tarka the Otter* has been a best-seller among children and adults since it was first published in 1927. However, his main work lay in the re-creation of his own life, his experiences on the Western Front during the First World War, and his attempts to restore a family farm in Norfolk. He hoped, through his fifteen-volume *Chronicles of Ancient Sunlight*, to present the causes of the deterioration and decay of a typical London family, and the source of his own failure, as he saw it, to reverse it. His nature books, his chronicle and the volumes of country tales all hammer out an environmental point of view: indeed, they are more seriously concerned with the need for rural revival and resettlement, unpolluted water, better use of physical resources and close contact with the countryside as a regenerative personal and collective force, than most ecological groups to-day, and the message is drawn from knowledge and experience of rural problems in a way seldom found among urban intellectuals. Williamson is the voice of the ecological movement in a way that Tolkien is not. Tolkien is doing something more when he creates an entire world-view, he is re-structuring European history by presenting a Norse/Catholic myth impregnated with Norse/Catholic values. But Williamson is offering a message of immediate relevance to anyone interested in environmental values and ecological ideas; a difficult, sour and demanding message, but one which omits no element of pain or failure, which strives above all for clarity, truth and justice.

Williamson began to plan his family chronicle – and made several false starts, of which the more popular and available four-volume series *The Flax of Dream*, is one, first published between 1921 and 1924. He wanted to show how the First World War had been caused by the spirit of lovelessness, and lack of thought for others, by a failure of 'truth and clarity', words which constantly recur in his books. He saw his own family history as a microcosm of this process, of hope crushed, land despoiled, and the sensitive victimized. Yet his work has nothing in common with the social novels and satires of the period, and he went out of the way to distance himself from works like John Galsworthy's *Forsyte Saga*, seeing them as superficial attacks on easy targets which lacked exactly that element of comprehension and empathy which he hoped to bring to his work. It took two decades to purge his work of the anger and resentment felt by someone who had always been isolated. Using his own and his family's journals, he began his work in the 1950s, and his last work was completed when he was seventy-five. The eventual picture is stunning but depressing. You cannot read it without a sense of having been touched by life, making Williamson one of the greatest English novelists of the twentieth century. It is Tolstoyan, and, as with Tolstoy, the personality of the author, awkward and messianic, and the message, or series of messages, cannot be expunged from the impact of the art. The First World War towers over his work. The experience of the war, volunteered for lightly out of an experience of suburban scouting and Territorial camps alongside his fellow London clerks, showed him discipline, courage and terror, and taught him empathic tolerance for those who had to suffer the intolerable, mixed with unforgiving impatience for the inadequate, the need for precision and exactitude. He suffered a kind of inner death during the war: its aftermath found him indifferent to physical suffering. He dated his spiritual re-birth to a chance reading of Jefferies in 1918. The capacity, or need, for endurance remained. Nothing, he would exclaim to himself, camping in a deserted barn while restoring his farm, or falling off a motorcycle into winter mud, could ever be as bad as the Flanders mud and the trenches. He felt a sense of guilt and a duty to those who had died. This burden of responsibility rescued him from Bloomsbury egocentricity and hedonism, and from escapist English charm, as well as from the fundamental failure to face reality of self-consciously 'reactionary' writers such as Evelyn Waugh. Whether or not one agrees with his ideas, they are far too deeply ingrained in the texture of his work to be brushed aside as the unfortunate excrescence of an eccentric naturalist. Indeed, one would not want to do so. No literature can be serious, just as no philosophy can be worthwhile, if it does not include the sense of wider interests known loosely as 'politics', based on an unreticent acceptance of one's own values, and a care for the spiritual and moral life of the nation.

His message is simple. The Western world is dying for lack of love, truth and clarity. These virtues are expressed in a well-ordered farm, in a well-ordered household, in a properly organized countryside. Order does not mean force: Williamson criticizes his own rages and attempts to produce order in others. A proper order arises from people's sense of harmony within themselves, from a loving upbringing, and from a feeling of responsiblity for the world around us. How was this to be made real? Williamson's picture of his hero, Phillip Maddison's life, is semi-autobiographical. Maddison is described as a cowardly, dishonest, tearful and sensitive small boy, who reacted against a stern father's coldness and bad treatment of a loving mother, – like so many intellectuals just before and after the First World War.

> The subdued expression of his face was characteristic of many children of the district in the first decade of the twentieth century: a remote look in the eyes, as though the living scene were generally being evaded; a pallor upon cheek and brow, due to long hours of sunlessness in school and to existence in a smoky, often foggy atmosphere during half the year; and on a diet the main food of which was bread whose composition lacked the beneficial germ, or 'sharp', of the white berry, being made of the interior filling whose whiteness had been enhanced by chemical bleaching.[9]

After four years war service, he suffered a complete physical and mental breakdown, and decided to try and re-build his character from scratch. Punished for his 'soft' impulses by separation from his mother, he could not find affection and comradeship with women: revealingly, he writes of his desire to 'punish', to 'pay back' a pretty cousin by seducing her. One pre-war novel implies a complete unfamiliarity with the female orgasm – yet Williamson had five children, one illegitimate! Torn between a desire for emotional self-sufficiency, and a romantic longing for companionship, he married a motherly, rather silly woman, and became, as it were, his father again, stern, demanding and insensitive with his own children, and shouting at his wife; this time not only, like his father, out of Victorian duty and repression, but from his sense of mission, his desire to create a new Europe in miniature. This new and better world could only emerge if each individual reformed himself, and the process should begin with the child. His restoration of a derelict and exploited farm, accompanied by his wife and four children, was to be a step towards this reform. A bloodless revolution was needed, the 'growing of young minds in a way entirely different from the past'.[10]

He had grown up on the edge of expanding London, and – something which seems a constant factor in twentieth-century country-lovers – saw with anguish his childhood fields become brutalised into garish shops and ugly suburbs. The villages and herb fields of Surrey became Greater London. Childhood holidays in Devon hinted at a different world. Scouting was a discovery. Williamson grew up a self-taught naturalist, saw himself as a recreation of Jefferies and Francis Thompson, and went to live in remote Devon after the First World War. At this stage in his life, he was a left-wing revolutionary typical of the time, hating capitalism, industrialists, and, above all, London.

> With the sun's disappearance there arose as out of sweating paving-stone, sooted building, wet bedunged asphalt street, and dripping branch of plane tree supporting puffed and dingy rock-dove...an emanation as of solar death. Sulphurous whiffs caught the breathing; acid inflamed the membrane of eyes; detritus lodged under lids, inflamed haws...The pea-souper dreaded...by two million Londoners, was beginning to drift in slow swirl and eddy...It was to be seen billowing past the street lamps, enclosing them at once in clammy thickness; it moved upon central London from its gathering places over the industrial east both north and south of the river, as though sucked upon the tide moving in from Gravesend and the marshes of Sheppey and distant Nore. *At six o'clock, when it was at its most dense, more than four hundred tons of organic and inorganic*

> *matter were in suspension within the area called Greater London; double night lay upon the City, more terrible because it was made by man who least desired it.*[11]

This is not Dickens' fog: the exact and disgusting detail I have italicised demonstrates the difference between the romantic Cockney approach and Williamson's. His early novels are a mine of detail about the physical, social and economic environment of urban life before the First World War. Londoners poured out on their free Saturday afternoons

> in droves and couples, or singly, all hurrying, staring ahead as with tinkling bells, backs bent, faces set as though they were in for a race, they crouched over handle-bars, while enormous bunches of bluebells, white clustered ends of long stalks dropping, were tied behind their saddles...the cyclists' faces were nearly as white as the stalks where they had been pulled out of the bulbs in the leaf-mould.[12]

Phillip Maddison mourned the execution of the Irish revolutionaries who assassinated Sir Henry Wilson. He supported Lenin. The 'hard-faced men' were responsible for the war. It was the white-faced worker in the urban slums who had suffered and fought, though also, and this probably stopped Williamson from becoming a serious Communist, the gentlemen from the Shires. The war taught him to 'fit in' with the county gentry he had never encountered before. The old families became a touchstone of comparison, a glimpse of an older, better world. Unlike many of the French fascists who had been through the war, Williamson did not come into contact with Marxist ideology or political sociology, and his left-wing tendencies were more of a gut reaction to the war and its aftermath than a system.

> The Corn Production Act was repealed in 1923, and farmers... found themselves facing ruin. Ex-soldiers were workless. In an effort to bring about the British Millenium, a General Strike was organised throughout England...Here and there...in the larger and unhappier towns, a motor-car, taking people to work, was overturned by the mob and set on fire. Most, if not all, working men, were animated by a vision of new hope, of new life, that was being stifled in their anguished breasts. The General Strike failed.[13]

Essentially, he was uninterested in party politics, and unable to lay blame on any group or class. He saw men as individuals each with a will and soul of his own. His sympathies, however, were with the Quixotic, chivalrous, natural men of the upper and lower classes. When he went to live in North Devon, his first project, never completed, was to create a full, complete picture of the life and world of the agricultural labourer, to bring up to date the picture of Hodge begun by Richard Jefferies.

He lacked the irritating romanticism of many writers about rural life because he had not only lived in the country, but lived as an economic equal with labourers. His exact descriptions and analyses were used to discuss their lot clear-sightedly; the minor tragedies, waste and hardnesses of village life. In his 1931 introduction to *The Labouring Life*, he wrote that if 'property was the root of all evil, then so was narrowness of interest'. The newspapers, wireless, higher wages, better food and clothing, that had revolutionised village life since the war, were a benefit, not a disaster. They temporarily removed 'the greatest enemy of mankind, fear'. Here, Williamson showed himself to be more humane than other rural writers, such as J. Robertson Scott, a disagreeably puritanical man, who thought compulsory church-going and porridge eating would revive village life.

Williamson penned the cruelty of the rural underworld, the kind impulses and stunted spiritual growth of the very poor. He wanted to show the heroic soul of the village labourer, but found himself writing about the petty meannesses of underdogs who turned on each other. This grasp of detail made him unique among nature writers.

> One small boy called Ernie, and a smaller, paler baby moving about from place to place in a lowly but rapid manner, a morsel of life, something entirely hidden, except for a small, pale face. . . in a bundle of rags. It was protected, in its shifting and crab-crawlings from cold lime-ash floor to damp stone drains, from streams or edge to garden rubbish-heap, in many layers or coverings of cloth, both wool and cotton, of various colours overlaid or dyed to the hue of ashes, coal, grease, gravy, jam, red mud from the loose and dark brown soil from the garden.[14]

In *The Labouring Life*, he described the sufferings and homesickness of a Maltese woman brought to the village by a sailor, the beatings and sexual repression of the children. This book, unfortunately out of print, lies behind the correlation of the small farm with Europe itself, which is revealed in his novel sequence. Williamson's stories of this time are perhaps his best work of all. His knowledge of agricultural history and economics become part of the scene he describes in a way that is unique. There is no romanticisation. When he describes a tree, you see not only a tree, but its context and meaning, embedded in a landscape that also possesses a past. *Tarka* got under the skin of an otter, but did not put it into a difficult and anguished context of human suffering. Hence its popularity, but Williamson became trapped by its innocuous success. His future work was usually greeted by requests to drop this political stuff and write another *Tarka* again. The 'political stuff' included support for Oswald Mosley and contributions to the *Anglo-German Review*.[15] Williamson, who was a quarter German himself, had been pro-German since the Christmas Day truce in 1914, the first Christmas of the First World War. Although he talked of a united Europe, it was really a united England and Germany that he envisaged. He visited Germany for the 1935 Nuremberg Rally, and was inspired by Nazi Germany's apparent success, the healthy youths in their labour camps and the lack of poverty and hunger. On return, all he could see was a decayed urban world, symbolized, above all, by London.

> They reached the area left ugly by the maulings of London; speculative hire-purchase housing 'estates' – all trees cut down – tens of thousands of cubic yards of coke-breeze blocks and pink heaps of fletton bricks piled up. Life is big business, fornication and death. Civilisation is chromium fittings, radio, love with pessary, rubber girdles, perms, BBC gentility and the sterilising of truth, cubic international-type architecture. Civilisation is white sepulchral bread, gin, and homosexual jokes in the Shaftesbury Avenue theatres. Civilisation is world-citizenship and freedom from tradition, based on rootless eternal wandering in the mind that had nothing to lose and everything to gain including the whole world. Hoardings, brittle houses, flashiness posing as beauty, mongrel living and cosmopolitan modernism, no planning, all higgledy-piggledy – thus the spiritual materialist approaches to London, the great wen, as Cobbett called it. Was the wen about to burst and pus to run throughout the body politic for the second time in his life?[16]

After *Tarka*, he had a similar success with *Salar the Salmon*, but eventually broke away from this false position by buying the run-down farm in Norfolk. Run-down is probably an understatement. At the height of the agricultural depression, with good farming land going for £10 an acre, Williamson managed to buy the only hilly, steep, difficult farmland in Norfolk, and he spent the next nine years restoring the land himself, and farming it organically. He was determined to restore the old four-year rotation system, of fallow, corn, small seeds and grazing, and bought one of the early small petrol-driven Ferguson tractors to help work the hilly land. He refused to put the land down to grass and run a dairy herd, thinking that this meant exploiting the land by exporting the fertility off the land with the milk, and importing artificial fertilisers and fodder. He saw the farm's history as symbolising England's:

> After centuries under a responsible landlord, when the place had order and design, the lands passed by mortgage to the 'Colonel'; thence to a London insurance company, which sold it in the depression upon 'the land fit for heroes', and so it fell into the speculator's market; and to dilapidation. And now, thought Phillip, to my microcosmic effect towards resurgence as damned and doomed as the European macrocosm.[17]

From naturalist to farmer was a difficult transition. Williamson's nature writings had hymned the wild countryside, while often resenting the farmer's eternal effects to control it.

> Which was the true way? Action and the market place: or inaction in retreat? The farm as it had been – a nature reserve reverting to wildness. . . or the farm civilized and brought back to culture, its wild flowers to be seen as weeds to be destroyed: the snipe bogs to become meadows for milk; the reeds pulled from the grupps, and the reed-warbler homeless?[18]

But restoring a family was to be a miniature lesson in Europe's resurgence. It was a way to break off from the overpowering, solitary ego town-dwellers were trapped in, the cause of war and hatred between nations.

> Were they, each one, crouching within the little ego, void of the still, small voice, the glimmer of each soul dulled-out under the bushel of circumstance – the circumstance of one business against another business, of each for himself, of unemployment, poor housing conditions, malnutrition, the wheat berry permanently stripped of its goodness, people fed on the destroying white bread of ordinary life, with its eternal wars, mutilations, its diseases and frustrations, until the final peace of death?[19]

Competition was solitary misery, and its effects social evil: co-operation would waste fewer resources, both human and physical. The white bread of the cities was not only a cause of war, but a symbol of the loss and destruction that deracinated men feel. In *The Phoenix Generation*, Maddison tells his wife of his wish to restore polluted land and water.

> One day our children...will see salmon jumping again in the Pool of London; and watch them...below the piers of London Bridge. One day our children...will save millions of pounds – the hundreds of millions of pounds' worth of factory waste, sewage sludge, and other valuable chemicals now cast into our rivers, and after treatment, put them on our land, our England – the great mother of our race.

Bringing in a typical Maddison/Williamson theme, he describes the leaping salmon as signifying the true, clear hope of the future.

> Anciently, the fish was the symbol of regeneration: as baptism is the symbol of the new consciousness of faith, of hope, of *clarity*. We are aspiring, struggling, learning – just beginning to believe we can build a fine new Britain. We are passing through an age of industrial darkness; but beyond it, I can see salmon leaping again in both the Rhine and its ancient tributary Thames.[20]

This strange mixture of Mosleyite political rhetoric with pantheistic longing for hope, faith and love, is typical of his work. The last phrase, the sting in the tail, refers to his longing to see a united Anglo-Germany.

His efforts to restore his farm organically and make a living from it broke against the stubborn wills of labourers perverted by a false, inhumane education, which cut them off from the rural world around them. 'Dead – dead – dead stuff, the blind trout slowly dying of inanition', he railed at the uselessness of the past.[21] He was obsessed with the loss of fertility through wasting human and animal excreta, joined to the pollution of the rivers and the sea. But the parish in which the farm lay had a bad local authority, which polluted streams and neglected its statutory duty.

> Phillip could not bear to look into the river; he felt its condition to be symbolic of the system, of the dark pollution of the spirit of Man, of the lack of honour in the body politic.[22]

Cheap grain still flooded England up to 1939. 'Could any man, small or great, stem the decline of a human culture?'[23] His own lack of experience, lack of capital and failure of will and concentration (partly due to the need to continue writing to earn a living) were other factors. 'That had been his ambition...to work to make a small parcel of England and water harmonious again, for its own sake.[24] During the war, part of the farm was requisitioned by the armed forces. After the war, he decided to retire and concentrate on writing, having decided that that was where his true metier lay.

> Farming is one long battle, most of it hidden behind the farmer's eyes. When I began. . .I believed then in the power of the will. . .Is to submit to be defeated? To learn that aspiration is of a man's aloneness, that the human will is not transferable directly, that endurance is by its very nature expendable? As the phoenix of resurgent Europe has sunk back into its own embers, so the family-farm idea had failed, and for the same causes in miniature, I cannot but believe.[25]

The story of the attempt to restore a family farm in Norfolk was told in a book published in 1941, the second year of the war. He was obliged to cut a chapter supporting Oswald Mosley and the B.U.F., a censorship he was to rectify to himself in later years by dedicating his book *A Solitary War* to the Mosleys. This action damaged his fortunes considerably – even an appreciative approach such as Keith's in *The Rural Tradition*, which describes Williamson as stylistically 'one of the purest writers of our time' and has a chapter on him, omits the novel sequence from his study.[26] Far more unacceptable ideas were to come. In his next book his battle to restore the farm ran parallel to what he saw as Hitler's attempts to foster the same rural and spiritual values in Germany. He eventually accepted that Hitler had been flawed, but occasionally still wrote of him as a flawed Christ, a saint killed by the lack of imagination of others.[27] Hence the 'Lucifer', of his penultimate book, *Lucifer before Sunrise*, a work which signalled the end of reviews and re-prints, and which has meant serious embarrassment for many of his fans.

Still, however historically unreal and naive his picture of Nazi Germany, Williamson was right to observe in it an interest in ecology and rural values. His error was rather in thinking that this was a major interest for Hitler, and in his romantic and absurd vision of Hitler as a simple old soldier, who wanted peace for Europe. The dimension of purely German nationalistic expansionism escaped Williamson entirely. He believed that Nazi Germany was curing the division between mind and body, by introducing the cult of physical labour. Hitler was a chaste saint, above earthly impulses. Williamson wanted to find a chaste spirit to follow – he saw T.E. Lawrence in this role, and believed him to be a non- or supra-sexual Ariel, a sprite, as did Robert Graves. Both, in a more innocent age, were unable to acknowledge Lawrence's homosexuality. Williamson's favourite music was Wagner, *Tristan and Isolde* and *Parsifal*, operas that inspired him at crucial moments of his life, before volunteering in 1914, or on his departure for Devon, and it is surely significant that he portrayed the announcement of Hitler's death on the German radio as being accompanied by the playing of *Siegfried*, the funeral march, – although in fact, it was Bruckner's 7th symphony.

> He had known that one day he would hear the music of the *Death-Devoted Heart, Love-Devoted Head* theme of Wagner's *Tristan*. And that would be followed by the music of the finale of *Götterdämmerung*-Valhalla of the gods wrecked and in flames, the world of men drowning in the rising waters of the Rhine. Wagner had seen it all, with the clairvoyance of genius: Siegfried, the pure hero, had, through arrogance, betrayed himself, and all about him.[28]

Williamson identified himelf and the ex-soldier Hitler as simple, holy, idealistic spirits. Both suffered a psychic wound, partly caused by the war, partly by a need to rise above the trivial demands of family and social life. Williamson compared his inadequacies in everyday life, his frequent failures, to a split between his capacities in daily life and his imagination, his failure to *realise* his imagination: like the wounded king in *Parsifal*, waiting for the healing holy Grail.

> Is it mere illusion to link the pollution of an English river with the general pollution of European vision, and attribute both to a cast of thought which accepts such things as ordinary, whereby the truths of the interior heart have been overlaid on the sandy bed of this brook with the sludge of dead life? Must a Christ perish in torment in every generation, because people have no imagination, as Bernard Shaw wrote in St Joan?[29]

Of course, Williamson did not expect his readers to accede to his rhetorical questions. With the end of the war and Hitler's suicide Williamson floundered among the wreckage of his world. His last book, attacked by some critics as a fantasy, shows the ruin of his Quixotic gentry as, variously crippled, impotent and incestuous, they come to the end of their lives. His old friend, the gallant young rake, Piers, returns to his family house, and, in an act full of symbolic meaning, strips off and sells the Georgian and Victorian outer shells, damaged by army occupation, to reveal a Jacobean farmhouse within. He is restored to 'his true self' by his girl-friend, a gentle, working-class girl, whose lover was hanged for murder, and the two begin to restore the vegetable orchard and garden. Maddison's girl-friend returns from India, her face scarred by a demented Indian soldier. His hill-top study has been occupied by troops and used for firing practice, his notes and belongings destroyed. The title, *The Gale of the World*, refers to the last words spoken by the Royalist Yugoslav leader, executed by Tito's men. Out of this numbing destruction, which is not so much an exaggerated as a puzzling remnant belonging to a hitherto untold history, Maddison/Williamson decides to write his series of novels. What had gone wrong? Returning to the belief in the clear, true self, obscured by the false ego, he writes. 'If the ego rules the mind, then the machine will rule the body. Is that what happened among men? Mankind mastered by the machine.'[30] The answer was not to avoid painful efforts to correct urban corruption in oneself or in others. After all, his own father, brought up in the country, had lost his link with the land and lived as a clerk in London until he retired, when he found himself unable to settle again in a village with his allotment: it was too late. People had to be taught the life of the farm while young enough, in farm labour camps if necessary, to retain this link with the land.

> The proper time to accustom. . . the body to the slow, satisfying, non-mental rhythm of sustained body-work was in boyhood and early youth. Properly organised, made interesting, such physical education would alter the secret mind-life of, and give calmness to, metropolitan man. . . dissolve the crystallised, or petrofact mentality of the towns. All boards of directors would know how to use. . . the shovel or the spade. . . For himself, he was part metropolitan waste-land – only part natural.[31]

The answer was to remember the past, and show it with the maximum clarity, so that others could learn that 'The grace of God is poetry – the spirit of love – the major spirit of Evolution.'[32] 'Fallible man must learn', he wrote in *The Children of Shallowford*. The salmon journeyed, the swallow voyaged, to raise their young, to face death, to 'give back what it has held, for a while, in trust for others of its kind'.[33] In his Mosley period, he had blamed capitalism, competition, the free market and lack of planning for pollution, white bread and stunted physiques. 'I knew that the haphazard economic structure was the cause of pale faces, bad teeth, fearful men and women, wars between European nations.'[34] The natural world was an orderly one: man had obtruded selfish disorder. The economic system produced disorder. Order was the framework needed for the 'natural man on his natural earth'.[35]

Williamson was naturally an optimist, burdened by the memories of his sad childhood, (though that was always gilded over by memory – 'the ancient sunlight'), by the war, and his sense of duty to the dead and their sacrifice, by his vision of loss and disaster, waste and destruction. Yet behind these themes run others, that 'the purpose of Nature is to create Beauty' (echoing Haeckel), that sunlight reveals truth, it 'saw no shadows', that the truth possesses order and integrity, an internal, necessary, truthful order.[36] The enemies of the sun and the beautiful were waste, short-sightedness, clumsiness, disorder, artificiality and the ego. These evils veiled the truth, veiled clarity, and its inherent orderly sensibility. There are no conflicting interests to be juggled by an invisible hand, no inherent clash between men, if they only faced up to their true selves. Maddison/Williamson assumed that all men were, like him, deeply riven: that, conscious of their bad, untruthful, insincere impulses, they could turn their back on this dark aggression, and become their good selves. It was vital to abolish the old education, which crushed intuition and replaced it with artificial 'dead stuff'. All his intuitions were correct, but one had to learn the courage to follow them, ignoring the clumsiness, stupidity and insensitivity of others.

> Indeed, so usual was the habit of despoiling his intuitions that it was with a considerable shock he had realized, after the Great War, that all the acts making his education . . . were not the true and authentic acts of himself. Instantly he had perceived Truth to be the realization of the Past, and he had begun to stammer.[37]

His obsession with clear, unpolluted water, as a symbol of truth, reality, and hope for the future, reappeared in his post-Second World War nature writings. Integrity, the state where 'the sun sees no shadows', remained the most that could be hoped for. He continued propagating ecological themes, and in a television programme shown in 1968 he expressed his approval of today's ecological awareness. The programme, made by Kenneth Allsop, failed to show the prominent fascist symbol painted on his farm wall, and was chided for whitewashing an old fascist. But what the programme could not have explained, even if the audience was ready to hear it, was that Williamson brought to his support of Mosley a bundle of 'soft' ideas, typical of the naturist thinker, despite his apparently collectivist and dictatorial desire for order and planning. He saw order as the natural state of things, which human error obstructed. He opposed frustration of the human spirit, especially in youth, and thought that natural man, treated and educated correctly, was essentially benevolent and sympathetic. A loving childhood was all-important. He had wanted to send his own children to the experimental 'free school' run by A.S. Neill but been unable to afford it.[38]

Meditating after the Second World War on his failure to change Britain, he concluded

> Water, like man, cannot be frustrated, by the nature of its energy, and like any human society, a river bed is always breaking down and re-making itself...Moving water is governed by the same laws which govern all the movement called life. Life is action, movement, progress as well as reaction, resistance, conservance; but action, movement, progress are alone of the Spirit that giveth life.[39]

Men and animals followed the same laws. Although bound by nature, they had individuality and feelings: 'the balance of nature is akin to the balance of a man's feelings', and he grew to resent those who tried to control the free flow and movement of nature, to gloat over their failure.[40] Civilization cut man off from the free flow of nature's instinct. Set against the physical world, man seemed nothing, his life of no more importance than the life of a fish or an insect. On a visit to North Florida, he found a sandy landscape, full of decayed tree-stumps. This seemed an enormity, a crime. The felled trees left an unforgiveable void, and only by planning land use so that each plant and animal had its rightful place could this wound be healed.[41]

Williamson donated many of his papers to Exeter University before he died, and observers recall an embarrassed Vice-Chancellor unsure what to say in his speech of thanks, but obviously reluctant to receive the gift. His books, especially the later ones, are hard to find. Yet, though unhonoured in any formal sense, he retains a cult following which is increasing as more people find their environmental and ecological interests reflected in his work. Williamson placed his hopes in youth, and demonstrated alongside self-conscious representatives of that creed in the Grosvenor Square anti-Vietnam demonstrations of 1968. Youth had begun to care about the environment. He was a sensitive friend to many such people. But he had seen his world come to an end in 1943.

> Small children growing up to be young men; season after season of corn turning to summer's gold; butterflies, birds, trees, faces of friends – all, all, drifting down the stream of Time which some men dread as death. A short-eared owl wafted down the sea-wall. Partridges had ceased to call on the stubbles. Night had come to the western hemisphere.[42]

The concentration on Gnostic psycho-analytical cults in *Gale of the World* mirrors the rapid shift from politics to meta-politics in 1945 which launched Jorian Jenks and others on to a spiritual ecologism. A retreat into the individual's own consciousness was the despairing Gramsciism of the defeated fascist.

In the end he adopted meta-political ends: deep breathing, Buddhism, 'diatonics' the need to re-create the past and make the dead live again in his work. He worked in a hut in a field in North Devon, where he grew vegetables and had a small orchard. The *Chronicles of Ancient Sunlight* emerged as the total recall of the century's experience. It is true to say it was 'as parochial as Homer'.[43] But, more importantly for our purpose, it was permeated with ecological motifs. The clear water, the shadowless sun, the kind harmony of nature, the need for whole grain and pure food, combine with the realistic detail of the naturalist and social chronicler to offer a convincing ecological vision. At his funeral, the Poet Laureate Ted Hughes described Williamson as a man who 'worshipped energy and. . .feared [entropy]. . .worshipped natural creativity'.[44] Hughes also comments that Williamson's views emerged from his love for a few simple things. Williamson's 'soft' politics could have led him to the left, as with T.H. White, anarchist pacifist, a writer whose tendency to seek lessons from the natural world, as well as his love of England, resembles Williamson.[45] Put into his correct category, as an ecologist of his era, those ideas of Williamson's which are intolerable to us today slot into place; as painful but entwined with his real beliefs, a society oriented around the natural man on the natural earth.

'AND LIFE CAN AFFORD TO BE WASTEFUL'

The second great writer who created an ecological ideology was the Norwegian, Knut Hamsun. He was born to a family of Norwegian peasants in 1859 and died in 1952. He became a Nobel Prize-winning novelist. His books were exceptionally popular in Germany, but were also translated into all major languages. He was one of the most praised novelists of his era. André Gide, Maxim Gorki, Allexandra Kollontai, H.G. Wells, Stefan Zweig, Ernest Hemingway, Henry Miller and Thomas Mann, all admired his work. Of the novel of peasant settlement, *Growth of the Soil*, Mann wrote,

> A splendid work, though completely apolitical, one in profound contact with all the present yearnings: glorification of the solitary farmer, of rustic self-sufficiency: hatred of the city, industry, commerce; ironic treatment of the state – all this is

> communism poetically conceived; or better; humanely poeticized anarchism. . . simplicity in it, goodness, health, humanity . . . *doubtless the spirit of the future.*[46]

Hamsun too was compared to Homer. But in 1945 he was declared a traitor and mad, and incarcerated in a clinic for both reasons. Nearly ninety, he published an account of his trial, to prove his sanity. He supported the Norwegian National Socialist Party during the war, but visited Hitler and Goering to ask for the dismissal of Josef Terboven, Gauleiter of Norway, because of his brutality towards the Norwegians. In 1945, his assets were seized and he became a bankrupt. It was many years before his works were to be republished in England, and, like the more political works of Henry Willamson, they are still hard to find.

Hamsun typifies the complexity that spanned simple left and right divisions in the first decades of this century. He was an individualist, but supported the untouched village community. He was a peasant without education, who became a Nobel Prize winner and unofficial Norwegian Poet Laureate. An anarchist, he admired the aristocratic values, chivalry, honour, independence, generosity, but painted a world where they always failed. He hymned the wanderer, the uprooted loner, but also showed the corruption caused by lost roots. He wrote of rural and fishing villages in decay, of emigration to America, of wandering pedlars, labourers and adventurers like himself, with empathy and tenderness, but his politics expressly opposed the wandering spirit.

A sensitive stylist, he also viciously attacked Ibsen and Strindberg, and the so-called 'social realist' school as neither realist nor social, but blind to human realities and instincts. 'They knew nothing of woman in her sanctity, woman in her sweetness, woman as a vital necessity. . .'[47] He wrote moving love stories, semi-autobiographical tales, but his best-known and most influential work was the story of an illiterate peasant settling uncleared ground in the Norwegian mountains, *Growth of the Soil* (1917).

He attacked the foreign ownership of Norwegian land and capital, but his support for autarky applied not only to nations but to villages. In one work he described his dislike of selling cows from one farm to another. But he was not a rural romantic. His picture of the 'folk' is as clear and sad as that of Williamson. Unlike the great Romantic writers, such as Victor Hugo, Hamsun could be truthful about people, but still love them.

Hamsun's importance here is not only as an early ecologist,

whose picture of the solitary, self-sufficient farmer caught the spirit of the age as no other, and with the total reforming vision which is one of the pre-requisites for the true ecologist; but also the demonstration of a clear link between support for what he perceived as the rural values of German and Norwegian National Socialism and his ecological world-view. However, Hamsun had put forward these ideas many decades before they were used by the Nazis. Between the wars, Hamsun, like Williamson, was to see Germany as the rescuer of the peasantry, and of the true European spirit. He may have a claim to have inspired much of National Socialist rural ideology, as Scandinavia and peasant novels were important to Nordicist Nazis such as Rosenberg, Hans Günther and Walther Darré. His English biographer points out that a wave of pro-Scandinavian sentiment hit Berlin in the 1890s. The fact that Hamsun owed his fame to early German appreciation of his work also affected him.[48]

From an early age, Hamsun wanted to write. He worked as a labourer to earn enough money to write, and emigrated to North America, where again he worked as a labourer, then as a secretary to a Scandinavian journalist in Minnesota. After falling ill, apparently with TB, he returned to Norway, where he underwent the experiences recorded in *Hunger*. He re-emigrated to North America where he fell in with a group of radical young Scandinavians, who denounced bourgeois culture and supported nineteenth-century progressive ideals, such as the temperance movement. Hamsun delivered a series of lectures on literature, ending with a denunciation of the North American business ethic and culture. (He forbade its re-publication.) He abhorred 'problem literature', and aimed at psychological realism and subtlety. Hamsun's early work concerned the wanderer, the artist-vagabond, rejected by bourgeois society. His hero was then the solitary writer, the anti-bourgeois radical, anxious to shock, the nihilist.

In his 1907 work, *The Wanderer*, Hamsun's outrageous vagabond turns into a more sympathetic figure. He learns to take pleasure in humble farm work, to make things *work*: he is the practical craftsman, whose quixotry is confined to a hopeless passion for the wife of his occasional employer. It is a farewell to his own youth, and an ode to the sweetness of women. In *On Muted Strings*, he describes the last love affair of his alter ego, the wandering labourer-cum-artist, who falls in love with a neglected married woman, who eventually drowns, with her unborn child. The wanderer sits in a cave in the snow-bound forest and muses on the loss 'Age confers no maturity; age confers nothing beyond old age.' Perhaps the nearest Hamsun approached to a social Darwinist position was when he meditated on this tragedy, the wasted life of a childless woman. 'And life can afford to be wasteful. . . It was mother and child that went to the bottom.'[49]

In 1911, Hamsun, like Williamson in 1935, bought a remote farm, and, again like Williamson, he became concerned with soil fertility and the relationship between farming, man and the soil.[50] He wrote numerous articles on the subject. In 1913 and 1915 he published his first books to deal with broader issues. He analysed the disintegration and degeneration of an entire community. *Children of the Age* and *The Village of Segelfoss* portray a Norwegian village transformed into a prosperous industrial centre by a successful emigrant, Holmengraa. He buys out the old landowning family and creates factories and a trading centre. The villagers forget their own skills and are corrupted by substitutes, such as margarine, bought-in boots, and various fripperies. Unlike the social realists, like Zola, or even Dickens, Hamsun's criticism of the spiritual decay brought about by industrial growth is, as one critic argues, a *total* criticism, which focuses not on specific problems, but on what he sees as the inherently alienating quality of trade.[50] This absolutist quality is another hallmark of the ecological thinker.

He defined what he saw as the problem of his era, the failure of the individualistic, aristocratic ethic of the uprooted wanderer, who loses his soul, and the failure of economic growth to restore it. He then set about showing the solution. This was the genesis of his greatest work, *Growth of the Soil* (1917), the story of a homesteader in the Norwegian mountains, who creates fertile and productive farmland from wilderness. He had killed off the dandy, that nineteenth-century ghost in the machine, and replaced him with the rooted peasant. A later work, *Wayfarers*, was to return poignantly to the theme of the uprooted versus the rooted, with what in hindsight emerges as a clear political message.

Up to the 1930s, Hamsun, apart from his pointed Anglophobia, seemed an apolitical writer, his moral aspect subsumed in his artistry, his early irony and savage humour mellowed by a Tolstoyan vision. His unsentimental vision of the uncorrupted peasant, the doomed villages, the spiritual beauties of the Norwegian countryside, suited the mood of post-1918 Europe. Pre-Second World War studies of his work naturally concentrate on this aspect. A recent Danish book about his post-war trial, and a new English biography both try to answer the question, how could such a sensitive artist ever have supported Hitler.[52]

Hamsun was always pro-German, and carried his pro-German

feeling at the time of the First World War up to the Second World War. He saw Germany as a young, expanding nation, cramped by the existing European Empires. Britain was a stale old colonial power. He opposed liberal democracy and the small-town mentality he found in Scandinavia. His dislike of the business ethic extended to England, which he described as the source of the Protestant free market enemy of all values, the 'Protestant Jews.' England was a colonialist oppressor, responsible for the deaths of tens of thousands of civilians during the Boer War.[53] Otherwise, he regarded himself as neither right nor left. He worshipped youth, which belonged to Persia, to Germany, anywhere except America and England, fat with success, the homes of sloth and the machine.[54] In his thanksgiving speech for his Nobel Prize, he toasted 'youth,. . . everything in life that is young'.[55] But Hamsun wrote about the solitary victim, the lonely, aristocratic failure. He did not support a hero cult. What he did find sympathetic in National Socialism was its support for the peasantry. Hamsun praised peasant virtues, resignation and content, peasant wisdom, the anti-hero. Was this National Socialism?

Yes, answered one biographer: not only was a belief in fate, resignation, acceptance of poverty and misfortune part of National Socialism, but it was 'an aim of what would to-day be considered the "ecological" side of National Socialism.' 'We see National Socialism retrospectively,. . . Hamsun saw it from its inception [von vorn], in the words of Thomas Mann, as "an attempt to take over the world in the name of thatched roofs, folk dances and solstice celebrations". He thought that in the fight between town and country, artificial and natural which had been the main theme of his life and work, Hitler indisputably was on the side of nature.'[56] Thorkild Hansen quotes the *Völkischer Beobachter* of 1920 calling for garden cities, to show the similarity between today's 'long-haired protest movement' and Hamsun's experience of National Socialism. Hansen interprets the Hitler Youth as a nature cult, and suggests that the peasantry were the object of the deepest emotion and propaganda efforts of the Nazis, and that *Lebnsraum* was not a desire for military expansion, but a call for new land to plough; a call for – as Hamsun expressed it – *Growth of the Soil,* literally *Segen der Erde,* that is, 'Seed of the Earth'.

But Hamsun had developed his ideas long before the First World War. What was a constant was the opposition to what Hamsun saw as the dominant forces of his day. His sympathy for the Chicago anarchists sentenced to death in 1889 expressed this, as did his later support for Russian populism.[57] It is probable that he supported Hitler also because of his loathing of England and opposition to free trade. The similarity is rather because much of his peasant ideology influenced rural Nazis than that Hamsun was inspired by Nazi ideology. Not only the early ideologues, but the German troops of the Eastern Front bought hundreds of thousands of his books. Jodl, Kaltenbrunner and Streicher all asked for and read Hamsun before their executions at Nuremberg.

His wife, an ex-actress, went on Hamsun lecture and reading tours during the Second World War, organised by the *Nordic Society*, founded in Lübeck in 1921 and patronised by Darré and Rosenberg. In Germany, to an attentive audience, she read extracts from Hamsun's works, the favourites being *Victoria* and *Growth of the Soil*. To a hushed room full of soldiers, she would read the opening pages of *Growth of the Soil*, which describe in precise but biblical language the peasant seeking for empty land to till, and the arrival of a woman,

> The man comes, moving towards the North . . . He is strong and thin, has a red beard . . . perhaps he is an ex-prisoner . . . perhaps he is a philosopher, who seeks peace; however, here he was, a wanderer in this enormous solitude . . .
>
> In the morning she stayed, nor did she leave during the day. She made herself useful, milked the goats and cleaned the stove with fine sand. She did not go away at all. She was called Inger. He was called Isak.

Hardened SS men and factory women in the Ruhr wept at the simple tale.[58]

Growth of the Soil could be interpreted as being about *Lebensraum*. However, Hamsun's main theme is the settlement of a wild stretch of country by a native peasant. Nothing is known of his past; he seems to have no family. He appears from nowhere with a bag of seeds and an axe, finds his chosen spot, and homesteads there. He traps animals and lives on barley bread and cheese. He finds a woman, Inger, who is disfigured with a harelip, but a good worker, a companion. When she becomes pregnant, they marry. Their idyll is disturbed by Inger's malicious and thieving sister. Through her interference, Inger murders her baby, also born with a harelip, and is sent to prison for some years. In a theme Hamsun takes up again and again, she is seen to return corrupted by the atmosphere of the town. She has discovered stockings, make-up and prostitution; she is now spoilt, dishonest, dissatisfied and worldly. Eventually she recovers her balance and love for Isak. The second symbolic intrusion is more benevolent. A likeable crook of an engineer, – again, the figure of the untrustworthy, but imaginative, unreliable but innovative confidence trickster appears often in Hamsun – persuades a company to take up a mining concession in the hills by planting ore samples. The company builds roads and opens up the land. They go bankrupt, but their fate receives no sympathy from the author. The engineer explains that he had deliberately cheated the company so that the rural wilderness would be settled by fine, productive peasants like Isak.

> Look at you folk at Sellanraa, now... living in touch with heaven and earth, one with them, one with all these wide-rooted things. No need of a sword in your hands, you go through life bareheaded, bare-handed, in the midst of a great kindliness. Look, nature's there, for you and yours to have and enjoy. Man and Nature don't bombard each other, but agree; they don't compete, race... but go together... Be content!... being born and bringing forth, you are the needful on earth. You maintain life. Generation to generation, breeding ever anew, and when you die, the new stock goes on.[59]

Like Williamson and the other ecologists, Hamsun believes that nature is benevolent if man accepts the discipline of its laws. *Growth of the Soil* also makes explicit the ambiguity of the ecologists' attitude to technology and progress. Technology is good if it can be lifted from its urban, corrupting influence, and used to benefit the countryman. The dishonest engineer, despite his boasting, drunken ways, is a hero because he uses the industrial system to benefit the peasant. Isak, though, maintains his integrity through remaining independent of the town. It is made clear that he can survive without towns and railways, but that they enable his abilities to be used to the full. Who are the villains? It is the small town and its stifling spirit, the petty bureaucracy, the rules and regulations. The town takes his two sons; debauches one and alienates the other, who emigrates to North America. There is creative, craft-oriented technology, which is of value, just as the earth's fruitfulness is creative. But everything urban is parasitical; newspapers, the law, small town society, and banks: 'sentimental feminist humanitarianism' and above all, 'progressive' literature.[60] (The self-taught Hamsun, like his hero in *Hunger*, hired a town hall to deliver an attack on Scandinavian literature.)

Because he was a great artist, Hamsun's messages are not over-simplified or didactic. *Wayfarers* (1927) is his clearest picture of the need to keep one's rural roots. Despite his dislike of the 'social' novel, this is just that, a picture of economic decay and sporadic prosperity in Norway's fishing communities at the turn of the century. It is the account of the education of a dreamy, imaginative village youth, Edvart, and his induction into the layers of dishonesty as he falls one by one down through the levels of society. Capitalist society, according to Hamsun, is a society of unstable, rootless, dishonest hucksters. He first encounters two pedlar tricksters; then a Jewish watch dealer, the most fraudulent, but the most capable of generosity (he leaves his money to Edvart). The apparently upright merchant is in contrast unimaginative, and ungenerous, whereas the wanderer Edvart is quixotry itself, the aristocratic value most prized by Hamsun. His first lover, Lovise, lies about her husband – he is in prison – and then, after some years in America, returns corrupted, an episode handled by Hamsun with the wry tenderness with which his work characteristically treats women. Edvart discovers that all his employers and workmates are dishonest. His best friend, like the engineer in *Growth of the Soil*, acts as a catalyst for slothful rural communities, pulling one area out of depression, through dishonest methods, and, for example, fooling a village into clearing a bog by pretending that it is haunted. He is a thief and a looter, but generous. The corruption helps to feed capital *into* rural life.

In this, as in Hamsun's other works, his perceptions raise his work far above easy attacks on urbanization and capitalist exploitation produced by socialist writers of the time. He shows a world of struggling small entrepreneurs, where everyone is a capitalist, everyone is corrupt, but everyone is capable of productive labour. The missing capital, controlled by the speculative companies and financiers, can be turned into productive capital. Similarly, we see the regenerative effect of rotten town money applied to the land, like compost. In *Chapter The Last*, a sanatorium is established (this book was published the same year as the *Magic Mountain*, and at times reads like a parody of it), by a gaggle of semi-crooked, incompetent doctors, and inhabited by pathetic, lying invalids and pseudo-invalids. Eventually the sanatorium burns to the ground. No-one is injured, and the doctors go back to the town. The heroine, an ex-patient now pregnant and deserted, fools a local farmer into marrying her. Hamsun's conclusion is unexpected. She succeeds in returning to the land, and makes the farmer happy as a husband and father. The sanatorium, symbol of useless modern medicine and urban hypochondria, disappears in chaos and bankruptcy, but a healthy woman and child have been restored to a sensible, primitive, rural life.

For Hamsun, as with Williamson, there are good and bad impulses mixed up in everyone. But the 'system' exacerbates bad things. The key theme in *Wayfarers* (1927) is – do not be tempted to wander. Edvart and Lovise, both villagers, and used to rural poverty, both become wanderers. They have the potential to become a settled, loving farming couple, but they lose their roots, which wither, and cannot be re-established. Edvart loses Lovise to America. He cannot settle to village life, and when she calls him, he goes. 'Lovise Magrete's roots had been torn up from their native soil, and now she belonged everywhere, belonged nowhere.'[61]

Edvart's brother, Joakim, a smallholder, tries to summarise the changes that have overtaken the village since Edvart and his friend, August, returned with their wealth and new ideas. His judgement carries a special moral force, since Joakim is a self-educated, improving farmer, not a yokel: – he 'reads and reads': he uses seaweed as a fertiliser, for example, because he read about it in his farming journals.[62]

> He was a stranger to us and he brought alien things into our lives. Now the people in the north of the district have started going in for calves. They fatten them up over a period and then sell them to the village people for slaughter. They make money out of it. . . 'There's something evil, something swinish indeed, about those calves,' Joakim says. 'First you raise them, then you get to know them, and then you dispose of them to the fine folk in the village for food! How were things before? Well, we bred our beasts and grew fond of them. And we never sold a cow without knowing how well it would be looked after in the new place. It was like letting one of our children go. But that's not how things are now. We've changed. . . I don't think anyone benefits by being homeless and wandering around. We should stay where we belong.'
>
> . . . 'The thing is whether we shouldn't try ourselves out to see where we belong best.'
>
> 'Don't you think we belong where we were put?. . . We don't become any happier in ourselves by being better off.'
>
> 'Then I don't understand why you want five cattle when Father and Mother were content with two.'[63]

The reader may wonder why more production is good if it is also immoral. Hamsun now brings in the theme of the national interest.

> In the first place,. . . there were just the two of them. . . but now there are four of us. . . Then there's the point that we ought to cultivate our own soil, Norway's soil; then we shouldn't have

> to buy so much of our food from abroad and suffer for it later in taxes and duties. But that's not all. The most important thing is that we avoid...being torn up by the roots from our own poor soil and set down in a richer one.[64]

There was a deep irony in this folk wisdom. Ecologists, like socialists, are making a moral claim, and one expects them to live according to their morality, within the practical limits imposed by the physical and economic infrastructure (– hard to use horses instead of cars when blacksmiths have become so scarce). Hamsun was himself an uprooted wanderer from a peasant family. He had taken on a peasant farm in a poor Northern part of Norway for some years, used it as inspiration for his novels, and then lived in luxury, feted by Europe's society. He despised the town, the literary establishment, emancipated women and 'bourgeois' society, but married first an heiress then an actress. Yet the continued quality of his artistry shows that he somehow maintained his integrity, avoiding the intellectual fashions of his time. His peasant stubbornness was perhaps the cause both of this independence and of his attachment to a Norwegian *völkisch* spirit. (Although Hamsun never seems to have joined the Norwegian Nazi Party, nor did he vote for it, his son and his wife were ardent supporters). Had he not known what it was to lose his 'roots' by becoming a writer, he could not have communicated his loss to others.

But while he avoided the trap of believing that such 'roots' could be artificially re-rooted, he was optimistic about the possibility of reviving rural communities, if done in a peasant fashion. But a farmer's energies had to be devoted to the soil. Local district councils were a waste of time, enabling pompous men to become malevolently destructive at the expense of productive farmers, yet the latter went gladly to their own destruction, exchanging the produce of their land and labour for shoddy goods. In *Hunger*, Hamsun's autobiographical study of a gifted writer slowly starving to death in Christiana, what he finds villainous is the spirit of provincial, petty obtuseness, rather than any particular malefactor or deliberate wrong-doing, – although in this work the psychological realism and subtlety of the work defy categorization.

Here is a passage quoted more briefly in Chapter Four.

> Isak at his sowing, a stump of a man, a barge of a man to look at, nothing more. Clad in homespun-wool from his own sheep, boots from the hide of his own cows and calves...a tiller of the ground, body and soul; a worker on the land without respite. *A ghost risen out of the past to point the future, a man from the earliest*

> *days of cultivation, a settler in the wilds, nine hundred years old, and, withal, a man of the day*... There was nothing left of the copper mine and its riches – the money had vanished into thin air... But the Almenning was still there, and ten new holdings on that land, beckoning a hundred more. Nothing growing there? All things growing there; men and beasts and fruit of the soil.[65]

This was the new man, the homesteader, untouched by past errors, untouched by tradition, come from nowhere, creating a new and fertile world. Hamsun's ideal was to increase the natural produce of the soil, to avoid corruption by outside and bought-in objects, and to use all natural resources to the full, but without despoiling them.

Were Hamsun alive today, he would certainly reject nuclear power and nuclear weapons, just as Williamson did. He would call for Norway's withdrawal from NATO. With his anti-authoritarian attitude, he would be a Green. His combination of cultural criticism and rejection of the trade ethic is typically ecological. The attachment to what he saw as a victimized spirit, the free peasant, is ecological. Bizarre as it may seem, and to his English biographer the 'Great Ideas' he pursues are indeed bizarre, his agrarian ruralism does cohere with his anarchist rejection of the international, the characterless.[66] His appreciation of craft and 'small' technology, too, is consistent with 'greenness'.

Above all, he portrays the ecological combination of a search for roots and a new start. Isak is a wanderer, but he is tribal. He both establishes a patriarchal family and comes to dominate the area. He is from away, but is in no sense 'other'. His name implies a biblical quality. It is perhaps not reading too much into it to suggest that Hamsun was offering a substitute Adam and Eve, a renewed Nordic *Genesis*, with the dominion of man over land and beasts given this time under the harsh Northern skies to Northern peasants.

CHAPTER EIGHT

Was there a Generic Fascist Ecologism?

During the inter-war period, most of the ecological thinkers examined in the last two chapters could be categorised as belonging to the soft, alternative Right. Anti-capitalist, anti-system and anti-Establishment, some described themselves as Tory anarchists, some as Cobbettian democrats and some as High Tories. No political party existed which could incorporate them. Such party activity as existed fluctuated between Independent Labour, Conservative, Liberal and Fascist. The political picture was complicated by the remnants of the nineteenth-century, intellectual, middle-class love affair with Germany. For many of these inter-war ecologists contact and cross-fertilization with German alternative ideas continued in the 1920s, and for some into the 1930s.

During the 1920s a tradition of liberal and pacifist internationalist pro-German feeling existed in Britain. German contacts were acceptable. The ecologists were, in any case, interested in values, and justifications for values, not programmes. Nevertheless, the link with Germany and its continuation into the 1930s is striking. It seems that German culture had a stronger leaning towards nature than others in Europe.

It has, however, been argued that radical fascism is always 'Catonist', in Barrington Moore Jr.'s derisive phrase.[1] According to Moore, 'Catonism' looks to the peasants as the saviours of the nation, and to peasant values as a corrective against urban corruption. This argument implies that the green streak in Nazism, which will be discussed in the next chapter, was generic to all European fascism. Ernst Nolte, too, has argued a similar case, in much more detail.[2] He believes that there was an anti-transcendance belief common to European fascism between the wars, and argues that fascist ideology rejected the old liberal ideal that man could rise above what was natural, or embedded in the laws of nature. A closer examination, however, brings out the interesting fact that between the wars German national socialism was alone among European fascist parties in expressing ecological concerns. For the purpose of the following discussion, no distinction will be made between national socialism and fascism. Although there are substantial differences, these are less important in the context of agrarian ruralism or middle-class ecological ideals than the similarities.

In looking for green roots among the European fascisms of the 1920s and 1930s, it is important to differentiate between ecological and peasant-oriented movements. All the successor states, except Czechoslovakia, had peasant-oriented policies, but no supporting ideology, so that once peasant demands on land reform had been met by expropriating or expelling ethnically different landowners, peasant parties tended to collapse. Even in Poland, where the Peasant Party was dominant in a democratic coalition in 1923, Marshall Pilsudski's nationalism had only hostility for the Polish Peasant Party.[3] The complexity of nationality, tribe and religion in Eastern Europe makes generalisations a problem. In some countries, the intelligentsia adopted a *narodnik* approach to the peasantry, that mysterious entity, still a separate caste. The Hungarian 'village explorers' were democratic agrarians. In Rumania, the Iron Guard were anti-liberal, anti-democratic peasant terrorists.[4] In some of their demands, for example, for an independent, productive and wealthy peasantry, the peasant national socialism of the Green Shirts in Hungary and Rumania might seem to resemble those of the ecological intelligentsia discussed in earlier chapters. Peasant radical fascism in Hungary, Rumania and Bulgaria was strongly anti-semitic and anti-capitalist, as well as being anti-communist. Rumania, especially, saw capitalism, which it partly identified with Jewish interests, as 'responsible for the destruction of the very fabric of traditional peasant life, be it the destruction of the ancient forests of Transylvania or the decline of the Orthodox Church'.[5]

Bulgaria defused peasant radicalism by the largest and most successful land reform in Eastern Europe, producing a nation of market gardeners by 1939. In Rumania, whose village fanatics present in some ways the closest approximation to early German Nazism, the Iron Guard consisted of fanatically Christian peasants (peasants made up some ninety percent of the country's population, a higher proportion than Turkey)! They saw terrorism as a means of divine retribution as well as a means to power. 'Up above, we will defend the life of the trees and the mountains from further devastation. Down below [in the towns] we will spread death and mercy.'[6] They called for national redemption and re-birth – the strength of their belief in individual redemption is indicated by their demand that their members give themselves up after each terrorist attack. Another similarity with Germany's 'Blood and Soil' intellectuals and Rumania is that they both opposed colonialism, and claimed a special status as a victim nation. On the whole, though, Eastern European radical fascism was a Messianic and apocalyptic creed with little urban or ex-urban component. The *narodnik* intelligentsia made little impression on the peasantry, who were often of a different religion and ethnic group. Furthermore, the intelligentsia concerned were likely to come from the land-owning gentry themselves, and hence were unlikely to glorify rural life.[7]

In Spain, similarities between early fascism and German National Socialism can be found. The closest link with German neo-conservative and radical right movements is through Ortega y Gasset, who studied in Germany before the First World War, and who went into exile under Franco. Ortega's politics were originally on the left, and it was the culture shock of finding Spain a despised poor relation of Northern Europe that turned his thoughts to the Paretoan view of power. In the 1920s, Ortega often referred to Hans Driesch, author of *The Philosophy of the Organic*, and was impressed by his biological teachings, as was Ernst Jünger, German neo-conservative. Ortega, though, was opposed to Spanish fascism from the first.[8] Jose Antonio, whose party but not whose policies were later to be subsumed in Franco's *Falange y Jons*, called not for land reform but for a transformation of rural-urban relationships. This included a guaranteed minimum price for farm goods, more agricultural education, more credit, rationalization of holdings, with the elimination of *latifundia* where inefficient, and the merging of inefficient small farms, the restoration of communal land, the abolition of rent, and general improvement of agricultural land through irrigation and afforestation.[9] This was a classic programme for general improvement, presented without ideological force or rhetoric, and not distinctively fascist, insofar as a belief in an interventionist, 'properly' planned economy was generic to the inter-war period. There was no emphasis on the need for a class of medium-sized or yeoman peasants, or on the need to retain a link with the soil. Indeed, although the anarcho-syndicalist nature of Spanish radical fascism might be expected to have entailed a revolt from organised technology, as well as from the usual concomitants of urban life, such as lawyers, parliaments and pornography, Jose Antonio stringently attacked the 'Blood and Soil' gut patriotism typical of Rumanian and German national socialism, together with Romantic nationalism and its emphasis on the pull of the land: 'The Romantics were keen on all things natural. Their slogan was a 'return to nature'. Thus they identified the nation with 'the birthplace'...The most pernicious nationalisms, because they are the most dissolvent, are those which take this view of nationhood.'[10] He called instead for the 'patriotism of the great heterogeneous units' and an awareness of historical destiny, while point three of the twenty-six points of the Falange, written in November 1934, declared that 'Spain's historical fulfilment is the Empire'.[11] His economic and social policies followed the modernizing path of Mussolini and the aims of Mosley. 'Patriotism' had to be 'anchored, not in the heart, but in the mind'.[12] The short-lived nature of this movement makes it hard to judge whether or not any serious conservationist or agrarian element would have been prominent in a genuinely fascist Spanish government. It is clear, however, that Jose Antonio's radical fascism does not correspond to the 'Catonist' model outlined earlier, nor is it oriented towards 'Blood and Soil', still less towards ecological ideas. Indeed, he goes out of his way to attack them.

Latin or Mediterranean fascism and its imitators had little in common with the Messianic religious peasant revolts of Eastern Europe. In England the British Union of Fascists, inspired by Mussolini were modernizers. They looked to technical advance, in agriculture as elsewhere. Heroic technology would free Britain from the stale burdens of the past. 'Our new Britons require the virility of the Elizabethan combined with the intellect and method of the modern technician.'[13] In the 1930s, although the rhetoric concentrated on national regeneration through spiritual rebirth and unity, actual B.U.F. policy concentrated on economic and social problems. An adequate food supply was to be ensured by the existence of a (largely white) British Empire, encouraged and aided by an extension of Imperial Preference and agricultural subsidies. Land reform was merely sketched in as a policy, while British self-sufficiency in agriculture was not envisaged.

Many supporters of the British Union of Fascists were drawn to it because they saw it as a way of using resources efficiently and properly. Unemployment and capitalist competition were both seen as prime areas of waste. But there was no equivalent of the large-scale agricultural settlement planned in Nazi Germany. Agricultural reform was integral to a grand plan to re-create British society and the economy. Land use throughout Britain was to be centrally planned and organised: re-afforestation, sewage disposal (to leave rivers clean and unpolluted), factory siting, and building motorways, would create jobs and re-cycle materials. One of the differences between the pre-war English groups described in an earlier chapter as 'High Tories' and the British Union of Fascists membership lay in this approach to the land. So few studies of B.U.F. membership and policy have been carried out that one cannot determine why this distinction existed.[14] However, exist it did. According to one study, interviews with surviving B.U.F. men produced only one reference to 'agrarian fascism' and 'peasant life', in opposition to the 'make full use of the land' policies of the B.U.F. As the author points out, this occurred in 1937, when several British fascists had been influenced by national socialist ideas encountered on visits to Germany. The interviewee himself referred to having encountered these ideas among anarchists at Hyde Park Corner, who were living a simple, peasant, agrarian, communard kind of life.[15] One can speculate that the sight of weed-strewn derelict acres in East Anglia, and other fertile arable counties, common after the collapse in land and produce prices after the abolition of corn price support in 1923, would not imply the need for the more intensive use of land which small-holder farming entails. Land lay under-utilised everywhere.

This emphasis on enlarging the urban home market, and getting 'back to work' as a cure-all for British agriculture was, of course, a short-term policy, but then, the inter-war Depression in arable farming lasted some fifteen years, a large part of a farmer's working lifetime. Does this account for the lack of 'Blood and Soil' ideology in British fascism? It could be argued that the social background of the membership was a relevant factor, that there were more landowners among the B.U.F.'s membership than agricultural labourers or small farmers, and that this led the B.U.F. to concentrate on agricultural price mechanisms rather than on land reform. But the group of ecologists centred around what was to be become Kinship in Husbandry and the Soil Association also included large landowners; indeed, men like Lord Lymington and Rolf Gardiner were the most prominent in the ecological movement. But Gardiner and Lymington were atypical 'sports', who fretted against the existing British agricultural establishment. (Gardiner also found the English Country Dance Association too respectable and conventional.) Perhaps Rolf Gardiner's criticism that Mosley's movement was too lower middle-class and urban is relevant here. He thought that national regeneration could only come about through an alliance of aristocrats and yeomen, by-passing the towns and especially, the new towns and suburbs.[16] Certainly, many B.U.F. members were proud of the accusation that they were 'lower middle-class', while their more wealthy landed supporters, according to MI5 files, were new landowners, whose money had come from the 'new' industries. Their industrial supporters were to a surprising degree the self-made men rather than the 'reactionary gentry' of left-wing fantasy.[17] The spirit of H.G. Wells can be found lurking behind some of the B.U.F.'s 1930s pronouncements, and this spirit was alien to the High Tories.

One exception to this tentative explanation may seem the presence of Jorian Jenks, the B.U.F.'s agricultural expert, because he was later to edit *Rural Economy*, produced as a 'club bulletin' from 1944 to 1951, and Eve Balfour's *Mother Earth*, both journals with a strong ecological interest. He was Secretary to the Soil Association.[18] Jenks was the author of pamphlets on the B.U.F.'s agricultural policy before the war. But his writings of the 1930s did not have an ecological or 'Blood and Soil' component. They followed Mosley's general economic and social policy closely. Foreign investment would be stopped, and an agricultural bank established, to invest in British and Dominion agriculture. The B.U.F. would restore the huge areas of land which lay wholly or partly derelict.[19] It would create an Agricultural Corporation, reduce foreign food imports, create an enlarged home market by raising industrial wages, and eliminate the middleman.[20] One policy that *was* similar to that of the National Socialists in Germany was to make land tenure hereditary 'provided the heir proves himself to be fitted to develop the land to the best purpose' but this idea was not worked out in any detail. It would have applied to all farms, regardless of size. In Germany, the Nazis planned to make only the 'hereditary farm', the *Erbhof*, inalienable, but the Junker estates were deprived of their inalienable entail. The B.U.F. intended to establish local councils to determine rents and wages, and 'plan' agricultural production, so that gluts and other marketing problems would be avoided, while at the same time production would be increased. Farmers and landowners would lose their land and estates if they were not well farmed, and absentee landowners would be expropriated. The vagueness of these proposals, typical of the naïvety of fascist economics, brings out the stress on 'proper' planning, the belief that good-will, dedication and team-work combined with a rebirth of nationalist feeling, could iron out all the alleged inefficiencies of individualistic, market-oriented production. There was a boy scout enthusiasm about the military attitude adapted towards some problems:

> Effective steps will be taken to cope with the host of rabbits, pigeons, rooks and other vermin, which now levy a heavy toll on our fields ... the Agricultural Corporation will maintain a

> corps of expert vermin-destroyers equipped with up-to-date apparatus, who will clear each district systematically.[21]

This militant problem-solving was *anti*-ecological in spirit, if anything. It was an attitude that disappeared during the early '40s. After the Second World War, Jenks published an article called 'The Homestead Economy' in a compilation of essays on agriculture and the small farmer edited by Hugh Massingham, which attacked 'Economic Man', predictions by socialist writers such as Rowntree and Lamartine Yates that there would be vast food surpluses after the war. He opposed the generic attack on 'backward, inefficient' peasant farming and desire for agricultural 'industrial efficiency' delivered by these advisers to the post-war British Socialist government. He called for an ecological balance in farming, regretted the disappearance of the four-year rotation of the high days of Victorian farming, and suggested that the future of improved agriculture lay in intensive peasant farming. Jenks' attitude towards natural resources was now that of the typical ecologist:

> Thus, the nineteenth century disequilibrium between 'industrial' and 'agricultural' countries is disappearing, and is being replaced by a new disequilibrium, that between the power-mechanisms and the natural resources which they have exploited only too successfully and without which they are useless.

and

> The limiting factor in civilisation now is *fertility*, which *is* capacity to create and sustain life...we have failed to notice the full significance of the many symptoms of flagging vitality – loss of soil, diminished resistance to pests and diseases, declining crop yields, falling birth-rates...No economy is worth considering that does not encourage the cultivation of *resources* that represent the springs of vital renewal...Our chances [in Britain] of survival depend very much upon the use we make of our own natural assets within the next ten or twenty years. It is not 'output per man' that matters now, but 'wealth per acre'.[22]

In the B.U.F.'s pre-war writings, the emphasis was on the ideal technocratic future: the garden city on stilts, walkways in the sky, and silent, clean, rapid public transport. Even in Williamson's work there is a constant tension between the vision of the untouched, richly-textured countryside (whether wild or farmed) and the roaring motor-cycle and sports car.[23]

Although Jenks was important enough to be interned during

much of the Second World War – and attended dinners in prison at which 'The Land' was toasted, – his policies and views remained peripheral to the B.U.F.'s chief interests before the war. His influence on the re-constituted Mosley movement after the war remains uncharted. One contributor to his *Rural Economy* in 1949 suggested paying agricultural workers dividends as well as wages, and creating a system of 'limited partnerships' between farmer and employee, an idea which has now found favour among progressive libertarian academics where industry is concerned, and which typifies the ability of the ecologists of the early post-war period to avoid the existing anti-rural economic orthodoxies.[24]

Jenks' shift from a belief in totalitarian team-work to a post-war belief in the individual small farmer, was marked, but does not seem to have affected his old colleagues, several of whom were landowners and practising farmers, using orthodox methods. *Feeding the Fifty Million* was produced by the 'Rural Reconstruction Association Research Committee on the Increase of Agricultural Production', a group which included several ex-B.U.F. members and Mosley supports, including D. Stukely, Robert Saunders, O.B.E., and Jorian Jenks. The book showed signs of dissension on issues like organic farming, a long discussion of which ended inconclusively. It limited consideration of ecological problems to one sentence on the ecological value of hedges and trees.[25] In calling for food and fodder self-sufficiency, the Committee echoed the preoccupations of the pre-war B.U.F., although the discussion, unlike pre-war pamphlets, was unpolemical and informed. Rural electrification and methane gas plants would help revive the countryside. 'Rural repopulation' was acceptable, providing it was carefully planned and 'not left to irresponsible economic forces'.[26] In supporting a family-worked farm of 50 to 100 acres, and in calculating productivity (both net and gross) according to the size of farm, it was building on the work of Danish and German agrarian reformers, including those who backed Walther Darré's peasant policies in the Third Reich, and the Danish smallholding movement of the 1920s. But the idea that in agriculture 'a measure of compulsion is necessary but just' had lost favour after the harsh war-time measures to increase self-sufficiency in British agriculture, which included totalitarian measures far exceeding anything the pre-war B.U.F. had dreamed of in agriculture and land tenure, not to think of rationing, quotas, civilian Land Armies and fixed prices.[27] These policies have now lost much of their novel thrust, and have an almost anodyne ring to them to-day.

In the case of Italy, lip service was paid to the peasantry throughout the life of Mussolini's regime. Mussolini fits the 'Catonist' model in that he always referred to the peasant as the backbone of the nation. The famous land reclamation schemes were carried out. By diminishing the power of the Mafia, the Fascist government eased some of the burdens of peasant life. Less successful attempts were made to introduce corporate and co-operative mechanisms to agriculture. Italy was almost as 'backward' as Spain, – or at least, had almost as high a proportion of peasants in the population. But the Fascist role-model was ancient Rome: youth, will and technological progress were the weapons to regain Italy's ancient glory. As with their imitators in Britain, the Italian Fascists emphasised in their political rhetoric a desire for imperial grandeur, won the support of the initiators of new industries (who were often from old families) – aircraft, electric light bulbs, chemists – and concentrated on public infrastructural works. They built, in short, motorways and harbours. There was no Fascist philosophy of nature, and, according to a recent 450-page biography of Mussolini which devotes a mere two brief paragraphs to the issue (the 'battle for wheat' of 1925, and Mussolini's decision, in 1939, to try to improve Sicily's fertility for purposes of self-sufficiency), there was little interest in agriculture, except where autarky was concerned.[28] Mussolini in his autobiography, does not refer to the concept.[29]

Insofar as there was a philosopher of the régime, this was the ex-liberal Giovanni Gentile (1875–1944), Idealist, Platonist and Hegelian, who became Minister of Public Instruction (Education) in 1923 under Mussolini and was fascism's most persuasive philosopher of corporate unity. In an earlier chapter, I described how the belief in an objective world, inherent in nature, came about in the nineteenth century, and looked at some of its epistemological consequences. The theoretical ecologist described in my model looks to nature for guidance. He believes in a finite, objective truth, in a single reality. In this, he is anti-transcendental. He rejects the belief that reality, embodied in nature, can be transcended. On this issue, Gentile expressed the opposite viewpoint, and this suggests that Italian fascism, certainly, did not share National Socialism's naturist bias.

Gentile denied the existence of an 'absolute Nature. . .against which the truth of experience can be measured.'[30] He wrote in his introduction to a Hegelian *Principle of Ethics* by Bertrando Spaventa, that art, philosophy and religion formed a great triad lying behind Logic and Nature, and commented that 'nowadays there is even a tendency to overemphasise the dependency of the latter [Nature] on the former [Logic]'; in other words, the spirit should not be dependent on nature.[31] The Fascist philosophy of the absolute and all-embracing state was the enemy of nature, and Sorel's attack on the dangerous and fundamental opposition of nature to man, which will be quoted in the next chapter, is further evidence of the essentially latin Fascist view of nature. Gentile believed that 'the absolute freedom involved in the identification of the rational individual with the State as an *ethical* reality requires that there be no pre-existing Nature behind . . . the Philosophy of Nature must disappear'.[32]

Gentile argued more directly for the totality of the identification of State and man as a political concept, in his late work *Genesis and Structure of Society*. 'And since we can also say that the State is man, it follows that nothing human can be alien to the essential nature of the State. For the State includes, unifies and fulfils every human activity, every form or element of human nature . . .'[33] He saw anarchy as the true alternative to a state-centred, totalitarian creed, not an organic tribalism. Anarchy, which he defined as the consistent and logical fulfilment of liberalism, would dismantle the framework in which human culture could survive and flourish. Anarchy was nature and nature anarchy. Nature was the enemy of human culture, and hence a danger to be fought. He even argued that nature was, through its anarchic and anti-étatist character, equivalent to evil. 'Evil is nullity. We might even say that it is nature . . .'[34] So not only did he maintain the supremacy of the state, he argued that nature threatened the autonomy of the state, and man's fully human culture.

This contradicts Nolte's anti-transcendentalist theory of fascism. For Gentile, the Hegelian, transcendalist idealist, nature is not an objective or, indeed, fully knowable state or thing. In direct contradiction to the natural scientists of the nineteenth century, he argues that nature is unknowable, that the only part of nature that can be known is that small part that can only be apprehended by becoming 'part of the personality of the knower'.[35] Not Nature, but Culture, was the watchword of Italian Fascism. The link between the two that was the heart of green Nazism, that the German philosophical anthropologists had argued was inevitable, that future ecologists would maintain was the motor of society, was rejected. At the heart of Italian Fascist philosophy lay a hostility to nature, despite the land reclamation and food subsidies. And 'to the humanism of culture, which was a great step in the liberation of man, there succeeds today or will succeed tomorrow the humanism of labour'.[36] This is surely the apotheosis of urbanism, the glorification of human labour which in this form became a mechanistic concept unconnected with its spiritual nature.

Thus, in this context, the philosophy of Italian Fascism had little in common with the German National Socialism with which it is so often linked. Italy was seen by Nazi intellectuals in the 1930s as too 'from above', too inorganic and inflexible. Otto Ohlendorf, a lawyer and economist who was head of the German Trade Council in 1936 (and later, of course, notorious as *Einsatzgrüppe* leader, besides being active in the Resistance against Hitler), visited Italy in 1934, as an active NSDAP party member, to examine Italy's economic and social policies. He concluded that they were too étatist, totally unsuited to the 'from below' strivings of German National Socialism.[37] The little-known philosopher of the Italian radical right, Julius Evola, was actually banned by Mussolini because of his pagan, rural philosophies and sympathies with national socialist naturist ideas. Evola criticised Darré's marketing organization for being too democratic. But, like the German ecologists of the time, he was drawn to Eastern religions, and wrote a book on Buddhism.[38] In December 1934, Mussolini tried to start a 'Fascist international', but Germany was not invited. Mussolini also attacked National Socialism, saying that the two movements were 'in many respects at opposite poles'.[39] Curzio Malaparte, journalist and novelist, described the new, mechanised, factory warfare introduced by Fascism.

> And below me, on both sides of the hill. . . I could see, slowly advancing, not an army, but an immense travelling workshop, an enormous mobile foundry, that stretched as far as the eye could see in either direction. It was as if the thousands of chimneys, cranes, iron bridges and steel towers, the millions of cog-wheels, the hundreds. . . of blast-furnaces and rolling-mills of the whole of Westphalia, the whole of the Ruhr, were advancing in a body over the vast expanse of corn-fields that is Bessarabia. It was as if an enormous Krupps Steelworks, a gigantic Essen, were preparing to launch an attack on the hills of Zaicani. . . Yes, that was it: I was looking not at an army but at a colossal steel-works, in which a multitude of workmen were setting about their various tasks with a streamlined efficiency which at first sight concealed the immensity of their effort.[40]

This picture of the German-Russian war was only partly accurate in that other observers saw a war fought partly with horse drawn troops – two million horses died in the first two years of the German-Russian war – and bicycles. Massive mechanisation and tank warfare came later. But the mistake itself is important, showing that Malaparte's memories of huge, factory-sized weapons lumbering across a great plain must have owed more to a theoretical assessment of modern fascist warfare than to the reality.

French fascism in the 1930s corresponds more to Stanley Payne's concept of the fascist negations than does the more programmatic Spanish and Italian variety. It was negative: it opposed. Struggle and action were its key-words. 'Any man who is both pessimistic and active is, or will become a fascist', commented André Malraux in the 1930s.[41]

A sense of the place of rural values *had* existed in the French Right. In the late 19th century, the novelist Barrés called for the provinces, especially his homeland, Lorraine, to become stronger, to regain autonomy, and break away from the powerful call of the capital, Paris. Regions, not nations, were the future of Europe for Barrés, especially under French guidance. '*Nous dépasserons notre nationalisme*', he wrote after the First World War.[42] It was Barrés, too, perhaps surprisingly for this fastidious, urban, sleek-haired dandy, who tenderly portrayed a tragic peasant family of semi-mystics, semi-money-grubbers, in *La Colline inspirée*. Barrés' analysis was not a political one, nor was it pessimistic. 'When the nightingale sings, you do not hear a word, or a song, but an immense hope.'[43] He pictured the pull and counter-pull of human values: the church on the hill, representing order and form, ('*la règle, l'autorité, le lien*'), and the free life of the flat fields below, ('*l'esprit de la terre et des ancêtres les plus lointains, la liberté, l'inspiration*'), with its heroes, Manfred, Prospero, Faust, who continually fight against the constraints of ordered human society.[44] Humanity needed both.

> Let the two antagonistic forces fight eternally, eternally prove themselves, but never conquer, and expand by their very struggle. One could not exist without the other. Of what value is enthusiasm which remains an individual dream? And what value an order if it is not animated by enthusiasm? The church is born from the fields, and nourishes it perpetually.[45]

The arid experiments of a disillusioned Drieu la Rochelle, leader of the post-Maurras French fascists, were of a different order. He and his group had much more in common with the French Communist intellectuals, in their hatred of the bourgeoisie, and their desire to destroy society, than with any existing French institutions. 'Was it possible to believe in fascism if you did not believe in communism?'[46] The drift towards Nazi sympathies came easily to a failed creed. Drieu, like others, appreciated the German's capacity for (apparent) success. However, they had hoped for a pan-European programme to emerge from the German conquest of France, which was supposed to lift France from its slough and stimulate a national re-birth. They were disillusioned.

Whatever the role of the First World War in creating this negative attitude, one has only to compare it with ex-soldier Henry Williamson's attempt to re-create a corner of Europe in the guise of a family farm to see the sharp difference. National Socialism attracted the French fascists by its success, but was philosophically and programmatically alien. The French intellectuals of *Action Française* found German eugenics comical, and had dreamed since 1918 of a united Europe. Nature was a bore, and peasants were something rather distasteful. Drieu played at adopting Northern racialism: he discarded a Jewish wife and lived with a Virginian woman. But when jilted, he joked that he felt like Madame Butterfly, not a comment that would have been permitted – or conceived, probably – in Germany at that time. The French fascist was locked into the very prison of urban individualism and irony he claimed to despise. There was only Culture, not Nature, to cling to, and an urban culture could not free him.

If nature was rejected by French fascists, was it of concern to the landed or rural interest? It appears that even agrarian radicalism failed to gain support in the Third Republic. The sporadic attempts to form a farmer's party, under, for example, Henri Dorgères, came to nothing. After the defeat of France, the Vichy Government's propaganda did stress the role of the sturdy peasant as well as rural life in general. However, given that this was during the war, Vichy propaganda must have been influenced by Nazi Germany.[47]

With the possible exception of Rumania's anti-colonialist, religiously fanatical, terrorist fascists, European fascism, where it had a programme, emphasised forward-looking, technological planning and urban development. Relatively developed countries, such as France, had this in common with less urbanised countries, such as Italy, and less technologically advanced countries, such as Spain. Germany was the exception, with a tradition, in practice as well as in theory, of looking to nature for philosophical guidance. It may be that similar evidence exists for Italy, the only other European nation which established a fascist government in peace-time. However, Italy did not have a bio-dynamic or organic or ecological lobby. Pending new evidence, I would conclude that from the stance of their public policy and their published ideology there was no ecological movement of any significance in Italy between the wars. In England, fascism followed the Italian model.

However, the Anglo-German sympathisers of the period were united by a common interest in nature and ecology.

Clearly, the shock of the First World War disoriented and alienated the intelligentsia who had experienced it. This trauma may have caused their inter-war support for fascism and communism. But this does not seem an adequate explanation for the different form taken by the alienation in different countries. It also clashes with the Weberian-Marxist explanation referred to earlier, that ecological ideas are a reaction to the anomic effects of industrialization and technology.

PART THREE

ECOLOGY: A GERMAN DISEASE?

CHAPTER NINE

The Chill of the Forests

> Of these cities there will remain what passes through them – the wind:
>
> (Bertolt Brecht, 'Vom armen B.B'.)

WAS THERE A GENERIC GERMAN NATURISM?

In my discussion on Haeckel, the influential neo-Lamarckian organicism of Hans Driesch was mentioned as the peak of the reaction in the natural sciences against mechanistic biology in Germany. Not only in Germany, of course; the growth of existentialist philosophy is a European phenomenon, but it has been argued that it was in Germany alone that 'life-philosophy tendentiously abolished the traditional difference between nature and culture, and thus facilitated the success of the general biologism in the theory of culture, which culminated in National Socialism'.[1] This chapter will look at some of the 'alternative' phenomena in 1920s Germany, to see whether the argument for similarity of content, if not form, of vitalist philosophy (*Lebensphilosophie*) and National Socialism, can be maintained. Driesch's influence certainly reverberated throughout the 1920s, – Ernst Jünger, for example, studied zoology with him in Leipzig in 1923–5.[2] Life-philosophy was a response to the revolutionary idea that man and world and nature were one. It gave birth to the philosophical anthropologists, philosophers who tried to make sense of the growth in biological knowledge and studies of animal behaviour, and the resulting implication that man's intellect was not autonomous. It certainly coincided with the rise of National Socialism, but the line of development was not a straightforward one, nor is there any apparent causal link. Other influences were

Nietzsche, Bergson and Spengler.

'In 1913, I composed...for the...Free German Youth...the essay 'Man and Earth', in which, on the basis of a terrible analysis of the rape of nature by humanity in the present day, I sought to prove that man, as bearer of the spirit, has torn himself apart along with the planet which gave him birth.'[3] This essay by Klages 'Der Mensch und das Leben', has been described as a 'brilliant essay about what we now call ecology'.[4] It had been written for a meeting of the Free German Youth held on the hill of Meissner, near Kassel. This gathering of 1913 was later seen as the peak of the Youth Movement's beliefs. Ironically, considering the passion with which many Youth Movement members were to throw themselves into war a year later, the conference had been called as a quasi-pacifist gesture, to counteract the centenary demonstrations for the Battle of Leipzig. Even more ironically, it was organized and hosted by Eugen Diederichs, neo-Conservative and *völkisch* publisher, later seen as an early Nazi. The meeting incorporated the mixture of radical nature-cult, community versus society, and youth versus age, typical of the youth movement. A group of German nationalist school teachers took part. Like Darré and Rosenberg later, they wanted to replace Christian traditions and myths with Germanic ones. The Holy Land was Germany: the holy symbol the swastika: the holy river the Rhine, the holy mountain the Wartburg.[5]

How could pacifist ecologists also be Germanic nationalists? They associated nature with the life-force, that existed independently of mankind, but made man into a vessel for its use. Man could express this autonomous force through dance, gesture, and poetry. He could satisfy it by living close to nature. What stopped people from living like this? Germans had been victims of forcible denaturalization from the days of the Roman Empire. The alien Christian-Judaic civilization had blocked man off from the natural world, and all the anti-life manifestations of urban living stemmed from this false ethic.

Another element in these pacifist 'Greens' which was repeated by some National Socialists and by post-Second World War ecologists was their theory of matriarchy. A German anthropologist, J. Bachofen, wrote in 1860 that pre-civilized society was based on a female-dominated religion and social system. Archaeological discoveries from the Bronze Age showed that a harmonious equality had reigned between the sexes, with women very slightly superior. Klages and Stefan George adopted this ideal in the early years of this century. To reject the dominant patriarchal principle meant rejecting exploitative, insensitive attitudes to nature. A neo-Conservative journalist of the 1920s, Paul Fechter, later a Nazi, wrote a science-fiction book after the Second World War, which portrays a matriarchal, tribal society.[6] The discoverer of the book interprets it as covert Nazi propaganda, in that Fechter is not a *real* feminist, but keeps woman in her place, the home, or rather, hut. Robert Graves' *The White Goddess* is an outright attack on late Greek, Roman and post-Roman civilization, male dominance, and the masculine spirit, in the name of the female muse and goddess, whether in the guise of blood-soaked matriarch or desirable succubus.[7] The identification of matriarchal ecological sensitivity and male destructiveness is too common today among feminist writers to need much comment here.

The similarity of Klages' argument to Nietzsche's is unsurprising. He was seen as Nietzsche's spiritual heir. One of the finest expressive dancers of the time would dance to a recitation of *Thus Spake Zarathustra*.[8] After the First World War, the cultural criticism of the earlier period seemed to have been only too unhappily fulfilled. In *Doctor Zhivago*, Pasternak quotes Blok's reference to the 'children of Russia's terrible years'.[9] For pre-war writers it was a metaphor. For the post-war generation it had become a reality. They *were* the orphaned children of the storm. Tens of thousands of homeless orphans roamed Russia in gangs. Many had to be shot. Similarly in Germany, the much mocked fear of steamroller pseudo-democracy, of anti-human technology expressed by the critics of 'bigness', or urbanism, was to be made manifest, embodied in the mindless mass slaughterings of the war. Although it could be seen as a vindication of their ideas, the trauma affected the sensitive matriarchites differently. Diederichs gave a memorial address to the war dead which was pagan and naturist.[10] For many, the sacrifices and death had to be retrospectively justified. Some rejected adult malehood altogether, clinging to a dream of youth and boyish comradeship: or a country ruled by a worker-soldier élite. The Youth Movement after the First World War was to fragment into political extremes. Some joined the neo-Conservatives, some the Nazis, others the Leninists, like Theodor Plievier and Johannes Becher, the left-wing anarchist who wrote a spectacularly bad paean to Rosa Luxembourg and an even more memorable ode to Lenin.[11] (Both went to Russia, and spent the war years there.) The voluntary hardships previously sought by pampered bourgeois children had became a necessity for the many penniless *nouveaux pauvres*.

Several Asconans had come from ethnic German communities in Transylvania or Czechoslovakia. Gräser, the poet-anarchist and Green, was one. Rudolph Laban was another. Among the

Auslander peasant anarchists was Dr Georg Kenstler, founder member of the *Artamanen*, and editor of the journal *Blood and Soil*, who was later to join Walther Darré in plotting a revolution to be fought by cells of disaffected peasant farmers. The name Artamanen derived from *Artam*, old German for a stretch of land, and meant tiller of the soil, according to the founder. The group consisted of a group of students and ex-soldiers, many from ethnic German communities who had lost German citizenship through the Weimar law of 1921, and were thus doubly aware of a loss of national status, and were continually harassed and moved on by the police when they tried to work as agricultural labourers.[12] Their mentors were Gandhi and Tolstoy. Their membership form asked not whether you were musical, but *which* musical instrument the applicant played. They wanted to settle the German east, which was losing its German character through Polish immigration, and this aim of racial defence and renewal drew comparisons from later historians with the S.S. Their art, postcards and illustrations, showed clear-eyed youths with page-boy haircuts, gazing over corn-fields and mountains.

Anarchists at Ascona had seen Cain, the murdering peasant, not Abel, the wandering pastoralist, as a hero, not so much because he was a peasant as because he was an individualist. Yet contemplative religions and cults such as Taoism, and Buddhism, were other influences. Julius Evola, the Italian pagan philosopher and Germanist, wrote a book on Buddha in 1937. Tagore's poems and music were danced to and recited at Ascona[13]

Engineers, geographers and *Auslanders* are prominent in the history of ecological thought. Ludwig Klages, author of 'Der Mensch und das Leben', neo-conservative philosopher, was trained as a natural scientist, and knew Stefan George, one of the founders of the German Youth Movement. His complex metaphysics can be summarised as a pro-life, anti-technology set of dichotomies; the title of his main work was *The Spirit as Adversary of the Soul* Klages decomposes the cosmos into spirit (*Geist*) versus object: spirit versus life. Life experiences pure being: the spirit, which one might also define as the intellect, comprehends what life lives directly. The spirit is anti-life, it judges the pure object of life-experience, and by mediating it, corrupts it. Life does not need the spirit, argues Klages, the spirit is parasitical on life. What is generally seen as the advance of history, or as progress, is in fact the gradual domination of the spirit over life, which must end with the annihilation of the latter.[14]

This view of history as having taken a wrong path, one where intellect increasingly dominated the vital spirit, owes something to Oswald Spengler's analysis of the cycles of history, whereby each period had a youthful, fresh, spontaneous culture, then froze into a technologically advanced civilization, then decayed. The new spirit dropped like manna on to a people, it grew, developed, flowered, became formalized and stratified, and died. Sometimes the death took a long time. Frequently it was unobserved and unrealised by the participants. Culture was as organic as a tree. Seen in the context of interpreting the cycle of Western civilization, Klages' cultural critique also resembled Heidegger's argument that the culture of the West had been flawed from Roman times, through Roman distortion of and misunderstanding of Greek ideas. '*Roman thought takes over the Greek words without a corresponding, equally authentic, experience of what they say, without the Greek word.* The rootlessness of Western thought begins with this translation.'[15] This flaw, inherent for Heidegger, in Western civilization, is the same as Klages' inauthentic intellect-spirit, which distorts life, and the transcendance which for Nietzsche was the ancient crime against Western culture.

Heidegger dedicated his 1929 book on Kant to Scheler, a follower of Klages, but opposed the claim by the philosophical anthropologist to have reached a final understanding of man's place 'in the Cosmos'.[16] His opposition seems based on an ambiguity. He did not wish to concede philosophy to natural scientists, as explained in his discourse, 'The Difficulties of Achieving a Natural Conception of the World', on the inadequacy of ethnology as a tool to understanding 'Being'.[16] Yet he conceded that 'In *biology* there is an awakening tendency to inquire beyond the definitions which mechanism and vitalism have given for "life" and "organism", and to define anew the kind of Being which belongs to the living as such.'[18] He shares with fascist writers the belief that new techniques require a new man, but unlike them does not welcome the idea: it is all part of the wrongness of our historical path.

> What Nietzsche already knew metaphysically now becomes clear: that in its absolute form the modern 'machine economy', the machine-based reckoning of all activity and planning, demands a new kind of man who surpasses man as he has been hitherto. It is not enough that one possess tanks, airplanes and communications apparatus: nor is it enough that one has at one's disposal men who can service such things; it is not even sufficient that man only master technology as if it were something neutral, beyond benefit and harm, creation and destruction, to be used by anybody at all for any ends at all. What is

> needed is a form of mankind that is from top to bottom equal to the unique fundamental essence of modern technology and its metaphysical truth; that is to say, that lets itself be entirely dominated by the essence of technology precisely in order to steer and deploy individual technological processes and possibilities...only the 'Over-man' is appropriate to an absolute 'machine economy,' and vice versa: he needs it for the institution of absolute dominion over the earth.

and

> Within the history of the modern age, and as the history of modern mankind, man...attempts to establish himself as midpoint and measure in a position of dominance...the new world of the modern age has its own historical ground in the place where every history seeks its essential ground, namely, in metaphysics; that is, in a new determination of the truth of beings as a whole, and of the essence of such truth.[19]

The ambiguous attitude expressed here to the 'new man' had become unambiguous opposition to technological domination and – especially – consumerism, by 1944.

> In place of all the world-content of things that was formerly perceived and used to grant freely of itself, the object-character of technological domination spreads itself over the earth ever more quickly, ruthlessly and completely. Not only does it establish all things as producible in the process of production; it also delivers the products of production by means of the market. In self-assertive production, the humanness of man and the thingness of things dissolve into the calculated market value of a market which not only spans the whole earth...but also...trades in the nature of Being and thus subjects all beings to the trade of a calculation that dominates most tenaciously in those areas where there is no need of numbers.[20]

Technology and the market corrupts. Everything has a market value; everything, including those things that should not be marketed, is for sale. This criticism was one of Heidegger's claims to an ecological ethic of life.

Klages was obviously influenced by Bergson's *élan vital;* but he extracted an anti-technological, pro-raw-experience message, that was, perhaps, too extreme to influence the mainstream philosophers of his time. Certainly, one commentator thinks that Klages's attack on 'spirit' as opposing intellect and technique removed any possibility of influencing 'the critique of culture, which could have been considerable in our own period of ecological, "green" and alternative ideas,' a comment which hints at the connection between today's cultural criticism of technology and the neo-conservative one of Weimar Germany, without really explaining why Klages should be seen as irrelevant to it.[21] Klages' criticism is in fact the essence of today's 'green' and ecological cultural criticism, which also attacks what is seen as excessive rationality.

Bergson's life-spirit also inspired Georges Sorel and his conclusions help to show the difference between German and Latin attitudes to the nature-culture issue. He disputed Bergson's contrast between intellect as a means of organising space (defined by Bergson as an essential part of the growth of civilization) and the vital life-force. Sorel saw this as a mere justification for mechanization, for capitalist division of labour and automation. For Sorel, this was out of date: the new capitalism was subject to the worker's will and creative impulse. What man could create was as 'vital' as raw nature. Unlike Bergson, Sorel rejected Darwinian analogies to explain society, because he saw society as a willed creation built on chaotic basic nature.[22] The interests of nature were opposed to man's: holistic theories tried to gloss over this chasm of struggle, to impose a pseudo-rationalism on raw reality

> The creation of an *artificial nature,* which appears during the feverish era of capitalism, assumes that men have become capable of imposing new directions on the movements of things [passage about hydraulic power & mines]. . . Nature does not let itself be reduced to the role of servant of humanity, without protesting. . . Nature never ceases working, with a crafty slowness, for the ruination of all our works. We buy the power of commanding in *artificial nature* by incessant labour; matter imposes its own laws when the mind withdraws. The true doctrine is that which juxtaposes *natural nature* and *artificial nature.*[23]

In this odd Marxian-fascist analysis, Sorel juxtaposes and alien nature with man's technological capacities and needs. He recognises a dichotomy between the two, but in the end supports man's dominance.

The permeation of the critique of technological culture in German thought at the time of Weimar is indicated by the attack by Ernst Niekisch – Niekisch was a National Bolshevik, who resisted Hitler. He inspired the Nouvelle Droite today, and went to East Germany after 1945. He wrote in 1931:

> Technology is the rape of nature. It brushes nature aside. It amounts to cunningly tricking nature out of the free disposal of one piece of land after another. When technology triumphs, nature is violated and desolated. Technology murders life by striking down, step by step, the limits established by nature. It devours men and all that is human. It is heated with bodies. Blood is its cooling lubricant. Consequently, war in this technological era is a murderous slaughter. . . The anti-life demonic quality of technology manifests itself most horribly in total war. In war, technology's productive capacity is so up-to-date that on the hour it is able to annihilate everything organic whatever it may be – suddenly, totally and precisely.[24]

Some neo-conservatives rejected nature as a philosophical guide – notably Spengler and Moeller van den Bruck. Spengler, indeed, commented to Eduard Spranger, the philosopher and education specialist, who wrote an influential book on the psychology of youth, that only Goethe's concept of the biological, or organic, was valid: that the idea did not mean the mechanistic biology of Darwin and his era, but a 'metaphysic of life'.[25] This was the fundamental difference between the idealistic, pessimistic neo-conservatives and those optimistic radicals who went on to accept the Third Reich.

Many of the traditional problems of philosophy ceased to have meaning when man was accepted as part of nature. 'Philosophical anthropology', was the new concept evolved by German philosophers in response to this challenge. Max Scheler was one of the most influential of this school. His posthumously published book of 1928, *The Place of Man in the Cosmos*, (misleadingly translated as *Man's Place in Nature* by the 1958 translator, which blurs the important change from Cosmos to Welt in Arnold Gehlen's *Der Mensch: seine Natur und seine Stellung in der Welt* (Berlin, 1940)) deals with the question of what is the essential nature of man, and his relationship to the world around him – perhaps the most pressing philosophical question that exists.[26] Scheler wrestles with the concept that man and nature are one, but emerges with a dualistic theory of man's *special* nature, one that rescues the religious cosmology while preserving scientific knowledge. For Scheler, man is different precisely because the cosmos has ordered it so. Man's tendency to develop a dualism, of body and soul, results from his capacity to be introspective, to think: he is the meditating animal. He deduced *differences* from the organic analogies between man and animal; man alone possesses 'spirit', a quality which in Scheler's schema encompasses will, making man 'open to the world', that is, able to reject or alter his surroundings.[27] In this, he was less subject to the world than animals, but more aware.

Arnold Gehlen, whose sociological work was published in wartime under the Nazis, and, as a leading conservative theorist, well into the 1970s, dismissed Scheler's attempt to maintain the existence of and justify 'spirit' as man's distinctive quality, and replaced it with a capacity to create social and familial institutions. He kept the belief in man's uniqueness, and argued that identifying man with animals too closely would blind people to what was distinct in man. He evolved a concept of a functional sociology which he called 'anthrobiology': this would analyse man in the context of his social relationships. Gehlen arrived at the same holistic view of man and human institutions taken by Weimar neo-conservatives, but by a very different path. His rested on an interpretation of nature supported by the most recent experiments in human and animal psychology; theirs rested on an emphasis on the non-animal, spiritually specific culture and will of man which derived directly from the Idealist tradition in German thought, especially the philosophy of history represented by Dilthey. Where animals had instinct, man had traditions. He had, as it were, genes for the ability to create traditions, which replaced genes for instincts.[28]

What, if anything, links the philosophical anthropologists and the ideologues of National Socialism? Certainly, Rosenberg, Goebbels and so on, do not appear to quote the works of Scheler and Gehlen. Indeed, Hitler directly attacked Haeckel's biographer, Bölsche, for writing rubbish designed to appeal to the urban masses.[29] Yet one can certainly elicit an appeal to 'natural laws', to accepting the way the world is, in Nazi writings, a rejection of transcendental doctrines which is quite separate from the Nazi approach to ecological politics. What was the common denominator? What – to return to a major theme in my argument – are the political implications of accepting nature's laws?

German naturist thought, from its inception in the late nineteenth century influenced a generation of well-meaning, earnest reformers. The German naturist thinker was opposed to Conservative thought, and also not utopian. The pacifist note of the meeting at Meissner in 1913, addressed by Klages, symbolised the yearning spirit of the youth movement. The first difference between German and English attitudes to nature and ecological ideas that strikes a student of these matters, is that German writings on nature seem not to have the sensuous element they have in England. The role played by nature in German literature, apart from lyric poetry, is not as great as one might expect. And while German poetry is often *based* on nature, it tends to have a didactic and teleological quality. The blue flower symbolises the unknowable, which is, finally, death. The bluebird means the unreachable, – perhaps, too, death. The wood, the forest, that potent element in German literature, implies a homeland, but also a way to lose the self. The bluebird, the wood, are symbols. They imply a certain relationship with the self, usually that of loss of selfhood, sometimes explicitly death.

There are significant differences between the English and German visions of what constituted the life of the peasant and yeoman. For example, German Romantic art (and one of its later variants, National Socialist painting) emphasises endurance, not jollity, and doom, not Arcadia, in its landscapes. German peasant painting was didactic and reformist. The sensuous luxuriating in rural beauty which characterises English landscape art is lacking. Why should this be? One, somewhat ethnocentric explanation, would be that the English countryside is more beautiful, although less wild and grand. That aside, however, what particular quality was being sought for in rural life in Germany? What did man's need for nature mean to them? It is hard to identify a specific change in late nineteenth-century German society that was responsible for the Wandervögel movement. Certainly there was no abrupt increase in industrialisation, urbanisation or technology at that time. Nonetheless, the Youth Movement, like German rural art, sought answers. It wanted to be taught.

One of the constant themes in German writings on nature is that it is seen as a pointer or a path. It goes somewhere. Nature is a teacher. Another theme is that there does exist a truthful, real world – identified with nature – which can be seized, grasped and verified, but which is veiled. The image of the veil which I mentioned earlier, first appeared in the nineteenth century. The veil has to be torn aside. This may seem a banal conclusion. Of course there is a real world. Of course one has to look for it. Yet the existence of reachability of an objectively other otherness has by no means always been granted by philosophy or religion. Nor is the symbol of veiled truth obvious in European thought before around 1800 – the date of Schiller's lovely poem.[30]

The concept of veiled nature-truth is not a conservative view of society or politics. In the realm of political ideas I would include as Conservative thinkers a rag-bag from Plato to Michael Oakeshott, who are self-defining, and include Hobbes, Burke, and perhaps some elements of Hegel's thought. Their main characteristic is that of *myth*-creating. Myths are needed either to convey a non-earthly or spiritual concept, or to maintain social stability and to protect society from excessive and destructive rationalism (constructivist rationalism, as defined by Hayek, and exemplified by Bentham). This is a constant in Conservative thought.

But the German naturist attitude prefers the 'real', the bed-rock, objective nature, to any structures and traditions built for human use. This is why naturists are drawn to unconventional and innovative ideas, although they are also looking for guide-lines. This leads to a form of centrist, but also radical attitude, that views political and social tradition and big institutions and structures with suspicion. They are seen as fossilised, and obscurantist: institutions, instead of being the guardian of the social memory, obstruct society, rather as Nietzsche saw the study of history as hampering a people's ability to create anew and yet continue their own history.

> The cure for an uncultured people? 'Know thyself.' The Greeks were faced for centuries by a danger similar to that which faces us; the danger of being overwhelmed by what was past and foreign, of perishing through history . . . But they learned to *organise the chaos* . . . thinking back to their real needs. Each one of us must organise the chaos within him by thinking back to his real needs.[31]

Traditions also veil reality, in a way that blurs comprehension and inhibits progress. The naturist does not live in the past although he rejects the present, and his frequent glances at earlier rural times are to eliminate the misdirecting signposts previous generations obeyed. That is because of the belief that in the past objects were more object-like, more real. The constant search for a bed-rock, true reality is not utopian. As Hannah Arendt writes, 'Conceptually, we may call truth what we cannot change; metaphorically, it is the ground on which we stand and the sky that stretches above us'.[32] The man seeking truth from nature usually comes from a mobile class background: certainly, he is not cushioned from insecurities by status and tradition. Perhaps that is why he searches for 'reality' more obsessedly, and seeks truth as a bulwark, for security. Something must be trusted, be hunted for as reliable. That intangible set of creative values that comprise the intimate, spiritual life of a nation matter more to the naturist than does national power. That is not a conservative position.

The naturist is a natural protestor. There can be no compromise where this objective world is concerned; yet one of its rules is constant change and growth. He is not a determinist, through religion or through genetical inheritance. The human spirit and will is all-important to him. Nature-based thinking tends, too, to optimism. In one sense it is 'forward-looking', partly because it is abjuring the outworn, out-of-date traditions, and partly because of the didactic element. As in von Humboldt's metaphor, nature is the teacher. When one learns from nature, as opposed to learning from one's parents, one learns something new and different. Optimism and novelty appeal to youth, and the generational split in European culture from around 1900 was sharp. With the German Youth Movement, the appeal of nature was bound up with a desire to escape from the old and outworn and look for a new path. The Art Nouveau artist who illustrated the works of the Youth Movement, Fidus, was seen wandering through the bombed ruins of Berlin in 1945, raising his arms, and saying, 'Now we can build afresh.'[33]

The lack of an Arcadian vision in Germany, the dark element in rural appeal, can be illustrated with two quotations here.

> From the dark opening of the worn insides of the shoes the toilsome tread of the worker stares forth. In the stiffly rugged heaviness of the shoes there is . . . her slow trudge through the . . . ever-uniform furrows of the field swept by a raw wind . . . In the shoes vibrates the silent call of the earth, its quiet gift of the ripening grain, and its unexplained self-refusal in the fallow desolation of the wintry field . . . the trembling before the impending childbed and shivering at the surrounding menace of death.[34]

This is Heidegger meditating on the implications of a small part of a Van Gogh painting and comparing the use-value of the painting of the shoes to the observer and the wearing of the shoes to the wearer. Whoever in England would have written that? We write about the sunflowers instead. Heidegger's late work includes an essay which consists of short nature poems, each one followed on the same page by didactic prose poems. For example,

> When the wind, shifting quickly, grumbles in the rafters of the cabin, and the weather threatens to become nasty . . .

is followed by:

> Three dangers threaten thinking.
> The good and thus wholesome
> danger is the nighness of the singing
> poet.
>
> The evil and thus keenest danger is
> thinking itself. It must think

against itself, which it can only
seldom do.

The bad and thus muddled danger
is philosophizing.[35]

The second quotation is Spengler describing the peasant's nature.

All effective history begins with the primary classes, nobility and priesthood, forming themselves and elevating themselves above the peasants as such...the peasant is historyless. The village stands outside world history, and all evolution...passes by these little points on the landscape...never touching their inwardness in the least. The peasant is eternal man, independent of every Culture that ensconces itself in the Cities. He precedes it, he outlives it, a dumb creature propagating himself from generation to generation, limited to soil-bound callings and aptitudes, a mystical soul, a dry, shrewd understanding ...the origin, the ever-flowing source of the blood that makes world history in the cities.[36]

The peasant, this undifferentiated blob, this crab-like plant person, is the foundation, the soil for the mysterious spirit that produces a Culture; but for Spengler, that is his sole important function.

The Wandervögel youth shared their love of the countryside with reformist views on society. The range of views was wide: from a Tolstoyan anarchy to communard Communism. After the First World War it encompassed racialist German settlement communes in the east to revolutionary Bolshevik and National Bolshevik activities. There were new settlements, communes built on youth movement ideology. All wanted their groups to be the seeds of a new world. One Back-to-the-Land prophet called for

A new belief in the greatness of humanity, a new courage to be free, the strength to search for truth...Not 'back to nature but forward to culture' is inscribed on our banner...Down with mechanical, dehumanising civilization. By culture we mean that state where man has a tight, personal link, a sensitive perception towards the things with which he is bound.[37]

The search for a bed-rock, objective reality meant a new sensitivity to cultural violation of the tangible. Rilke praised the thingness of things, a quality which materialistic mass production destroyed. Things had to be rooted in real meaning, in their links with the past, with the maker, with the owner. Things only possessed meaning if they emerged from a nexus of meaning.

> Even for our grandparents, a house, a well, a familiar tower, their very dress, their cloak, was infinitely more, infinitely more intimate; almost everything a receptacle in which they both found and enlarged a store of humanness. . . Now there are intruding, from America, empty, indifferent things, sham things, *dummies* of life. . . A house, etc., as the Americans understand it, has *nothing* in common with the house into which the hope and thoughtfulness of our forefathers had entered. The animated, experienced things that share our lives are running out, and cannot be replaced. *We are perhaps the last to have known such things*[38]

This poignant assertion can perhaps be illustrated by considering the question of real and fake works of art. What Rilke and Heidegger were saying was that, even if a work of art were imitated so well as to be completely identical with the original, it would still not *be* the original, and that quality that made it objectively not the original was the quality that mattered. Furthermore, thingness affected and was affected by the relationship between the object and the owner, or, in the case of a work of art, between the object and the understanding observer, not to think of the maker. In denying empirical materialism and substituting thingness, or Being, these writers postulated a new dimension, neither mind-mind, or mind-body, or all body, but the cobweb of links existing in a hidden reality, occasionally sun-flecked, as it were, where caught by the light. In Heidegger's extraordinary passage about Van Gogh's portrait about a peasant woman, he defines the relationship between the observer of a work of art and the thingly quality of the painting as one of the qualities that makes a work of art art.

For Heidegger, the quality that goes to make a poem or a painting is its degree of thingness, its substance, its reality, and its truth. We at once see that for the Conservative, this craving for rock bottom, objective truth does not exist. Michael Oakeshott's definition of poetry and other works of art is that they express a myth: and far from being a higher, purer form of truth, they provide a dimension of escape, a golden myth, a transcendental other to comfort and to solace, to help to maintain society. For the pessimistic Conservative, the truth is hardly bearable; for the naturist radical, it is the true end of endeavour. As Rilke, again, writes:

What is your most grievous experience?
If the drink is bitter, become wine . . .
And if forgotten by the earthly world,
Say to the still earth that you flow on.
Tell the running water that you be.[39]

Going back to nature in this context is hardly about nature at all. It is about being versus thinking: being inside the egg not outside it. It expresses an ancient dichotomy in Western political life, that between the Grand Inquisitor and Jesus, between Descartes and Spinoza. This is hinted at by one sympathetic and knowledgeable observer of German Conservatism, who objects to a close analogy between conservatism and fascism, although he considers, as I do not, that both share a pessimistic view of human nature. Klemperer argues that 'the conservative's opposition to a one-sidedly optimistic faith in man was connected with his organic view of life . . . Man was shaped by his past, and, therefore, subject to tradition.'[40] At first, this sounds like our hypothetical naturist: but being bound by tradition was precisely the concept that such people opposed.

Utopian and mystical are words often used to define odd and unfamiliar ideas, but if one accepts the definition of utopianism as the attempt to escape from the wheel of fate, naturist reformers cannot be defined as utopians.[41] They do not want to cling to an inevitable and pre-determined fate. They go to nature to learn, and return with the recommendation that one clings to the wheel because it is the most sensible path of action. To do so requires the sweeping away of past identities, past traditions and past errors.

This line of thought fitted the mood of 1920s Germany. German nature-based thinking had a practical, social-problem base that it did not have elsewhere in Europe. 'Blood and Soil', a phrase invented in the early 1920s, was a code word implying the protection of a real personality. It stressed the kinship element, and the peasant's demographic role. City-dwellers did not breed – peasants did. They were the life-blood of the nation in a literal sense as well as its spiritual and cultural basis.

The cultural criticism of this period in Germany has two faces. On the one hand there was the desire to escape from the burden of the past; on the other hand a sense of loss so acute as to induce nihilism. This apparent contradiction stems from the reality of the loss of the past. One could accept and rejoice or one could mourn. The fact of the loss was put into poetic and philosophic form by

Rilke and Heidegger. The need to replace what had been lost was emphasised by German conservatives. Sometimes the losses seemed merely the doorway to something dazzlingly new.[42]

Material losses had occurred. A war had been lost, and with it territory, goods, industry and a system of government. But the tangible loss about which we know was not only what was mourned. The poets and philosophers did not discuss these specifics, but instead the spiritual problems of the new era. That technology, for example, had to be discussed and analysed so often gives a clear picture of the impact of change. However, why this impact should have taken place in the 1920s is difficult to understand. There was, after all, technology in the nineteenth century. If anything, the 'heavy metal' artefacts of those days, – railways, lathes and factories – were fiercer and more frightening. By contrast, the technology linked with the 1920s, telephones, radio and aeroplanes, was clean, efficient and usable. The nineteenth century gloried in detail, complexity and effort: its machines are found drawn in detail in encyclopaedias like Dürer etchings. The more advanced technology of the 1920s was simpler, and more acceptable. Possibly this made it seem more de-humanised – one can only surmise. The gulf between what observers claim to observe and what is perceived as real is a problem of intellectual history. It is easy to assume that because the issue of technology obsessed German politicians and philosophers in the 1920s, there was some real and quantifiable increase in technology's alien and harsh nature. But it seems rather that 'The defense against the cultural and political effects of modernity on the body politic [was] thus thought to require a homeopathic absorption of the organisational and technological hallmarks of modernity.'[43]

Certainly, this period found Germany suffering a loss of identity. The outburst of creative modernity before 1914 had petered out, countered by a hunt for older values. Despite the superficial success of the Wilhelmine Empire, its unity fragmented after 1918. For the radical intelligentsia, it had never satisfied their yearnings for a fully German identity: the hunt for a definition of what was uniquely *their* Germany continued. This aspect of the Wilhelmine period still leaves room for research. Attention has focused on Marxist and Social Democratic theorists, while those searching for a German identity tended to be subsumed under the general rubric of proto-Nazi, nationalist, or anti-semitic. Although these facets existed, they were not confined to the radical conservative German intelligentsia.[44]

The radical nationalists included those with progressive, social reformist ideas. The warlike Professors, conservative landowners, Catholic reactionaries, and other figures who receive a bad press in most history books, were in a minority. Theosophy became popular: Gerhard Hauptmann wrote 'problem plays' on alcoholism, others on euthanasia. Many of this group of vegetarians, temperance activists, utopian eugenicists and communards, were connected by marriage, others by university education and their joint victimization by Bismarck's anti-Socialist laws. In their search for identity, many looked to India, – after all it was Max Müller, a German, who first developed the science of comparative philology and Indo-European linguistics from studying Sanskrit. India was a place of romance in the German popular imagination, and in poetry. 'Aryanism', and especially the pan-Aryan variant, was to catch on because of this fundamentally sympathetic attitude to North Indian culture, of which Hinduism was seen as a variant. Tagore, the Indian poet and nature-mystic, received a rapturous reception in Berlin in the 1920s, and had a status similar to that of Count Keyserling and Rudolf Steiner.[45] Some of the messianic gurus of the Weimar period dressed up in loose, dhoti-like clothing.

This sense of a lack of cultural identity, of insecurity, can be found in Thomas Mann's works. Mann, the half-Brazilian outsider, aware of the dichotomous impulses in his own character and upbringing, expresses in his novels a disturbing insecurity. His heroes always yearn after the 'other', sometimes transcendental, sometimes not. In *The Magic Mountain*, the blonde, simple Castorp from the North German plains, yearns for an untrammelled, feckless 'bad Russian' carelessness, in the form of a slant-eyed Russian woman. His will has been sabotaged by an early love for an utterly 'other' slant-eyed Russian boy. In other works he portrays the yearning of the complex, dark, earth-bound, introspective, for the blonde, healthy, carefree, callous Northerner. In the 1920s, an age axis enters. A three-year-old girl falls in love with a young man; an ageing musician with a fourteen-year-old boy. A fifty-year-old woman desires a youth in his early twenties: her passion seems to lead to a cancerous tumour. The various longings in *Doctor Faustus* end in death or suicide. What is yearned for is never achieved, and it is implied that it never can be. The 'other' is a threat because it involves a sense of incompleteness and inadequacy on the part of the lover, and although Mann presents his suffering anti-heroes with irony, there is nevertheless something unsatisfactory in this situation. Before the First World War it could be subsumed in the general ferment of the time.

> Men of practical enterprise joined forces with the men of intellectural enterprise...The Superman was adored, and the Subman was adored: health and the sun was worshipped, and the delicacy of consumptive girls was worshipped; people were enthusiastic hero-worshippers, and enthusiastic adherents of the creed of the Man in the Street; one had faith and was sceptical...one dreamed of ancient castles and shady avenues, autumnal gardens, glassy ponds, jewels, hashish, disease and demonism, but also of prairies, vast horizons, forges and rolling mills, naked wrestlers, the uprisings of the slaves of toil, man and woman in their primeval garden, and the destruction of society.[46]

In the 1920s, a return to simplicity, to Indian peasant life, to anything, as long it did not breathe the air of past disasters, seemed the answer. And not only the sensitive neo-conservative yearned for nature, and felt a sense of loss. Who is this whom we hear bewailing the loss of his birthright, the forest?

> 'I, Bertolt Brecht, cast away into the asphalt cities out of the black forests when I was in the womb...'[47]

Yes, it is none other than the tough apostle of alienation, anti-individualism and Marxist collectivism: prophet of *asphaltindividualismus*, later known as Bert Brecht, partaking of the *Zeitgeist*.

> 'I, Bertolt Brecht, come from the black forests. My mother took me into the towns while I was in her womb. And the chill of the forests will be in me until I die'.[48]

CHAPTER TEN

The Steiner Connection

METHODOLOGY

How relevant were ecological ideas to the Third Reich? Discussions of theory and practice under the Nazis tend to dissolve into schoolmen-type arguments about ideology and practice. But we all know what we mean by ideology, even though it is difficult to judge precisly how Nazism was perceived at different times by its various supporters. There is a body of speeches, books and pronouncements which, in common sense terms, constitute Nazi ideology. It is not complete. Hitler's speeches have never been collected and published in full, even in their original German. What exists is sometimes fraudulent or of dubious origin. Nonetheless, there is some basis from which to deduce an ideology, a collection of texts, although some are authorised and some are not. Further, there are intellectual forefathers. Traditions can be identified. Historians of ideas would be silenced indeed if, for every allegation that the Third Reich was for example influenced by, or a product of, the French Enlightenment, or perversions therefrom, evidence had to be produced to show that Rosenberg or Hess had studied Diderot, Voltaire or Condorcet. Ideas are held to permeate or saturate other ideas. They are, in the telling phrase, 'in the air'. To measure the influence ideas have on practice is more difficult. Fortunately, though, we do not need to strain at gnats to show that there was a strain of ecological ideas among Nazis: the evidence is ample. It would be better known if it were to be found in the more well-known of the authorised texts referred to above, but it does exist in the ministerial, planning and personal archives of the Third Reich.

The problem arises when one is trying to determine whether a concept or policy existed contemporaneously outside Germany. Equally, a concept may seem specifically German but be not necessarily specifically Nazi. Two cross-axes of comparison have to be brought to bear. This process has been continuing for some years, and is known as the 'historicization' of the Third Reich. National Socialist welfare policies, for example, have been compared to those proposed by Beveridge – a cross-country comparison. Nazi war aims have been found comparable to those of Germany in the First World War – a comparison of a different kind.

A further problem is how peripheral these ideas were to National Socialism. If they were part of a separate current of ideas, then their practitioners would have held ecological beliefs whether or not the Third Reich had come to power; – the argument for continuity in this area of German life, as in other intellectual and academic spheres, is a powerful one. If the ideas were central and not peripheral, then the onus is on students of comparative fascism to explain why similar themes were not embodied in other fascist movements. The following discussion should help to shift the debate from morphological to structural points.

The argument for continuity has to answer the problem that there was top-level Nazi support for ecological ideas – especially if one incorporates the attitude of Hitler and Himmler on vegetarianism and animal rights, issues which are not covered in this book.[1]

A discussion of the element of green and ecological ideas in Nazism is bound to have an explosive effect. There are also possible political consequences for Germany. The Green Party in today's Germany is popular among many disaffected intellectuals, because it appears to be pure and untainted by the past. The Green Party is a potential ally of the SPD, and therefore opposed to the Christian Democrat right. In short, its heart appears to be in the right place, that is, on the left, and it has adopted the 'soft' values of today's far left – feminism, egalitarianism, and anti-nuclear action. So a link between today's fashionable green ideas and the Nazis can meet with displeasure or even vituperation.

Given that ecological ideas in Germany did not begin with the Nazis, would their proponents have come to power in any case under a non-Nazi government? Would their policies have been made law? Was a radical revolutionary government necessary for the activists to attain office? The answer is probably yes, on the analogy on Roosevelt's New Dealers, where it took a collectivist interventionist government to impose anti-erosion and peasant settlement ideas on an uninterested populace (an area of historical comparison which deserves more attention than it can receive here); but perhaps the *ideas* would eventually have affected government policy whatever the government.[2] Again, how far was there continuity of ideas and personnel with the past, or should all legislation and activity under the Third Reich be seen as manifestations of Nazism? Another problem is how important the various ecological legislation and activities were in terms of the overall programme. So far, they have been dismissed as trivial and irrelevant. Was this true, or was this dismissal because academics did not want to draw comparisons with today's green ideas? Has there been a paradigm shift? How far did the Nazis implement their ecological policies? These are questions which are not always posed in discussions of ideology and practice, but they are important, and all discussions of this issue (or any other regarding radical politics in power) need to take account of methodological difficulties, which will be borne in mind as the account continues.

There were two levels of ecological support in the Third Reich. The first was at ministerial level, the second was at planning and administrative level, in the new party organs. The two ministers concerned were Rudolf Hess, Hitler's deputy, and Walther Darré, Peasant Leader and Minister of Agriculture between 1933 and 1942, while Fritz Todt, founder and head of the Todt Organisation, a civil engineer, was also an ecologist. Hess was a follower of Rudolf Steiner and a homeopath. A naturist hospital was named after Hess (although it was renamed after his flight to England in 1941). Hess's office contained several ecologists, including Antony Ludovici, who wrote on the need for carefully planned, 'organic', ecologically sound land use and planning. There were two thousand bio-dynamic farmers registered in the Nazi 'Battle for Production', probably an under-statement of the real figure, in view of the known hostility from Goering, Goebbels and Bormann to bio-dynamic methods. Martin Bormann, who replaced Hess as leader of the Reich Chancellory, was sufficiently alarmed about the number of alternative practitioners close to Hess to circulate a memorandum to all Gauleiters – some days before Hess's flight to England – asking them to ban 'confessional and occult circles'. He drew a contrast between the 'slogans of politicking soothsayers' and 'the solid National Socialist *Weltanschauung* founded on a scientific knowledge of the laws of race, life and nature'.[3] This attack emphasises the split within National Socialism, between the practical men, and the alternative, individualist rebels against the Weimar structures, whose ability to conform to the strictures and precepts of the Third Reich was tempered by their own strongly held beliefs.

Alwin Seifert, a member of the Todt Organisation, was a

motorway architect who specialised in 'embedding motorways organically into the landscape'.[4] He took the then unfashionable ecological position that monoculture damaged disease resistance among plants and animals, as well as diminishing land fertility. The interests of man, even German man, did not come first for him. He also argued against land reclamation and drainage, claiming that Germany's water table depended on her wild countryside. His arguments were sufficiently persuasive to make Hitler order that such programmes of moorland drainage should cease. This caused considerable anger among the Ministry of Agriculture leaders, including Herbert Backe, who had prepared a plan in 1942 to drain and reclaim moorland in Schleswig-Holstein, and Willikens, who in 1937–8, had a similar programme under way in Frisia. Seifert was also a follower of Steiner, and bombarded Walther Darré with Anthroposophical papers and long letters about the need to retain wild plants to form a bank of plant genes and resistance potential. He sent Darré unpublished papers by Steiner, including one on magnetism and its effects on agriculture. One paper by Seifert himself argued that 'classical scientific farming' was a nineteenth-century phenomenon, unsuited to the 'new' era; that imported artificial fertilisers, fodder and insecticides were not only poisonous, but laid an extra burden on agriculture through transport and import costs. It was dangerous to depend on these products in wartime. He called for an agricultural revolution towards 'a more peasant-like, natural, simple' method of farming, 'independent of capital'. Again, typically for the biodynamic reformers, he emphasised the need for a total rethinking of agricultural methods, rather than a simple reversion to the primitive. 'A mere re-building of the old peasant methods cannot help, because the internal connectedness of the old ways has gone. The ground that was healthy then is now sick in many ways.'[5] The land-planning department in Hess's office used similar language, which is unsurprising, since it included men of a similar cast of mind and background to Seifert, who was a trained architect; he worked for the Todt Organisation, and Todt found him 'a knowledgeable co-worker'.[6]

> Rural land created [erfasst] the landscape as a natural, organic, vital [lebendige] world, ploughed fields, meadows, pastures and woodland. It is the soil as bearer [Träger] of organic nature, the ground which bears the harvest, ...bound to the landscape...the foundation of the formation of a community...of neighbourliness. The agricultural community is bound to this land. The land determines labour and economy...[7]

Thus wrote the Representative for Settlement who was also the land planning officer, as in Hess's office the term included rural and urban building.[8]

Given the split between Hess and the increasingly powerful Bormann, the subject of bio-dynamic agriculture was a sensitive one. One Gauleiter, an ex-Keeper of the Seal for the National Peasant Council, wrote to Herbert Backe in 1940, in guarded terms, about this issue. The letter hints at dissensions.

> You are probably aware that after the war Dr Todt [at this date still alive] will have control of all Germany's technology. All the more vital, then, that each Ministry should have people in it who are trusted by him...There has been a complete revolution in the question of bio-dynamic farming. After [Hess] in very odd circumstances repudiated the results drawn from a study of organically farmed units by Darré's staff, the renewed investigation in 1939 by Darré's staff office has come down quite clearly on the side of bio-dynamic agriculture...The SS have already installed their own agricultural and market gardening enterprises, and it really looks as though leadership has been transferred to Himmler...With the recent drought in North Germany, the superiority of organic farming methods as opposed to artificial fertilisers has made itself apparent in no uncertain fashion.[9]

But despite the battle waged at Reich Chancellory level, actual government policy continued to support rural conservation. Nazi Germany was the first country in Europe to form nature reserves. (America had done something similar, on a much larger scale, in the nineteenth century.) It was the first country to insist, in 1934, that new tree plantations should include broad-leaved, deciduous trees, as well as conifers (a decision not yet formalised in law in Britain), while hedge-row and copse protection ordinances were passed in 1940 'to protect the habitat of wild-life'.[10] Anti-vivisection laws were passed. Ninety per cent of all Prussian government-owned land in East Prussia was forest, and some eighty per cent of community and local authority land over the rest of Germany. Despite the general belief that Germany was desperately short of land, land with trees on it was seen as sacrosanct. Not only was it *not* planned to cut down trees, but landowners offered to exchange their arable land for publicly owned forest, so that they would own trees, and the public authorities could settle peasants on the cultivated land: nobody seemed to think this an odd proposal. When part of Poland was incorporated into Germany as the Warthegau, after 1939, fifteen per cent of the usable arable land was set aside to be afforested. According to one economic historian, two-fifths of German land consisted of forest in the 1930s: while today, it is still one-third.[11] According to a 1984 German opinion poll forests were of great concern to seventy four per cent of those questioned, and ninety nine per cent of Germans had heard of the dying trees, threatened by acid rain. 'West Germans show a deep rooted love of forests' was the unfortunate newspaper title.[12] The oak leaf was a symbol of the SS.

Tension between Germany and Italy intensified when Mussolini persisted in cutting down trees in the South Tyrol. German spies in Poland in 1937 saw an outbreak of pine bud mite, which destroyed vast tracts of forest along the German-Polish border, as tantamount to an act of war – the Poles had not only taken their trees, they had neglected and destroyed them.

'THE ERA OF THE PEASANT'

'A new era is upon us, which will be the era of the Peasant.'[13]

Between the end of the First World War and the Nazi takeover, the idea that the peasantry had a special 'mission' was widespread.[14] A reaction against the use of artificial fertilisers also occurred. Rudolf Steiner, founder of Anthroposophy, became its leader, before his death in 1925, and inspired the founding of a new school of farming known as 'bio-dynamic agriculture'. In Easter 1924, a meeting of Anthroposophical farmers took place at a Silesian estate owned by Count Keyserling, belle-lettrist, poet and nationalist author of *Das Reisetagebuch eines Philosophen.* Here Steiner delivered eight lectures calling for self-sufficient farms, which preserved the spirit of the soil and were tilled in accordance with his vision of the life-forces and magnetic influences of the cosmos. Artificial fertilisers were rejected because they were alien to the land, man-made, or at least, man-extracted, and dead. The earth was alive: the soil was like an eye or ear for the earth, it was 'an actual organ'.[15] Humus in the soil had to be built up naturally, through compost made from living matter. Steiner's followers believed that the build-up of chemical fertilisers was harmful to human health, and could eventually destroy human civilization through damaging the human nervous system and brain. Agriculture should be part of a world-earth organic unit; Goethe, who thought nature should be viewed through its inherent morphology – the acorn *has* to grow into an oak – was seen as a forebear, and Steiner's building was called the Goethenaeum. The symbol for their farm produce, and later title of their journal, was Demeter, goddess of fruitfulness, the corn-harvest, and mother of Persephone. It ran from 1930 to 1940, when Himmler seized all copies, and ordered the SS to destroy them.[16] This journal, in content and format, was very like the later *Soil Association* magazine, and showed pictures of hedges, copses and well-farmed land. It carried reports of productivity and protein equivalent grown on each acre of the experimental farms. A Society for the Furtherance of Bio-Dynamic Agriculture was formed, and no less a figure than the former German Chancellor, Georg Michaelis, became its leader in 1930.

Throughout the 1930s, Anthroposophist farmers, whose system of bio-dynamic farming was, in practical terms, close to what is today called organic farming, tried to publicise their results and ideas, especially to the Nazi leadership. The most active farmer and propagandist was a Dr Eduard Bartsch, who started an organic farm at Marienhöhe, in East Prussia, after hearing Steiner's lectures on bio-dynamic farming. He was chairman of the Union of Anthroposophist farmers, which was banned by the Gestapo in 1935, as tainted with excessive individualism, international Freemasonry, pacifism, and Judaism. The National Union for Bio-dynamic Agriculture, however, survived, and in 1935 merged with the German Society for Life Reform. It was to reappear as a force in top government circles at a most surprising moment in time, well after the invasion of Poland. The bio-dynamic farmers were, however, harassed, and in some cases arrested, in 1941, after Hess's flight to England. Dr Bartsch was held, as was Dr Hans Merkel, later to be Darré's defence lawyer at Nuremburg. Darré was rumoured to have been briefly arrested, but despite his attempts to protect his Anthroposophical farmers, remained in office. Anyone linked with Hess's ideas, – he was a homeopath and naturist – was suspect. Hermann Goering and Martin Bormann opposed any attempt to move to a system of organic farming, Goering because he feared a drop in German food production, Bormann for ideological reasons.[17]

Hess himself, who was then Hitler's representative, ordered, soon after the Nazi *Machtergreifung*, that there should be no division between concepts of 'organic' land use and planning, and farming. The intensive experimentation in bio-dynamic farming that continued till about 1942 had first Hess's blessing, and later Darré's.[18] In 1937, a meeting took place between Hess, Bormann and Darré to discuss farming, and at this meeting Hess complained that the farming advisory service of the National Food Estate was interfering with bio-dynamic farms.[19] Between 1936 and 1939, experiments were carried out on feeding infants with organically grown food. Official instructions on agricultural practice began to take account of the need to form humus in the soil. The land planning officer under Himmler, Konrad Meyer (sentenced to seven years at Nuremberg), impressed by the results of the experimental feeding programme, called in 1941 for chemical fertilisers to be forbidden.[20] Meyer, though, disliked the Steiner connection, and preferred 'organic farming' to 'biodynamic agriculture'.[21]

But there was conflict within the Ministry of Agriculture itself on the issue of organic farming. Herbert Backe 'hated the mystic twilight', and wanted the agricultural advisory officials to concentrate on orthodox productivity increases.[22] It was Backe who initiated and publicised the 'Battle for Production' in 1934 (the *Erzeugungschlacht*), a campaign which, despite its militant and grandiose title, included advice on keeping rabbits, hens and geese, and growing fruit trees and fruit bushes. Picture books were produced showing farmer's wives how to do these things. This campaign to use each corner of the farmland and farmyard intensively was successful. Visitors to Germany in these years recall the cabbages planted on roadside verges, while the production figures for rabbit and poultry breeding show substantial growth. The Four-Year Plan, with its étatist, interventionist approach, exacerbated the bias towards scientific farming and mechanisation. In order to induce German farmers to use more chemical fertilisers, there were proposals to lower fertiliser prices by fifty per cent, and increase state credit for mechanising peasant farms: this would release land used for growing fodder for horses.[23]

Backe disagreed with Darré about organic farming: he believed in increasing artificial fertiliser use, though it should be borne in mind that the canons of good farming technique at the time – with which Backe was certainly familiar – called for a balanced use of different kinds of fertilisers (nitrogen, potash and phosphate), not a crude dosing with nitrogen alone. But in practice, Darré's apparent dottiness on this issue ('Darré muttering about organic farming', groaned Backe) would have helped Germany's war effort.[24] Germany exported most of her nitrogen during the war, and war-time productivity began to drop after 1943. A system of organic farming, if adopted well before the war to allow for the temporary drop in productivity caused by the new techniques, would almost certainly have improved agricultural self-sufficiency.[25] The gap between technocrats and organicists was forced wide open by the war. 'It is always the same. Backe thinks in terms of paper and facts, he is étatist and statistical, but not bio-dynamic in orientation', noted Darré in 1940.[26]

Darré, Minister of Agriculture between 1933 and 1942, devoted his last two years as Minister, at a time when his effective power was over, and he had nothing more to lose, to conducting a campaign for organic farming in 1940 and 1941, against the wishes of Backe, Heydrich, Bormann and Goering. In May, 1940, he circulated all members of the National Peasant Council, a group which included Gauleiters, *Reichsleiter*, and *ad hoc* dignitaries, on the desirability of bio-dynamic farming, which he decided to re-label 'organic farming' (*lebensgesetzliche Wirtschaftsweise*), to avoid the connection with Steiner.

> In 1933, my first task was to secure Germany against a blockade. It had to be as quick as possible; there was no time to worry about the right and wrong method. . . I left the question of bio-dynamic farming open, and gave it no publicity. But after the Armistice with France, the danger of Germany's hunger receded, though a continental European blockade was still possible. . . On June 18th, I visited. . . Marienhöhe, and established that is [Steiner's] method is the best. The results speak for themselves. If the scientists and past agricultural teaching cannot explain it, that is their problem. The achievement and the result are ours. I have decided to support bio-dynamic agriculture, without altering my previous course.[27]

This last phrase meant that the Ministry of Agriculture's commitment to the 'Battle for Production' would remain. Darré was, still, at least on paper, a Minister presiding over the fourth largest spending Ministry of the régime, and the care with which he prepared the groundwork for his campaign, – obtaining a broad permission from Goering, who did not realise what was happening – shows his awareness of his weak position.

Darré received comprehensive reports from the Gauleiters of various areas, which showed that many peasants, as well as large farmers, were switching to organic farming techniques. Not all their reports were positive: the Chief of the Civil Administration in Alsace, Wagner, commented in November 1941, that in Baden there were some seventy to eighty peasant farms, and one of 100 ha, which had gone over to bio-dynamic farming, but that performance had dropped by twenty to twenty-five per cent. He pointed out that productivity appeared to drop substantially on a changeover from inorganic to organic methods. On the other hand, the Gauleiter of Koblenz-Trier, an acquaintance of Alwin

Seifert's, was impressed by what he had heard and seen of organic farming.[28] Darré's staff circulated a letter from the chemical giant I.G. Farben, allegedly plotting against organic farmers. The letter disappeared from the files, but was mentioned in a *Der Spiegel* article on Anthroposophy and the National Socialists.[29]

Although warned by Backe that Hitler had advised against protecting members of the now dissolved Reichsverband für biologisch-dynamische Wirtschaftsweise, Darré continued his questionnaire campaign until June 1941. He was sure that he had the support of Himmler. Indeed, one third of the top Nazi leadership supported Darré's campaign: one third only declined to lend support because of the link with Rudolf Steiner and Anthroposophical ideas, and only one third were hostile. A similar result in other countries seems improbable, especially during war-time, and demonstrates the extent to which interest in organic farming had permeated the Nazi as well as the German establishment.

Himmler established experimental organic farms, including one at Dachau, which grew organic herbs for SS medicines. The head of the SS Race and Settlement Office, Gustav Pancke, visited Polish farms in October and November 1939, two months after the German invasion and conquest of Poland, in search of farms that could be farmed organically, and sent detailed reports to Himmler on each one, its fertility, productivity and potential. Himmler's staff sent him papers on B vitamin shortages as a cause of matriarchal societies, together with more serious scientific studies on the effects of trace mineral deficiency on plant genes.[30] Studies were made on the degenerative effect of artificial fertiliser.[31] Himmler looked at the efficacy of nature cures for cancer.[32] In 1943, Himmler's staff commissioned a report on the possibility of making protein from cellulose waste products and yeast.[33] A complete list of all homeopathic doctors in Germany, with their political leanings and biographical details, was compiled for Himmler in 1942 .[34] On Himmler's insistence, anti-vivisection laws were passed. SS training included a respect for animal life of near Buddhist proportions. Konrad Lorenz, who was originally inspired to study zoology by Bölsche's biography of Ernst Haeckel, was able to continue his scientific research after the *Anschluss*, while biological research institutes, like the Kaiser Wilhelm Institute, attracted overseas scholars, who found the emphasis on a holistic approach sympathetic.[35]

Clearly, there was an element of simple continuity in National Socialist support for ecologically sound land planning and organic farming. As in other areas, such as the teaching of history in universities, discontinuities under the Nazis have been exaggerated.[36] Still, the existence of ecological ideologues among the Nazi leadership does show that National Socialism was perceived at the time as a system which had room for ecological ideas. Certainly, Nazism opposed the liberal belief, entrenched under many political labels, that nature and its laws could be transcended by human society. Like ecologists to-day, the nazis opposed capitalism and the consumer-oriented market mechanism. In theory, if not in practice, they supported critiques of mercantilism, and claimed to serve ideals of long-term responsibility, duty and service for the community.

Nonetheless, ecologists were eventually seen as hostile to Germany's national interests by the technocrats among the leadership, especially Heydrich, who interpreted the search for ecological values as essentially treacherous: part of the pre-Third Reich yearning for a pan-Aryan, non-national identity of a 'soft', oriental kind. He set the Security Service to harass organic farmers, as well as fringe groups such as the nudists. But this was shortly before Hitler's invasion of Russia, at a time of national emergency, and Hess's flight to England was obviously a factor in tainting all such groups with treason in the eyes of the Gestapo. Was this the triumph of one ideology over another? Surely, it should rather be seen as a result, temporary and non-contingent, as it would seem, of the imperatives of war-time.

I described earlier how the agricultural adviser for the British Union of Fascists moved in about 1944 from a polemical and technocratic programme to a strikingly ecological, 'soft' attitude. The same cannot be said of Walther Darré. His views remained the same mixture of practicality, rejection of Steiner as unproven, and support for small farmers, as before. However, he was enthusiastic over the writings of Lady Eve Balfour, whose book *The Living Soil* he reviewed in 1953, and the English Soil Association. He attempted to start a similar group for Germany after his release from prison, when his first contact was with a biodynamic farmer, but decided that his connection would lend it a 'Nazi taint'. His protection for Anthroposophists during the war was repaid greatly by their help and support for his family and for him immediately after his release. The utterly unpolitical nature of Steiner's followers, their rejection of organised activity and disdain for external labelling, can be seen by their dedication both in continuing to oppose the Third Reich when it was in power, and – at a small but significant level – in repaying help from one of its leading members when he was sick and powerless.

Anthroposophists were present at a meeting held in England in 1950 to propagate a joint Anglo-German venture for ecological ideals. They included Ehrenfried Pfeiffer, author of a book on biodynamic farming in 1938, inspirer of Lord Lymington. The Catholic Minister for Refugees, Professor Theodore Oberländer, who had visited Russia in 1931 to examine their agriculture, and had been an adviser for the SS and the National Food Estate during the war, was also present. (He was later to resign his office when his war-time position was publicised by the East Germans.) The initiative petered out, but contacts remained.[38]

It was in its 'Back to the Land' programme that the Third Reich achieved its greatest and most puzzling mixture of continuity, similarity with other countries, and drastic differences. It also presents a confused picture of success and failure.

The land settlement programme was essential for Nazi plans to create a rural Germany. It would sweep away the old nobility by enforcing land division. It would install a new peasant nobility. However, between 1933 and 1938 the number of new small farm units created annually declined. The failure to implement the programme has been attributed to Junker power, to re-industrialisation and to rearmament, with its resulting shortage of agricultural labour and land. However, a study of it shows that institutional and financial factors were more important. These problems were embedded in the basic concept of the Back-to-the-Land movement in Germany, and to this extent it was a flawed vision.

The major difference between the Nazi programme and Britain's, for example (as exemplified in Britain's Smallholding Act and later agricultural protection) is the racial emphasis of the former. The racial-cum-tribal element in Britain was hardly ever articulated. But in both countries such an emphasis was redundant. While land was a favoured investment in England and to some extent Germany, in neither country did immigrants wish to settle as agricultural labourers or farmers on small, fixed-tenure, non-alienable holdings. It was the descendants of those who had left the land, decades or generations ago, who wished in England to return.

Some aspects of this agrarian revival are comparable to Eastern Europe, Bulgaria, Hungary and Poland; others relate to the post-First World War distaste for the industrialised world seen in Britain at the same time. In the 1920s, land settlement was part of utopian left as well as nationalist right programmes; the German allotment movement acquired a wide following. Planned demographic consolidation of thinly populated farmland had been German policy since Frederick the Great's time; he had imported Dutch and Frisian colonists to settle the Mark of Brandenburg.

Loss of agricultural labour, to emigration abroad and to towns, had diminished the tax base of several German states. Fear of Polish migration from the East was another factor in encouraging the promotion of rural settlement. During the 1920s the Polish government established armed 'Poniatowski' villages on its border with Germany, after buying out German farmers (with worthless government scrip). Although Weimar Germany maintained the rhetoric of anti-Polish demographic settlement, they did not have the clout to enforce it. The Third Reich did, but this time the emphasis was on creating a yeoman peasantry all over Germany, not only in the relatively under-populated Eastern areas.

What was distinctly ecological about the planned creation of a new German peasantry was the reasoning behind it. Agrarian radicals saw the American dust-bowl and agricultural depression as the vindication of their dislike of capitalistic agriculture. The creation of a strong, self-reliant class of yeomen peasants was seen as a cure-all for various social, economic and moral evils.

The Weimar Constitution had contained a clause promising smallholdings to all applicants, and during the Depression the rural population had been swelled by returning industrial workers. But while numerically impressive, these holdings were small and under-capitalised. The rhetorical thrust of the radical agrarian Nazis was rather different. They wanted Germany to be part of a Northern Europe peasant international. The unit of settlement was the medium-sized farm of 7 to 125 hectares. Earlier settlements were to be enlarged and improved to conform to this ideal. In order to prevent foreclosures and partition, farms were to be inalienable. Banks could not foreclose upon them, and descent was to the eldest son. Sub-division was forbidden, but younger sons had first call upon new settlements. If farms were not run to the satisfaction of a local committee of agricultural advisers and experts, they could be seized. Finally, farmers had to be of 'German or similar' descent.

This incorporated a large-scale attack on capitalistic economic and property relationships. The belief was that foreign trade and industrialisation had been designed by manipulative capitalists to force the rural population into towns to produce finished industrial goods in order to export them in exchange for raw materials. The system, they believed, had been expressly intended to prevent local autonomy, barter and self-sufficiency. The remedy, they believed, was the ruralisation of Germany. This was not seen as merely a distant utopia. It was thought that the industrial world, whose infrastructural base had substantially diminished during the Depression, was not sustainable.

Apocalyptic conclusions were drawn from the American experience of the period – the dust-bowl, the apparent seizure of an advanced technological society, just as the oil-price increases of the 1970s fed apocalyptic fears of energy starvation. The specific and characteristically National Socialist argument was that second and third generation city dwellers were deemed to have lost their capability to live on the land as German peasants. Once the network of kinship and tradition had been broken it could not be restored simply by moving city-dwellers to the land and telling them they were peasants again. Nazis like Darré stressed the distinction between their vision of a peasant Europe, in which cities would have decayed and disappeared, and the 'urban intellectual homestead romanticism' which by creating suburbia on the land would merely corrupt the countryside.[39] This was an ideological development that had not taken place in England, but which resembles arguments used about peasant life in the Third World today.

PART FOUR

THE NEW AGE

CHAPTER ELEVEN

Greens, Reds and Pagans

But tell me Nymphs, what power divine
Shall henceforth wash the river Rhine?

(S.T. Coleridge, 'Cologne')

What produced the flowering of the ecological movement? In the early 1970s the finite resource arguments fused with the biological argument. Today it is often thought that the oil crisis of the early 1970s seemed to prove the economic ecologist argument beyond doubt. The West's dependence on this finite resource seemed very clear when an abrupt rise in price created shortages and economic depression. The long-term implications of a shortage of mineral resources could be impressed clearly on the public mind.

However, the emergence of finite resources as a global issue predated the oil crisis. In 1972 a report was presented to the United Nations World Conference on the Human Environment by Barbara Ward and Rene Dubos.[1] It argued that man had to replace family or national loyalties with a sense of allegiance to the planet. It preached imminent doom through man's technological capacity. The book prophesied that children alive then would see the global crisis take inescapable shape. The Club of Rome was also founded in 1972. It too prophesied imminent global catastrophe, unless resource use was curbed, and resources shared .

The ideal of global planning of resources had emerged well before the Second World War. Later bodies that embodied this ideal, like the United Nations and its subsidiaries, had begun the post-war era full of hope. Yet their scope had grown in almost direct proportion to their increasing powerlessness over Third World countries. Fears of their over-population increased in the 1960s.[2] Theories of increasing immiserisation continued in parallel with increasing population growth and prosperity. The stage was set for academic arguments about inter-generational allocation of resources to affect the public. To do this the media had to present ecological issues seriously. The mass media had not done so before. It was helped to do so now by well-organised, massively-financed conferences, conference reports and press releases from authoritative-sounding bodies. The mixture of vague alarm about forthcoming doom and convincing statistics extrapolated from current experience proved irresistible. Instead of having to deal with isolated or irritable conservative thinkers who puzzlingly bucked the progressive trend, the media now dealt with intellectuals who spoke and understood the jargon of growth, but turned it on its head. Those who absorbed economic ecologism did so because of their values, their love of countryside and animals. They found in economic ecologism a legitimation of these values, which were no longer presented as a selfish, middle-class luxury. Here were scientifically backed and quantified arguments. Instead of feeling guilty for wanting to preserve nature, that desire was a means to save the world from catastrophe. The oil crisis of 1973–4 seemed a rapid vindication of economic ecologism. The fusion of green values with resource fears had taken place.

It was also necessary that the ecological movement be freed of the elements that had been mocked or feared previously.[3] Up to the end of the 1960s the link between far right groups and alternative, organic movements was stressed by those interested in the characteristics and psychology of extremism. In Europe and in North America during the 1960s, the major political parties were committed to growth, size and efficiency. Labour and Conservative parties vied to capture this ground. To make ecologism acceptable to the media and the intelligentsia of the time, it had to lose its middle-class values-oriented image, and, in Britain, drop any vestige of English cultural nationalism. It had to become universalist. It had to move into acceptable patterns of political discourse, and, ironically, could only do so by becoming left-radical. Some existing forms of alternative politics could be absorbed. Celtic nationalism, feminist exclusivism and anti-paternalism fitted the pattern of opposition to what was presented as the Western values of paternalism, greed and exploitation. The process of matching radical politics to the new ecologism differed in different countries.

The German connection with ecology was partly through the holistic and organic tradition of German medicine and biology and partly through bio-dynamic agriculture. It encompassed a current of agrarian ruralism shared spiritually with England, and finally the philosophical and cultural yearning for Greek or Buddhist oneness with nature.

In pursuing the genesis of post-war ecologism, the German influence re-emerges in the shape of anti-Nazi emigrés. Fritz Schumacher, author of *Small is Beautiful,* arrived in England in 1939, and worked as an agricultural labourer for some time during the war, before being whisked to high office as an economist for the nationalised coal industry after the war. Schumacher was, of course, opposed to Nazism. However, he came with a full complement of the German intellectual luggage of his time. He became chairman of the Soil Association in 1971, and the Schumacher Society Lectures, which have publicised a range of alternative ideas, were established in his memory.[4]

In post-war England, reconstruction was based on the welfare-state plans of utopian socialists. The rhetoric of a New Jerusalem suggested Blake, Ruskin and the early Morris. It implied a return to rural life and pre-industrial values. However, the rhetoric was appropriated and enunciated by left-wing intellectuals such as Harold Laski and E.H. Carr, in whom the 'Little England' cultural patrotism and nationalist idealism of the earlier Labour Party were absent.

The new town planners despised rather than admired Gothic architecture and thatched cottages. The new towns built after the Second World War showed no trace of Ruskin's influence. The small-scale rustic charm of Bournville and Letchworth was absent in Stevenage, Basildon and Bletchley. There was a real hatred of everything Victorian. The honesty of concrete replaced the honesty of stone and timber. The plans for a new world expressed only the ugly side of the collectivist, socialist tradition, a side that was to culminate in the wholesale destruction of British towns and cities in the 1960s. The vision of Ruskin and Morris had little to do with the socialism of Balogh and Kaldor, with the five-year plans proposed in *Picture Post.*

> In presenting the sun-lit Britain of the future. . .an aerial view of an existing town with its streets of little terrace houses on one page faced on the next *an architect's vision of tomorrow's city of glass and concrete geometrically laid out in wide grassy spaces.*[5]

The search for English values, for English spirit and nature-tradition which had dominated conservationist sentiment in the 1930s and early 1940s was moribund. For many involved and influential people the desire to find and preserve rural values and roots was tainted by the image of the Third Reich. Public expression of this urge was killed stone dead by the revelations about

Nazi atrocities appearing almost daily. For the home-grown English folk movement, as for the school of 'organic' biologists in Chicago, it was fatal. The foundation of specifically English patriotism that underlay the conservationist movement was cut away. From 1944–5 on many of its adherents moved away entirely from politics or ideas of political action.[6]

In spite of the reliance on scientists and their wisdom which characterised the post-war world, some conservationist initiatives emerged. In 1949 the Nature Conservancy Council was established. Its brief included the creation and management of nature reserves and ecological research. One of its founders, Professor Charles Elton, had written standard university works on animal ecology. He extrapolated from animals to man in his interest in preserving a stable and balanced environment.[7] But during the 1950s, after over ten years of rationing, shortages and general if low-grade privation, few in Britain were interested in preservation. The Nature Conservancy Council experienced an important internal revolution in the late 1960s, designed to change it, according to the radicals, from a powerless, underfunded group of elderly conservationists to a politicised, dynamic pressure group, worried about mounting threats to the biosphere.

The Nature Conservancy Council was a statutory agency developed with pressure from the Royal Society for Nature Conservation.[8] With less land in the hands of large estates and more run by practising farmers, the structure of agricultural marketing and land use was possibly more relevant to the preservation of the countryside. In this sector, pre-war price maintenance and marketing boards survived. A policy of protecting marginal hill farms was pursued, while a system of price subsidy helped British farmers and kept food prices low. Smallholding legislation was kept on the statute books, and the small number created were successful, although their envisaged purpose of providing a stepping-stone from small to large farms failed.

However, government quangos of all kinds were powerless to halt the infrastructural development of the 1950s. Where they had power, competing lobbyists and pressure groups rendered them inoperative, as their role could only be virtually to sabotage the efforts of governments devoted to growth, size and social reform of various kinds.

Media (if not public) imagination was caught more by the intermediate technology initiatives of Schumacher and John Papworth, adviser to Kenneth Kaunda of Zambia after independence, pacifist, and editor of *Resurgence*, an anarchist and pacifist journal in the 1960s.[9] The Intermediate Technology (IT) movement opposed much of the big-is-beautiful ethic of its time. It was an ethic that assumed, in a crude extrapolation from Marxist ideology, that large firms must crush small firms; that the independent small business, like the individual, was finished. Intermediate Technology was directed at the Third World, and argued that development projects geared to heavy industry, advanced technology and the 'big' were unsuitable to the social infrastructure of undeveloped countries (as they were then known). Schumacher's group wanted well made fishing nets instead of factory fishing ships; wells and pumps instead of dams and hydroelectricity plants. It implied, too, that the West was guilty in forcing its high-technology projects on to poor countries, and that the cultural destruction involved was too high a price to pay for a progress that was in any case largely illusory. IT was not just a criticism of unsuitable aid projects but a criticism of the technology and ethic that had created them Not only was the West guilty of creating poverty through colonialism, it compounded the guilt through destroying the habits and milieu of simple peasants. That such destructive effects should be envisaged through exporting Western culture implied a loss of faith in it. One reason for doubt was that after the Second World War, expensive technology was identified with the USA. It was therefore seen as alien to Europe. Thus the entire anti-American lobby was available for mobilization on this issue.

But if washing machines and cars were deleterious to Africans, were they suitable for Surbiton? As the standard of living rose in Britain and America, the problem of the positional good arose, too. By this was meant the conundrum that some goods could only be enjoyed if they were confined to a few; cars and motor travel were the classic example. Some libertarian writers attributed aristocratic malice to the socialist anti-technology movement. It was alleged to want a world of impoverished serfs in which only th educated planner-king enjoys port and motor-rides to the rural heartlands. However, anyone who lived through the cultural decline of the 1950s and 1960s can very well understand why it should have found opposition. The conceptual problem lay in trying to stem techological advance at any one time. Small computers are as beautiful as small wells.

THE ORGANIC FARMING MOVEMENT IN ENGLAND

Disparate alternative groups were shattered by the war until the

1960s; pacifism, conscientious objection and conservationism had emerged as the most unpopular pressure groups. But the period 1944–5 saw the founding of an important single-issue group which kept ecological issues alive during the 1950s and 1960s. Lady Eve Balfour, niece of Arthur Balfour, started the Haughley experimental farms in 1939 to test the claims that organic matter incorporated into the soil produced better results, and inorganic fertilisers, pesticides and weed-killers worse results. The farms were brought into existence by a sympathetic woman landowner, who donated two farms at Haughley for this purpose. Followers of Rudolf Steiner gradually increased in number, and formed a powerful network of alternative sympathisers, some of whom were involved in the Soil Association.

The importance of the Soil Association is that it brought together at the end of Second World War the various groups and people worried about soil erosion, soil fertility, pollution and chemicals-based agriculture. They described themselves as ecologists. The Soil Association is still in existence. Together with various research groups such as the Henry Doubleday Association, it concentrated on research into the effects of chemical pollutants, advice to members, the circulation of books and pamphlets and locally based groups. Organic farmers could be put in touch with each other through the Association. Many family farms which had always farmed according to older ways were helped to survive by SA advertising and publicity for their products.

This group, the first effectively organised ecological pressure group in the United Kingdom, had its genesis among the pre-war ecologists described earlier. In 1938, the Earl of Portsmouth held a conference at his house to plan organic experiments. From this emerged the Kinship in Husbandry circle run by Rolf Gardiner. Several of the landowners present did establish organic methods on their own estates. Lord Northbourne, Sir Albert Howard, George Stapleton (as early as 1935) and Lord Lymington had all written books before 1940 which opposed mechanisation and chemicals in farming, wanted Britain to be self-sufficient in agriculture, and spoke of ecological dangers. In 1944 a book appeared which brought together the ecological sympathisers. Lady Eve Balfour described in *The Living Soil* the web of energy use and fertility creation, from sun to soil, to micro-organisms and worms, to plant and animal life, finally to man. Her picture of the ecological food chain conformed to extant 'normal' biological descriptions, but had a persuasive moral force. She used the work of Howard in India to urge the virtues of compost heaps and organically-grown food. Monoculture was attacked. The Haughley farms were designed to complement the Rothamstead experimental soil plots, which had experimented with the effects of chemical fertiliser and organic manures since the early 1800s. The Haughley group criticised Rothamstead for errors of methodology; the plots were too small and new seed was used each year, variables which they claimed affected the experiments. The Haughley farms followed the German Anthroposophical farms of the 1930s in their composition and experimental method, although the bio-dynamic element in organic farming was generally played down. However, the ecological vision was the same; Alwin Seifert's bio-dynamic paper and appeals to the German Ministry of Agriculture in 1936 stressed the same belief in mulching, non-ploughing farming methods, the same opposition to single crops and weed eradication. The existence of this group, and especially the arguments in Lady Eve Balfour's book of 1944, emphasise the long tradition of ecological awareness.

In June 1945 the Soil Association was formally created. Lord Teviot was the first president. Jorian Jenks, formerly agricultural adviser to Mosley, was editorial secretary of the Soil Association journal, *Mother Earth*, until 1963. During this period he published several ecological books, including *We are What We Eat*, an influential study of the effect of pesticides and additives on man. Rolf Gardiner and Lord Lymington were on the Council, together with Laurence Easterbrook, ex-agricultural correspondent of the *News Chronicle*, who edited *Feeding the Fifty Million* in 1955. Jenks advised Easterbrook about the practicality of its recommendations, which included measures to help the rural population with electrification and cheap energy methane gas plants.[10] A prominent supporter of Anthroposophy, Maye Bruce, was also on the Council, and her influence apeared from time to time in the journal with articles on vegetarian compost made with yarrow flowers gathered in moonlight.

The members of the Soil Association were described in interviews in 1970–71 as criticising orthodox science, as looking for a creed of 'wholeness'. Members referred to vitalist Hans Driesch and Bergson, the existentialist philosopher, one member indeed describing the Soil Association's philosophy as 'neo-vitalist'.[11]

Towards the end of the 1960s the Soil Association leadership shifted emphasis. Barry Commoner, the American environmentalist who saw multi-national corporations as responsible for forcing unwanted and unnecessary technology down people's throats, became Vice-President. Commoner took the left-wing side in the debate about scarce resources which developed in the 1960s. Garrett Hardin, a right-libertarian ecologist, wrote in an influential arcticle that without property rights resources, especially land, would not be used economically and with care for its future.[12] Population pressure was cited at this time as a cause of imminent over-population and famine. Anti-capitalist ecologists argued rather that distribution was at fault, and Commoner was at the forefront of the drive to take control of technology and production from 'big business'. Michael Allaby edited the journal, renamed in 1968 *Journal of the Soil Association*, from 1971 to 1973–4. He developed a left-ecologist viewpoint. He was to become involved in Edward Goldsmith's *Ecologist*, and in 1981 was co-author of *The Politics of Self-Sufficiency*.

With Schumacher's appointment a key change of attitude had taken place among the conservative conservationists. Practical agrarian reform and organic farming was soon replaced as a political aim by the egalitarian socio-economic re-structuring we associate today with ecologists. The Soil Association now published a handful of articles admiring Mao's communes, and suggesting that plots of land a few acres in size be distributed among the population. The self-sufficiency books of John Seymour, who described how to run a small-holding, were attacked by radical reformers who thought that small-holdings of 60 acres should be parcelled out among ten families.[13] Under the later guidance of Secretary David Strickland the Soil Association reverted to its original preoccupation, organic farming. The gap between farming organically and growing small vegetable plots and gardens was, however, hard to bridge, and dislike of 'muck and mystery' persisted among farmers and Ministry of Agriculture officials. But with persistence and amid growing publicity about the harm of pesticide residues and food additives, the health food movement began to expand towards the end of the 1970s.

A smaller version of the Soil Association existed in France. Its journal, *Nature et progrès* was like a carbon copy of *Mother Earth* and both resembled the German *Demeter*, which had begun again in the 1950s. The French version was completely independent, but used the same bio-dynamic works of Pfeiffer and others as inspiration. In Germany 'Demeter' became the name of a health food chain and organic movement in general, and branches were opened overseas. Demeter remained an Anthroposophical group, although it did not attempt to recruit for the movement as such.

The intellectual core of the British ecological movement during the 1960s and 1970s was with the *Ecologist*, a journal edited and financed by the brother of Sir James Goldsmith, the multimillionaire businessman. The most cogent arguments for ecological problems and policies, drawn from writers familiar with philosophical traditions as well as scientific data, appeared in his journal. The American influence on the treatment of the subject in the British media has led to an undervaluation of Edward Goldsmith's work, but his *Blueprint for Survival*, with its draconian policies for cutting population numbers, does face up to the problems inherent in cutting down on resource use and mechanised food production.

THE GREENS IN GERMANY

The relationship between the health food movement in German and the green movement is more complex. The green protest movement emerged from the organised left-wing student protest movement of 1968. Anthroposophists were a particular target of the protesters in German universities, and bitter attacks were launched on them for their alleged authoritarian tendencies and 'social fascist' beliefs.[14] What was anarcho-communism in the Berkeley of 1968 split between organised terrorism (Hitler's Children, as one author called them) and alternative groups, Marcuse's Children, perhaps.[15] During the 1970s, anti-nuclear movements, anti-American groups, the feminist movement, all the so-called 'citizen's initiatives', had no clear focus, but mobilised between them a large number of middle class supporters. Opposed to authority and what were seen as patriarchal, middle-class values, many of the protesters moved into communes. By independent routes, they came to the same concern for environmental values as their grandparents. The rhetoric of environmentalism carried uncomfortable overtones for the German conservative. Calls for the German soul, for re-unification of East and West Germany, for neutralism, for a 'Third Way', were too similar to the 1920s for comfort. Where had late capitalist society gone wrong, to be so criticised? The theory of marginality was produced. The functional logic of late capitalist society, argued academics, alienated certain marginal groups; the physically handicapped, the mentally handicapped, the unemployed and – the ecologists.[16] However, far from being a marginal part of German society, the new ecologists represented its most secure and comfortable section, the middle-class *Beamten*; the schoolteachers and civil servants who made up the majority of the alternative supporters.

Indeed, straight ecological issues re-emerged in mid-1970s Germany as a conservative cause. It was Herbert Gruhl, member of the Christian Democratic group, whose *The Plundering of a Planet* became a bestseller in 1975. Gruhl, who had been involved in the Club of Rome's 1972 *The Limits to Growth*, was pessimistic about growth and economic competition. Capitalism and Communism were fighting to plunder and destroy the eco-system. In becoming anti-earth they had become anti-human. In 1976, opinion polls in Germany among the young showed that technology was seen as a boon by fifty per cent. By 1981, it was thus seen by only by thirty per cent.[17]

In 1977, anti-nuclear 'citizen's initiative' groups moved from mass demonstrations and other pressure group activity in the early 1970s to *Land* (state) candidatures. The first 'Green List' party was in Lower Saxony, with a strong environmental protection slant. A year later, the resignation of the leader expressed the shift to a more concentrated anti-nuclear platform. In 1978 Hamburg saw a convention of various alternative list groups. This convention was named the Rainbow group, because all the alternative groups had their own colours; purple for the women's movement, black for the anarchists and so on. The German Communist Party attended the convention. One of their publications in October 1978 even claimed that the alternative list had been 'subsumed by the CP'.[18] The Maoists of Hamburg were also represented in the alternative list, and are unlikely to have remained in a group controlled by the Communist Party. Their joint inclusion, however, is of some significance.

The name 'Green' struck a chord in Britain, but the instinctive sympathy felt towards them rested in part on a cultural confusion. 'Green' in English carries a connotation of old rural myth. The Green Man was the god of the woods. 'Green' is linked with late spring. It is the colour of English meadows, the prevailing colour of the countryside. In Germany the word was more of a convenient label, an equivalent to the purple, the black and the red. Since a colour had to be found, 'Green' was used. If anything, it carried an ironic tinge of rural idiocy. Green Henry, a German-language folk hero, was an innocent fool, a saintly rural simpleton.

The Rainbow List received three and-a-half per cent of the Hamburg vote and the Green List, still conservative-oriented, only 1 per cent. The Berlin alternative list was Maoist-dominated in 1978, but later attracted Socialist Bureau members. The Schleswig-Holstein Green List had a more agrarian flavour, one missing from other Green groups, then and now; it was led by a practising farmer, who wanted to ban fascist and communist members.

In June 1979 the Greens became a Party. The Green Party first fought the European Parliamentary election in 1979, and then the German federal elections in 1980. Their delegates came from anthroposophical groups in Baden, Gruhl's Green Future Action, the Green Alternative List and the Action Association. Herbert Gruhl, Rudolf Bahro and Otto Schily were the best-known members. It thus included a wide cross-section of political views.

However, the conservative element soon left, while the Greens found that they had attracted unexpected support from the far Right. Anti-capitalist German nationalists formed themselves into a Green cell in Berlin. When uncovered, they were expelled, but the fact that they could present themselves as Green without causing comment is of itself significant. One Green representative resigned after a row erupted over his past as an SS man in the 1930s. The clash between the fundamentalist ideals of the Greens and the democracy of Parliamentary processes put their potential co-operation in some doubt, while the refusal of the Green leadership to disavow militancy led to some commentators in the early 1980s seeing them as dangerous revolutionaries. In their early days in Parliament organised heckling and self-conscious ridiculing of governmental methods were common with Green representatives and their followers. They have on the whole, however, adopted the non-violent mass protest tactics of the CND, not the violent student protests of 1968.

In the non-party political sphere, Left and Right meet on the issue of ecological values. Yet to determine these values remains difficult. Green policies focus on the issue of nuclear power and nuclear bombs. There is concern about acid rain and the Black Forest. But calls for one car-free day a week, and for no more motorway building are far from the radical socio-economic proposals of ecologists elsewhere. Instead, the left-oriented Greens call for participatory democracy, egalitarianism within the movement, women's rights and an end to unemployment. Green representatives display impressive debating skills when dealing with the kind of politician who will explain to them that they represent marginalism in late capitalist society. But they seem less impressive at producing proposals for general environmental improvement. What ideas about, for example, the need for a Social Wage do demonstrate is the Greens' inheritance of egalitarian left-wing energy economics. Popper-Lynkeus was cited by the speaker for the Greens in the Baden-Württemberg Parliament in 1986 as the progenitor of this idea (although, as Milton Friedman was also called in to add credit to green economics, some doubt remains about the validity of this claim).[19]

In short, the German Greens do not seem very green at all compared to single issue ecological groups; and the most green element in them, Gruhl's conservationist movement, split off in 1981. Given the evidence of opinion polls on green issues, especially the German forest it is surprising that the Red-Greens and Green-Reds have come to dominate their party.[20] Much of the remaining left-wing ideology was made acceptable through charismatic leaders like Petra Kelly, and the religious poetics of Rudolf Bahro.

Kelly is one of the best known Green leaders, together with the Party's fundamentalist ideologue, Rudolf Bahro, who resigned in 1984. Bahro was a dissident in East Germany, where he was imprisoned for some years. His book *The Alternative in Eastern Europe* was a best-seller in the West. His works are sometimes almost imcomprehensible, with their Marxist terminology forced to accept non-Marxist meanings, and sometimes full of the declamatory rhetoric which characterises the German radical. Bahro was one of the first Greens to realise that party-political participation would render Green ideology impure through compromise with 'the system'.

Kelly is an attractively sincere orator, who was brought up and educated mostly in America. Despite an American political style of lobbying and campaigning, and an American set of political left-liberal values, she has, paradoxically, captured the anti-Americanism of German youth. Her political position is presented with a simple emotion rather than argument. She is not an intellectual, and lacks any compensating component of common sense or analytical ability. Her account of the sufferings of female secretaries in the EEC (they have to commute, sit still all day, type letters), who notoriously earn a great deal for doing very little, is an example of the crude feminism of her arguments, as is her claim that the thalidomide tragedy 'shows how lethal the policies of male researchers and male politicians have been'.[21] But her speeches brought together the general feeling that something was wrong, without alienating the general public through specific proposals. Her political naivety and freshness, too, helped the Greens avoid being seen as a sinisterly committed radical left group.

The well-known 'rotation' rule of the Greens provides another clue as to their increasing popularity. There is little doubt that cynicism about party politics exists. The spectacle of Green representatives actually giving up position so that their comrades can have their turn impresses, even if it meant classing Petra Kelly as an honorary man to let other women have their turn.

The chief representatives of the realist wing are Joschka Fischer, who by 1987 was Minister of the Environment in Hesse, and Otto Schily, representative in the German Federal Parliament. Schily's parents belonged to the upper echelons of German industrial society and his father is said to be an Anthroposophist. They were educated at a Rudolf Steiner 'Waldorf School'. (Schily's brother recently founded one of West Germany's few private universities.) Schily was a left-wing lawyer who appeared on behalf of German terrorists in trials during the 1970s.[22]

The disaster at Chernobyl in 1986 led many observers to expect a rush of support for the Greens. The Greens took advantage of this fulfilment of one of their main prophecies to launch a full economic party-programme, and decide against coalition with the S.P.D. The programme called for full employment and nationalisation of the steel industry, neither policy remotely green. However, in the *Land* elections of the summer of 1986 they did less well than expected. The January elections of 1987 produced a vote averaging eight per cent, better than before but less high than had been hoped. In Hesse, May 1987, it was 9.4 per cent.

Currently, the Greens have successfully overcome the first hurdle of radical parties, multiple fission. Their coalition contains the Red-Greens, the Green-Reds, the eco-libertarian wing represented by Hasenclaver, the eco-socialists like Schily, fundamentalists, realists and Buddhist revivalists. What is more of a problem is that the major German parties have stolen many of their green clothes, and now talk about qualitative not quantitative growth, and the need to curb pollution. A change of atmosphere and piecemeal reform are not enough for the alternative movement, who demand job quotas for women and an end to American bases in Europe.

Another problem is that the split between Green factions represents a deeper clash of attitudes than can easily be contained by one party. For example, there is an element of folk-nationalism in the Greens, focused on the old peasant ideal. Antje Vollmer, one of the *Frauenliste* representatives, supports a policy of agricultural subvention, and her department was responsible for a poster showing what another Green critic described as an 'idealised peasant, a phallic German acorn and the obligatory sunflower'.[23] Her critic here, Jo Müller, was a representative of urban Green socialism, while Vollmer has called on Gruhl, the conservative ecologist, to rejoin the Greens. Vollmer also suggested that subsidies currently paid to the deep-sea fishermen of Bremen should be paid instead to farmers, on the grounds that the personnel manning the fishing-boats were not German.[24] Clearly a potential rift exists in policy between those who want the egalitarian sharing of scarce resources, on an international basis, using the tools, techniques and rhetoric of traditional economic socialism; and those who, in accordance with what is for many the green image, seek a local, ethnic or tribal autarkic protectionism.

It is perhaps a fear, indeed a terror, of this potential return to small-scale European nationalism that has caused the Greens to be attacked as potential terrorists and anti-semites from time to time, since such a system tends towards exclusivity. One such attack was from Israel's ambassador to Bonn in 1984, after Greens planned to meet the PLO.[25] A Freudian psychiatrist, Jannine Chasseguet-Smirgel, accused the Greens of wanting to write out of history the Nazi murders of the Jews; and claimed that Green interest in air pollution was a sub-conscious reference to the gassing of the Jews, and that they claimed that Germans were in danger of suffocation through air pollution in order to hide their feelings of guilt at having (via their parents and grandparents at least) gassed the Jews.[26] Whatever one may think of the idea that sub-conscious guilt feelings can be passed down through the generations – via the blood, the genes or the collective subsonscious is not explained – it is plain that by some Greens are seen as in danger of breaching one of the main conventions of Western democracy since the war, the centrality of the Jewish experience under the Nazis. This is not because there is actual anti-semitism among the Greens, or support for Nazi crimes such as Auschwitz, but because they implicitly turn their backs on so many of the old Enlightenment ideas: progress, emancipation, growth and utilitarianism.

Yet in some ways the German Greens *do* correspond to the model of the traditional urban radical. When the Greens first breached the five per cent barrier and qualified for public funding, they immediately donated much of the money to typically left-wing causes and groups. The anti-nuclear groups, Third World lobbyists and immigrant workers all received funds. This was not obviously in accordance with ecological policies. Had the money gone towards tree-planting or river cleaning the ecological stance would have been more convincing. And after all, Green power does not depend on the support of marginalised groups such as foreign workers, who do not have a vote in Germany, or the disabled, who are not politically mobilised. Their attempt to create a new socialist order based on compassion for these groups is therefore not essential for their power base. Their leftward emphasis may be linked with the influence on the socialist Greens of the economists and philosophers emerging from the failed (and polluting) socialisms of the Eastern bloc. That third way so much sought after this century is put forward not only by disenchanted ex-Marxists like Bahro, but also by men like Ota Sik, the 'reform communist' who tried to give Czech socialism a human face.[27] Realos, apparently moderates in their support of parliamentary proceedings, include originally far-left figures like Frankfurt communard, Danny Cohn-Bendit, ex-student leader in the violent protest movement of 1968, and Otto Schily. But the call for a third way is also seen as a means of avoiding the past.

The most telling criticism of the Red-Green path is the defection of Bahro, the movement's philosopher. Bahro, unlike many Greens, has been searching for a broad green tradition. He quotes Thoreau, Robert Graves and Lao Tse, as well as Rilke, Hölderlin and Thomas Münzer, leader of the sixteenth-century peasants revolt. Through writing and lectures, his influence, unlike other German Greens, is powerful outside Germany, and especially in America.[28]

THE AMERICAN MOVEMENT

After the failure of the student movement of 1968, some Berkeley activists found a new cause. Marxist criticisms of alienation and reification combined with a Reichian critique of hard, paternalist insensitivity. Rachel Carson's 1966 *Silent Spring* had demonstrated the existence of an astonishing degree of pollution of North America's vast and fertile sub-continent. The young radicals now claimed that it was multi-national capitalism that was responsible for pollution. It was the positive value behind this socialist criticism that provided a non-party, catch-all popularity among America's affluent middle-class. At last radical socialism could combine with aesthetic values. The urban proletariat was no longer God; it would, indeed, be abolished altogether. Political action in the form of campaigning against ecological damage could now morally be carried out from a comfortable suburb. The 'pink-diaper babies' found Marcuse more spiritually appealing than Marx. While reputable scientists like the Ehrlichs and Barry Commoner drew attention to pollution that was real enough (however unreal and indeed disproven their prophecies of disaster), anarcho-communist Murray Bookchin, his books circulated by the Schumacher Book Centre, wrote of a utopian communard future in which scarcity would disappear, when man returned to living close to the land.

Since 1970, and Charles Reich's *The Greening of America*, which foretold a return to rurality which has not occurred, the American ecological movement has gone through many stages, in a weirdly speeded-up version of the slow growth and development of ecologism elsewhere. The American feminists took up ecology. It fitted their belief that there had once been a matriarchal paradise, which nurtured the earth and encouraged universal harmony. Technophobe ecologists, who praised the most marginal Third World tribes, but could not manage on their communes without washing machines and videos, clashed with technophiles, who saw solar power and computers as energy efficient. 'Deep ecology', a non-party political search for Buddhist-type harmony soon had its violent splinter movement, the eco-teurs, who specialised in sabotaging industrial plants.[29] With technocratic gusto, plans for 'bio-regions' were drawn up by men who had never heard of Lewis Mumford. These regions would be self-sufficient areas which provided their own water and fuels, converted their sewage and garbage to usable fertiliser and heating, and grew their own crops. Gardens in towns would grow vegetables and fruit trees.

One of the important aspects of the bio-region plan is that nation-state and other boundaries would be superseded by geopolitical ones. Who is to plan these new areas, how large they are to be, and who is to police the boundaries to make sure that no apples are transported beyond them is neither disclosed nor costed. So far, these plans have not been quantified in terms of population-carrying capacity. Certainly, there seems no reason why ecologists should not establish such areas in the fertile parts of America or Africa, just as ecological and anthroposophist merchant banks have been established in Europe, and barter areas set up in an island off Vancouver. However, for some reason Greens appear bad at self-sufficiency. Some alternative communes are unable to support themselves on three hundred acres of land, although Cobbett's smallholders could do it on five. Ecologists seem to need more of earth's resources than other people. One reason may be the participatory democracy, because attending meetings every evening is time-consuming.[30]

The various Ecotopias (and the *Blueprint for Survival* drawn up by Goldsmith in England) do assume that the limit for population has been reached. Many ecologists argue that to be viably self-sufficient, countries like England are over-populated. The ideal population for North America has not been stated, but the ecotopias presume a low-density population, something that seems to beg the question, for if industry, towns and mechanised farming can support a larger population than low-density housing and peasant farming, what then becomes of the argument that they are a means of exploiting and worsening the environment of the masses?[31]

American ecologists seem to have come to the movement afresh. More than in Europe they have ignored their ancestors. In a continent and a culture frequently renewed by migration it is understandable that little memory of the past should linger, more surprising that the ideas of geographers and economists should have been virtually lost to the academic community. Not only have they lost sight of their own nineteenth-century forebears, not to think of other countries', but they forget their own prophecies. The apocalyptic visions of twenty years ago (hundreds of millions dead of famine, infertile soil, climatic disaster) have not come true. That is not to say, of course, that they never will.[32] In any case, purified by their rebirth from the Atlantic, ecological lobbies have returned to influenced Europe since 1970.

ECOLOGY IN EUROPE

Concern about the land in Europe today takes many forms. A rebirth of the agrarian ruralism of the inter-war period appeared in Bulgaria, Czechoslovakia and East Germany. The East German Communist Party recently reversed its policy of extreme agricultural monoculture and specialization, and began to appeal to the 'peasant ethic'. The inauguration of the *Bauernkongress* in 1970 was itself significant, as between 1945 and 1970 the peasant was suposed to behave like an industrial worker. The East German Minister for Agriculture now called for 'pride' in the peasant's occupation.[33] The Soviet Union has held off firmly – even under Gorbachov – from pandering to the bourgeois reactionary nature of the peasant. The Soviet envoy to Bulgaria complained in 1985 that Bulgarian workers were insufficiently proletarianised; they saw factory jobs as subsidiary to tilling their plots.[34] However, the disparity between successful peasant production and disastrous collective farm production in the USSR, must eventually weaken the politico-moral fear of the individualist, of roots, of folk memory, which has prevented rational agrarian reform in Russia to date.

Green parties as such have emerged in several European countries. Despite the success of the German Green Party, it is not typical of European ecological parties. These include ones that developed from small socialist parties (Denmark and the Netherlands), parties which are specifically geared to ecological/environmental issues and liberal agrarian parties (Sweden) which adopt environmental issues. The membership tends to a leftward position where young, and a more right-wing position where old. Italy's radical left ecological party elected eighteen candidates to the national parliament in 1979.[35] In France, ecological candidates first stood in 1973; one received 6.5 per cent of the vote in a 1976 bye-election, and ten per cent in 1977 in the municipal elections. An umbrella organization was formed in 1978, the *Collectif Écologie*. Their standard green policies included the protection of the environment, the conservation of energy resources, economic social and sexual equality, a 'new culture', no more nuclear power or bombs, and decentralisation. From a low of 2.22 per cent in 1978 the French ecological vote climbed to nearly four per cent in 1981, while in the European Parliament elections of 1979 *Europe-Écologie* won the fifth largest vote in France (4.39 per cent).[36] Nuclear power was the main issue in Sweden, Switzerland and Austria; in the latter two countries a referendum was held on the question.

In Austria, Greens have won representation in provincial parliaments, but not yet in the main parliament. Greens there have a more conservationist policy, focusing especially on plans to develop the unspoilt forests of the lower Danube. Although the Austrian Greens are a conservative group, they have co-operated with Austrian trade unions on such single issues. The Greens captured some seven per cent of the vote in Belgium in 1981; it has remained static since then. In Finland an ecological party has the support of seven per cent of the electorate, and two Green M.P.s.[37] The static nature of the green vote in countries (outside Germany) with proportional representation seems to show that ecological issues are strong values for some, but a lower priority for most voters.

England's two-party system militates aganist the success of a third or fourth party. It has the Ecology Party, the first of that name. It was founded in 1973, and changed its name in 1986 to the Green Party. It fought its first election under that name in June 1987. It grew out of the 'Movement for Survival', launched in 1972. The Friends of the Earth, the Soil Association and the Conservation Society supported the Movement, which was in part modelled on Edward Goldsmith's *Blueprint for Survival*.[38]

It is some indication of the leftwards shift of the green movement that in 1973 two of the three groups were conservatively (if passionately) conservationist, while the Green Party is now competing with the Labour Party as a radical movement. Friends of the Earth, formed in 1970, was a single-issue pressure group devoted at that time to landscape and energy conservation. Their good-humoured demonstrations calling for the re-cycling of glass bottles and bio-degradable food wrapping drew attention away from their economic energy argument that the energy input into capital infrastructure could never be returned by energy output in terms of income. (Thus, it would be as pointless to dig an allotment as to build a new cow-shed; the energy units expended could not be recovered – a comically wrong-headed argument.) The green umbrella organization and alternative voice in Britain, the Schumacher Society, seems to have expunged the older conservationists from its memory. This is despite the fact that Schumacher was President of the Soil Association. It is probably not surprising that they do not publicise the works of Lord Lymington and Rolf Gardiner, with their pre-war support for Germany. But it is a surprising shift of emphasis that in 1986 out of a hundred and five of its recommended green books, only four covered organic farming. Out of the original founders of the movement only the works of Schumacher himself and Ananda K. Coomaraswamy, a member of the Lymington circle, were circulated, the latter possibly because the current head, an ex-Jain monk, is of Indian origin. Eve Balfour's *The Living Soil* was not included. Jungian mysticism and feminism as well as American anarchocommunism seemed to dominate.[39]

The Ecology Party called for participatory democracy as well as decentralisation, for increased aid to the Third World but no trade with them at all, and for full sexual equality. As some three million people are estimated to be active supporters of environmental groups, clearly greenness has potential support in Britain. Here too, however, there was clothes-snatching. The Conservative Party developed an environmentally-conscious wing after 1983, with South of England Tories opposing new development in their constituencies. Some Tory 'wets' were closely connected to the Rowntree Trust, which houses and helps to fund pressure groups such as the Friends of the Earth and Greenpeace. The old Liberal Party, based in the Celtic fringe and the countryside, always had an environmentalist element. The Alliance (the Liberal Party in short-lived coalition with the SDP) stressed participatory politics and local issues in a way that could lead to a green stance if this were to become a majority view. In 1984, the National Front, an amalgam formed in the 1960s from the League of Empire Loyalists and the British National Party, decided to focus on green issues, a decision greeted by Jonathon Porritt with dismay.[40] This move was apparently prompted by increases in membership in country towns and rural countries, and the interests of new recruits. Since 1984, the influence of continental anti-urbanism has increased, and may lead to a split within the party, as may pressure to take up an anti-nuclear stance.

'PAGANS AGAINST NUKES'

In the sphere of single-issue campaigns ecologists have been successful. They have aroused public and media interest, even if their policies have not always themselves succeeded. Greenpeace and its Save the Whale campaigns, recycling bottles, Friends of the Earth and their specific and localised anti-pollution campaigns, anti-nuclear-waste actions, all these have caught the public imagination, and appeal to the prevalent sense that the valuable and beautiful rural world is being laid waste. When the issue is presented in terms of destroying ancient forests around the Danube, or building a hydro-electricity dam, it seems that public opinion can be aroused to protest. However, the sphere of action of single-issue pressure groups is limited. Despite the Marxist belief that only capitalist societies are uncontrollably polluting and exploitative, Soviet fishing fleets prove much less responsive to Greenpeace's campaigns than American ones. Air and water pollution from the factories of Eastern Europe is horrific, especially considering their much lower density of population than Western Europe.

However, environmental movements are strongest in North America and Western Europe. In part this is because of the Transcendentalist tradition of these areas, and the moral residue of the Protestant ethic – Waste not, Want not. It is a reaction to the perceived wastefulness of the planned state by young radicals, influenced by the pacifist tradition. There is also a more unstructured cultural criticism involved, which relates to the political condition of today's Europe.

George Orwell said during the Second World War that H.G. Wells's dream of a New Utopia pre-supposed an antithesis between the scientist working for a planned world state and the 'reactionary who is trying to restore a disorderly past'. Wells opposed 'war, nationalism, religion, monarchy, peasants, Greek professors, poets, horses'.[41] Romantic nationalism, 'the atavistic emotion of patriotism, . . . racial pride', Orwell points out, was the chief force that kept England and Russia fighting Germany.[42] There are two paradoxes in this analysis insofar as modern ecological politics are concerned. The first is that both scientists working for a planned world state *and* atavistic poets have come together in the ecological movement, with the scientific planners currently in the ascendancy ('scientific' here referring to a cast of mind, not a guarantee of quality). The second is that in 1945, in contrast to the restorations of 1815, there was no restoration of the ideals of sword, honour, church and tradition. The nationalism called into service during the war in the Allied nations was promptly discarded.[43] But it remains true that man does not live by Wellsian values alone. In the bombed-out ruins of Europe those who had linked ecological values with the far Right began to rethink their positions, and retreat into pessimistic isolation. Heidegger's critique of technology and consumerism belong to this war-time era. Those who were born one or two generations later came newly-minted to the desire for cultural values, for roots, national memories, and the mystic symbols of ancient European tribes.

Today's Back-to-the-Land movement presents these symptoms of loss across the political spectrum. Among the green movements mentioned earlier, such manifestations of 'folkness' tend to be jeered at or written out by the media, as with the Morris-dancing of earlier decades.[44] And the Red entryism, which is obviously just at its inception, will have nothing to do with such matters. It is found, however, in the minority European nationalisms. Where once the Nordic League brandished its mystic Eastern symbols, today's Celtic nationalists brandish their own, similar, three-legged symbol; the CND itself has made the death-rune famous. Basque and Breton nationalists use the flags, symbols and pre-Christian rituals.

Green culture today ranges from CND to the European *Nouvelle Droite*. It incorporates the new pagans, such as the nomadic bands of witches, who visit Stonehenge for the solstice and follow the astral plane across Britain's sacred land, the matriarchal witches who worship at exactly the same standing stone in Germany as did the pagan Nazis, although rejecting the patriarchy of the Nazis.[45] The pagan movement in Britain and America has grown from matriarchal feminism and anti-nuclear movements, together with the astrological and nature-worshipping tendencies of the naturist movement this century. Such revivals are not new. The Druid cult, appearing to us now in tamed form of bespectacled, neatly collared men in flowing white gowns, had found an echo all over Europe in the late eighteenth century, when nations vied for the honour of being the most truly celtic, ('Wizardry, myth and ritual 'was claimed as the Celtic inheritance in a pop-history series on BBC 2, 21 May 1987.) The last Druidical group in Germany was closed down by the Nazis in 1934. However, Druidism was exclusivist; in Britain, at least, it was geared to the Welsh. The new paganism, often based on Atlantean theories of a lost Golden Age, and theories of cultural diffusion via a vanished super-race, is open to all, and especially attractive to the semi-educated, semi-rational product of today's de-naturing educational process, stripped of religion, reason, tradition and even history.

The *Nouvelle Droite*, strongest in France, Italy and Belgium, is green in its cultural critique. It upholds Hellenic values (including Hellenic paganism), and supports geo-political thinking, a form of decomposition of national boundaries for reasons of geographical determinism, which loosely resembles the 'bio-regions' of American ecologists. The *Nouvelle Droite* is anti-American, sharing in this one of the chief components of Greens today. They want American missiles out of Europe, and are hostile to nuclear power, while suspecting the Left Greens' opposition to both. Some ecological activists are hard to categorise. Peter Cadogan, CND anarchist, organised a European ecological anti-nuclear group that co-operated with John Papworth's long-standing *Resurgence*. Opposition to environmental pollution and landscape destruction is an automatic part of their values. In the tradition of European conservatism, they are anti-capitalist, because of the alienation and rootlessness they see as its consequence. Unlike European conservatives, they have adopted socio-biological arguments to stress the uniqueness of each race and culture. Like E.M. Forster and Gobineau, however, they oppose slavery, colonisation and empire. J.R.R. Tolkien is the object of a political cult in Italy, where, as mentioned earlier, hobbit camps teach bomb-making and runes. Hobbit newsletters and hobbit tee-shirts are circultated by the Italian radical right, while *Nuova Destra* carries a feature entitled 'Hobbit, Hobbit'.

In Germany, the radical right journal *Mut* is pacifist and pro the ecological movement. *Neue Zeit* describes itself in its advertising as being 'ecological, – but not against technology. For the social revolution – but aganist Marxism'. The radical left journal *Aufbruch* demands the re-unification of Germany, and this folk nationalism is strong amongst non-party intellectuals. Peter Brandt, the son of Willy Brandt, said that Germans could 'not talk about returning to their roots without recognising' their 'own nationality', while Henning Eichberg, a left-wing sociologist, argued that 'nationalism is not out of date' but was essential to the attack on bureaucracies, dynasties and alienation.[46] One neo-Nazi novel, published, apparently, by an underground Californian press in 1966, offered a vision of the ecological bio-region of South America. A task-force of joint East and West Germans, numbering three, push a corrupt and crime-ridden North America into self-destruct mode with ease. The team take time to complain that the car lobby conspired to destroy a viable, public transport network in Los Angeles. They then return to their South American base, herd the natives into sexually segregated camps (so that they cannot breed), and make them replant the forests of the Amazon, to restore the ecological balance of the country.[47] There exists stil a group of Indian Nazis who believe that a Hindu-German alliance would save the world from pollution and industrialisation.[48] Indeed, neo-Nazi movements in general all seem to be inspired by a strong ecological input. How far this relates to the original ideology of Nazism, how far it is a result of opposition to today's world driven underground, or how far there has been a change of ideology resulting from the defeat of imperialist Nazism in armed combat is an open question.

Ideological continuity of a related kind has been found among the New Right in Russia. One opposition group of the early 1970s, *Veche*, which was closed down by the KGB in 1973, called for the renasissance of a peasant Russia, possibly located in Siberia, with European Russia left to the Marxists.

> A nation resettled into cities is doomed to extinction. All patriotism is inseparably linked to love for the land, for the sower and protector of the land, the peasant. All cosmopolitanism is equally inseparably linked to hatred of the peasantry – the creator and preserver of national traditions, the national morality and culture. . . The peasant is the most morally unique type.[49]

This 'liberal utopia', which demanded the de-urbanization of Russia and a reverse migration away from the cities, derives from Danilevsky, the biologist and pan-Slavist discussed earlier. The more recent and apparently apolitical Committee for the Protection of Russian Monuments (Pamyat) has taken up environmental and ecological issues. It attacks pollution and the cult of ahistorical ugliness and 'modernity' in today's Russia. While some commentators have perceived this movement as sinisterly illiberal and anti-Western, to share in today's ecology movement is a sign that Russia is still part of European culture.[50]

Given the witches, the CND, the neo-Nazis and the French professors, though, can one really talk of a common green ethic, a joint ecological cultural criticism? In fact they do have points in common, despite the unlikelihood of any joint future co-operation. They are all anti-capitalist and anti-growth-ethic. They are pacifist, both with regard to unilateral nuclear disarmament but also in that they believe that a decomposition of nation-state boundaries will remove the causes of war. They oppose the market economy on principle, and object to man's attempt to escape from the laws of nature. They favour a long-term view. There are apocalyptic expectations of desertification and mass famine. There is support for a return to tribal society ('the global village') and communes. Obviously cities must go; man must return to the land, to rebuild a new age, a new culture and a new world.

I referred earlier to the ecologists' paradox; that living in a natural way is seen as better, more 'economical', more enjoyable and more productive, while the way to this new life is to be planned for us by the very kind of scientific, or pseudo-scientific, mental attitude that inspires small boys to fiddle with watches and break them, and, of course, led to wasteful use of resources in the first place.

Eco-socialism has produced a new paradox. Earlier ecologists argued that we were living too well; earth's resources were being over-used and wasted. Energy economists claimed that we were in danger of running out of energy, and a form of rationing should be introduced to use existing resources sparingly. Social life should be re-organised and directed from above to ensure its continuation. But socialist suggestions for environmental improvement want more of the same. To provide 'free' transport would mean its over-use. Government-subsidised airlines, as John Papworth points out, fly half-empty all round the world. The public purse is seen as bottomless, and is the most uneconomical possible way to use any resource, especially when one considers the manpower involved in re-directing and supplying all resources used by humanity. It is no accident that such utopias emerge from a generation of political activists who have worked in the public sector only, sometimes leaving for the charity sector when life becomes too bureaucratic and wasteful. All the contributors to Weston's *Red and Green* are public sector officials. Some red ecologists try to escape from this paradox by advocating anarchic, co-operative socialism, on the lines of Godwin and Robert Owen (whose free-enterprise ideas and belief in hard discipline would not fit their ideology). While rights-based anarcho-socialism has always appealed to decent and serious reformers, the result of the anarchist communes established over the last hundred years is not impressive. Either an egalitarian ethos is adopted, in which case Veysey shows the result to be a grey, ant-like submissiveness to the group, or a charismatic authoritarian leader is needed to hold the group together. Neither, presumably, would be acceptable to the anarcho-socialist, with his regard for individuality. Religious communes have a higher rate of success, as well as economic self-sufficiency. Religious tribal groups, like the Amish in America and the Doukhoubours, work best, and do not depend on the state sector. The Basque Mondragon co-operative schemes are also tribal, established in an intensely nationalistic area, and run on a tribal capitalist basis.

The claim has been mentioned that the Labour Party's welfare state incorporated 'the most wide-reaching environmental measures ever enacted in Britain.'[51] Here we see ecological values abandoned. Even if we are to adopt anthropocentric living standards as an index of ecological virtue, did the post-war welfare state really contribute more than piped sewage, clean water, market gardening, sewing machines, bicycles and timber-framed houses? Even as I write, the last physical remnants of those days are being thankfully destroyed; the council complexes, the low-grade spectacles and appalling dentistry, the atrocious school buildings, the destruction of entire viable communities in the name of slum clearance, the corruption, all created at vast cost out of the last remnants of British prosperity, itself the creation of two hundred years of working-class and lower-middle-class savings at painfully low interest rates, the ten years of food rationing, the queues, – all the remnants of a callous disregard for human and natural values which characterised post-war collectivism.

In reality, it is socialist planning and economic policies, both under socialist and corporative capitalist parties, that have proved to be the most wasteful consumers of resources. The billions of dollars' worth of aid that disappeared into arms purchases and gold bath-taps; Mercedes for the concerned Third World leaders and American-financed land nationalisation for the masses; the unnecessary maintenance of resource-heavy primary production, both in mines and in factories; wasteful education policies that keep healthy, intelligent individuals compulsorily at school and then in tertiary education for one third of their useful working lives; the hideous and expensive concrete factories and houses which collapse after twenty years and which no-one wants to live in; the unnecessarily ugly squalor of those parts of our lives owned and directed by the public authorities, from roads to new shopping precincts; this is the fruit of the collectivist *Zeitgeist* of earlier decades. Given these phenomena of the planned state, the claims by the new Red ecologists that more of the same – 'changing social relations of property,' 'taking resources from private ownership' will somehow produce an ecological millenium, show that ecologism has already lost its way.

If single-issue groups become subsumed in a radical new Green Party, much of the value of the ecological critique will be lost.

Their policies have little to do with real green values, while the anti-Western stance which characterises the European left points to another danger. For ecologism is a phenomenon of the despised 'Northern White Empire'. It is not – as yet – prominent in the newly emerging prosperous nations elsewhere. The question is whether, if ecologism returned to being a non-party matter, Western man could restore his sense of values, while surviving in a world dominated by anti-ecological ideology, and potentially dominated by the expanding economies of nations like Japan and Indonesia, Brazil and Korea, who do not share the culture-specific ecological concerns of the West.

CONCLUSION
The Political Economy of Ecologism

> Boswell: 'So, Sir, you laugh at schemes of political improvement?'
> Dr Johnson: 'Why, Sir, schemes of political improvement are very laughable things'.
>
> (Boswell, *Life of Johnson*.)

I We have arrived at a set of historical data with which to check my preliminary typology of ecologism. This is not intended to be, and can hardly be, an exercise in finality. Although the historian is always tempted to be dogmatic about his intuitions, facts require humility. However, I have compiled sufficient expository material to commence the voyage of interpretation, which must leave areas of ambiguity, must remain partly uncharted. This interpretation is an act of creation, not a judgment, a vision to be shared with the reader.

Ecologism appears to me to be a convincing box in which all kinds of alternative ideas and people fit, and which begins to take on its current form and clearly identifiable content in the late nineteenth century. It is a box that contains anarchist and proto-fascist, Marxist and liberal, natural scientist and visionary alike; not because their world-views were identical, but because all shared an idea which by them was perceived as primary, although its secondary manifestations may have differed. In one book it has been impossible to deal with all the manifestations of the phenomenon of ecologism. The details of the anti-vivisectionist movement, of the commune movement, of vegetarianism and animal rights, receive treatment elsewhere, and I have merely sketched in their connection with ecologism. These movements, though deeply connected with the ecological world-view, can exist without a total commitment to global ecologism. I have concentrated here on what seem the more vital links between ecologists and land and resource use, ecologists and biological studies.

Ecological values have the force of a religion. But there is no reason why religion should not be subjected to critical analysis like any other belief. One can sympathise with people's values without believing that cultural relativism prevents an examination of the implications of their credo.

In the last chapter, I described how, in the 1970s, a major change came over the ecological box. The force of the new Greens came from a fusion of the two roots of ecologism; the biological root and the economic root. The holistic values of the new biological science proved, justified and utilised man's links with nature. It emphasised our interdependence with soil, air and food. It showed the importance of instinct and inbuilt patterns of behaviour. It did so 'scientifically', that is, it utilised rational ways of thought, testable hypotheses and experiments to show that man's genetic potential included a grammar of behaviour as powerful as his inborn sense of language.

After 1880, 'green' biology would offer a real alternative. Konrad Lorenz and Eugene Marais, Whitman and Eibl-Eibesfeld, would produce a scientific explanation of the living world not only different from but demonstrably better than the experimental results of Skinner's rats in mazes, or Zuckermann's chimpanzees in captvity. It was a more satisfying picture of the world than the earlier holistic philosopher, Goethe, had ever offered, despite the poetic genius of his vision. It also suggested a vindication of the claim of the German vitalists. By admitting into the picture the intuition of the observer, science thus became more scientific. Had there not been this valid basis for the cultural criticism of today's Greens, it would have remained a luxury for the few. But the perceived inadequacies of the orthodox science world-picture were both shown and cured by the new holism.

This rediscovery of man avoided determinism by emphasising his powerful will. By utilising his pattern of development to avoid the traps set by artificial civilization, his potential could be fulfilled, but his aggressive and destructive capacities short-circuited. The new biology implied that man could be improved, even perfected, but only in relation to his natural capacities. Acceptance of the real would mean greater, not less, freedom. This shift of values in the biological sciences meant that for the first time man was free from the dreadful bondage of his alleged dual nature. The ideals of progress and improvement were no longer linked with the ideal ant-state the technocratic communists like J. D. Bernal and Herman Muller had foreseen. If his values and instincts were integral to man, essential to his full development, the burden of sin, of centuries of wrong-headed repressions, had gone, vanished in the light of the new sun-worship.

Hence some of the apparent paradoxes I have examined in the political development of ecologism. Planning and anarchy; the tribal village and the global village; humanism versus anti-humanity; materialism versus spiritualism, all depend on the blurring of the old boundaries between world and human, being and time, matter and spirit, produced by the realisation that we are all part of the one earth. What they have in common is a mutual rejection of the traditional, the existing political system, and a set of values which, while not unique to ecologists, are put first by them.

The economic and geographical theories that provide the second root of ecologism seem less valid, partly because normative economics and geography cannot be demonstrated by experiment in the same way as the animal sciences. The same belief in the validity of the scientific method leads to the assumption that 'rational' economic policies of redistribution and reorganisation can solve what are seen as resource shortages and inequality. The cost of the redistribution is either not quantified, or counted in as a necessary sacrifice towards improving the quality of people's lives. When the concept of economics is extended to include the 'household management' implicit in *Oekonomie*, economists do not always seem to realise the political dimension, of control, order and paternal (or maternal) forward planning that is, for better or worse, inherent in the household state.

The belief that trained minds can plan life better than those just living the life stems from the formative influence of a specific global village, that of the university-trained intellectual. Green biologists often had to work away from recognition, from outside the traditional system. They failed for decades to break into orthodox science, even to the extent of the hapless suicide of a Marais. Where experimental animal biologists worked outside laboratory confines in as natural an environment as they could find, economists do not. Thus, the academic economists retain their cabalistic character, and faith in their own diagnoses and prescriptions. The new economics of food production, of the bio-region, comes from the thoughtless rejection of what does not belong to the cabal. Further, cabals are always set against the tribe, the rooted group, the loss of whose roots I have hinted at earlier as another factor in ecologism. But economists do have loyalties; they are firmly attached to their global vision, and the re-ordered global system will be supra-tribal, because that is where their faith lies.

Oppositional economists may jib at being described as a global cabal, when their own self-image is one of internal exile, of perpetual dissidence. But there is no real conflict here. All orthodoxy derives from heresy. Bacon, Galileo and Copernicus were heretics in their time. The advocates of Third-World self-sufficiency are happily moling away in the World Bank, while opponents of the Green Revolution (that is, advances in crop breeding and food production) are cheerfully ensconced in the Food and Agriculture Organisation. While economic ecologists would probably put their hand into the fire without a qualm for their ideas, they are still heretics securely embedded in the very system they attack.

The anti-capitalist, anti-growth distributionists do point up the inadequacies of neo-classical economic models, as models. Yet the criticisms of a Ballod, a Soddy or a Podolinsky, remain just that, criticisms, unable to offer convincing alternative models or precise suggestions. The onus is on those who wish to replace the impersonal and costless theory of the system to produce viable alternatives. This ecological economists have not yet done, though because many of their criticisms can be used against the West, international trade and other objects of Marxist and Third-World hatred, their criticisms have convinced researchers, and have been propounded in numerous feature articles and books, and documentaries and educational programmes on radio and television.

The moral criticisms of trade, which imply imbalance, greed and resource exploitation to the ecological economist, are contrasted with a hypothetical, but unspecified, viable moral economic order. The confusion of arguments which support this dogma is itself significant. We are told that there will be less food in the near future, but that there is too much food, grown at the cost of fertility. There are too many people in the world, and those here are about to die in their billions of famine. Within the same Green Party manifesto, entirely conflicting scenarios will be found. Existing national borders should be replaced by bioregions, which are self-sufficient. No clue is given as to who is to decide them, or on what grounds, or what the carrying capacity of the region will be. Who will police the borders; why trade within a region should be permissible but not outside the region; who is to take the food that is too important to be treated as a mere commodity and given to whom by whom; not to question these policies is to accept indeed the benevolent nature of man, and his harmony of interests. Self-sufficiency is desirable, but aid to the Third World, or at least that dwindling part of it still unaffected by prosperity, must increase without, of course, strings. Would the cabal of planners, foreseen by Bernal and Muller, partly implemented under Roosevelt, ever dissolve itself, or would it remain as a permanency? It would be an irony if the implicit anarchy of the ecological movement were to end subject to such a system, and yet it would also be in accordance with some of the earlier political manifestations of ecologism outlined previously. For here is a re-working of geo-politics, but without the sense of history, in a sense fascism without the nationalist dimension. Ecological economics, as enunciated so far, inherently oppose the values of political ecology.

These criticisms may seem harsh. The rhetoric and values of a political party do customarily attract more attention than its detailed policies, which are often improvised after a party reaches office. However, radical groups with a moral critique need to explain the practical effects of their policies more stringently than parties who believe in continuing the old system, or in muddling through somehow, in being pragmatic, unideological, 'natural' in short. As soon as ecological movements become political parties they have to turn against their own values, and the more 'apolitical' in party terms they aim to be, the more ideological they become. It was barely four decades ago that Joseph Schumpeter, the great economic historian, feared that the grey centralised socialism he saw creeping over the West would prove more efficient than capitalism at managing an advanced industrial society. We no longer think so. But will it be necessary to repeat this error, to spend another few decades in struggling with corrupt, cumbersome international bureaucracies, planned by well-meaning ecologists, run by 'qualified' bureaucrats, whether or not so envisaged by the Green Parties?

But, the ecologist may ask, how 'natural' is it to exploit and pollute our earth, to cut down trees, to erect ugly and wasteful buildings, to make an environment so hateful and ugly that human beings cannot function within it?

While in times of crisis – the Ice Age, the great neolithic flint wars, the twentieth century world wars, – survival must come first, no civilization, no culture can truly survive which ignores the human spirit and human values. The habit of English businessmen of returning to their rural homeland as soon as possible – so bewailed by critics for over two hundred years – shows that the first 'good' that is purchased after one's sustenance is the quality of life we associate with the countryside. And the nurture of the countryside is the first long-term aim of those who live in it, belong to it and wish to transfer it intact to their heirs. Whether a new rural proletariat, previously unemployed in the towns, inhabiting small, nationalised units of land, working farms organically, would offer such a nurture seems to me doubtful. The experience of the radical German agricultural programme described earlier indicates that while highly capitalised peasant settlement, complete with price subsidies and low-interest loans, is viable, it does not attract the masses in the insecurity of a mixed economy. Given socialist certainty, where forced collectivization is concerned, whether communist, or socialist, as in Tanzania, to force the masses to go to the land has been seen to lead to the solution of Pol Pot; a far cry from the vision of Kropotkin, Soddy or Schumacher.

So the lesson of the Third Reich in peasant-oriented land reform is an important one, and, given the link between a 'Germanic' ideology, the Protestant transcendentalism of Northern Europe and her children overseas, and the current popularity of ecological ideas, one that should be considered. However, the atrocities of the Third Reich are probably still too close to make it easy to render a balance sheet of its share in the themes of the time.

II Among the disparate groups who were the first ecologists, some have become forefathers, and some have been forgotten. In part, this is because of profound diffferences. The shift of political categories that has taken place outside ecologism has deeply affected the self-image of the ecologist. The earlier ecologists would probably support those of today, but in many cases the recognition would not be reciprocated. Seen in terms of the categories with which we are more familiar, it seems bizarre to group together, for example, the scientific bureaucratic would-be overlords and the pro-peasant anarchists. Yet the common bundle of characteristics elicited and described, and the lack of fit with other political boxes, help to prove that a new political category is at issue here. The outlines of a political box, and its typology, have emerged.

There are several reasons for re-categorising the past. One is pure curiosity: who was this person, why did they think what they did? Allied by necessity to this is the problem as to why their thought has become neglected, or misrepresented; how it does not, or perhaps does, fit into today's problems. Another drive to re-interpret is to clear away misconceptions: it is an act of mental hygiene. A more usual motive is the polemical one.

Undoubtedly, the link between a German ideology and green ideas has been used in this way, and will continue to be so used in the future. Anything to do with National Socialism must carry overtones of a polemical interpretation, for the simple reason that National Socialism is the demonic figure of our time, and plays a vital psychological role in the health of society, quite apart from its role in legitimizing the post-war settlements and systems. We need a figure to represent evil. Although there is bound to be a negative element in these re-interpretative acts, the links which I have delineated should be seen in their context, as part of a broader movement.

III We have arrived at some strange developments since I laid out some of the defining qualities of the ecologist. One of these qualities was that of seeking after truth. Ecologists believe in an objective reality. They oppose dualism, implicitly or explicitly. Ruskin was described as being such a man, and his theory of aesthetics as well as his politics rested on this belief. It was an element in his writings that particularly inspired the first ecologists. Erahim Kohák, the philosopher, in his book on man and nature, described his meditations in a hut in the woods, his vision of the boundless moral sphere embodied in the stars and the sky. According to his vision, there were 'no conditions more basic to authentic humanity than *to live in truth*'.[1]

Why is it that the search for truth, for objective reality, can, and does in any other than the aesthetic sphere, lead to unreality? How does Rilke's anti-consumerist man-object shift to a primitivism focussed on the Ghanaian drums of the global village? The conservative and the libertarian would answer that any faith in 'scientism' must lead to error. But why the desire for such alternative world-views?

Ecologists believe that society has taken a wrong path. As ecologists are a phenomenon of Western society, their search for the guilty party concentrates on Western society. Some place the wrong turning with the Roman Empire: some with the Iron Age's victory over the Bronze Age: some with the beginning of the Industrial Revolution, and others with the end of the mediaeval age. All look elsewhere for salvation. Although nature must not and cannot, according to this creed, be transcended, the desire for transcendance is still present. They seek the transcendental 'other' in primitive tribes. The noble savage belief was a powerful myth of Rousseau's, whose benevolent Nature we have seen extending its wings into the twentieth century, a belief which has survived in popular fiction in England, Germany and North America. The influence of Lao Tzu and Buddha is another transcendental 'other' which seems especially prominent in today's fundamentalist German Greens and in America's deep ecology, but which has not yet struck root in England. The contemplative and rural aura of Hinduism offers another escape from a guilty

Western identity. The ecological far Right in Europe differs from the *Nouvelle Droite* in emphasising this spiritual, apolitical dimension, just as does the ecological far Left. Matriarchy offers another escape for 'guilty', 'dominant' Western man. Thus, nature is accepted, but the urge which leads the ecologist to accept nature makes him abandon his own self.

Ecologists' solutions differ. Some, like Ernst Haeckel, thought society lagged behind scientific knowledge about man's nature, and society should be geared to the necessities of the biological drive. For him, that meant a centralised, liberal, progressive, strong nation-state. This is alien to today's ecologists. Both left and right ecologists today support the decomposition of society into small communities, either as minority tribes (Bretons and Basques, Welsh, Orinoco Indians) or on a basis of size alone, as when Bahro suggests 3000 as a maximum for any community. In theory, communes could be self-motivating; in practice, a network of international communities and contacts exists, whose pressure groups and members create the atmosphere of a church, mutually supportive, full of faith and good works, but dependent on jet planes and telephones.

A typical example of the anti-trade bias of ecologists is Knut Hamsun's peasant, who complained that cows were sold off callously from one village to another, whereas once each farm kept its cows, knew them and cared for them. Ecologism is anti-trade, and while the weight of argument is directed usually against international trade, the logic of the creed is indeed against trade between villages.

Here again 'Right' and 'Left' meet. International trade has been presented as exploitative since Hobson and Lenin's theories of imperialism. It is obviously a theme that appeals to the Left, broadly speaking. But it is not part of Marx's doctrine. Marx's model of commodity exchange assumed that value was exchanged against value. The measure of the value involved was the value of the labour. The exchange of labour itself, as a commodity against money wages, produced exploitation, because here value was *not* exchanged against value. Labour had a dual quality, the 'dual commodity value', by which the labourer received only his subsistence value, while the added value of his labour produced the surplus that became the employer's profit. The supposedly free market for labour concealed an inherent bias, due to the monopoly purchasing power of the capitalist. This technical exploitation has a lesser emotional force than Marx's theory of alienation, whereby the worker becomes alienated from the result of his labours under the wage system and division of labour. The object he makes does not belong to him. It has only a short connection with his life, and leaves him for the hands of others. Marx is not objecting that the worker has no property right vested in the object; but uses the tools of German idealism to express the idea that the connecting web between worker and product is broken. It is this part of Marx's theory that has remained a powerful criticism of the capitalist economy.

In 1920s Germany the separation of object and meaning apparently caused by technology was opposed. It was linked with a loss of identity. Heidegger's critique of consumerism is the same; that objects become separated from producer and consumer, through mass production and technology, and lose meaning, and Heidegger, after all, was described as 'the metaphysician of ecology'. It is here too that the Left and the Right meet, in an attack on alienation of man and thing, man and the world, man and nature, derived from the same source, the anti-liberal tradition of Hegelian idealism. That is why both Bahro and Heidegger cite Hölderlin, the melancholy singer of the death of the pagan world. Ecologists object to consumerism not because it is too materialistic, but because it is not real materialism. Real materialism, an understanding of things, possesses a sensitive understanding of and respect for the real, material and natural world. The religion of greed is, they argue, what is nonmaterialistic.

The theory of exploitation through trade, then, argues that monopoly purchasers can beat down unorganised producers. Trade *must* exploit. The profit made from re-sale is the result of exploitation. In order to increase exploitation, people invest in the Third World. If their investment is in urban factories, they exploit labour on the Marxist model, but a new dimension of guilt appears, white is allegedly exploiting black, and cultural oppression appears. Capitalist trade corrupts as well as exploits. Further, the economic changes that will arise are said to damage rural life in the Third World. If investment is rural, it much more clearly distorts and corrupts. If the big is favoured, the small goes under. In this simple model, any economic contact between one culture and another, first world and third world, exploits and corrupts.

Add to this the idealistic belief in exploitation through reification, and the impetus of the message becomes clear; that human lives and natural resources are being destroyed to pander to unnecessary consumerist fripperies in the West. This guilt at wasting resources helps explain the religious dimension, its force and fervour, and the link with the Marxist, the proto-fascist and the High Tory criticism of the mercantile world.

There may seem to be a gulf between the small-nation patriotism then and the global dimension of today's ecologists. It is true that pre-First World War thinkers tended to be Euro-centric, if European, or oriented towards the frontier society, if North American. But both were anti-imperial, and today's dream of an empire of good works, mysteriously non-coercive but effective, led by a Western intelligentsia open to non-Western values, is still consistent with ecological ideas.

IV The claim that man could feed himself from poor land living a pastoral life was made certainly as early as 1920; while in 1980 Allaby and Bunyard reported that 'scientists' had discovered that wild wheat in Turkey produced more edible corn for pastoralists than wheat grown as a crop.[2] The hope inspired by these fantasies is telling. Ecologists have failed to compute the relative fertility of the soil or explore the repeatable nature of the exciting discovery or take into account the fact that most of the world's population does not live in Turkey. All reason is abandoned at the sight of an apparently scientific legitimation of the modern ecologists' dream that the hunter-gatherer life is viable, that agriculture, with its property rights, its discontents, its brutalities, was never necessary.

The question has to be put, why is it that so many able, intelligent and learned men have deceived themselves in this way? Unless one assumes conspiracy theories of fantastic proportions, the answer can only be that disaffection with the extant has been of such an order as seriously to impair their sense of reality. After all, many ecologists gave and give their entire lives to trying to replace what to them was immoral and hideous; not with easy escapism but with passionately held visions of a purer and more resource-efficient world. That this particular biped had 'advanced' to the point where he could not sustain himself 'naturally' for a fortnight unless he reduced his numbers by at least three-quarters, was something many ecologists have been unable or unwilling to grasp. That five billion people can exist on earth today is a direct consequence of the technical advances made by agronomists, including the so-called agricultural Green Revolution.

The sad fact is that ecological movements have been given impetus and organization by the recent left-wing entryism. But this has not clarified their millenarian beliefs in an enhanced potential for survival. Such a scenario would, according to them, be mysteriously rendered possible throughout the globe by measures of egalitarian self-sufficiency financed, somehow, by an equally self-sufficient West. This agenda would only be destructive if put into effect. It would result in waste and squalor, not environmental improvement. The attribution of pollution and ecological damage to capitalism and greed is significant. The blindness to the environmental pollution in the Eastern bloc, where capitalism and private exploitation can be punished by death, demonstrates a dyslexia of categories which is not new in radical politics.

Truth is not only a matter of the private sphere. The public sphere too has to have a regularity, reciprocity and security in which man's creativity can flower. The philosophical anthropologists and the 'green' biologists argue that man's animality both sets the problem and enables him to solve it. Ethologists hope that a universal comprehension of instinctive social relationships will enable man to control what nature had left uncontrolled; that his primate curiosity can lead to self-knowledge to control his destructive side.

Comtean scientific ecologists believe that the reforms they want are obvious; that only people of ill-will would deny their validity. Yet their writings which concern the reconstruction of the public sphere are worryingly imprecise. Imprecision of word can arise from vagueness of thought. It can also arise from a desire to manipulate language. Language is one of the main social bonds with the past, it is an area of contemporary reciprocity. Given the cultural shifts this century, the domination of American culture in Europe – especially Britain – via the media, the slow but final removal of meaning from many of our institutions (church, family, law) which has already amounted to a revolution; the dissolution of language and meaning is another blow to the public sphere.

In the language of economic ecologism today, its relativism is intended to create a world where symbols produce an instant response. It is one of those campaigns, typical of our century, where a negative common-sense, an incredulous rejection, is the only possible response. There is unlikely to be an articulate and organised opposition to economic ecologism; there is even the hope of gain (moral and aesthetic) for individuals through single-issue campaigns (although the whales are still killed by Japanese and Russian fleets, and large-scale urban green-field development continues).

The twentieth century was the century of socialism; between 1880 and 1980 the West and its areas of cultural export experimented with various forms of collectivism, social planning and Marxism. Ideology began it, ideology was abandoned. Perhaps the next hundred years will be the century of the global ecologist – only in those areas which have already looted themselves for socialism, and regret it.

In the meantime, there are the sufferings of the Communist-ruled nations, where the attack is on individual conscience and autonomy. In the attempt to attach itself to the guilt festering in the West, ecologism is attacking the roots of individual moral integrity, and substitutes a nebulous societal guilt. It is yet another paradox of the ecological movement – that the call to individual moral truth should finish as a global religion. Despite its rejection of organised and traditional Christianity, the ecological movement still carries the burden of its heritage, the legacy of the crucifixion, symbol of death, suffering and self-surrender.

What after all today's ecological movement is advocating is a return to primitivism, and the abandonment of treasure and knowledge to tribes and nations in foreign lands who pose no threat to us. Consciously or otherwise, this is a death-wish. We are not talking here about eschewing food additives and colouring matter, whole food in a whole land, as were the earlier ecologists, but something different – and deathly. For today's ecologists, their hope of regeneration presupposes a return to primitivism, and thus, whether they wish to enunciate it or not, concomitant anarchy, the burning before the replanting, the cutting down of the dead tree. The father of the movement is an utter rejection of all that is, and for at least three millenia all that was.

NOTES

Chapter One

1. For example, Ursula le Guin's feminist utopias; Brian Aldiss's Gaia in *Helliconia Winter* (London, 1986).
2. The Gaia concept was first made explicit in J.E. Lovelock, *Gaia. A New Look at Earth* (Oxford, 1979).
3. See Juan Martinez-Alier with Klaus Schlüpmann, *Ecological Economics. Energy, Environment and Society* (Oxford, 1987), pp. 237–9; he also cites T. O'Riordan's bibliography of environmental writings and its focus on Britain and the U.S.A. A. Mohler, in *Der Traum von Naturparadies. Anmerkungen zum ökologischen Gedankengut* (Munich and Berlin, 1978), p.9, stresses the Protestant character of the 'triangle between San Francisco, Zurich and Stockholm' which he sees as the area where ecological beliefs are found.
4. Anne Chisholm, *Philosophers of the Earth. Conversations with Ecologists* (London, 1972), p. xi. A. Toynbee, *Mankind and Mother Earth* (Oxford, 1976), p.5, introduces his world history with a discussion of the ethical and historical dilemmas offered by biological science. He places his account of great civilizations in a framework of references to the biosphere, man's place among other species as the child of Mother Earth, and man's choice between 'matricide' through misuse of technology, and the overcoming of his 'suicidal, aggressive greed', pp. 595–6. He sees the 'Oikoumene's peasants' as 'saddled with the burden of having to support a superstructure of civilization', p.591. The sense that real values are produced only by the peasant is fundamental to the ecological thinker. But it is also something that Toynbee has effortlessly absorbed into his otherwise straightforward survey of world history.
5. *The Times*, 20.10.84.
6. D. Bellamy and B. Quayle, 'The Green Rustling', *Sunday Times*, 3.2.85. I owe this reference to Geoffrey Ahern's 1985 unpublished paper on modern ecological values.
7. Avner Offer, *Property and Politics, 1870–1914* (Cambridge, 1981), chapters 20 and 21.
8. Ibid., p.341, but cf. the reference to Jefferies in Paul Meier, *William Morris, the Marxist Dreamer* (Hassocks, Sussex, 1978), pp. 68–9, where Jefferies is described, surely correctly, as an inspirer of Morris's utopian Socialism.
9. Mohler, *Der Traum von Naturparadies*, describes Friedrich Georg Jünger as a founding father, although his chronology includes both Rousseau and Darwin. On p.19, he describes how Jünger protested in 1946 against the reconstruction of German industry.
10. D. Pepper, *The Roots of Modern Environmentalism* (London, 1985).
11. D. Worster, *Nature's Economy. The Roots of Ecology* (San Francisco, 1977), p.2.
12. Martinez-Alier, *Ecological Economics.*
13. P. Lowe and J. Goyder, *Environmental Groups in Politics* (London 1983).
14. See M. Allaby and P. Bunyard, *The Politics of Self-Sufficiency* (Oxford, 1980), p. 20, and esp. p.25, and p.130, 'Carry Carlyle through to Nietzsche and it is but a short step to Hitler.' The authors are clearly disturbed by the connota-

tions of 'back to nature' and the implications as regards Germany, p.31.

15. F. Nietzsche, 'Ecce Homo' in L. Forster ed. *The Penguin Book of German Verse* (Harmondsworth, 1974), p.374, my translation.
16. Heidegger as the metaphysician of ecologism, see G. Steiner, 'The House of Being', *Times Literary Supplement* 9.10.81. Professor Steiner thinks that Heidegger's 'alarm' and then isolation at the prospect of world-wide pollution and alienation was influential in his brief entry into the Nazi Party. Those works of Heidegger which bear most closely on ecological issues seem to date from a later period, during the war in fact. Heidegger's most striking and pessimistic ecological criticism is 'Overcoming Metaphysics', *The End of Philosophy* (London, 1975), published in German in 1954 but written at the end of the Second World War. For Heidegger's demand that man become the shepherd of the earth, see p.109. Surprisingly for its early date, the essay also includes an attack on 'the artificial breeding of human material, based on present-day chemical research' p.106.
17. A. Bramwell, *Blood and Soil. R. Walther Darré and Hitler's 'Green Party'* (Bourne End, 1985).
18. M. Hauner. 'A German Racial Revolution?' *Journal of Contemporary History*, 1984, vol. 19, p.685, n.46.
19. See for example. H. Graml and K-D Henke, eds., *Nach Hitler. Der Schwierige Umgang mit Unserer Geschichte. Beiträge von Martin Broszat* (Munich, 1985); R. Bessel, ed., *Everyday Life in the Third Reich* (Oxford, 1987); I. Kershaw, *The 'Hitler Myth'. Image and Reality in the Third Reich* (Oxford, 1987).
20. T. Mann, *Diaries, 1918–1933* (ed. H. Keston) (London, 1983), *passim*.
21. Eg., Peter Medawar, *Pluto's Republic* (Oxford, 1982), pp.242–51 and 253–62, vigorously attacks the cosmology and philosophy of Teilhard de Chardin and the spiritualism of Arthur Koestler. He warmly supports the economic ecologism expressed in Barbara Ward and Rene Dubois's *Only One Earth* (London, 1972).
22. The Pol Pot analogy comes to mind from the current fashion for ecology among revolutionaries; e.g., the comment by a 'Senior Officer' in the National Resistance Army of Uganda, 'I have killed many men. What I want now is a degree in ecological and conservation studies.' *Daily Telegraph*, 1.2.86. A recent attack on nature-based values, which he links with Nazi ideology, is in R. Pois, *National Socialism and the Religion of Nature* (London, 1985), pp.155–6; and see the attack on the 'New Right' by the British Association for the Advancement of Science, reported in the *Times Higher Education Supplement*, 30.8.85, for believing in an 'immutable nature'.
23. B. Moore, Snr., editor of *The Ecologist*, 1915, 'ecology...a point of view', quoted in Worster, *Nature's Economy*, p.203; though Worster, p.391, gives the date as 1920.

Chapter Two

1. C. Glacken, *Traces on the Rhodian Shore. Nature and Culture in Western Thought from Ancient Times to the End of the Eighteenth Century* (Berkeley, 1967), p.70, and quote, pp.704–5.
2. Ibid., p.58.
3. D. Worster, *Nature's Economy. The Roots of Ecology* (San Francisco, 1977), on White *passim*, and for gap between name and thing, p.192.
4. Ibid., p.20.
5. Lowe and Goyder, *Environmental Groups in Politics*, p.16.
6. Ibid., p.19.
7. Lynn White, 'The Historical Roots of Our Ecological Crisis' *Science*, 1967, vol. 155, pp.1203–7.
8. J. L. Talmon, *The Origins of Totalitarian Democracy* (London, 1970), p.249.
9. Susan Griffin, 'Split Culture', in S. Kumar, ed. *The Schumacher Lectures* (London, 1984), p.181.
10. Glacken, *Traces on the Rhodian Shore*, pp.471–2.
11. R. Bahro, *The Logic of Deliverance. On the foundations of an ecological politics* (Schumacher Society Lecture), 1986, p.20.
12. T. Huxley, *Science and Culture* (London, 1881), pp.241–6.
13. J.J. Bachofen, *Myth, Religion and Mother Right* (London, 1967). Harvey Greisman, in 'Matriarchate as Utopia, Myth and Social Theory', *Sociology*, 1981, vol. 15, pp.321–6, discusses the emer-

gence of theories of matriarchal origins of civilization, early feminist science fiction, and the re-emergence of matriarchy as part of a campaign against exploitative paternalism. Interestingly, those who toyed with matriarchal theories before Bachofen included John Ray, the biologist.

14. Jost Hermand, 'All Power to the Women: Nazi Concepts of Matriarchy', *Journal of Contemporary History*, 1984, vol. 19, pp.649–50: and see P.V. Glob, *The Mound People. Danish Bronze-Age Man Preserved* (London, 1974).
15. C. Merchant, *The Death of Nature. Women, Ecology and the Scientific Revolution* (New York, 1980), p.xix.
16. See Greisman, 'Matriarchate', and Mary Daly, *Gyn/Ecology* (London, 1981). Caroline Merchant uses Marxist criticisms of Hobbes as legitimiser of 'possessive individualism', while glorifying mediaeval communalism.
17. Monica Sjoo, 'The Unofficial Herstory of the Externsteine, Ancient Sacred Rocks of Germany', *The Pipes of Pan* (Journal of Pagans Against Nukes), 1985, no. 19, p.4.
18. See H. Adams, *Mont St Michel and Chartres* (New York, 1980) and *The Education of Henry Adams; an Autobiography* (London, 1961). See too for the cult of the Virgin Mary, Marina Warner, *Alone of All Her Sex* (London, 1978).
19. Bahro, *Logic of Deliverance*, p.4.
20. R. Bahro, *Building the Green Movement* (London, 1986), p.95 An example of the ahistorical polemic of the ecological feminist is the work of the American writer, Susan Griffin. 'Like the Inquisition and the witchburnings, the slave trade began at the time of the scientific revolution, the 16th century', 'Split Culture', p.191. Like other feminist historical analogies, each of these is inaccurate. The Inquisition was not founded in the sixteenth century. The slave trade goes back as far as recorded human history, as anyone who has heard of the Roman and Greek empire will recall; the Phoenicians and Egyptians had slaves. If we look at the Arab slave trade in Africa, given that Griffin is exclusively concerned with 'the Jew or the Black or the women,' (p.184) as victims of patriarchal oppression, it goes back many centuries before the sixteenth century. Unfortunately, nobody seems prepared to apply the most minimally critical methodology to these polemics.
21. Griffin, 'Split Culture', p.198.
22. Klaus Thewelweit, *Männerphantasien*, 2 vols, (Frankfurt, 1977–8).
23. See B.M. Lane and L. Rupp, *Nazi Ideology Before 1933* (Manchester, 1978), pp.18–26.
24. Glacken, *Traces on the Rhodian Shore*, pp. 276–7.
25. Quoted by Bahro, *Logic of Deliverance*, p.5.
26. Ibid., p.5. I am not sure why free competition between Indo-European petty kings and warriors and expansion is very different from other prehistorical epochs, e.g. Papua New Guinea, which did not develop capitalism. Compare here Walther Darré, who argued that the robber-baron spirit entered North Western Europe through Teutonic knights, who caught it in Sicily from the Arabs, but claims capitalism was essentially ungermanic.
27. Bahro, *Logic of Deliverance*, p.6.
28. R. Graves, *The White Goddess* (London, 1986), pp.10, 486. Graves is cited by Bahro, *Logic of Deliverance*, p.5.
29. Malcolm Chapman, *The Gaelic Vision in Scottish Culture* (London, 1978), examines the Celtic myth in Britain.
30. K. Thomas, *Man and the Natural World* (London, 1983), p.89.
31. F. Hayek, *The Counter-Revolution of Science. Studies in the Abuse of Reason* (Glencoe, Illinois, 1952), pp.51–2, 55–6, 110–11.
32. Ibid., and see especially Hayek's criticisms of Condorcet, Bentham and Comte.
33. H.L. Parsons, *Marx and Engels on Ecology*, (Westport, Conn., 1977); M. Prenant, *Biology and Marxism*, (London, 1938); Prenant was Professor of Zoology at the Sorbonne, Paris. There are several recent works which deal with the need to take over the ecological movement for Marxism. Some of the essays in Joe Weston, ed., *Red and Green. The New Politics of the Environment* (London, 1986), argue this cause forcibly. However, I have confined my examples to Prenant and Parsons because they both, although writing from different scientific disciplines, concentrate on Marx and Engels and biology and ecology specifically. Pre-

nant was published by Lawrence and Wishart, the party-line publishers, which lends it an extra authenticity within that context. Parson's book incorporates and discusses most of the work on Marx and ecologism. An updated New Left interpretation of Marx, ecology and modern German politics is in W. Hülsberg, *The German Greens. A Social and Political Profile* (London, 1988).

34. 'Thus, Marx and Engels had an understanding of an approach to ecology before...Haeckel coined the term Oekologie in 1869, and long before the current 'ecological crisis', Parsons, *Marx and Engels on Ecology*, p. xi. Engels included Haeckel in his plan of the contents of *Dialectics of Nature* (written 1873–1882), see *Marx and Engels, Collected Works*, vol. 15, (London, 1987), p.314., but did not write the section.
35. Ibid. intro., *passim*.
36. Ibid., pp.8–10.
37. F. Engels, *Dialectics of Nature*, pp.330–1, my italics. Engels argues in this work, p.323, that the first breach with a rigid concept of nature appeared in 1755, with Kant's work, *Allgemeine Naturgeschichte und Theorie des Himmels*. Although Engels emphasises man's superiority over the animals in his ability to control nature, he also comments on the environmental damage done by man's actions, pp.460–1.
38. Prenant, *Biology and Marxism*, p.44. In 'The German Ideology', *Marx and Engels, Collected Works*, vol. 5 (London, 1976), pp.39–40, Marx attacks Feuerbach's concept of a 'harmony of all parts of the sensuous world and especially of man and nature'. Marx comments that the natural world is 'an historical product' an ever-varying thing, created by man's labour. He argues that the 'celebrated "unity of man with nature" has always existed in industry...and so has the struggle of man with nature, right up to the development of his productive forces on a corresponding basis.' This vision of struggle rests on a rejection of the idea of a benevolent nature. It seems to me to be opposed to ecological thinking.
39. Prenant, *Biology and Marxism*, pp.47, 49.
40. F. Engels, *Origin of the Family, Private Property and the State. In the Light of the Researches of Lewis H. Morgan, Marx, Engels, Selected Works*, vol. 3 (Moscow, 1970), p.331, quoted by Prenant, *Biology and Marxism*, p.64. Hermand, *'All Power to the Women'*, p.653, shows how Engels drew on Bachofen. Engels' own preface to the fourth German edition of *Origin of the Family*, op. cit., pp.194–6, stresses the importance of Bachofen.
41. Parsons, *Marx and Engels on Ecology*, pp.40–1.
42. Quoted by David Mitrany, *Marx Against the Peasant. A Study in Social Dogmatism* (New York, 1961), p.91.
43. Parsons, *Marx and Engels on Ecology*, pp.40–1.
44. K. Marx, 'The British Rule in India', *Marx and Engels. Basic Writings on Politics and Philosophy* (London, 1969), pp.517–18;

    we must not forget that these idyllic village communities, inoffensive though they may appear, had always been the solid foundation of Oriental despotism, that they restrained the human mind within the smallest possible compass, making it the unresisting tool of superstition, enslaving it beneath traditional rules...We must not forget the barbarian egotism which, concentrating on some miserable patch of land, had quietly witnessed the ruin of empires ...We must not forget that this undignified, stagnatory and vegetative life, that this passive sort of existence evoked on the other part, in contradistinction, wild, aimless, unbounded forces of destruction and rendered murder itself a religious rite... We must not forget that these little communities were contaminated by distinctions of caste, and by slavery, that they subjugated man to external circumstances instead of elevating man into the sovereign of circumstances, that they transformed a self-developing social state into a never changing natural destiny, and thus brought about a brutalising worship of nature...

    See too F. Engels, 'On Social Condition in Russia', *Basic Writings*, pp.507–8, ascribing 'Oriental despotism' in Russia, India and other nations to the low level of development induced by the communal ownership of land characteristic of peasant society.

45. Point 9 of the *Communist Manifesto* in *Marx and Engels. Basic Writings*, p.70.
46. Parsons, *Marx and Engels on Ecology*, p.42.
47. Mitrany, *Marx against the Peasant*, pp.36–7.
48. M. Almond, unpublished seminar paper delivered to the Wellcome Unit for the History of Medicine, Oxford, 1986, and Thomas on Schopenhauer, *Man and the Natural World*, p.23.
49. K. Marx, 'On the Difference Between the Democritean and Epicurean Philosophy of Nature', *Marx and Engels, Collected Works*, vol. 1 (London, 1975), pp.29–105. Compare to Marx's dislike of rural idiocy the telling passage in ultra-libertarian, pro-capitalist Ayn Rand's *Atlas Shrugged* (New York, 1957), pp.266–7, when the heroine and her lover drive into an abandoned industrial area, covered now with trees and bushes. There are no bill-boards. They view the scene with horror. Of those who complain that bill-boards ruin the country-side, the heroine muses 'They're the people I hate.' Later they spot a derelict petrol pump. The horror of the trees and shrubs is all the greater. Rand fears nature as the voracious destroyer of human energy and individual initiative; Marx fears it because it endangers his vision of historically-determined progress. There is more in common between Marx and Randian libertarians than the parasitical symbiosis between Marxism and capitalism. The dislike of environmental and rural values is one such factor.
50. Quoted in Michael Allaby and Peter Bunyard, *The Politics of Self-Sufficiency* (Oxford, 1980), p.45; the practical problems of ploughing virgin soil, by hand, are obviously unknown to Mumford. With a wobbly strip of upturned soil constantly falling back, grass upwards, only the most determined Freudian could have seen anything phallic in the exercise. Ploughing, in any case, followed hand cultivation; it did not precede it.
51. For example, Jean Auel's best-selling series, *Earth's Children* places 35,000 BC Cro Magnon man as potentially more destructive than the earlier Homo Sapiens he replaced. Her tribes inhabit a matriarchal system, based on the worship of the Mother Goddess, where rape and violence are virtually unknown. The series is well-researched and claims a certain scholarly status. In C. Harness, *The Paradox Men* (London, 1949) the hero, in order to save mankind from nuclear extermination, returns through time to the dawn of the Palaeolithic era, to prevent the extermination of Neanderthal man by Cro-Magnon man. He believes that if this turning-point can be averted, paternalist violence will not triumph in later millenia.

Chapter Three

1. That is not to say that comparisons between human and animal societies were not made before the 1880s: Mandeville's *Fable of the Bees* does so, but the starting point is the fabulous nature of animals. Neither Condorcet nor Burke, for example, look at the 'natural world' as natural scientists.
2. R.C. Stauffer, 'Haeckel, Darwin and Ecology', *Quarterly Review of Biology*, 1957, vol. 32 pp.138–44. The OED gives 1873 as the first mention of the word, while Worster, *Nature's Economy*, p.192, gives 1866. C.J. van der Klaauw's detailed search for the origins of ecology gives similar definitions under the title of ethology and economy, but no earlier use of the word, in C.J. van der Klaauw, 'Zur Geschichte der Definition der Oekologie...', *Sudhoffs Archiv für die Geschichte Medizin*, 1936, vol. 29, pp.136–77. The authorities seem to agree on Haeckel as the first user of the word, and a date of either 1866 or 1873. However, Thoreau mentions 'Ecology', in conjunction with Botany and in a context that suggests a plant or geological science. This reference appears in a letter written in 1858 (see his collected *Letters* (New York, 1958) p.502) but was not published until 1958. The OED 1971 Supplement contains it. Thoreau was a classical Greek scholar – he translated Sophocles' *Seven Against Thebes*. Did he coin the word himself from the Greek root *Oikos*, meaning home? Klaauw suggests that one early meaning of ecology is bio-geographics, the homeland of the plant and animal, and this meaning would explain the

parallel 'invention' of the word. Another possibility is that the word was already in use in America, but had escaped the notice of dictionaries and historians of biology. D. Worster's examination of Thoreau's link with ecology, *Nature's Economy*, pp.59–111, does not refer to a contemporary use of 'ecology'. F. Egerton comments in 'A Bibliographical Guide to the History of General Ecology and Population Ecology', *History of Science* 1977, vol 15, p.195 that, according to Walter Harding, one of the editors of Thoreau's correspondence, the correct reading of the manuscript shows 'Geology' and not 'Ecology'.

3. Stauffer, 'Haeckel, Darwin and Ecology', p.140. See also D.R. Stoddard, 'Darwin's Impact on Geography', *Annals of the Association of American Geographers* 1966, vol 56, p.688, which has a reference to 'Haeckel's new science of ecology' dated 1869.
4. See D.F. Owen, *What is Ecology* (Oxford, 1980), pp.1–28.
5. Worster, *Nature's Economy*, p.198.
6. Van der Klaauw, 'Zur Geschichte', pp.139–40.
7. Ibid.
8. Ibid.
9. M.B. Petrovich, *The Emergence of Russian Pan-Slavism, 1856–1870* (New York, 1956), p.66.
10. A Yanov, *The Russian Challenge* (Oxford and New York, 1987), p.47. This collection is given the title 'Political and Economic Essays' (the Russian title in both references varies accordingly) in Robert MacMaster's bibliography in *Danilevsky. A Russian Totalitarian Philosopher* (Cambridge, Mass., 1967), p.319. Danilevsky is discussed at greater length in Chapter Four.
11. Worster, *Nature's Economy*, p.193.
12. W. Johnson, *Gilbert White* (London, 1928, this edition 1978), p.58, and see also Keith Tribe, *Land, Labour and Economic Discourse* (London, 1978), pp.81–2, on Aristotle and the *oekonomie* of the French physiocrats.
13. J. Durant, 'Innate Character in Animals and Man: a Perspective on the Origins of Ethology', in C. Webster, ed., *Biology, Medicine and Society, 1840–1940* (Cambridge, 1981), p.162.
14. Wilhelm Bölsche, *Haeckel, His Life and Work* (London, 1909); R. Chickering, *We Men who feel most German. The Pan-German League, 1886–1914* (London, 1984), pp.146 and 150n; P. Weindling, ''Darwinismus' and the Secularization of German Society', in J.R. Moore, ed., *The Humanity of Evolution. Perspectives in the History of Evolutionary Naturalism* (Cambridge, 1989). For his early Protestantism, see E. Haeckel, *Story of the Development of a Youth. Letters to his Parents, 1852–1856* (New York, 1923).
15. E. Haeckel, *The Wonders of Life* (London, 1905), p.157.
16. E. Haeckel, *Monism as Connecting Religion and Science. The Confession of Faith of a Man of Science* (London and Edinburgh, 1894), pp.1–5.
17. Haeckel, *Monism as Connecting Religion and Science*, pp.7, 9.
18. Ibid., pp.16–24.
19. Ibid., pp.17, 49–50, 62–3.
20. E. Haeckel, *The Riddle of the Universe* (London, 1900), p.363.
21. Haeckel, *Riddle*, pp.359–60, 365, 389.
22. J. Durant argues that Catholicism was more anti-nature, in 'The Meaning of Evolution. Post-Darwinian Debates on the Significance for Man of the Theory of Evolution, 1858–1908', Ph.D. Thesis, Cambridge, 1977; C. Merchant, *Death of Nature*, pp.10–11, 16–18, describes a Neoplatonist tradition of a female cosmos, and an alchemist belief in an androgynous god deriving from gnostic texts.
23. Worster, *Nature's Economy*, p.27.
24. Glacken, *Traces on the Rhodian Shore*, pp.152–3.
25. R. Gruner, 'Science, Nature and Christianity', *Journal of Theological Studies*, 1975 vol. 26, pp.55–81. A recent example is P. Santmire, *Travail of Nature. Ambiguous Ecological Promises of Christian Theology* (n.p., 1985), which argues that the view of Christianity as anti-ecological is over-simplified, and that pro-ecological strands exist. I owe this reference to Trevor Williams, of Trinity College, Oxford. See Sean McDonagh, *To Care for the Earth* (London, 1986), who argues that the Catholic Church should take up the challenge of ecological decay. This book, by a Franciscan monk, has a good historical summary of naturist ideas. David C. Lindberg and Ronald L. Numbers, eds, *God and Nature. Historical Essays on the Encounter Between*

History and Science (Berkeley and London, 1986), survey the debate to this date.
26. Worster, *Nature's Economy*, p.29.
27. Durant, 'The Meaning of Evolution', p.10.
28. C. Darwin, *The Origin of Species* (London, 1859), p.63.
29. T. Huxley, quoted in Durant, 'The Meaning of Evolution', p.19.
30. Ibid., p.31.
31. See for Carrel p.121 below; P. Carus, *The Surd of Metaphysics* (Chicago and London, 1905), pp.75–7, and *The Monist*, 1890–1, vol. 1, pp.229ff, 552ff.
32. N.R. Holt, Ernst Haeckel's Monist Religion'. *Journal of the History of Ideas*, 1971, vol. 32, p.272.
33. T.H. Huxley, *Science and Culture* (London, 1881), pp.232–3, 241–6.
34. Martinez-Alier, *Ecological Economics*, p.202; Bölsche described as a reactionary, p.203.
35. Joseph le Comte, *The Monist*, 1890–1, vol.1, pp.334–5.
36. Haeckel, *Monism as Connecting Religion and Science*, p.64.
37. Haeckel, *The Wonders of Life*, pp.48–50.
38. Ibid.
39. Haeckel, *Monism as Connecting Religion and Science*, pp.64.
40. Ibid., p.82; Haeckel, *Riddle of the Universe*, p.352.
41. Haeckel, *The Wonders of Life*, p.137.
42. A. Kelly, *The Descent of Darwin. The Popularization of Darwin in Germany, 1890–1914* (Chapel Hill, 1981), p.121.
43. Ibid., pp.17–18; the reference to Vogt and terrorism I owe to Mark Almond, of Wolfson College, Oxford.
44. Ibid., pp.38–9, 127.
45. Ibid., pp.39, 108, 127. On August Forel, D. Gasman, *The Scientific Origins of National Socialism. Social Darwinism in Ernst Haeckel and the German Monist League* (London and New York, 1971), pp.103 n.52, 145.
46. For Ossietsky and Hirschfeld, see Kelly, *Descent of Darwin*, pp.120–1; W. Ostwald, *Natural Philosophy* (London and New York, 1911), p.185, 'the present social order is 'barbarous'...'progress depends much less upon the leadership of a few distinguished individuals than upon the collective labor of all workers.' He foretold 'a time... when the social organization therefore demands and strives for as thorough an equalization as possible in the conditions of existence of all men'.
47. Schopenhauer, in *The World as Will and Idea*, vol 2, quoted in H. Driesch, *The History and Theory of Vitalism* (London, 1914), p.121.
48. C.K. Ogden, intro. to Driesch, *History and Theory of Vitalism*, p.v; Soil Association members and Driesch, see V. Payne, 'A History of the Soil Association', M.A. Thesis, University of Manchester, 1971, p.59.
49. K. Popper, *Unended Quest. An Intellectual Biography* (London, 1982) p.137. Popper describes Schrödinger as inspired by Schopenhauer, p.135.
50. Ibid.
51. Ibid.
52. Coincidentally, a von Uexküll is today a representative of the German Greens, and founder of a Right Living Foundation at Bradford University. See p.272 below.
53. W. Köhler, *The Mentality of Apes* (London, 1973). Lorenz himself, in *Behind the Mirror. A Search for a Natural History of Human Knowledge* (New York and London, 1977), p.128, ascribes this comment to Karl Böhler.
54. A. Nisbett, *Konrad Lorenz* (London, 1976), p.21.
55. Conversation with Sir Charles Elton, January, 1987.
56. K. Lorenz, *On Aggression* (London 1966); ibid., *King Solomon's Ring. New Light on Animal Ways* (London, 1952). In the introduction to the latter by W. Thorpe, Lorenz is quoted as saying that behaviourists could never have asserted that complex behaviour patterns were conditioned if they had only once reared a young bird in isolation, and referred to his disillusionment at finding out that the 'great authorities' were wrong, p.xviii. Bruce Chatwin in 1974 (*Sunday Times*, 1.12.74) suggested that a 1942 article of Lorenz's, which was decorated with pictures of Greek statues, expressed Nazi ideology about race, Aryans and physical beauty. The question of Lorenz's Nazi membership after 1938, and his articles of that period, is discussed by Alec Nisbett, *Konrad Lorenz*. He argues, pp.81–5, 87, that serious mistranslations and selective quotations by North American scientists of a 1940 paper were the basis for attacks on Lorenz but adds,

pp.134–5, that Lorenz's war-time work uses Nazi terminology. Theodora Kalikow adopts Gasman's misleading interpretation of Haeckel as a *völkisch*, anti-Enlightenment precursor of Nazism. She argues that Lorenz certainly read of Haeckel via Bölsche, and therefore shares his proto-Nazi qualities, in 'Die ethologische Theorie von Konrad Lorenz', in, H. Mehrtens and S. Richter, eds., *Naturwissenschaft, Technik und NS-Ideologie. Beiträge zur Wissenschaft des Dritten Reiches* (Frankfurt-am-Main, 1980), p.198. As an example of the allegations, Lorenz's 1935 article suggesting that domesticated animals become over-specialised and need influxes of 'wild' genes to improve them is presented as a Nazi theory. But the Nazis did not think that domesticated man should be improved by genes from wild stock, quite the contrary. If Lorenz is supposed to have been implicitly and subtly toadying to Nazi ideas, why should he not have done so openly and explicitly? Lorenz's use of physical beauty as a genetic marker in 1940 and 1942 was not presented as an exclusivist racial argument but as an argument against domesticisation.

57. See papers by Eibl-Eibesfeldt, 'Ritual and ritualization from a biological perspective' and by Paul Ekman, 'About brows; emotional and conversational signals', in M. von Cranach, K. Fopa, W. Lepenies and D. Ploog, eds., *Human Ethology. Claims and Limits of a New Discipline* (Cambridge and Paris, 1979).
58. Lorenz, *Behind the Mirror*, pp. 178, 233.
59. Ibid., pp.174–82.
60. Ibid., pp.175, 178–9, 245.
61. Ibid., p.245.
62. Ibid.
63. Ibid., pp.129, 183, 248–9.
64. Nisbett, *Konrad Lorenz*, p.176. Since writing this book, Konrad Lorenz's *The Waning of Humaneness* (London, 1988), has appeared, in which he specifically addresses environmental and ecological questions, and stresses his ecological sympathies.
65. Lorenz, *Behind the Mirror*, p.21; nature of man, 148–9.
66. Ibid., pp.148–9.
67. D. Stoddard, *On Geography* (Oxford, 1986), p.240.
68. Ibid., p.237.
69. Chisholm, *Conversations with Ecologists*, p.237; K. Boulding, 'The Economics of the Coming Spaceship Earth' in H. Jarret, ed., *Environmental Quality in a Growing Economy* (Baltimore, 1966).
70. Quoted in Stoddart, *On Geography*, pp.231–7.
71. J. Grinevald, 'Vernadsky and Lotka as source for Georgescu-Roegen's Economics', draft paper delivered to the Second Vienna Conference on Economics and Ecology, Barcelona, 1987.
72. For the pessimism of Henry Adams and an account of Bernard Brunhes, see Martinez-Alier, *Ecological Economics*, p.126.
73. For Henry Adams' theory of history and energy, see *The Education of Henry Adams* (London, 1961), pp.474–98.
74. For the argument that trees have standing, see C.D. Stone, 'Should Trees have Standing?', *Southern California Law Review*, 1972, vol. 45, cited and discussed in Thomas, *Man and the Natural world*, p.302,; the standard text on animal rights is P. Singer, *Animal Liberation* (London, 1976), while J. Passmore, *Man's Responsibility for Nature. Ecological Problems and Western Traditions* (London, 1974), sets the problem in philosophical perspective. The argument that affection for the weak and powerless is linked with aggression is made by Yi-Fu Tuan in *Dominance and Affection. The Making of Pets* (New Haven, 1984). His point is that domesticating and civilizing natural objects, even rivers, streams and plants, involves force and a violent change to their nature that expresses a fundamental sadism on the part of the perpetrator (farmer, gardener). To anyone who has shuddered at the sight of a bonsai tree the argument carries a certain force.

Chapter Four

1. On the implication of the second law of thermo-dynamics, a considerable literature has appeared since the late 1960s. A good source for the contemporary discussion is N. Georgescu-Roegen. *The Entropy Law and the Economic Process* (Cambridge, Mass., 1971). His theory resembles the earlier work discussed in H. Daly 'The Economic Thought of Frederick Soddy', *History of Political*

Economy, 1980, vol 12, pp.469–88. Georgescu-Roegen wrote the afterword to J. Rifkind and T. Howard's *Entropy. A New World View* (London, 1985), which delivers the ecological energy critique in a green context; see Chapter 11 below. See too J. Raumoulin, 'L'Homme et la Destruction des Ressources Naturelles. La *Raubwirtschaft* au tournant du siècle', *Annales, Intersciences*, 1984, vol. 39, pp.798–819.

2. W. Ostwald, *Natural Philosophy* (London and New York, 1911), p.184.
3. The eighteenth-century writer, Jean Baptiste Say; his 'law' that factors of production must always equal factors of consumption (the so-called circular-flow theory) helped to confirm the optimistic assumptions of the neoclassical economists about the long-term efficiencies of the market.
4. M. Breitbart, 'Peter Kropotkin, the Anarchist Geographer', in D.R. Stoddart, ed., *Geography, Ideology and Social Concern* (Oxford, 1981), p.40.
5. Podolinsky, the Ukrainian landowner, populist and socialist, constructed a table of energy inputs and concomitant production for French agriculture. He allowed 2550 kcal. per kilogramme of wood, hay and straw, and 3750 kcal. per kilogramme of wheat. The energy inputs of man and horses were also granted a calorific value. He concluded that forest and natural pastures produced wood and hay for nil energy input, while sown hay and wheat produced roughly twenty and ten times as much respectively as the calorific value of the energy used in the production process. See Martinez-Alier, *Ecological Economics*, p.48. For Bernal and Muller, see W.H. G. Armytage, *Yesterday's Tomorrows* (London, 1968), pp.150–2.
6. Pseud. J.J. Conington, *Nordington's Million* (London, 1923). One unintentionally ironic passage shows a recruiting agent sent to a cannibalistic, famine-ridden London. The hero travels from one side of London to the other in safety, through the simple expedient of *wearing a Red Cross armband*.
7. A. Trollope, *He Knew He Was Right* (St Lucia, Queensland, 1974), pp.220–1, expressed the more conventional point of view: that of the Victorian gentleman faced with intensive Italian peasant cultivation, catch-crops and intercropping.

   On this side of the house the tilled ground, either ploughed or dug with the spade, came up to the windows. There was hardly even a particle of grass to be seen.... The occupiers of Casalunga had thought more of the produce of their land than of picturesque or attractive appearance.

8. E. de Lavelaye, 'Land System of Belgium and Holland' in (Cobden Club), *Systems of Land Tenure in Various Countries* (London, 1870), pp.242–3.
9. Allaby and Bunyard, *The Politics of Self-Sufficiency*, p.31.
10. De Lavelaye, op. cit., p.229.
11. Readers who have encountered Marx's animadversions on capitalist agriculture, which plundered the graveyards of Europe for bones to nourish the soil of England, will be relieved that this adventurism was not in fact confined to the likes of Turnip Townshend.
12. On Rousseau and the peasants, and his erroneous observation on the living conditions of free and unfree peasants on the two sides of Lake Geneva, see D.G. Charlton, *New Images of the Natural in France. A Study in European Culture* (Cambridge, 1984), p.192.
13. K. Hamsun, *Growth of the Soil* (tr. W. Worster) (London, 1980), pp.316–17.
14. De la Vigne Eckmannsdorf, 'Blut und Boden', paper sent to Walther Darré, 7.12.31, Federal Archives, Koblenz, NL94/1.
15. Von Bernhardi, *Versuch einer Kritik der Gründe die für grosses und kleines Grundeigentum sprechen* (St Petersburg, 1849); examples of the doctoral theses are, Huschke, 'Landwirtschaftliche Reinertragsberechnungen bei Klein-Mittel- und Grossbetriebe' (Jena, 1902); Luberg, 'Vergleichende Untersuchungen über Wirtschaftsergebnisse und Wirtschaftsbedingungen kleiner, mittlerer und grosser Besitzungen unter dem Einfluss niedriger Getreidepreise' (Allenstein, 1898); Stumpfe, 'Über die Konkurrenzfähigkeit des kleinen und mittleren Grundbesitzes genenüber dem Grossgrundbesitze', *Thiels Landwirtschaftliche Jahrbücher* (1896); Klawki, 'Über die Konkurenzfähigkeit des landwirtschaftlichen

Kleinbetriebes', *Thiels Landwirtschaftliche Jahrbücher* (1899); Dr Julius Faucher on the Russian *mir*, 'Russian Agrarian Legislation of 1861', in (Cobden Club), op. cit., R. Drill, 'Soll Deutschland seinen ganzen Getreide bedarf selbst produzieren?' Inaug. Diss., Munich and Stuttgart, 1895.

16. For a discussion of Gladstone and Ireland, and Balfour's support of state-aided land purchase for English smallholders in 1909, see Offer, *Property and Politics*, p.357; example of Irish land reform, and need to avert possible Socialism in Great Britain by land redistribution, Long to Balfour, September, 1910, Offer, op. cit., p.362; Lord Salisbury supports Joseph Chamberlain and the Smallholding Act of 1892, Offer, op. cit., p.353.
17. Offer, *Property and Politics*, p.351; J.S. Mill on emigration scheme, E.S. Halevy, *The Philosophic Radicals* (London, 1972), pp.60–2.
18. Outline of Lloyd George's proposals, Offer, *Property and Politics*, p.360. The comparison with the British Union of Fascists is my own.
19. Breitbart, 'Kropotkin, Anarchist Geographer', p.140, describes how Kropotkin was honoured by a special banquet of the Royal Geographical Society of Great Britain in the 1890s. See G. Woodcock and I. Avakumovic, *Kropotkin, the Anarchist Prince* (London, 1950) p.59, for Kropotkin's reaction to the failure to carry out other reforms he advocated, through vested interests, bureaucratic sloth and squandering of money.
20. Ludwig von Mises attacked Kropotkin for this interpretation in *Socialism. An Economic and Sociological Analysis* (London 1936), p.319; 'a fact which clearly exposes the decay of sociological thought in recent decades is that people now begin to combat sociological Darwinism by pointing to examples of mutual aid (symbiosis)... Kropotkin, a defiant antagonist of liberal social theory,...found among animals the rudiment of social ties and set these in opposition to conflict.'
21. Breitbart, 'Kropotkin, Anarchist Geographer', p.139.
22. Cf. *Resurgence*, 1986, no. 118. The whole number is devoted to 'Education on a Human Scale'.
23. Lewis Mumford, *The Culture of Cities* (London, 1940), refers to Kropotkin, pp.339–40. C. Ward, in a stimulating commentary on and introduction to P. Kropotkin, *Fields, Factories and Workshops* (London, 1985), p. v, discusses Kropotkin's relevance to today's ecologists; also p.195 on Ebenezer Howard; p.81 on Blatchford.
24. Thomas Jefferson, communication from Heinz Haushofer; J.Q. Adams, *Letters from Silesia* (London, 1800).
25. J. von Thünen, *The Isolated State* (London, 1966), pp.229, 246.
26. Attack on marginalist economics, see K. Tribe and A. Hussein, unpublished paper presented at a Conference on German Rural History, University of East Anglia, 1979; N. Vlengels, 'Thünen als deutscher Sozialist', *Jahrbuch für National-Oekonomie*, 1941, vol. 153, pp.339–62. The Universty of Rostock organized a bicentennial celebration of Von Thünen in 1982.
27. Von Thünen expressed a stadial theory of history. In his introduction to the second part of *The Isolated State*, pp.246–58, he argued that:

    An ancient myth pervades our agricultural writings that whatever the stage of social development, there is one valid farming system only, – as though every system that is more simple, every enterprise that adopts extensive methods to economise on labour, were proof of the practising farmer's ignorance...A human being changes at the various stages of his life – how much more so will the succeeding generations be different from their predecessors.

28. Ibid., p.194.
29. Ibid., p.252.
30. Ibid., pp. 245–7.
31. For the debate in Germany over protectionism and agriculture versus industry, see K. Barkin, *The Controversy over German Industrialisation 1890–1902* (Chicago, 1972); for Rodbertus, the only English work is C. Gonner, *The Social Philosophy of Rodbertus* (London, 1899); G. Ruhland wrote a pamphlet on the evils of speculation and the futures market, which is supposed to have caused the closing down of the Berlin futures market, see C.W. Smith, introduction to G. Ruhland, *The Ruin*

of the World's Agriculture and Trade (London, 1896). For Ehrenberg and the Thünen-Archiv, see Haushofer, *Ideengeschichte der Agrarwirtschaft und Agrarpolitik*, vol. 2, *Vom Ersten Weltkrieg bis zur Gegenwart* (Bonn, 1958), p.40.

32. C. Rose, 'Wilhelm Dilthey's Philosophy of Historical Understanding. A Neglected Heritage of Continental Humanistic Geography', in Stoddart, *Geography, Ideology and Social Concern*, p.99.
33. Details about Ratzel and other geographers are from Raumoulin, 'L' Homme et la Destruction', pp.798–801. The comments are my own.
34. G.S. Dunbar, 'Élisée Reclus, an Anarchist in Geography', in Stoddart, *Geography, Ideology and Social Concern*, p.157.
35. G. Woodcock, *Anarchism. A History of Libertarian Ideas and Movements* (Harmondsworth, 1975), p.150; T. Zeldin, *France, 1848–1945. Intellect and Pride* (Oxford, 1980), p.35; Dunbar, 'Élisée Reclus', op. cit., pp.156, 161–2. I am grateful to Lord Beloff for the reference to Reclus and the Russian geographers.
36. Raumoulin, 'L' Homme et la Destruction', pp.799–800.
37. Ibid., pp.803 ff. Colin Ross, *Das Unvollendete Kontinent* (Leipzig, 1930), and see Modris Ekstein, 'When Death was Young...German Modernism and the Great War', in H. Pogge von Strandmann, A. Nicholls, et. al., eds., *Ideas into Politics* (London, 1985), pp.25, 33.
38. Raumoulin, 'L' Homme et la Destruction', pp.803, 807.
39. R. MacMaster, *Danilevsky. A Russian Totalitarian Philosopher* (Cambridge, Mass., 1967), p.80. See also pp.17, 22–7, 51, 78–9; the stadial theory of human history, pp.7, 81–2, 93, 95, 102–3; Danilevsky abandons Comte, p.169; on evolution, p.172.
40. For Danilevsky as a major figure in Pan-Slavism, theoretician of history, botanist and ichthyologist, see M.B. Petrovich, *The Emergence of Russian Panslavism, 1856–1870* (New York, 1956), esp. pp.65–75.
41. P. Boardman, *The Worlds of Patrick Geddes* (London, 1978), pp.9, 404–5.
42. Ibid., p.405.
43. P. Geddes, *Cities in Evolution* (London, 1915), *passim*; P. Mairet, *Pioneer of Sociology. The Life and Letters of Patrick Geddes* (Westport, Conn., 1979), pp.153–5.
44. Geddes' two articles are quoted and discussed in Boardman, *Worlds of Patrick Geddes*, pp.404–5.
45. L. Mumford, *The Culture of Cities* (London, 1940), p.302.
46. Ibid., p.495–6.
47. B.T. Robson, 'Geography and Social Science. The Role of Patrick Geddes', in Stoddart, *Geography, Ideology and Social Concern*, pp.187, 204. On the other hand, Mairet, *Pioneer of Sociology*, p.204, stresses Geddes' support for the cottage garden city ideal as opposed to apartment settlements: he preferred cottages to flats.
48. Robson, 'Geography and Social Science', p.204.
49. Boardman, *Worlds of Patrick Geddes*, p.405; on Gräser, see M. Green, *Mountain of Truth. The Counter Culture Begins. Ascona, 1900–1920* (Hanover and London, 1986), p.53.
50. Mairet, *Pioneer of Sociology*, p.155.
51. N. Pevsner, quoted in David Watkin, *Morality and Architecture* (Oxford, 1977), p.95. Pevsner was an advocate of *Jugendstil*, or Art Nouveau. The style was attacked in its day as decadent, alien and destructive. Pevsner became a Modernist, emigrated to Britain, and ended as a famous architectural *savant* and historian. He ceaselessly argued on behalf of unpopular modern architecture. More damagingly, he tried to write out of history those English architects who did not accept this tradition, or who, like Lutyens, could not be fitted into this picture.
52. Watkin, *Morality and Architecture*, p.95. Watkin stresses that Pevsner would not have wished to identify himself with either Bolshevism or National Socialism.
53. Ibid., p.88.
54. Ibid., p.89.
55. H. Agar with Lewis Mumford, *City of Man. A Declaration of World Democracy* (New York, 1940).
56. Mumford, *Culture of Cities*, p.388, and see also pp.495–6.
57. Mumford, *Culture of Cities*, pp.495–6.
58. G. Auty, *Spectator*, 26.10.85.
59. Daly, 'The Economic Thought of Frederick Soddy', p.469. See also Martinez-Alier, *Ecological Economics*, pp.140–1.
60. F. Soddy, *Cartesian Economics* (London, 1922), p.2; Martinez-Alier, *Ecological Economics*, pp.129–35.

61. Soddy does not seem to have speculated that the 'capital' aspect of corn lay in its use as seed corn, and the long-term planning and activity needed to plant and harvest it.
62. Gasman, *Scientific Origins of National Socialism*, p.69, see especially connection between Ostwald's remarks on the sun and poems and solstice ceremonies. For the complex connections between mysticism and scientific materialism, see N. Goodrick-Clarke's discussion of Lanz von Liebenfels attraction to 'idealistic monism', *The Occult Roots of Nazism* (London, 1985), p.102. For Ostwald's theories of energy, see Martinez-Alier, *Ecological Economics*, pp.183–6.
63. Soddy, *Cartesian Economics*, pp.22, 30.
64. Daly, 'Economic Thought of Frederick Soddy', pp.476–81.
65. For Soddy and solar energy, see Martinez-Alier, *Ecological Economics*, pp.136–7.
66. Ibid., p.142.
67. Soddy, *Cartesian Economics*, p.7.
68. Ibid., p.15. Soddy paraphrased Ruskin's *Unto This Last* as follows;

    Ruskin appears to have had a very much clearer conception of the real nature of wealth than either earlier or later economists. He points out...that the art of becoming rich was to get more *relatively* than other people, so that those with less may be available as the servants and employees of those with more. In this acute and original analysis of the real nature of the individual's wealth-power over the lives and the labour of others – Ruskin disclosed probably the most important difference between the interests of the individual and the interests of the State, and the main reason why the mastery of man over nature has hitherto resulted in so meagre a contribution to the perfection of human life. ...Of what use are the discoveries of scientific men of new modes and more ample ways of living so long as the laws of human nature turn all the difficultly won wealth into increased power of the few over the lives and labours of the many?

69. Ibid., p.32.
70. Martinez-Alier, *Ecological Economics*, pp.144–8. He argues, pp.145–7, that the resource economics technocrats 'realised that the ecological approach' led to 'egalitarian principles of distribution.'
71. K. Popper, *Unended Quest. An Intellectual Biography* (London, 1982), pp.11, 127. See also pp.12–13, where Popper mentions that 'Popper-Lynkeus had a considerable following among the Monists of Vienna'; a comment which adds weight to my interpretation of Monist politics, see Chapter 3 above.
72. See J. Weston, ed., *Red and Green. The New Politics of the Environment* (London, 1986), and M. Bookchin, *Post-Scarcity Anarchism* (Berkeley, 1971).
73. Wolf-Dieter Hasenclever, Speaker for the green section in the Baden-Württemberg Landtag between 1980 and 1984, *Die Zeit*, 2.5.86.
74. Martinez-Alier, *Ecological Economics*, pp.199–206.
75. Early anarchist programmes are described in A. Masters, *Bakunin* (London, 1975), pp.250–2, 'On Building the New Social Order', programme by James Guillaume, and Bakunin's *The Revolutionary Catechism*, pp.168–9. Masters discusses Bakunin's sympathy for peasants, greater than that of Marx, pp.103–4.
76. A.V. Chayanov, *A Theory of Peasant Economy* (ed. D. Thorner et al.) (Madison, Wisconsin, 1986).
77. Information in a paper circulated by A. Stobart.
78. G. Stapledon, *Disraeli and the New Age* (London, 1943), pp.116–17.
79. Ibid., p.20.
80. Ibid., pp.49–50.
81. Ibid., p.133.
82. Ibid.
83. Ibid., p.115.
84. Ibid., p.116. Stapledon's biographer, Robert Waller, argues in his introduction to Stapledon's *Human Ecology* (London, 1964), p.34, that by 1945 Stapledon had changed his 1912 belief in technology as a weapon of construction, and no longer defined himself as a social engineer. However, on p.62 of his 1964 book, written some years before publication, Stapledon called for more planning. His aim was to 'steer a middle course between the all-out... ruralism and craftsmanship of the countryside as depicted by...men like Hugh Massingham and Rolf Gardiner

and . . . the all-out mechanization of agriculture and industrialization and urban alienation'. He wanted to define the correct balance between land and nature on the one hand, and 'concrete, the artificial and creature comforts' on the other. Stapledon's belief that the destiny of man trembled in the balance until this dilemma was solved is an example of early apocalyptic nullity.

85. Stapledon, *Disraeli*, p.123.
86. See for example, J. Beresford, *The Long View* (London, 1944).

Chapter Five

1. See W.H.G. Armytage, *Yesterday's Tomorrows. A Historical Survey of Future Societies* (London, 1968), and F.E. and F.P. Manuel, *Utopian Thought in the Western World* (Oxford, 1979), for an interesting survey of utopias; the Manuels' book looks most closely at Europe between 1500–1800, with some coverage of the nineteenth century.
2. For a contemporary account of radical communities of the United States in the nineteenth century, see Charles Nordhoff, *The Communistic Societies of the US* (New York, 1875; this edition New York, 1960). For the Doukhoubours, see George Woodcock and Ivan Avakumovic, *The Doukhoubours* (London, 1968).
3. Andrew Rigby, *Communes in Britain* (London, 1974), pp.2–3. A study of these groups would be informative for the sociologist or anthropologist, but such studies have for the most part been undertaken by 'believers' (as with Andrew Rigby, historian of alternative hippy communes, whose books are redolent of such phrases as 'where it's at', and 'getting it together'). The excellent study by Lawrence Veysey, *The Communal Experience. Anarchist and Mystical Counter-Cultures in America* (New York, 1973), is an exceptionally open, honest and well-informed work which combines an overview of American radicalism with anthropological descriptions of communes, observed over some years.
4. H.D. Thoreau, *Walden, or Life in the Woods* (first published 1854: this edition New York, 1961), pp.24, 32 (he *borrows* an axe), 34, 38.
5. R. Bahro, 'Fundamental Thoughts on the Crisis of the Greens', in *Building the Green Movement* (London, 1986), p.159.
6. Veysey, *Communal Experience*, p.32.
7. Ibid., p.23.
8. Ibid., p.3.
9. See discussion in Everett Webber, *Escape to Utopia. The communal movement in America* (New York, 1959), pp.418–19.
10. Arthur Christy, *The Orient in American Transcendentalism. A Study of Emerson, Thoreau and Alcott* (New York, 1932).
11. See G, Orwell, 'Helen's Babies', in *Collected Essays, Journalism and Letters*, vol. 4. *In Front of Your Nose* (Harmondsworth, 1970), p.286, 'uncorrupted . . . integrity or good morale, founded partly on an unthinking piety . . . an underlying confidence in the future, a sense of freedom and opportunity'.
12. H. George, *Progress and Poverty* (London, 1951), p.2: 'Could he have conceived of the hundred thousand improvements which these only suggest, what would he have inferred as to the social condition of mankind? . . . How could the vice, the crime, the ignorance, the brutality, that spring from poverty and the fear of poverty, exist where poverty had vanished? *Who should crouch where all were freemen? Who oppress where all were peers?*' (my italics).
    George briskly disposes of Malthusian prophecies; man is the only animal who has the ability to increase his food production with his population increase, pp.55, 59. George's opposition to Darwinian evolution is based here on the presumption that man is quantitatively superior to the animals in technology and reasoning; it is not based on a moral distaste for competition, see also Offer, *Property and Politics*, pp.344–5, on George's 'pantheistic religion'.
13. W.H.G. Armytage, *Heavens Below. Utopian Experiments in England, 1560–1960* (London, 1961), p.308.
14. Ibid., p.316; Veysey, *Communal Experience*, p.45; and see Offer, *Property and Politics*, chapters 20 and 21.
15. Veysey, *Communal Experience*, p.10. G. Woodcock, though, in his standard work *Anarchism. A History of Libertarian Ideas and Movements* (Harmondsworth, 1975), omits this aspect of anarchy.

16. See Armytage, *Heavens Below*, p.292, and see Jan Marsh, *Back to the Land. The Pastoral Impulse in Victorian England, 1880 to 1914* (London, 1982) for a detailed study of Ruskin-inspired communes and the Salvation Army land colonies. Clark C. Spence, *The Salvation Army Farm Colonies* (Tucson, 1985) is a fascinating account.
17. Paul Meier, *William Morris, the Marxist Dreamer* (Hassocks, Sussex, 1978), pp.68–9.
18. Armytage, *Heavens Below*, p.307.
19. H. Rider Haggard, *A Farmer's Year* (London, 1899), pp.421, 439.
20. A.N. Wilson, *Hilaire Belloc* (Harmondsworth, 1984), pp.292–3.
21. Ibid., p.293.
22. Orwell often referred to Chesterton's hopeless lack of progressive spirit. The most accessible account is in *Collected Essays, Journalism and Letters*, vol. 4, *In Front of Your Nose*, pp.123–4.
23. Cited in Armytage, *Heavens Below*, p.407.
24. Ibid., p.395.
25. Marsh, *Back to the Land*, passim.
26. Paul Weindling, unpublished lectures at the Wellcome Unit for the History of Medicine, Oxford, 1985.
27. See Ulrich Linse, ed., *Zurück o Mensch zur Mutter Erde. Landkommunen in Deutschland, 1890–1933* (Munich, 1983), intr., and for George and the single tax in England, see Offer, *Property and Politics*, p.345.
28. For a full account see B. Zablocki, *The Joyful Community. The account of the Bruderhof. A Communal Movement now in its Third Generation* (Baltimore, 1971).
29. See Bundesarchiv, Koblenz, Artamanen file, NS 1285. They talk, too, about 'awakened racial consciousness', an unusual phrase for the period. The passage runs;

    Artam – tillers of the soil, fighters for honour, ...land and *Lebensraum*. Artam means the renewal of the people ...The most holy revolutionary will was expressed by the first Artamanen in the deed. (zur Tat) Youth's early instinct...led us to Mother Earth. Without programmes, or great speeches...the blood-red swastika banner...was the symbol of awakened racial consciousness'; quoted in Linse, op. cit., p.331, my translation.

    This extract was published in a 1934 document, and may therefore not be entirely reliable.
30. See R. Sheldrake, 'Mother of All', in S. Kumar, ed., *Schumacher Lectures* (London, 1984) pp.219–51.
31. Quoted in Rigby, *Communes in Britain* pp.109–10.
32. See John Higham, 'The Reorientation of American Culture in the 1890s', in John Weiss, ed., *The Origins of Modern Consciousness* (Detroit, 1965), who saw continuity since the 1890s in 'back to nature' ideals; and an interesting account of individualistic anarchists who started with calls for general strikes, and became neo-fascist in a Sorelian spirit, in Michael Wreszin, 'Albert Jay Nock; the Anarchist Elitist Tradition in America', *American Quarterly*, 1969, vol. 21, pp.165–89.
33. Veysey, *Communal Experience*, p.469.
34. See Arthur E. Morgan, *The Small Community* (New York, 1942) and Newlyn R. Smith, *Land for the Small Man. English and Welsh Experience with Publicly Supplied Smallholdings, 1860–1937* (New York, 1946).
35. Veysey, *Communal Experience*, p.43.
36. Webber, *Escape to Utopia*, pp.418–19; Veysey, *Communal Experience*, pp.317–20.
37. See C.E. Ashworth, 'Flying Saucers, Spoon-Bending and Atlantis: a Structural Analysis of New Mythologies', *Sociological Review*, 1980, vol. 28, pp.353–76. In *The World and I* (Washington, 1987), pp.627–643, Richard Rubinstein writes on 'Religion and the Rise of Capitalism; the Case of Japan': 'Unlike every nation of Judaeo-Christian inheritance, the Japanese alone remained in contact with their oldest sources of religious and cultural values' (p.638). Rubinstein is writing about nationalism, but the point is valid generally.
38. W.A. Hinds, *American Communities and Co-operative Colonies* (Philadelphia, 1978); Webber, *Escape to Utopia*, pp.418–19.

Chapter Six

1. See J.M. Winter, 'Military Fitness and Civilian Health in Britain during the First World War', *Journal of Contem-*

porary History, 1980, vol. 15, pp.211–45.

2. A. Sutcliffe, *Towards the Planned City. Germany, Britian, the United States and France, 1780–1914* (Oxford, 1981), p.77.
3. Lowe and Goyder, *Environmental Groups in Politics*, pp.15–21.
4. C. Barnett, *The Audit of War* (London, 1987), pp.12–14.
5. Worster, *Nature's Economy*, pp.329–31.
6. J.L. Finlay, 'John Hargrave, the Green Shirts and Social Credit', *Journal of Contemporary History*, 1970 vol.5, p.54; J. Hargrave, *The Confession of the Kibbo Kift. A Declaration and General Exposition of the Work of the Kindred*, (London, 1927); the work begins with a quotation from Lao-Tzu, 'production without possession, action without self-assertion, development without domination'.
7. D. Prynn, 'The Woodcraft Folk and the Labour Movement, 1925–1970', *Journal of Contemporary History*, 1983, vol. 8, pp.79–95.
8. Finlay, 'John Hargrave,' p.54.
9. M. Green, *Mountain of Truth. The Counter-Culture Begins. Ascona, 1900–1920* (Hanover and London, 1986), pp.29–31, and *passim*.
10. M. Straight, *After Long Silence* (New York and London, 1983), pp.32, 34.
11. F. Grover, *Drieu la Rochelle and the Fiction of Testimony* (Berkeley, 1958), p.45; M. Young, *The Elmhirsts of Dartington* (London, 1982), pp.89–90.
12. According to B. Morris, 'Ernest Thompson Seton and the Origin of the Woodcraft Movement', *Journal of Contemporary History*, 1970, vol. 5, p.193, Paul, the founder of the Woodcraft Folk, was more pacifist.
13. Finlay, 'John Hargrave', p.55; Morris, 'Ernest Thompson Seton', p.189; Prynn, 'The Woodcraft Folk', p.84.
14. C.B. Macpherson, *Democracy in Alberta. Social Credit and the Party System* (Toronto, 1962), p.113, and see his chapters IV and V for an exposition of Douglas's theories and their effect on Hargrave; see also pp.108–9.
15. Ibid.; pp.108–9.
16. See H. Kenner's description of Pound's interpretation of Douglas, *The Pound Era* (London, 1975), pp.301–18.
17. Finlay, 'John Hargrave', pp.56, 63.
18. MacPherson, *Democracy in Alberta*, p.134 n. 69.
19. I am grateful to S. Cullen, of Nuffield College, Oxford, for this information.
20. J. Webb, *The Occult Establishment*, vol. 2,*The Flight from Reason* (Glasgow, 1981), pp.89–91. In 1976 a rock musical appeared at the Edinburgh Festival called 'Kibbo Kift!', occasioning a one-page, sympathetic interview with Hargrave, in *The Guardian*, 10.6.1976.
21. Quoted in H.R. Gardiner, *World Without End* (London, 1932), p.37.
22. D.H. Lawrence, *Kangaroo* (London, 1923), p.106.
23. R. Ebbatson, *Lawrence and the Nature Tradition* (Hassocks, Sussex, 1980), pp.38, 71, 240.
24. Green, *Mountain of Truth*, p.230.
25. E.g., D.H. Lawrence, *Women in Love* (London, 1980), pp.26–8; idem, *The Captain's Doll* (London, 1980), p.507.
26. D.H. Lawrence, *The Rainbow* (London, 1980) p.861.
27. Lawrence, *Women in Love*, p.49.
28. H.R. Gardiner, *Water Springing From* the Ground (ed. by A. Best) (Fontmell Magna, Dorset, 1972), p.xi.
29. W.J. Keith, *The Rural Tradition* (Hassocks, Sussex, 1975), p.257.
30. Gardiner, *World Without End*, pp.36–7.
31. Keith, *The Rural Tradition*, p.255.
32. H.R. Gardiner, *The English Folk Dance Tradition* (London, 1923), p.29.
33. Ibid., pp.30.
34. Ibid., p.24.
35. Ibid., p.12.
36. Ibid., p.19.
37. H.R. Gardiner and H. Rocholl, eds., *Britain and Germany. A Frank Discussion* (London, 1928), pp.121–2.
38. Gardiner, *English Folk Dance Tradition*, p.30.
39. Ibid., p.5.
40. Gardiner, *World Without End*, pp.33–4.
41. H.R. Gardiner, *England Herself. Ventures in Rural Restoration* (London, 1943), p.14.
42. Griffiths, *Fellow Travellers of the Right*, p.144.
43. Gardiner, *England Herself*, p.14.
44. Ibid., p.87.
45. Gardiner, *Britain and Germany*, p.127.
46. Gardiner, *World Without End*, pp.41–3.
47. Ibid., p.43.

48. Gardiner, *Britian and Germany*, pp.261, 134; other contributors to the symposium, *passim*.
49. Gardiner on the Nordic Race, 'A Common Destiny', in *Britain and Germany*, p.256. A bizarre footnote to the theme of race, empires and planning is afforded by *Bio-Economics* (London, 1938) by Joseph Yahuda, a barrister and supporter of eugenics, who had written earlier criticisng democracy as a basis for government. He argued that economic and social principles rested on evolutionary biology, and that society was divided not only into classes but into categories of fitness (Upper Fit, Upper Unfit; Lower Fit and Lower Unfit). He offered a programme of 'regeneration of the human stock', based on sound natural economy, which, unlike 'economic individualism' depended more on the qualities of virtue and duty. He saw industry and civilization as sapping racial vitality. The 'racial reserves' and 'racial resources' of Britain had been drained by her role as world leader. Yahuda argued for planned British emigration to the Dominions, in conjunction with immigration into Britain from Europe. He attacked the 'grotesque racialism' of National Socialism (while admiring what he saw as its cult of physical health and classlessness), but hoped that a new world order based on peaceful co-existence with the fascist countries would emerge. This little-known author used a language of 'racial survival' and decay associated today with social Darwinism. He opposed economic individualism and democracy. But his suggestions for reallocating human and physical resources throughout British-ruled territory rested on the same belief in planning, public service and duty as that of the Fabians. Yahuda's combination of biology and economics had an ecological quality, although he does not use the term.
50. Earl of Portsmouth, *A Knot of Roots* (London, 1965), p.126; R. Thurlow, *Fascism in Britain. A History, 1918–1985* (Oxford, 1987), p.44; Webb, *The Occult Establishment*, vol 2, pp.102, 134.
51. Griffiths, *Fellow Travellers of the Right*, pp.324–6.
52. *New Pioneer*, 1939 vol. 1, pp.152, 163.
53. Ibid, 1939, vol. 1, p.199.
54. *New Pioneer*, 1938, vol. 1, p.2.
55. Ibid., p.6. This article is unsigned, but is in Gardiner's prose style.
56. Ibid.
57. Portsmouth, *Knot of Roots*, pp.89–90; *Biologists in Search of Material. An Interim Report on the Work of the Pioneer Health Centre, Peckham* (London, 1938).
58. *New Pioneer*, 1938, vol. 1, p.16.
59. Ibid., pp.17ff.
60. G.V. Jacks and R.O. Whyte, *The Rape of the Earth* (London, 1939), pp.80, 82, 163, 180, 251.
61. G.T. Wrench, *The Wheel of Health* (London, 1938), p.51.
62. Ibid., p.52.
63. Portsmouth, *Knot of Roots*, p.37.
64. Ibid., p.85.
65. The first meeting of the Kinship in Husbandry was in Blunden's rooms. All kinds of fantastic rumours were attached to the members of Kinship in Husbandry after the Second World War, because of the cross-membership between them and the English Mistery and English Array. George Thayer, in *The British Political Fringe* (London, 1965), pp.104–6, reports a rumour that the Array plotted together to murder Britain's Jews. No source is given for this allegation, which was also not mentioned in Blunden's obituary when he died in 1974. Some such rumour may have been responsible for his relinquishment of his Merton Fellowship during the Second World War. He was not interned during the war. He went to the Far East soon after it, and, indeed, spent most of his working life abroad. Thayer's book, while castigated by Skidelsky for its treatment of Mosley and British fascism, does offer a glimpse into the mentality and political assumptions of his time and place. He associates 'Nature, the sun, the soil' with the post-war far right, and claimed that 'a belief in Soil, Health and Organic Farming. . . Muck and Mysticism' characterised the anti-democratic, anti-Communist, anti-semitic and anti-banking lobbies.
66. Michael Beaumont was later to be on the board of the Rural Reconstruction Association. For information on the Rockefeller file on Carrel, I am grate-

ful to Paul Weindling, of the Wellcome Unit for the History of Medicine, Oxford.
67. *Anglo-German Review*, 1939, vol. 3, p.142.
68. C. Ward, commentary on *Fields, Factories and Workshops*, pp.115, 119,n.
69. Maurice Hewlett, *Rest Harrow* (London, 1912).
70. Maurice Hewlett, *Song of the Plow: a Chronicle of England* (London, 1917) p.viii.
71. Ibid., p.222.
72. Webb, *The Occult Establishment*, vol. 2, p.89.
73. S.L. Bensusan, in *Latter-Day Rural England, 1927* (London, 1928), took the Rural Reconstruction League, 'largely Labour in its sympathies', as 'ample evidence that Labour is learning' the importance of the agricultural sector; p.220.
74. M. Fordham, *Rebuilding of Rural England* (London, 1924), p.66.
75. M. Fordham, *The Restoration of Agriculture* (London, 1945), pp.4–5.
76. Ibid., p.18.
77. Ibid, p.21; M. Fordham, *The Land and Life. A Survey prepared for the R.R.A* (London, 1942), p.84.
78. Fordham, *Rebuilding*, pp.50, 205–6.
79. Fordham, *Rebuilding*, introduction; idem., *Land and Life*, p.23.
80. H.J. Massingham, *Remembrance. An Autobiography* (London, 1941), pp.59–60.
81. H.J. Massingham, *The Tree of Life* (London, 1943), p.166.
82. Ibid., p.62.
83. Massingham, *Remembrance*, p.62.
84. Ibid, p.6.
85. Ibid.
86. Ibid., pp.31–3.
87. Ibid., p.42; R. Tomalin, *W.H. Hudson, A Biography*, (Oxford, 1984), pp.25, 146–9.
88. Massingham, *Remembrance*, p.42.
89. Ibid.
90. H. Rauschning, *Make or Break with the Nazis* (London, 1941), pp.123–5, 212ff.
91. Massingham, *Tree of Life*, p.176.
92. Massingham, *Remembrance*, pp.142–3.
93. Ibid., pp.143–4.
94. Ibid., p.144.
95. Ibid., p.146.
96. F. Fanon, *The Wretched of the Earth* (London, 1965), pp.27–74, 169–70.
97. H. Carpenter, *J.R.R. Tolkien. A Biography* (London, 1977), p.51.
98. Ibid., pp.21, 89–90.
99. J.R.R. Tolkien, letter to Milton Waldman, of Collins, not dated, probably late 1951, in H. Carpenter, ed., with assistance from Christopher Tolkien, *The Letters of J.R.R. Tolkien* (London, 1981), pp.144–5.
100. Carpenter, *Tolkien*, p.187.
101. J.R.R. Tolkien to Michael Tolkien, 9.6.41, *Letters*, pp.55–6.
102. M. Green, *Mountain of Truth*, p.231.

Chapter Seven

1. Chronicles such as that by R.K. Delderfield, to the aficionado of Williamson, seem but stale imitations. Compare the treatment of a remembered idyll in John Fowles' *Daniel Martin* with any similar passage in Williamson's books to see how original and precise the latter's work is. On the pre-First World War, and its glow of remembered sunlight, the unsentimental and non-rural Rebecca West, in *This Real Nght* (London, 1984), refers to the post-war period as 'the Lent that was to endure all our lives' after 'this time of Carnival', p.217.
2. See Introduction above, notes 5 and 6.
3. Ebbatson, *Lawrence* and *the Nature Tradition*, p.2, and on Jefferies, pp.129–37.
4. All quotes from *Nature and Eternity* are taken from Edward Thomas, *Richard Jefferies* (London, 1978), pp.176–7. The essay is also to be found in R. Jefferies, *The Hills and the Vale* (Oxford, 1980), pp.284–305.
5. Ebbatson, *Lawrence and the Nature Tradition*, pp.129, 137.
6. Keith, *The Rural Tradition*, p.15.
7. Thurlow, *Fascism in Britain*, who discusses Williamson's politics and his involvement with Mosley, argues that 'Williamson's romanticism and nature-worship...was to owe much to the books of Richard Jefferies, in particular the sunlight imagery of much of his work', p.42; Keith, *The Rural Tradition*, pp.14–15, 140; J.W. Blench, who is writing a critical study of Williamson's work, has given a detailed account of this issue in 'The Influence of Richard Jefferies on Henry Williamson', Part I, *Durham University Journal*, 1986, vol. 79,

and Part II, *Durham University Journal*, 1987, vol. 79. He stresses Williamson's desire to bring Jefferies' *Hodge* up-to-date, and examines the debt Williamson's apprentice nature writings owed to Jefferies. He traces a continuous line of inspiration through *The Flax of Dream* and the later novels.

8. H. Williamson, *The Phoenix Generation* (London, 1965), pp.144–5
9. H. Williamson, *Young Phillip Maddison* (London, 1985), p.30.
10. Williamson, *Phoenix Generation*, p.48.
11. H. Williamson, *Donkey Boy* (London, 1984), p.122, my italics.
12. Williamson, *Young Phillip Maddison*, p.72.
13. H. Williamson, *Lucifer Before Sunrise* (London, 1967), pp.423–4.
14. H. Williamson, *The Labouring Life* (London, 1932), p.109.
15. Williamson was briefly interned at the beginning of the Second World War, and by 1944, the BBC had forbidden him to broadcast. See copy of BBC memo, published in *The Henry Williamson Society Journal*, 1983, p.21. Thurlow, in *Fascism in Britain*, pp.26–7, thinks that 'it is his support for Mosley which goes some way to account for the continuing neglect of his work by much of the literary establishment', and adds that a writer specialising in First World War literature, Paul Fusil, ignores Williamson's war books. Thurlow regrets this, commenting that Williamson's accurate reporting of social classes under the impact of war helps to explain why 'idealists and embittered individuals' should have turned to fascism between the wars.
16. Williamson, *Phoenix Generation*, pp. 373–24.
17. Williamson, *Lucifer* p.313.
18. Williamson, *Phoenix Generation*, p.307.
19. Ibid., p.376.
20. Ibid., pp.144–5.
21. Ibid., p.150.
22. Williamson, *Lucifer*, p.76.
23. Ibid., p.313.
24. Ibid., p.467.
25. Ibid., p.498.
26. Keith, *The Rural Tradition*, pp.213–31, esp. p.229, and see note 15, above. Williamson's dedication to Hitler was in the 1930s, and *Good-bye West Country* (London, 1937), carried a favourable account of the Nuremberg Rally, but the climate of opinion was different before the war, when many dignitaries like Lloyd George visited Nazi Germany and expressed approval of the country and its policies.
27. Williamson, *Lucifer*, p.466.
28. Ibid., p.480–1.
29. Ibid., p.466.
30. Ibid., p.490.
31. Ibid., p.101.
32. Ibid., p.487.
33. H. Williamson, *The Children of Shallowford* (London, 1939), p.227.
34. Ibid., p.34.
35. Williamson, *Goodbye West Country*, p.283.
36. H. Williamson, *The Gold Falcon* (London, 1933), p.142.
37. Ibid., p.33.
38. H. Williamson, *Story of a Norfolk Farm* (London, 1941), and cf. Admiral Sir Barry Domvile, Mosley follower interned during the war, who sent his two children to Dartington Hall in the 1920s. According to Michael Straight, *After Long Silence*, p.43, Domvile withdrew them after what he claimed were Black Magic practices came to light. A libel writ ensued.
39. Williamson, *A Clear Water Stream* (London, 1958), pp.33–4, 71.
40. Ibid., pp.40, 83.
41. Ibid., pp. 205–6, 222.
42. Williamson, *Lucifer*, p.515.
43. R. Mortimore, 'Henry Williamson and 'A Chronicle of Ancient Sunlight': an Appreciation', in B. Sewell, ed., *Henry Williamson. The Man, the Writings. A Symposium* (Padstow, Cornwall, 1980), p.135.
44. T. Hughes, 'A Memorial Address', in B. Sewell. ed., *Symposium*, p.162.
45. Cf. T.H. White, *The Fifth Book of Merlin* (London, 1948), pp.144–5, for lessons drawn from the wild geese. White's *The Sword in the Stone* shows Arthur being prepared for kingship by living among animals, and comparing their different societies. White admired the wild geese, because they had no nations and no frontiers. He wanted man to become a migrant again and thereby avoid property and territoriality, which White saw as the causes of war. Although Williamson was a nationalist, there were similarities between him and White, especially in their internal contradictions. After discussing 'natural morality', Merlin concludes' I am an anarchist, like any sensible person',

p.172. White's book is almost embarrassing in its English patriotism (presumably flavoured by the war, which he spent in Ireland); e.g., a hedgehog, representing the spirit of the English agricultural labourer, sings *Jerusalem* to Arthur, who has a vision of the land of England.

46. T. Mann, *Diaries, 1918–1939* (ed. H. Keston) (Londdon, 1983), pp.42–3, 44–6; entries for 31.3.1919 and 12.4.1919, my italics.
47. K. Hamsun, *The Wanderer* (tr. O. and G. Stallybrass) (London, 1975), p.250.
48. R. Ferguson, *Enigma. The Life of Knut Hamsun* (London, 1987), p.119.
49. Hamsun, *Wanderer*, pp.247, 245.
50. A. Gustafson, *Six Scandinavian Novelists: Lie, Jacobsen, Heidenstam, Selma Lagerlöf, Hamsun, Sigrid Unset* (London, [1968]), p.248.
51. Ibid., pp.240–1.
52. Robert Ferguson, *Enigma*, and T. Hansen, *Der Hamsun Prozess* (Hamburg, 1979). Translations from Hansen's book are by me.
53. Hansen, *Der Hamsun Prozess*, pp.50–1.
54. Ibid., pp.50–3.
55. Gustafson. *Six Scandinavian Novelists*, p.267; Ferguson, *Enigma*, pp.262–3. Hamsun spent his Nobel Prize and writing money during the 1920s and 1930s restoring an old mansion, and reclaiming the surrounding moorland, Ferguson, *Enigma*, pp.270–1.
56. Hansen, *Der Hamsun Prozess*, p.56–7.
57. Ferguson, *Enigma*, pp.94, 96, Hamsun wore black ribbons in mourning for the executed anarchists.
58. Hansen, *Der Hamsun Prozess*, pp.365–7.
59. K. Hamsun, *Growth of the Soil* (tr. W. Worster) (London, 1980) p.312.
60. Gustafson, *Six Scandinavian Novelists*, p.284.
61. K. Hamsun, *Wayfarers* (tr. J. McFarlane) (London, 1982), p.279.
62. Ibid., p.375.
63. Ibid., pp.373–5.
64. Ibid., p.376.
65. Hamsun, *Growth of the Soil*, pp.316–17, my italics.
66. Ferguson, *Enigma*, pp.293–4, and *passim*.

Chapter Eight

1. B. Moore, Jr., *Social Origins of Dictatorship and Democracy. Lord and Peasant in the Making of the Modern World* (Harmondsworth, 1974), pp.491–6.
2. E. Nolte, *Three Faces of Fascism* (New York, 1969), pp.537–42; fascism historically specific, p.570 and *passim*. Nolte's use of 'transcendental' seems not to be connected with Emersonian Transcendentalism.
3. A. Polonsky, *The Little Dictators* (London, 1975), pp.35–6.
4. Ibid., p.7.
5. S. Cullen, 'Leaders and Martyrs. Codreanu, Jose Antonio and Mosley', *History*, 1986, vol. 71, pp.408–30.
6. Ibid., p.8.
7. Not only Rumania but other post-imperial states can be compared with post-colonial Third World nationalism, a comparison I drew in an earlier work, *Blood and Soil. R. Walther Darré and Hitler's Green Party* (Bourne End, Bucks, 1985), pp.6, 199.
8. R. Wohl, *The Generation of 1914* (London, 1980), pp.128–9 and p.272, n.31.
9. H. Thomas, ed., *Jose Antonio Primo de Rivera. Selected Writings*, (London, 1972), p.30.
10. Ibid., p.10.
11. Ibid., pp.101, 102, 132.
12. Ibid., pp.75–6.
13. Quoted in Cullen, 'Leaders and Martyrs', p.7.
14. See S. Cullen, 'The Development of the Ideas and Politics of the British Union of Fascists, 1932–1940', *Journal of Contemporary History*, 1987, vol. 22, pp.115–136.
15. Mr Cullen kindly made available to me transcripts of his interviews with ex-members of the B.U.F. A more detailed account of this issue can be found in S. Cullen, 'The Development of the Ideas and Policies of the B.U.F.' M.Litt thesis, Oxford, 1987.
16. H.R. Gardiner, *World Without End* (London, 1932), pp.36–7.
17. E.g., the editor and deputy director of *Flight* magazine, Donald Campbell, whose *Bluebird* flew the Fascist flag along with the Union Jack when it broke the world speed record: Saunders, of Sander Roe aircraft, and modernizing military strategists.
18. R. Skidelsky, *Oswald Mosley* (London, 1981), p.302; Webb, *The Occult Establishment*, p.127.
19. J. Jenks, *The Land and the People. The British Union Policy for Agriculture* (London, no date).

20. *Fascism and Agriculture*, British Union pamphet (London, no date).
21. Jenks, *Land and the People*, p.7.
22. J. Jenks, 'The Homestead Economy', in H. Massingham, ed., *The Small Farmer* (London, 1947), pp.163–4.
23. Compare here the pleasure in fast motorcycles and sports cars taken by Henry Williamson's hero in the *Chronicles of Ancient Sunlight*; Maddison's lifestyle even after buying a run-down farm in Norfolk requires constant visits to London and Devon. These are accomplished by fast driving along empty roads, an experience repetitively and lovingly described.
24. P. Derrick, *Rural Economy*, March, 1949, quoted in L. Easterbrook, *Feeding the Fifty Million*, London, 1950, pp.73–4.
25. Ibid. *passim*.
26. Ibid., pp.69–70.
27. J. Jenks, *Spring Comes Again* (no place, 1939), p.60.
28. D. Mack Smith, *Mussolini* (London, 1983), pp.60, 140, 285.
29. Mussolini, *Autobiography* (London, 1935), p.37, describes how his stay in Switzerland (to attend Pareto's lectures) left him unaffected by its scenic beauty or political economy. Switzerland confirmed him in his belief in 'the function of Latinity'.
30. H.S. Harris, *The Social Philosophy of Giovanni Gentile* (Urbana, Illinois, 1960), pp.18–19: 'It is in this sense that actual idealism affirms transcendence...experience begets reality.'
31. Ibid., pp.40–1.
32. Ibid., p.78.
33. G. Gentile, *Genesis and Structure of Society* (Urbana, Illinois, 1966), p.135.
34. Ibid., pp.116–7.
35. Harris, *Social Philosophy*, p.109n.84; anarchy, pp.180–1.
36. Gentile, *Genesis and Structure*, p.171.
37. O. Ohlendorf,. *Testament* (Nuremberg, 1947), p.17; cf. R. Pois, *National Socialism and the Religion of Nature* (London, 1985), pp.66–7, Nazis against totalitarianism.
38. N. Goodrick-Clarke, *The Occult Roots of National Socialism* (Wellingborough, 1985), p.190; J. Evola, *The Doctrine of Awakening* (London, 1937).
39. Mack Smith, *Mussolini*, p.216.
40. C. Malaparte, *The Volga Rises in Europe* (London, 1957), p.47.
41. Quoted by R. Winegarten, 'The Fascist Mentality – Drieu la Rochelle', in H.A. Turner, ed., *Reappraisals of Fascism* (New York, 1975), p.216.
42. Quoted by R, Traz in his introduction to Maurice Barrés, *La Colline Inspirée* (Geneva, 1912), p.13.
43. Ibid., p.325 my translation.
44. Ibid., p.326.
45. Ibid., p.327 my translation.
46. Drieu la Rochelle, *Gilles* (Paris, 1939), p.604.
47. I am grateful to Dr Peter Tame, of Queen's University, Belfast, for this reference, and for discussion on the role of nature in French fascist literature of the period.

Chapter Nine

1. H. Schnädelbach, *Philosophy in Germany, 1831–1984* (Cambridge, 1984), p.149.
2. R. Wohl, *The Generation of 1914* (London, 1980), p.240.
3. Ludwig Klages, 1931, quoted in Schnädelbach, *Philosophy in Germany*, p.150.
4. Green, *Mountain of Truth*, p.140. A 1913 essay by Klages 'Mensch und Erde', in *Mensch und Erde* (Jena, 1929) pp.1–41, contains most of the themes of today's ecologists; that matriarchy is better than patriarchy, that numberless animal species have been exterminated by man, that the fur and feather trade is wicked, that civilisation and *Kultur* kills the spirit, that economics is opposed to real values. This popular collection of essays was reprinted several times in the 1920s. In his foreword to the 1920 edition, reprinted in the edition cited above (p.8), Klages points out that he foresaw the First World War in 1913 when he wrote of the 'unbounded exterminatory urge inherent in civilization' ('Die "Zivilisation" trägt die Züge *entfesselter Mordsucht*'...).
5. Ibid., pp.140–1.
6. For Klages, George and matriarchy, ibid., pp.161–2. For Fechter see Jost Hermand, *'All Power to the Women*. Nazi Concepts of Matriarchy', *Journal of Contemporary History*, 1984, vol. 19, pp.649–68, esp. pp.649–50.
7. R. Graves, *The White Goddess* (London, 1986), pp.461–2, 486.
8. Green, *Mountain of Truth*, pp.10, 199.

9. B. Pasternak, *Doctor Zhivago* (London, 1963) p.506.
10. Green, *Mountain of Truth*, p.151.
11. There is a nice continuity in the fact that Rudolf Bahro wrote his doctoral thesis on Becher, the Marxist Wandervögel.
12. J. Fox, 'Jews in Weimar Germany', unpub. paper, Conference on European and Middle East Refugees, Oxford, August 1985.
13. Green, *Mountain of Truth*, pp.112, 165. For Evola, see p.above.
14. L. Klages, *Der Geist als Widersacher der Seele*, 2 vols, (Munich and Bonn, 1954), vol. 1, pp.342–445. Vol. 2, pp.1251–1400, discusses the so-called Pelasgian tradition, a prehistoric matriarchal world which Klages sees as distorted by Greek and Roman patriarchy.
15. M. Heidegger, *Nietzsche*. vol. 4, *Nihilism* (New York, 1982), pp.96–7, Heidegger's italics, and see Heidegger, 'The Origin of the Work of Art', *Poetry, Language, Thought* (New York, 1975), p.23.
16. Schnädelbach, *Philosophy in Germany*, p.219; D. Levy, 'Max Scheler: Truth and the Sociology of Knowledge', *Continuity*, 1981, vol. 3, pp.91–104.
17. M. Heidegger, *Being and Time* (Oxford, 1967), p.76.
18. Ibid., p.30.
19. Heidegger, *Nihilism*, pp.116–17, 100.
20. Heidegger, 'What are Poets For?', in *Poetry, Language, Thought*, pp.114–15.
21. Schnädelbach, *Philosophy in Germany*, p.151.
22. G. Sorel, *From Georges Sorel* (ed. by J. Stanley) (New York, 1976), pp.51–2, 53–4.
23. Ibid., p.290, Sorel's italics.
24. Cited from K. Prumm, *Die Literatur des Nationalismus*, vol. 1, p.376, in J. Herf, *Reactionary Modernism. Technology, Culture and Politics in Weimar and the Third Reich* (Cambridge, 1984), p.39.
25. O. Spengler, 5.4.36, *Briefe, 1913–36* (Munich, 1963), p.773, my translation; see also p.538, Spengler to E. Förster-Nietzsche, on Steiner.
26. D. Levy, 'The Anthropological Horizon. Max Scheler, Arnold Gehlen and the Idea of a Philosophical Anthropology', *Journal of Anthropological Studies at Oxford*, 1985, vol. 16, p.170, note 2.
27. Ibid., p.177, and see Lorenz on Gehlen, Chapter Three.
28. Ibid., p.182.
29. H. Rauschning, quoted in Kelly, *The Descent of Darwin*, p.121. While Rauschning is not a reliable guide for exact quotations, as he was seldom present at his 'reported' conversations, he was good at collecting gossip, and there is probably substance to this comment.
30. F. Schiller, 'Das Verschleierte Bild zu Sais' *Sämtliche Werke*, Erster Band, *Gedichte, Dramen* I, Munich, 1958, p.224.
31. F. Nietzsche, 'The Uses and Abuses of History for Life', *Untimely Meditations* (Cambridge, 1983), pp.122–3.
32. H. Arendt, 'Truth and Politics', in P. Laslett and W.G. Runciman, eds., *Philosophy, Politics and Society* (Oxford, 1969), p.133.
33. Fidus was the pseudonym for Hugo Höppener. See J. Hermand, 'Meister Fidus. *Jugendstil*-Hippie to Aryan Faddist', *Comparative Literary Studies*, 1975, vol. 12, p.301.
34. Heidegger, 'The Origin of the Work of Art', pp.33–4.
35. Heidegger, 'The Thinker as Poet', in *Poetry, Language, Thought*, p.8.
36. O. Spengler, *The Decline of the West*, vol. 2 (London, 1971), p.96.
37. Quoted in U. Linse, *Zurück O Mensch zur Mutter Erde. Landkommunen in Deutschland, 1890–1933* (Munich, 1983), pp.343–5.
38. Quoted in J. Leishman, introduction to *Rilke. New Poems* (London, 1979), p.17.
39. Rilke, 'Sonnets to Orpheus' no.xxix, *Duineser Elegien. Die Sonette an Orpheus* (Ulm, 1976), p.88, my translation.
40. K. von Klemperer, *Germany's New Conservatism* (Princeton, 1968), p.29.
41. F.E. and F.P. Manuel, *Utopian Thought in the Western World* (Oxford, 1979), introduction and *passim*.
42. The desire for new institutions is emphasised in Jerry Muller, *The Other God that Failed. Hans Freyer and the Deradicalization of German Conservatism* (Princeton, N.J., 1987), p.53.
43. Ibid., p.20.
44. Julius Langbehn's famous *Rembrandt als Erzieher* (Leipzig, 1888), a work which helped to inspire the Youth Movement, contained no anti-semitic passages in its first two editions (1888 and 1890). Such passages were added after pressure from Langbehn's publisher. On the other hand, Marx's attacks on Jews appeared as early as 1844; see 'On the Jewish Question', *Collected Works*, vol.

3 (London, Moscow and New York, 1975), pp.146–75. The inventor of the term 'anti-semitism', Wilhelm Marr, was a radical socialist, expelled from several European countries for left revolutionary activity.

45. U. Linse, *Barfüssige Propheten* (Berlin, 1983), pp.33, 52.
46. R. Musil, *The Man Without Qualities*, quoted in J.M. Ritchie, *Periods in German Literature* (London, 1953, pp.230–1.
47. B. Brecht, 'Vom armen B.B.', in, L. Forster, ed., *Penguin Book of German Verse* (Harmondsworth, 1974), pp.439–40.
48. Ibid.

Chapter Ten

1. Hitler's and Himmler's vegetarianism is widely known. What is less widely known is their opposition to Hess and Darré on a wide range of 'Green' issues, extending to Heydrich's arrest of Darré and others of the Hess circle after Hess's flight to England, and his harassment of the organic farmers.
2. Roosevelt's smallholder programme achieved a mere 3000 settlements, which demonstrates a substantial difference between Roosevelt's New Deal and Nazi policy on this issue, despite similarities of rhetoric, see J. Garratty, 'The New Deal, National Socialism and the Great Depression', *American Historical Review*, 1973, vol. 78, pp.907–43.
3. For the Bormann quote, see J. von Lang, *The Secretary* (New York, 1979), pp.160–1. For Fritz Todt, see K. Ludwig, *Technik und Ingenieure im Dritten Reich* (Munich, 1975), pp.337–40. See, too, Bramwell, *Blood and Soil. R. Walther Darré and Hitler's 'Green Party'*, pp. 171–80, 195–200.
4. Ludwig, *Technik and Ingenieure*, p.339.
5. Federal Archives, Coblenz, hereafter referred to as BA (Bundesarchiv), Darré papers, II/1.
6. Ludwig, *Technik und Ingenieure*, p.338. There were disagreements between Todt and Seifert over Seifert's attacks on techology and his 'fanatical attitude' to landscape protection; Todt told Seifert that their joint enemies were the bureaucrats and lawyers; ibid., p.339.
7. A. Ludovici, 'Skizze zur Gliederung der Bodenordnung', no date, probably 1935, BA NS2/272.
8. Ludovici submitted papers to Hitler's Adjutant, BA NS2/53; for articles by Ludovici on ecological themes, see BA NS26/948.
9. Backe papers; BA NL75/10, undated addition to letter of 19.4.40, possibly misfiled, but certainly 1939 or later.
10. 24.1.40, BA, NS10/37.
11. C.W. Guillebaud, *The Economic Recovery of Germany, 1933–1938* (London, 1939), p.143.
12. *Financial Times*, 14.9.83.
13. Heinz Haushofer, *Ideengeschichte der Agrarwirtschaft und Agrarpolitik im deutschen Sprachgebiet*, vol. 2, *Vom ersten Weltkrieg bis zur Gegenwart* (Bonn, 1958), p.260.
14. Ibid., pp.260–1.
15. Ibid., p.87.
16. BA NS2/296.
17. For discussion of relations between followers of Steiner and the regime, I am grateful to Anthroposophist members of Darré's staff and others for interview.
18. Haushofer, *Ideengeschichte*, p.270.
19. Darré's diary, 10.11.37; the original of this diary was read by various historians and the archivists at Coblenz. It was then bought back by Darré's second wife and burnt. The typed version consists of passages preserved and edited by friends and colleagues of Darré. It is lodged in the City Archive, Goslar. The point about Hess is confirmed in a letter from Dr Hans Merkel to the author, 21.7.81.
20. BA, Darré's papers, II/1a; Darré to Hess, 17.1.40, ibid., Hans Merkel to the author, 21.7.81, Haushofer, *Ideengeschichte*, p.270, and K. Meyer, 'Unsere Forschungsarbeit im Krieg, 1941–3' (mimeographed report in Koblenz Federal Archive).
21. Questionnaire response, BA, Darré's papers, II/1a.
22. Interview with Mrs Backe, 6.1.81.
23. Memo by von Zitzewitz-Kottau, 12.11.37, BA NS10/103.
24. Mrs Backe's diary (in her possession), 19.6.40.
25. A.C. Bramwell, 'Small Farm Productivity under the Nazis', *Oxford Agrarian Studies* 1984, vol. 13, pp.1–19.
26. Darré's diary, 18.6.40.
27. Darré papers, BA, II/1a.

28. Ibid.
29. P. Brügge, 'Die Weltplan vollzieht sich unerbitterlich', *Der Spiegel*, 28.6.84.
30. BA NS19(neu)/1632, undated report.
31. BA NS19(neu)/1313, 22.3.41.
32. BA NS19(neu)/222, 4.1.38.
33. BA NS19(neu)129/11.3.43.
34. BA NS19(neu)/578, 11.8.42.
35. See for an example of this attraction K.R. Manning's biography, *Black Apollo of Science. The Life of Ernest Everett Just* (New York and Oxford, 1983). Just spent some years working in the Kaiser Wilhelm Institute in the 1920s, and claimed to have received more intellectual stimulus and appreciation there than in the USA, pp.188, 194. Although he left Germany for Italy after the Nazi takeover, he 'made excuses' for and produced rationalisations for Germany in 1936, p.290.
36. See, e.g., K. Barkin, 'From Uniformity to Pluralism; German Historical Writing since World War One', *German Life and Letters*, 1980–1, vol. 34; cf. R. Pois on the surprising degree of scientific openness at German universities after 1933, *National Socialism and the Religion of Nature* (London, 1985), p.74, and see G. Cocks, *The Göring Institute* (New York, 1984), which shows how despite the destruction of Freudian analytical science, psycho-therapy and analysis continued, with papers by Karen Horney being read as late as 1936.
37. Darré, notes on forming a German version of the Soil Association, to be called *Mensch und Heimat*, Goslar, 19–20.2.52, p.2, in author's possession.
38. Webb, *The Occult Establishment*, p.103.
39. Darré, memorandum to W. Willikens, 27.6.34, BA, NS26/946.

Chapter Eleven

1. B. Ward and R. Dubos, *Only One Earth* (London, 1972). This chapter can only be an overview of events in the ecological movement after the Second World War. In order to examine the roots of a movement the shape of the movement has to be indicated. A comprehensive treatment would require a book to itself.
2. G. Hardin, 'The Tragedy of the Commons', *Science*, 1968 vol. 162, pp.1243–8, offered a model of the effect of overpopulation on a limited resource. The 'Spaceship Earth' concept stressed the finite nature of land compared to population. Economic ecologists were hostile to the 'Lifeboat syndrome', because they saw excessive and unequal use of resources by the rich countries as the real threat, a theme that became more prominent from 1972, before the oil crisis. E. Goldsmith's 'Blueprint for Survival' issue of the *Ecologist*, January 1972, argued that expansion of numbers and resource use could not continue indefinitely. E.F. Schumacher,. in a speech given to the Human Rights Society (published as *Population and World Hunger* (London, 1973) thought (pp.2–3) there was no clear link between 'population and world hunger'. 'There would still be a population problem, even if the possibilities of food production were infinite, which of course they cannot be; and there would still be a food-production problem, even if the population were stationary or shrinking.' On p.8 he identified as a more serious problem 'a consumption-explosion among the rich,' which threatened us all with 'pollution, resource-depletion,'. . .For the same point, using the thermo-dynamic argument, see J. Rifkind with T. Howard, *Entropy. A New World View* (London, 1985), pp.238–40.
3. See G. Thayer, *The British Political Fringe* (London ,1965), discussed in note 65, p.264 above. For many, *Cold Comfort Farm* demolished the pretensions of the English blood-and-soil novel typified by Mary Webb; this process of jeering the rural novel out of fashion seems not to have happened in Germany, where peasant novels continued to appear throughout the 1920s. For a conservative attack on growth, one not taken up or publicised much at the time, see E.J. Mishan, *The Costs of Economic Growth* (London, 1967) and idem., *Growth. The Price We Pay* (London, 1969).
4. E.F. Schumacher, *Small is Beautiful* (London, 1973). For biographical details of Schumacher's life, see Barbara Wood, *Alias Papa* (London 1984). Ironically, German ecologism was itself American-oriented. Nearly 400,000 cop-

ies of *Global 2000* were sold in Germany; see H. Mewes, 'The West German Green Party' *New German Critique*, 1983, vol. 28, p.78.

5. C. Barnett, *The Audit of War. The Illusion and Reality of Britain as a Great Nation* (London, 1987), p.21, my italics.
6. Worster, *Nature's Economy*, p.330. Some socialists claim, however, that Beveridge and Attlee produced an environmental improvement, see P. Pender, quoted by David Pepper in 'Environmentalism and Labour', in Joe Weston, ed., *Red and Green. The New Politics of the Environment* (London, 1986). p.118. Pepper argues on pp.117–20 that Porritt's claim that decentralisation and internationalism is uniquely green ignores Kropotkin, Godwin, Proudhon, Morris and Robert Owen. While this is true, the British Labour Party's post-war policies emphasised overall state planning, extreme collectivism and hostility to the individual. The 'white-heat of technology' and industrial growth at all cost, appear unrelated to the ideas of Kropotkin, Godwin, Proudhon, Morris or Robert Owen.
7. C. Elton, *Animal Ecology* (London, 1935), p.vii.
8. Lowe and Goyder, *Environmental Groups in Politics*, pp.152–7, threats to the biosphere, p.155.
9. See John Papworth, *New Politics* (New Delhi, 1982), for a statement of his position.
10. The information about the structure and membership of the Soil Association comes from V. Payne, 'A History of the Soil Association', M.A. Thesis, University of Manchester, 1971. Payne does not mention the previous political affiliations of the Council members, but discusses their pre-war ecological writings. Colin Ward refers to Easterbrook's book in his edition of Kropotkin's *Fields, Factories and Workshops Tomorrow* (London, 1985), p.119.
11. Payne, 'History of the Soil Association', p.59.
12. Hardin, 'The Tragedy of the Commons'.
13. J. Seymour, *The Forgotten Arts* (London, 1977); Payne, 'A History of the Soil Association', pp.36–40.
14. Interviews with green supporters, 1985–6.
15. J. Becker, *Hitler's Children* (London, 1977).
16. J. Esser. 'The Future of the Greens in West Germany', unpublished paper delivered at All Souls College, Oxford, 25.2.86.
17. G. Langguth, *The Green Factor in German Politics. From Protest Movement to Political Party* (Boulder, Colorado, 1986), pp.4, 6. See too Elim Papadakis, *The Green Movement in West Germany* (London, 1984).
18. Langguth, *The Green Factor*, pp.8–9.
19. *Die Zeit*, 2.5.86. According to Mewes, 'West German Green Party', p.63, only six out of the forty-eight pages of the Green programme discuss environmental issues such as 'the protection of air, water, plant and animal species and specific natural or [sic] ecosystems'.
20. *Financial Times*, 12.11.84; *The Times*, 25.6.85.
21. P. Kelly, *Fighting for Hope* (London, 1984), p.107; see also pp.105–7. Possibly Kelly believes that all the researchers and officials concerned with the development of thalidomide were men, although she does not offer any evidence to this effect. It may be fair to suggest that the development and testing of drugs takes place in a male-dominated environment. How things would be different in a non-male dominated environment is not explained. Would there be no new drugs? Would they be tested on humans instead of animals, as thalidomide was? Would the process of testing and development be more efficient? Would pregnant women be discouraged from taking drugs – something that could be done even in a patriarchal society? Or would women not need tranquillisers in a society where they were dominant? The picture of passive pregnant woment and a male-dominated medical/drugs establishment, who do not care whether their drugs produce deformed babies or not, is not proven. Certainly, to take drugs while pregnant may be wrong, but it is feminists who insist that women have the right to ease their mental and physical suffering at whatever cost.
22. *taz* (Berlin-based journal of the Green movement), 21.5.86 and 10.5.86. In an interview in *Green Line* (May, 1987, no. 51), p.4, the Oxford-based Green

alternative voice, one Green representative, Jacob von Uexküll, said surprisingly bluntly that the Greens in Germany had deliberately chosen to seek out minority groups and keep left, because commentators had pointed out that ecological statements had been made by Nazi and Fascist governments.

23. *taz*, 10.5.86, an interview with Antje Vollmer.
24. Ibid.
25. *The Times*, 15.12.84.
26. See Janine Chasseguet-Smirgel's paper to the Institute of Contemporary Arts, 'The Green Theatre' (1986), pp.10–11, 21–24. and her emphatic criticism on page 27, *'the Jews are never mentioned* in the brochures of the Green Movement. A strange silence reigns over the Jewish question'. (Underlining in original). She interprets the German ecological movement, especially its anti-nuclear stance, as a sub-conscious attempt to pretend that Germans can be victims as well as villains.
27. *taz*, 10.2.86.
28. See Bahro's main books, *Building the Green Movement* (London 1986), and *The Alternative in Eastern Europe* (New York, 1979). His Schumacher Lecture of 1986 refers to Rilke, Hölderlin, Thoreau, Joachim di Fiore, Thomas Münzer, etc.
29. See *New Internationalist*, 1987, no. 171, pp.10–11. The issue was devoted to Green politics.
30. Ibid., p.1 and *passim*.
31. E. Goldsmith, *Blueprint for Survival* (London, 1972); E. Callenbach, *Ecotopia* (London, 1977).
32. E.g., see the prophecies of mass famine by 1985 made in 1966, quoted in Armytage, *Yesterday's Tomorrows* (London, 1968), p.204: world food production could not increase by more than one per cent a year, while population would double in thirty-three years, so calorie intake would have to fall. Peter Medawar, *Pluto's Republic*, p.280, quotes Barbara Ward's *Only One Earth* approvingly;

    The two worlds of man-the biosphere of his inheritance, the technosphere of his creation – are out of balance, indeed potentially in deep conflict. And man is in the middle. This is the hinge of history at which we stand, the door of the future opening onto a crisis more sudden, more global, more inescapable and more bewildering than any ever encountered by the human species and one which will take decisive shape within the life span of children who are already born.

    The vein of apocalyptic nullity referred to earlier is even more noticeable here. Ward compares two worlds, which in her metaphor balance, with man in the middle. The 'technosphere' is not really a world, but a capability; the analogy between two worlds – even on a metaphorical level – is false. The conflict between the biosphere and the technological capacity is not explained, though the inherent opposition is assumed. The crisis glimpsed through the door opening on the hinge of history is so vaguely expressed as to be meaningless. Peter Medawar examined the opposition to Ward and Dubos, in J. Maddox, *The Doomsday Syndrome* (London, 1972), but concluded that Maddox was 'hopelessly sanguine', p.283. It is an interesting example of the gullibility of trained scientists that Medawar thought that 'death by starvation and infectious disease is already commonplace in over-populated parts of the world', p.283. Death by starvation takes place in areas less highly populated than Europe. There are no famines in Britain or Holland today. The toll of infectious disease is substantially lower in the Third World than in 1900. The startling rise in population in Third World countries this century alone is evidence that something is wrong with these assumptions. In comparison, many European countries took three hundred years to regain the loss of population following the Black Death. J. Simon and H. Kahn, in. eds., *The Resourceful Earth* (Oxford, 1984) examined in detail the prophecies of doom made in *Global 2000 Report to the President*, a 1980 American report. In their introduction, pp.1–49, Simon and Kahn concluded that where prophecies were expressed in precise form or could be quantified, the evidence showed that the predictions were false.

33. *Neues Deutschland*, 4.1.82, speech inaugurating the XII Bauernkongress; I

am grateful to L.R. Colitt for this information.

34. *Financial Times*, 15.8.85. Alec Douglas-Home recalled Khrushchev's disillusionment with professional agronomists, who advised him to plough up large tracts of Central Russia. A local peasant told him not to, as the top-soil would blow away: the land was ploughed, and the top-soil did blow away. (27.12.83, interview with Alec Douglas-Home, British Overseas Service, 'Time Remebered').
35. F. Müller-Rommel, 'Ecology Parties in Western Europe', *Western European Politics*, 1982, vol. 5, pp.68–74.
36. J–F. Pilat, 'Democracy or Discontent? Ecologists in the European Electoral Arena', *Government and Opposition*, 1982, vol. 17, pp.222–33. At cantonal level in spring, 1987, Green candidates in Eastern France received ten per cent of the vote, while the Fronte Nationale had about six per cent. A poll on second preferences showed that only one per cent of the two parties would support the other, *Le Monde*, 27.5.87.
37. *Sunday Telegraph*, 11.11.84.
38. Lowe and Goyder, *Environmental Groups in Politics*, pp.72–3.
39. See Schumacher Society Book List, 1986. A recent (and welcome) initiative by Green Books Ltd has altered the balance. The works of H.J. Massingham together with an anthology of the writings of several early organic farmers are among the 'Green Classics' to be published by them in September 1988.
40. *The Times*, 20.10.84.
41. George Orwell, *Collected Essays, Journalism and Letters*, vol. 2, *My Country Right or Left*, (Harmondsworth, 1970), pp.168–9. 'The energy that actually shapes the world springs from the emotions – racial pride, leader worship, religious belief, love of war – which liberal intellectuals mechanically write off as anachronisms', p.168. Orwell did not particularly approve of these qualities; he was arguing that a view of life which included them had a better prophetic and explanatory power than one which did not.
42. Ibid, p.168.
43. An example of war-time patriotism is the English Association's *England* (ed. by Harold Nicolson) (London 1944). The English Association was established to study and preserve the language. The anthology deals with English qualities such as humour, character, courage, etc.
44. See e.g., editorial in *New Internationalist* as cited above which admits to omitting mystical elements in green ideas, and typical tongue-in-cheek interview with Porritt, *Sunday Telegraph*, 17.4.83.
45. See note 17, p.251, above.
46. Quoted in *Scorpion*, June, 1984, no. 5, p.8.
47. F. Thomson, *The Chosen One* (California International Award Press, no place, 1966).
48. See for example S. Devi, *Pilgrimage* (Calcutta, 1958). D. Pepper in *The Roots of Modern Environmentalism*, pp.204–13, describes survivalists, Hardin and Ecotopias as 'ecofascism'. The category is surely better kept for real ecofascists and econazis.
49. Yanov, *The Russian Challenge*, p.135.
50. Ibid., pp.135–7, 149–51.
51. Weston, ed., *Red and Green*, p.118.

Conclusion

1. E. Kohák, *The Ember and the Stars. A Philosophical Enquiry into the Moral Sense of Nature* (Chicago, 1984), p.80.
2. Allaby and Bunyard, *Politics of Self-Sufficiency*, pp.39–40.

Bibliography

Journals

Anglo-German Review
Anthroposophical Review
Demeter
Green Line
Journal of the Soil Association
Mother Earth
Nature et Progrès
Resurgence
Rural Economy
taz
The Monist
The Ecologist
The New Pioneer

Manuscript sources

Information on ecological ideas under the Third Reich came from the private papers and letters of Walther Darré and Herbert Backe, both lodged at the Federal Archives, Coblenz. The Backe papers are restricted. Walther Darré's diary is in the City Archives, Goslar; it too is restricted. The diary consists of an edited, typed, version produced after Darré's death from an original which was read by archivists and historians, then repossessed by Darré's widow and burnt. I have not relied on it as a source unless there was confirmatory material elsewhere. I am grateful to former colleagues of Darré for supplying me with a copy of Darré's handwritten notes on the formation of a German Soil Association, and to Mrs Backe, who permitted me to read and quote from her diary. Material from the Himmler file on organic farms and similar matters together with mimeographed reports by A. Ludovici and others referred to in the text and notes is to be found at the Federal Archives, Coblenz, as is other unpublished material concerning the Third Reich.

Books, theses and articles

H. Adams, *The Education of Henry Adams*, London, 1961.
J.Q. Adams, *Letters from Silesia*, London, 1800.
H. Agar and Lewis Mumford, *City of Man. A Declaration of World Democracy*, New York, 1940.

M. Allaby and P. Bunyard, *The Politics of Self-Sufficiency*, Oxford, 1980.
F. Alley, *Back to the Land: Now and How*, no place, [Australia], 1931.
W.H.G. Armytage, *Heavens Below. Utopian Experiments in England, 1560–1960*, London, 1961.
——, *Yesterday's Tomorrows; a Historical Survey of Future Societies*, London, 1968.
C.E. Ashworth, 'Flying Saucers, Spoon-Bending and Atlantis. A Structural Analysis of New Mythologies', *Sociological Review*, 1980, vol. 28, pp.353–76.
W. Ashworth, *Genesis of Modern British Town Planning*, London, 1954.
J.J. Bachofen, *Myth, Religion and Mother Right*, London, 1967.
R. Bahro, *Building the Green Movement*, London, 1986.
——, *The Alternative in Eastern Europe*, New York, 1979.
——, *The Logic of Deliverance. On the foundations of an ecological politics* (Schumacher Society Lecture), London, 1986.
——, 'Socialism, Ecology and Utopia', *History Workshop*, 1983, vol. 16, pp.91–9.
Lady Eve Balfour, *The Living Soil*, London, 1944.
Ian Barbour, *Western Man and Environmental Ethics*, Reading, Massachusetts, 1973.
K. Barkin, *The Controversy over German Industrialisation, 1890–1902*, Chicago, 1972.
C. Barnett, *The Audit of War. The Illusion and Reality of Britain as a Great Nation*, London, 1987.
James Barr, *Christianity and Ecology*, Manchester, 1983.
John Barrell, *The Idea of Landscape*, Cambridge, 1972.
Hellmut Bartsch, *Erinnerungen eines Landwirts*, Stuttgart, no date [c. 1948].
D. Bateman and A. Vine, 'Organic Farming Systems in England and Wales', University of Wales M. Sc. Thesis, 1981.
S.L. Bensusan, *Latter Day Rural England, 1927*, London, 1928.
J.D. Bernal, *The Social Function of Science*, London, 1939.
W. Birklin, *The Greens and the New Politics* (European University Institute Working Paper no. 7), Florence, 1982.
J.W. Blench, 'The Influence of Richard Jefferies upon Henry Williamson', Part 1, *Durham University Journal*, 1986, vol. 79, pp.79–89.
——, 'The Influence of Richard Jefferies upon Henry Williamson', Part II, *Durham University Journal*, 1987, vol. 79, pp.327–47.
P. Boardman, *The Worlds of Patrick Geddes*, London, 1978.
W. Bölsche, *Haeckel, His Life and Work*, London, 1909.
Murray Bookchin, *Post-Scarcity Anarchism*, Berkeley, 1971.
P.J. Bowler, *Evolution. The History of an Idea*, Berkeley, 1985.
A.C. Bramwell, *Blood and Soil. Walther Darré and Hitler's 'Green Party'*, Bourne End, Bucks, 1985.
——, 'A Green Land Far Away. A Look at the Origins and History of the Green Movement', *Journal of the Anthropological Society of Oxford*, 1986, vol. 17, pp.191–206.
——, 'Darré. Was This Man 'Father of the Greens'? *History Today*, 1984, vol. 34, pp.7–13.
——, 'Widespread Seeds of the Green Revolution', *Times Higher Education Supplement*, 20.11.87.
M. Breitbart, 'Peter Kropotkin, the Anarchist Geographer', in D.R. Stoddart, ed., *Geography, Ideology and Social Concern*, Oxford, 1981.
J.D. Brewer. *Mosley's Men. The British Union of Fascists in the West Midlands*, Aldershot, 1984.

British Union, *Fascism and Agriculture*, London, no date.
R. Bubner, *Modern German Philosophy*, Cambridge, 1981.
A.L. Caplan, *The Sociobiology Debate. Readings*, New York, 1978.
F. Capra and C. Spretnak, *Green Politics*, London, 1984.
H. Carpenter, *J.R.R. Tolkien. A Biography*, London, 1977.
P. Carus, *The Surd of Metaphysics*, Chicago and London, 1885.
G. Cavaliere, *The Rural Tradition in the English Novel*, London, 1977.
M. Chapman, *The Gaelic Vision in Scottish Culture*, London, 1978.
D.G. Charlton, *New Images of the Natural in France. A Study in European Culture*, Cambridge, 1984.
J. Chasseguet-Smirgel, 'The Green Theatre', unpublished paper presented at the Institute of Contemporary Arts, May, 1986.
B. Chatwin, 'Man the Aggressor', *Sunday Times*, 1.12.74.
R. Chickering, *We Men who feel most German. The Pan-German League, 1886–1914*, London, 1984.
A. Chisholm, *Philosophers of the Earth. Conversations with Ecologists*, London, 1971.
A. Christy, *The Orient in American Transcendentalism. A Study of Emerson, Thoreau and Alcott*, New York, 1932.
W. Cobbett, *Rural Rides*, Harmondsworth, 1967.
——, *Cottage Economy*, Oxford, 1965.
(Cobden Club), *Systems of Land Tenure in Various Countries*, London, 1870.
J. Collings, *Land Reform*, London, 1906.
R.G. Collingwood, *The Idea of Nature*, Oxford, 1945.
J.J. Conington (pseud), *Nordington's Million*, London, 1923.
Sir W.E. Cooper, *The Murder of Agriculture. A National Peril. Disastrous Results to the Nation. Being an Earnest Appeal to the People to demand Land, Tariff and Poor Law Reform*, Letchworth, 1908.
A. Coomaraswamy, *The Transformation of Nature in Art. Theories of Art in Indian, Chinese and European Medieval Art*, Cambridge, Mass., 1934.
S. Cotgrove, *Catastrophe or Cornucopia. The Environment, Politics and the Future*, Chichester, 1982.
Cotgrove and A. Duff, 'Environmentalism, Values and Social Change', *British Jorunal of Sociology*, 1981, vol. 32, pp.92–110.
R.N. Coudenhove-Kalergi, *Revolution durch Technik*, Leipzig, 1932.
S. Cullen, 'The Development of the Ideas and Policies of the British Union of Fascists, 1932–40', *Journal of Contemporary History*, 1987, vol. 22, pp.115–36.
——, 'Leaders and Martyrs. Codreanu, Jose Antonio and Mosley', *History*, 1986, vol. 71, pp.408–30.
H. Daly, 'The Economic Thought of Frederick Soddy', *History of Political Economy*, 1980, vol. 12, pp.469–88.
M. Daly, *Gyn/Ecology*, London, 1981.
C. Darwin, *Autobiography*, Oxford, 1974.
Ibid., *The Origin of Species*, London, 1859.
C. Decovan *La Dimension Écologique de 1'Europe*, Paris, 1979.
D.J.K Depew and B.H. Weber, eds, *Evolution at a Crossroads. The New Biology and the New Philosophy of Science*, Cambridge, Mass. 1985.
H.N. Dickinson, *The Business of a Gentleman*, London, 1914.
H. Driesch, *The Philosophy of the Organic*, London, 1909.
——, *The History and Theory of Vitalism*, London, 1914.
G.S. Dunbar, 'Élisée Reclus, an Anarchist in Geography', in D. Stoddart, ed., *Geography, Ideology and Social Concern*, Oxford, 1981.
J. Durant, 'Innate Character in Animals and Man. A Perspective on the Origins

of Ethology', in C. Webster, ed., *Biology, Medicine and Society, 1840–1940*, Cambridge, 1981.

——, 'The Meaning of Evolution. Post-Darwinian Debates on the Significance for Man of the Theory of Evolution 1858–1908', Cambridge Ph D. Thesis, 1977.

L. Easterbrook, ed., *Feeding the Fifty Million*, London, 1905.

R. Ebbatson, *Lawrence and the Nature Tradition*, Hassocks, Sussex, 1980.

F. Egerton, 'A Bibliographical Guide to the History of General Ecology and Population Ecology', *History of Science*, 1977, vol. 15, pp.189–215.

——, 'Changing Concepts of the Balance of Nature', *Quarterly Review of Biology*, 1973, vol. 48, pp.322–50.

I. Eibl-Eibesfeldt, 'Ritual and ritualization from a biological perspective', in M. von Cranach *et al*, eds., *Human Ethology. Claims and Limits of a New Discipline*, Cambridge and Paris, 1979.

P. Ekman, 'About brows: emotional and conversational signals', in M. von Cranach, *et al*, eds., *Human Ethology*, see above.

C. Elton, *Animal Ecology*, London, 1935.

F. Engels, *Dialectics of Nature*, in *Marx, Engels, Collected Works*, vol. 25, London, 1987.

——, *Origin of the Family, Private Property and the State. In the Light of the Researches of Lewis H. Morgan*, in *Marx, Engels, Selected Works*, vol. 3, Moscow, 1970.

R.I. Evans, *Konrad Lorenz. The Man and his Ideas*, London, 1975.

R. Ferguson, *Enigma. The Life of Knut Hamsun*, London, 1987.

J.L. Finlay, 'John Hargrave, the Green Shirts and Social Credit', *Journal of Contemporary History*, 1970, vol. 5, pp.53–71.

M. Fordham, *The Land and Life. A Survey Prepared for the Rural Reconstruction Association*, London, 1943.

——, *The Rebuilding of Rural England*, London, 1924.

——, *The Restoration of Agriculture*, London, 1945.

M. French, *Beyond Power. Men, Women and Morals*, London, 1985.

R.G. Frey, *Rights, Killing and Suffering*, Oxford, 1983.

J. Fuellenbach, *European Environmental Policy East and West*, Bonn, 1981.

H.R. Gardiner and H. Rocholl, eds., *Britain and Germany. A Frank Discussion*, London, 1928.

H.R. Gardiner, *England Herself. Ventures in Rural Restoration*, London, 1943.

——, *Forestry or Famine?*, London, 1949.

——, *The English Folk Dance Tradition*, London, 1923.

——, *World Without End*, London, 1932.

——, *Water Springing From the Ground*, ed. by A. Best, Fontmell Magna, Dorset, 1972.

J. Garratty, 'The New Deal, National Socialism and the Great Depression', *American Historical Review*, 1973, vol. 78, pp.907–45.

D. Gasman, *The Scientific Origins of National Socialism. Social Darwinism in Ernst Haeckel and the German Monist League*, London and New York, 1971.

P. Geddes, *Cities in Evolution*, London, 1915.

A. Gehlen, *Der Mensch: seine Natur und seine Stellung in der Welt*, Berlin, 1940.

G. Gentile, tr. H.S. Harris, *Genesis and Structure of Society*, Urbana, Illinois, 1966.

A. George, 'Back to the Land', M. Sc Thesis, Oxford, 1979.

H. George, *Progress and Poverty*, London, 1951.

C. Glacken, *Traces on the Rhodian Shore. Nature and Culture in Western Thought from Ancient Times to the End of the Eighteenth Century*, Berkeley, 1967.

E. Goldsmith, *Blueprint for Survival*, London, 1972.

——, 'Superscience; its mythology and legitimisation', *The Ecologist*, 1981, vol. 11, pp.228–41.
R. Graves, *The White Goddess*, London, 1986.
M. Green, *Mountain of Truth. The Counter-Culture Begins. Ascona, 1900–1920*, Hanover and London, 1986.
H. Greisman, 'Matriarchate as Utopia, Myth and Social Theory', *Sociology*, 1981, vol. 15, pp.321–36.
S. Griffin, 'Split Culture', in S. Kumar, ed., *The Schumacher Lectures*, London, 1984.
R. Griffiths, *Fellow Travellers of the Right*, London, 1980.
J. Grinevald, 'Vernadsky and Lotka as Source for Georgescu-Roegen's Economics', unpublished paper presented to the Second Vienna Centre Conference on Economics and Ecology, Barcelona, 1987.
F. Grover, *Drieu la Rochelle and the Fiction of Testimony*, Berkeley, 1958.
R. Gruner, 'Science, Nature and Christianity', *Journal of Theological Studies*, 1975, vol. 26, pp.55–81.
A. Gustafson, *Six Scandinavian Novelists; Lie, Jacobsen, Heidenstam, Selma Lagerlöf, Hamsun, Sigrid Unset*, London, no date [1968].
E. Haeckel, *God-Nature*, London, 1914.
——, *Last Words on Evolution*, London, 1906.
——, *Monism as Connecting Religion and Science. The Confession of Faith of a Man of Science*, London and Edinburgh, 1894.
——, *Story of the Development of a Youth. Letters to his Parents, 1852–1856*, New York, 1923.
——, *The History of Creation*, London, 1876.
——, *The Riddle of the Universe*, London, 1900.
——, *The Wonders of Life*, London, 1905.
K. Hamsun, *Chapter The Last*, tr. A.G. Chater, London 1930.
——, *Mysteries*, tr. G. Bothmer, London, 1973.
——, *The Wanderer*, tr. O. and G. Stallybrass, London, 1975.
——, *The Wayfarers*, tr. J. MacFarlane, London, 1982.
——, *Growth of the Soil*, tr. W. Worster, London, 1980.
T. Hansen, *Der Hamsun Prozess*, Hamburg, 1979.
G. Hardin and J. Boden, eds., *Managing the Commons*, London, 1978.
G. Hardin, 'Genetic Consequences of Cultural Decisions in the Realm of Population', *Social Biology*, 1972, vol. 19, pp.350–61.
——, 'The Tragedy of the Commons', *Science*, 1968, vol. 162, pp.1243–8.
D. Hardy and C. Ward, *Arcadia for all. The Legacy of a Makeshift Landscape*, London, 1984.
J. Hargrave, *The Confessions of the Kibbo Kift. A Declaration and General Exposition of the Work of the Kindred*, London, 1927.
H.S. Harris, *The Social Philosophy of Giovanni Gentile*, Urbana, Illinois, 1960.
H. Haushofer, *Ideengeschichte der Agrarwirtschaft und Agrarpolitik*, vol. 2, *Vom Ersten Weltkrieg bis zur Gegenwart*, Bonn, 1958.
F. Hayek, *The Counter-Revolution of Science. Studies in the Abuse of Reason*, Glencoe, Illinois, 1952.
M. Heidegger, *Being and Time*, Oxford, 1967.
——, *Poetry, Language, Thought* New York, 1975.
——, *The End of Philosophy*, London, 1973.
——, *Nietzsche*, vol. iv, *Nihilism*, New York, 1982.
J. Herf, *Reactionary Modernism. Technology, Culture and Politics in Weimar and the Third Reich*, Cambridge, 1984.

J. Hermand, *'All Power to the Women.* Nazi Concepts of Matriarchy', *Journal of Contemporary History*, 1984, vol. 19, pp.649–68.
M. Hewlett, *Rest Harrow*, London, 1912.
——, *Song of the Plow. A Chronicle of England*, London, 1916.
J. Higham, 'The Reorientation of American Culture in the 1890s', in J. Weiss, ed., *The Origins of Modern Consciousness*, Detroit, 1965, pp.25–48.
N. Holt, 'The Social and Political Ideas of the German Monist Movement to 1914', Ph.D. Thesis, Yale, 1967.
——, 'Ernst Haeckel's Monist Religion',*Journal of the History of Ideas*, 1971, vol. 32, pp.265–80.
A. Howard, *An Agricultural Testament*, London, 1940.
E. Howard, *Garden Cities of Tomorrow*, London, 1902.
W. Hülsberg, *The German Greens. A Social and Political Profile*, London, 1988.
T. Huxley, *Autobiography*, London, 1890.
——, *Science and Culture*, London, 1881.
G.V. Jacks and R.O. Whyte, *The Rape of the Earth*, London, 1939.
L. Jebb, *The Smallholdings of England*, London, 1907.
R. Jefferies, *The Hills and the Vale*, Oxford, 1980.
——, *The Life of the Fields*, Oxford, 1983.
J. Jenks., *Farming and Money*, London, 1935.
——, *Fascism and Agriculture*, London, no date.
——, *From the Ground Up*, London, 1950.
——, *Spring Comes Again*, London, 1939.
——, 'The Countryman's Outlook', *Fascist Quarterly*, 1936, vols. 3–4.
——, 'The Homestead Economy', in ed. H. Massingham, *The Small Farmer*, London, 1947, vol. 2, pp.396–404.
——, *The Land and the People. British Union Policy for Agriculture*, London, no date.
H. Jonas, *The Imperative of Responsibility*, Chicago, 1984.
F.G. Jünger, *Die Perfektion der Technik*, Bonn and Munich, 1946.
T.J. Kalikow, 'Die ethologische Theorie von Konrad Lorenz', in H. Mehrtens and S. Richter, eds., *Naturwissenschaft Technik und NS-Ideologie des Dritten Reiches*, Frankfurt-am-Main, 1980.
W.J. Keith, *The Rural Tradition*, Hassocks, Sussex, 1975.
A. Kelly, *The Descent of Darwin. The Popularization of Darwin in Germany, 1890–1914*, Chapel Hill, 1981.
P. Kelly, *Fighting for Hope*, London, 1984.
C.J. van der Klaauw, 'Zur Geschichte der Definition der Ökologie, besonders auf Grund der Systems der zoologischen Disziplinen', *Sudhoffs Archiv für die Geschichte Medizin*, 1936, vol. 29, pp.136–77.
L. Klages, *Der Geist als Widersacher der Seele*, 2. vols., Munich, 1953.
——, *Mensch und Erde*, Jena, 1929.
K. von Klemperer, *Germany's New Conservatism*, Princeton, 1968.
E. Kohák, *The Embers and the Stars. A Philosophical Enquiry into the Moral Sense of Nature*, Chicago, 1984.
P. Kropotkin, *Fields, Factories and Workshops Tomorrow*, ed. C. Ward, London, 1985.
——, *Mutual Aid as a Law of Nature and a Factor of Evolution*, London, 1902.
G. Langguth, *The Green Factor in German Politics. From Protest Movement to Political Party*, Boulder, Colorado, 1986.
D.H. Lawrence, *Kangaroo*, London, 1923.
D. Levy, 'The Anthropological Horizon. Max Scheler, Arnold Gehlen and the idea of a Philosophical Anthropology', *Journal of the Anthropological Society of*

Oxford, 1985, vol. 16, pp.169–87.
——, 'Max Scheler: Truth and the Sociology of Knowledge', *Continuity*, 1981, vol. 3, pp.91–104.
U. Linse, *Barfüssige Propheten*, Berlin, 1983.
——, *Die kommune der deutsche Jugendbewegung*, Munich, 1982.
——, *Zurück O Mensch zur Mutter Erde. Landkommunen in Deutschland, 1890–1933*, Munich, 1983.
J. Williams Lloyd, *The Natural Man. A Romance of the Golden Age*, Newark, New Jersey, 1902.
——, *The Dwellers in Vale Sunrise*, Westwood, Mass., 1904.
K. Lorenz, *Behind the Mirror. A Search for a Natural History of Human Knowledge*, New York and London, 1977.
——, *On Aggression*, London, 1966.
——, *King Solomon's Ring. New Light on Animal Ways*, London, 1952.
A.F. Lovejoy, *The Great Chain of Being*, Cambridge, Mass., 1974.
J.E. Lovelock, *Gaia. A New Look at Life on Earth*, Oxford, 1979.
P. Lowe and J. Goyder, *Environmental Groups in Politics*, London, 1983.
Viscount Lymington (Gerard Vernon Wallop, later 9th Earl of Portsmouth) *Famine in England*, London, 1938.
——, *Horn, Hoof and Corn: the Future of British Agriculture*, London, 1932.
R.E. MacMaster, *Danilevsky. A Russian Totalitarian Philosopher*, Cambridge, Mass., 1967.
C.B. Macpherson, *Democracy in Alberta. Social Credit and the Party System*, Toronto, 1962.
P. Mairet, *Pioneer of Sociology. The Life and Letters of Patrick Geddes*, Westport, Conn., 1979.
T. Mann, *Diaries 1918–1939*, ed. H. Keston, London, 1983.
F.E. and F.P. Manuel, *Utopian Thought in the Western World*, Oxford, 1979.
E. Marais, *My Friends the Baboons*, London, 1971.
J. Marsh, *Back to the Land. The Pastoral Impulse in Victorian England, 1880–1914*, London, 1982.
J. Martinez-Alier, with Klaus Schlüppmann, *Ecological Economics. Energy, Environment and Society*, Oxford, 1987.
H. Massingham, *Downland Man*, London, 1926.
——, *Remembrance, An Autobiography*, London, 1941.
——, ed., *The Small Farmer*, London, 1947.
——, *The Tree of Life*, London, 1943.
——, *Through the Wilderness*, London, 1935.
C.F.G. Masterman, *The Condition of England*, London, 1909.
A. Masters, *Bakunin*, London, 1975.
E. Mayr, *The Growth of Biological Thought. Diversity, Evolution and Inheritance*, Cambridge, Mass., 1982.
P. Medawar, *Pluto's Republic*, Oxford, 1982.
P. Meier, *William Morris. The Marxist Dreamer*, vol. 1, Hassocks, Sussex, 1978.
C. Merchant, *The Death of Nature, Women, Ecology and the Scientific Revolution*, New York, 1980.
H. Mewes, 'The West German Green Party', *New German Critique*, 1983, no. 28, pp.51–85.
D. Mitrany, *Marx Against the Peasant. A Study in Social Dogmatism*, New York, 1961.
A. Mohler, *Der Traum vom Naturparadies. Anmerkungen zur Ökologischen Gedankengut*, Munich, 1978.

B. Moore, Jr., *Social Origins of Dictatorship and Democracy; Lord and Peasant in the Making of the Modern World*, Harmondsworth, 1974.
A.E. Morgan, *The Small Community*, New York, 1942.
B. Morris, 'Ernest Thompson Seton and the Origins of the Woodcraft Movement', *Journal of Contemporary History*, 1970, vol. 5, pp.183–94.
W. Morris, *News from Nowhere*, London, 1891.
J. Muller, *The Other God That Failed. Hans Freyer and the Deradicalization of German Conservatism*, Princeton, N.J., 1987.
F. Müller-Rommel, 'Ecological Parties in Western Europe, *West European Politics*, 1982.
H.J. Muller, *Out of the Night. A Biologist's View of the Future*, London, 1936.
L. Mumford., *Technics and Civilization*, New York, 1934.
——, *The Culture of Cities*, London, 1940.
A. Nisbett, *Konrad Lorenz*, London, 1976.
E. Nolte, *Three Faces of Fascism*, New York, 1969.
J. Norr, 'German Social Theory and the Hidden Face of Technology', *European Jounal of Sociology*, 1974, vol. 15, pp.312–26.
Lord Northbourne, *Look to the Land*, London, 1930.
A. Norton, *Alternative Americas*, Chicago, 1986.
A. Offer, *Property and Politics, 1870–1914*, Cambridge, 1981.
T. O'Riordan, 'The natural Habitat for Green Politics', *Times Educational Supplement* 26.10.84.
G. Orwell, *Collected Essays, Journalism and Letters*, vol. 2, *My Country Right or Left*, Harmondsworth, 1970.
——, *Collected Essays, Journalism and Letters*, vol. 4, *In Front of Your Nose*, Harmondsworth, 1972.
W. Ostwald, *Natural Philosophy*, New York and London, 1911.
——, *Die energetische Imperativ*, Leipzig, 1912.
——, *Die Philosophie der Werte*, Leipzig, 1913.
E. Papadakis, *The Green Movement in Germany*, London, 1984.
J. Papworth, *New Politics*, New Delhi, 1982.
H.L. Parsons, *Marx and Engels on Ecology*, Westport, Conn., 1977.
J. Passmore, *Man's Responsibility for Nature. Ecological Problems and Western Traditions*, London, 1974.
N. Pastore, *The Nature-Nurture Controversy*, New York, 1949.
D. Pepper, *The Roots of Modern Environmentalism*, London, 1985.
M.B. Petrovich, *The Emergence of Russian Panslavism, 1856–1870*, New York, 1956.
E. Pfeiffer, *Bio-Dynamic Farming and Gardening*, 1938.
D. Phillips, 'Organicism in late 19th and early 20th century Thought', *Journal of the History of Ideas*, 1970, vol. 31, pp.413–32.
J-I. Pilat, 'Democracy or Discontent? Ecologists in the European Electoral Arena', *Government and Opposition*, 1982.
The Pioneer Health Centre, Peckham, *Biologists in Search of Material. An Interim Report on the Work of the Pioneer Health Centre, Peckham*, London, 1938.
R. Pois, *National Socialsim and the Religion of Nature*, London 1985.
J. Popper-Lynkeus, *Die allgemeine Nährpflicht als Lösung der sozialen Frage*, Dresden, 1912.
K. Popper, *Unended Quest. An Intellectual Biography*, London, 1982.
Earl of Portsmouth (Gerard Vernon Wallop, 9th Earl), *A Knot of Roots*, London, 1965.
M. Prenant, *Biology and Marxism*, London, 1938.
I. Prigogine, *From Being to Becoming*, San Francisco, 1980.

D. Prynn, 'The Woodcraft Folk and the Labour Movement, 1925–1970', *Journal of Contemporary History*, 1983, vol. 8, pp.79–95.
E. Rádl, *History of Biological Theories*, London, 1930.
J. Radcliffe, 'The Politics of Ecology', M.Sc Thesis, University of Wales, 1981.
J. Raumoulin, 'L' Homme et la Destruction des Ressources Naturelles. La *Raubwirstchaft* au tournant du siècle', *Annales; Intersciences*, 1984, vol. 39, pp.798–819.
H. Rider Haggard, *A Farmer's Year*, London, 1899.
J. Rifkind and T. Howard, *Entropy: A New World View*, London, 1985.
A. Rigby, *Communes in Britain*, London, 1974.
B. Robson, 'Geography and Social Science. The Role of Patrick Geddes', in D. Stoddart, ed., *Geography, Ideology and Social Concern*, Oxford, 1981.
Drieu la Rochelle, *Gilles*, Paris, 1939.
——, *Récit Secret*, Paris, 1950.
C. Ross, *Der unvollendete Kontinent*, Leipzig, 1930.
Rothamstead Experimental Station at Harpenden, *Rothamstead Conferences*, vols. 1–20, London, 1926–36.
Rothamstead Experimental Station at Harpenden, *Rothamstead Memoirs on Agricultural Science*, vols. 8–9 London, 1902–16.
J. Ruskin, *Unto This Last, and other writings*, Harmondsworth, 1985.
P. Santmire, *Travail of Nature. Ambiguous Ecological Promises of Christian Theology*, Fortress Press, no place, 1985.
H. Schnädelbach, *Philosophy in Germany 1831–1984*, Cambridge, 1984.
E.F. Schumacher, *Small is Beautiful*, London, 1973.
——, *Population and World Hunger*, London, 1973.
G.R. Searle, 'Eugenics and Politics in Britain in the 1930s', *Annals of Science*, 1979, vol. 36, pp.159–69.
H.P. Segal, *Technological Utopianism in American Culture*, Chicago, 1985.
B. Sewell, ed., *Henry Williamson. The Man, the Writings. A Symposium*. Padstow, Cornwall, 1980.
R. Sheldrake, *A New Science of Life: The Hypothesis of Formative Causation*, London, 1987.
J.L. Simon and H. Kahn, eds., *The Resourceful Earth. A Response to 'Global 2000'*, Oxford, 1984.
P. Singer, *Animal Liberation*, London, 1976.
N.R. Smith, *Land for the Small Man, English and Welsh Experience with Publicly Supplied Smallholdings, 1860–1937*, New York, 1946.
F. Soddy, *Cartesian Economics. The Bearing of the Physical Sciences upon State Stewardship*, London 1922.
G. Sorel, *From Georges Sorel*, ed J. Stanley, New York, 1976.
D. and E. Spring, *Ecology and Religion in History*, New York, 1974.
M. Stanley, *The Technological Conscience*, New York, 1978.
G. Stapledon, *The Land, Now and Tomorrow*, London, 1935.
——, *Disraeli and the New Age*, London, 1943.
——, *Human Ecology*, ed. R. Waller, London, 1964.
R. Stauffer, 'Haeckel, Darwin and Ecology', *Quarterly Review of Biology*, 1957, vol. 32, pp.138–44.
R. Steiner, *Two Essays on Haeckel*, New York, 1936.
J. Stewart Collis, *The Worm Forgives the Plough*, Harmondsworth, 1973.
D. Stoddard, 'Darwin's Impact on Geography', *Annals of the Association of American Geographers*, 1966, p.683–98.
——, ed., *Geography, Ideology and Social Concern*, Oxford, 1981.

——, *On Geography*, Oxford, 1986.
M. Straight, *After Long Silence*, New York and London, 1983.
P. Tame, *La Mystique du Fascisme dans l'oeuvre de Robert Brasillach*, Paris, 1987.
E. Thomas, *Richard Jefferies, His Life and Work*, London, 1978.
K. Thomas, *Man and the Natural World*, London, 1983.
H.D. Thoreau, *Walden, or Life in the Woods*, New York, 1961.
J. von Thünen, *The Isolated State*, London, 1966.
R. Thurlow, *Fascism in Britain. A History, 1918–1985*, Oxford, 1987.
N. Tinbergen, *The Study of Instinct*, New York and Oxford, 1974.
J. Turner, *Reckoning with the Beast. Animals, Pain and Humanity in the Victorian Mind*, Baltimore and London, 1981.
L. Veysey, *The Communal Experience. Anarchist and Mystical Counter-Cultures in America*, New York, 1973.
K, Vogt, *Lectures on Man: His Place in Creation*, London, 1863.
R. Waller, *Prophet of a New Age*, London, 1962.
J. Webb, *The Occult Establishment*, vol. 2. *The Flight from Reason*, Glasgow, 1981.
E. Webber, *Escape to Utopia. The Communal Movement in America*, New York, 1959.
P. Weindling, '"Darwinismus" and the Secularization of German Society', in J.R. Moore, ed., *The Humanity of Evolution. Perspectives in the History of Evolutionary Naturalism*, Cambridge, 1988.
J. Weston, ed., *Red and Green. The New Politics of the Environment*, London, 1986.
L. White Jr., 'The Historical Roots of our Ecological Crisis', in J. White, ed., *Machina ex Deo*, Cambridge, Mass., 1968.
H. Williamson, *A Clear Water Stream*, London, 1958.
——, *Good-bye West Country*, London, 1937.
——, *Life in a Devon Village*, London, 1945.
——, *Tales of Moorland and Estuary*, London, 1981.
——, *Tales of a Devon Village*, London, 1945.
——, *The Gold Falcon*, London, 1933.
——, *The Children of Shallowford*, London, 1939.
——, *The Labouring Life*, London, 1932.
——, *The Story of a Norfolk Farm*, London, 1941.
——, *Chronicles of Ancient Sunlight*, 15 volume novel series. Individual novels cited in the text are given a full reference *in situ*.
R. Wohl, *The Generation of 1914*, London, 1980.
G. Woodcock and I. Avakumovc, *The Doukhoubours*, London, 1968.
——, *Kropotkin, the Anarchist Prince*, London, 1950.
G. Woodcock, *Anarchism. A History of Libertarian Ideas and Movements*, Harmondsworth, 1975.
D. Worster, *Nature's Economy. The Roots of Ecology*, San Francisco, 1977.
G.T. Wrench, *The Restoration of the Peasantries*, London, 1941.
——, *The Wheel of Health*, London, 1938.
M. Wreszin, 'Albert Jay Nock; the Anarchist Elitist Trdition in America', *American Quarterly*, 1969, vol. 21, pp.165–87.
J, Yahuda, *Bio-Economics*, London, 1938.
A. Yanov, *The Russian Challenge and the Year 2000*, Oxford and New York, 1987.
B. Zablocki, *The Joyful Community. The account of the Bruderhof. A Communal Movement now in its Third Generation*, Baltimore, 1971.

Index